Tug of War

The Allied Victory That Opened Antwerp

Denis Whitaker
and
Shelagh Whitaker

Beaufort Books edition published in 1984

Published in 2000 by Stoddart Publishing Co. Limited
34 Lesmill Road, Toronto, Canada M3B 2T6

Distributed in Canada by:
General Distribution Services Ltd.
325 Humber College Blvd.
Toronto, Canada M9W 7C3
Tel. (416) 213-1919
Fax (416) 213-1917
Email cservice@genpub.com

Distributed in the U.S. by:
General Distribution Services Inc.
PMB 128, 4500 Witmer Industrial Estates
Niagara Falls, New York 14305-1386
Toll-free Tel.1-800-805-1083
Toll-free Fax 1-800-481-6207
Email gdsinc@genpub.com

04 03 02 01 00   1 2 3 4 5

Canadian Cataloguing in Publication Data
Whitaker, Denis
Tug of war: the Allied victory that opened Antwerp
2nd ed.
Includes bibliographical references and index.
ISBN 0-7737-3226-8 (bound)

1. Scheldt River Estuary, Battle of, 1944.
2. Canada. Canadian Army – History – World War, 1939–1945.
3. World War, 1939–1945 – Campaigns – Belgium.
4. World War, 1939–1945 – Campaigns – Netherlands. I. Whitaker, Shelagh. II. Title.
D756.5.S34W57 2000   940.54'21   C87-093292-6

U.S. Cataloguing in Publication Data (Library of Congress Standards)
Whitaker, Denis
Tug of war: the Allied victory that opened Antwerp /
Denis Whitaker, Shelagh Whitaker. – 2nd rev. ed.
[480] p.: ill. ; cm. (maps)
Originally published: 1984.
Includes bibliographic references and index.
Summary: The Allied armies' mission to clear the approach to the
port of Antwerp, and the subsequent Battle of the Scheldt.
ISBN: 0-7737-3226-8

1. World War, 1939–1945 – Campaigns. 2. World War, 1939–1945 – Canada.
I. Whitaker, Shelagh. II. Title.
940.542 21   2000   CIP

Jacket design: Bill Douglas @The Bang
Text design: Joseph Gisini/Andrew Smith Graphics Inc.

THE CANADA COUNCIL | LE CONSEIL DES ARTS
FOR THE ARTS | DU CANADA
SINCE 1957 | DEPUIS 1957

*We acknowledge for their financial support of our publishing program the Canada Council
for the Arts, the Ontario Arts Council, and the Government of Canada through the
Book Publishing Industry Development Program (BPIDP).*

Printed and bound in Canada

In memory of our fathers

Major Guy Shewell Whitaker
and
Colonel James Moore Dunwoody, DSO, DCM, ED, CD

Contents

List of Maps

Acknowledgements

*T*UG OF WAR IS THE EXPRESSION OF THE THOUGHTS AND EXPERIENCES of the one hundred and seventy-five men who were interviewed in some depth for these pages. To these men, who *are* the book, must go our first thanks.

The search for these men encompassed eight countries and required a considerable outlay of time and resources in establishing personal contacts on such a broad scale. This was made possible by generous grants from the Social Sciences and Humanities Research Council of Canada and by the Ontario Heritage Foundation of the Ministry of Citizenship and Culture. For their continuing encouragement and guidance, we are deeply indebted to Dr. W.A.B. Douglas and Brereton Greenhous of the Directorate of History, Department of National Defence, which has contributed so much towards documenting Canada's role in World War II. We are grateful, too, to Colonel Charles Simonds for lending us his father's unpublished papers.

For some twelve months, *Tug of War* functioned from the back seat of a small car. The simple logistics of moving this operation — personal computer, boxes overflowing with transcripts and files, and luggage for two persons over a one-year period — to and around Europe was made the easier by the help of several associates: Burns Fry Ltd. of Toronto and London was of invaluable assistance in this, as was Mr. Michael Bell of Federal Commerce & Navigation Ltd. of Montreal.

Locating contacts in each country and oftentimes translating their interviews were facilitated by the help of a number of friends, such as Major General Peter Bush of London; Colonel Eugene Colson of Antwerp; the Canadian Attaché to Hamburg, Germany, Mr. Ron Berlet; Mr. Erwin Jaeger and F.K. von Düsterlohe of Hamburg; Mr. Leo Timmermans in Zeeland; Mr. Camille Vervarcke of Knokke; Mr. Etienne van de Walle in Brugge. Several noted international historians, authors, and British and Canadian senior military commanders were kind enough to take an interest in *Tug of War* and, in some cases, offer their comments on segments of the manuscript: Major General Eric Sixsmith, Colonel C.P. Stacey, Mr. Eversley Belfield, Professor Leon Charles, Dr. L. de Jong, Dr. Carlos Vlaemynck, Major General J.L. Moulton. In addition, directors of the archives which are noted following the List of Interviews were unfailingly cooperative and helpful.

Finally, and gratefully, we acknowledge the support and forbearance of all our family during our twenty-four months' absorption in this single battle and, in particular, our daughter Mrs. Martha Ann Hooker, currently studying for her Master's Degree in Canadian Military History at Carleton University, whose contribution in historical research and editing was only eclipsed by the devoted interest and encouragement she gave us; and our son-in-law, Dr. Ian Shaw, Associate Professor of English at Brock University, whose objectivity and creative talents were deeply appreciated.

Prologue

THIS BOOK IS DEDICATED, IN PART, TO A YOUNG CANADIAN WHOM WE met in 1983; we never learned his name.

On 2 November, 1983, we had gathered with many hundreds of others at the Canadian Military Cemetery at Adegem in West Flanders, Belgium. The rain that had lashed out at the Canadian troops who had fought through this same country in November, 1944, seemed as unrelenting now as we stood, Canadians, Belgians and Dutch, in silent thought. Here, thirty-nine years later, we assembled to honour the Canadian dead who liberated the areas of Zeeland and West Flanders bordering the Scheldt Estuary.

On the previous day, twelve hundred men, women and children, civilians and soldiers, had joined hands symbolically on the annual thirty-two-km Canadian Liberation March from Hoofdplaat in Holland to Knokke in Belgium, following the same route — then so costly and difficult — of the liberating Canadian Army. The procession stopped along the way to honour the Resistance fighters and civilians of Holland and Belgium who gave their lives in battle.

Then, at the cemetery, the marchers filed through a column of yew trees toward a tall white cross. On both sides were the graves, over one thousand, lined up in rows, their stark stone whiteness relieved by colourful and sweetly scented flowers and the deep green of the grass. Only the young lie buried at Adegem, and this youth is the pathos of its message. Soldiers of nineteen and twenty died miserably in the sodden polders of Zeeland. The survivors could only think, "They were but boys."

A platoon of Canadian soldiers formed the Honour Guard as the Canadian Ambassador to Belgium, d'Iberville Fortier, joined the dignitaries from all the surrounding towns in presenting wreathes. The "Last Post" echoed across the graveyard; no one spoke or moved.

A man approached us. "My father was killed on Friday, October 13th, in the Battle of the Scheldt," he said quietly. "He was a private soldier, young, a runner for a platoon in the Black Watch Regiment. I never knew my father. I am trying to find out the circumstances of his death."

He left without giving his name. His answer is in this book. It is not a reassuring answer, but it is truthful. And it is ugly, just as war is.

Dolle Dinsdag

"DOLLE DINSDAG" — "CRAZY TUESDAY," 5 SEPTEMBER, 1944 — WAS a day burned into the memories of the Netherlanders. It was the day the Dutch people went mad.

Listening furtively to the BBC evening broadcast on Radio Oranje, they had learned that the advancing British troops had captured the Belgian city of Antwerp the previous day. The BBC had further reported that the 2nd British Army was pushing across the Dutch border just a few kilometres beyond Antwerp, and speeding through the Netherlands to bring about the liberation that these people had almost stopped believing in.

And the people believed, because they wanted and needed to. They knew that the great port of Antwerp was useless to the Allies until its approaches had been cleared of the enemy. For although Antwerp was in Belgian territory, its harbour lay some eighty-five km inland, fed by the icy waters of the River Scheldt as it snaked lazily through the city before flowing through German-occupied Holland toward the North Sea. Now, with their own eyes and ears, they could see the Germans on the run, hear the British guns coming ever closer. After four years of occupation by the loathed German Army, Holland was to be free again.

Hour by hour, on that Crazy Tuesday, the feelings of optimism swelled, until finally the Dutch exploded in a frenzy of celebration — and vengeance. Quiet village squares erupted as Resistance fighters joined their families in joyful reunion. The fears bred by four years of occupation turned to bravado as Germans were bodily booted out of town by unarmed citizens. Nazi collaborators were rounded up and publicly abused by indignant and angry citizens. Women who had consorted with German soldiers were stripped and force-marched down the main streets with scalps shaven clean and bodies smeared with lurid paint.

But the madness was short-lived. Euphoria plunged into despair as the distraught Netherlanders witnessed the sudden return of the German conqueror. In terms of devastation of the spirit, few events can rival *Dolle Dinsdag*. The day will always be remembered.

———•———

While the Dutch rejoiced over their phantom liberation, the people of neighbouring Belgium also celebrated the event that they, too, called Mad Tuesday, as their towns and cities were liberated. Here, too, heads were shaven in vengeance, and quislings were hounded and jailed, or shot.

Here, too, the despised Germans would try to return, but they would not succeed in reoccupying Belgium. The freedom the Belgians celebrated was a true freedom, and a lasting one — not the by-product of the Dutch people's foolish hopes caused by ill-fated rumours.

———•———

Dolle Dinsdag, this single day of madness, was to become in the following weeks a symbol of a liberation euphoria that was not to be contained within the boundaries of the Lowlands. It spilled over to leave its ugly stain on the Allied commanders and key decision-makers in the European conflict, now into its fifth year.

The careless optimism, the recklessness, the vindictiveness and anger, the jealousies and self-aggrandizement that were demonstrated in Holland and Belgium that day were mirrored in the actions of the Allied governments in Paris, London, Washington and Ottawa. In those days of madness, a bare handful of men spoke up about the possibility of finishing off hostilities — but no one was listening. At Supreme Headquarters of the Allied Expeditionary Forces (SHAEF), men of brilliant military skill who had commanded scores of thousands of troops shrewdly and with verve would now be caught up in the headiness of the moment. It was a time, as one British Guardsman described it, of "a very dangerous state of elation."[1]

In the wake of this perilous mood came the blunders — blunders caused when concentration wavers, when subjective opinion usurps good judgement. The German, on the edge of catastrophe, kept his reason. The Allies, sensing victory, lost theirs. And in the ensuing confusion, they lost the opportunity to end the war quickly.

Countless thousands of troops would die needlessly on Europe's battlefields as this war dragged on. Uncounted numbers of civilians, in homes, on streets — and in concentration camps — would lose their lives. And Canadian and Allied soldiers under the command of the Canadian Army would fight a wholly unnecessary battle, along the banks of the Scheldt River.

The military leaders are nearly all dead now, and each man deserves all the accolades that history has heaped on him. They served their countries with skill and loyalty. Our tragedy is that they too were overcome by the madness of a single day: *Dolle Dinsdag*.

———————

The liberation of Paris on the 25th of August had sparked a new wave of hope for all the Allies that the enemy was close to defeat. In the ensuing sweep through France and Belgium, the Allied armies had thrust deeper and deeper into German-occupied territory, almost outstripping their own supply lines. Entire divisions were strung out, flanks unprotected, well ahead of their rear echelon, with perhaps one day's supply of petrol in their tanks, and no more. Rash? Probably. Successful? Wildly so.

On the 30th of August, 1944, at 1615 hours, Lieutenant General Sir Brian Horrocks summoned Major General G.P.B. (Pip) Roberts, the thirty-seven-year-old commander of the crack British 11th Armoured Division, to his command headquarters of XXX Corps of the 2nd British Army. The two men met at the edge of a field in the Seine Valley, conferring in a makeshift office in the bowels of a tank, with the armament removed to make room for one small table.

There, protected from the steamy August downpour through

which the tank corps had advanced during the long day, Horrocks issued an order that was to initiate what he later described as "the most exciting and exhilarating period of my life."[2] He was to discover soon enough that the order would culminate in what also must be the greatest disappointment of this astute general's life: the lost opportunity to finish off the war in 1944.

In the course of the previous two days, the tank drivers had been on the move for some thirty-six hours, advancing, often with bitter fighting, from Vernon, on the Seine, toward Amiens near the Somme River. They had pushed on through the heavy rains of northeastern France as they attempted to close the gap between themselves and the fleeing enemy. Now, dug in for the night, they looked forward to the rarity of a good hot meal. A few enterprising men had liberated enough French chickens and ducks to ensure a tasty dinner.

But their gain of thirty-five km had not satisfied the commander of XXX Corps. ("A tall, lithe figure," historian Chester Wilmot describes him, "with white hair, angular features, penetrating eyes and eloquent hands, Horrocks moved among his troops more like a prophet than a general."[3] His orders from his senior officer, General Bernard Montgomery, were unequivocal: he was to advance quickly and capture Antwerp. The enemy is in full retreat, he was told, there is to be no relaxation of pressure by day, or, if necessary, by night. "The Germans are very good soldiers," Montgomery had reminded his veteran commander from the North African campaign, "and will recover quickly if allowed to do so. All risks are justified. I intend to get a bridgehead over the Rhine before they have time to recover."[4]

Horrocks was well aware of the critical shortage of supplies. The Allied Expeditionary Force (AEF) had, by now, almost two months after the D-Day invasion of Normandy, outstripped its supply lines by some 650 km. Supplies and reinforcements were grounded at port for lack of transport to the front line. Petrol, ammunition and arms were doled out on a meagre ration, with intense rivalries and even some hijacking developing between units on allocation of supply.

The problem would be solved, Horrocks realized, with the capture of Antwerp, whose docks would permit the off-loading of supplies almost directly to the front. The urgency, then, was to capture Antwerp before the enemy was fully alerted to the British advance.

Without question, the Germans were keenly aware of the need of the Allies for a deepwater port, and they would certainly have made provision for the destruction of the port facilities if attacked.

So came the order from General Horrocks that unleashed a marathon drive seldom experienced in modern warfare. Some four hundred tanks and twenty thousand men gave chase to a retreating enemy across 560 km of German-held territory, showing a capacity for movement and exploitation that even the American High Command termed "electrifying."[5] Following on the heels of the armour, the infantry divisions of XXX Corps mopped up pockets of enemy resistance which the tanks had skirted. On one occasion, the 11th Armoured's advance was so rapid that the commandant of the German 7th Army, General Hans Eberbach, was captured still in his pajamas. For six days and nights, sleeping only in snatches, XXX Corps made its historic thrust towards the Rhine, Horrocks's command-post tank never far behind the lead squadrons.

The dramatic chase compelled the British to advance their tanks at night, a feat that few commanders would demand, and a stratagem that Horrocks had employed in only two previous operations. A large mass of armour was exceedingly vulnerable when moving at night. Driving through utter blackness, with both flanks exposed, navigating through a narrow observation slit in what was essentially the interior of a large dark tin can, was an unnerving experience. But an armoured attack in darkness provided the advantage of surprise over an enemy unversed in such unorthodox tactics. (The innovative use of tanks by night was first demonstrated on the European front at Normandy by Lieutenant General Guy Simonds, a Canadian who would play a determining role in this battle-in-the-making during the coming weeks.)

The dash across France and Belgium was not without incident; the 11th Armoured met small pockets of opposition, which were at times intense. At a road junction, in one instance, several German vehicles inadvertently joined the long column of Allied tanks and trucks picking their way through the inky blackness. During a periodic halt, a British soldier seated at the back of a truck noticed one of the newcomers walking around the British vehicle, trying to make out its identifying signs.

Recognizing him as a German, the Englishman grabbed a shovel and dealt the enemy soldier a blow to the head. At once a short but brisk fight with grenades and machine guns broke out, ending with destruction of several German vehicles.

On Sunday, the 3rd of September, at 1330 hours, the Guards Armoured, a sister division to the 11th Armoured, crossed the Belgian frontier, a fact reported by the British Broadcasting Corporation to Belgian civilians who were monitoring the signal on contraband radios. Later that afternoon, Brussels fell. Horrocks insisted that members of the Belgian Secret Army join their Allied comrades in the triumphant entry into the city, the troops "alternately drinking toasts in champagne and firing at the pockets of enemy who still remained."[6]

By 1200 hours on Monday, 4 September, the tanks of Roberts's 11th Armoured Division were poised triumphantly on the outskirts of the city of Antwerp. By evening, the city was in Allied hands. But on Tuesday, Crazy Tuesday, the tenacity of the prophet Horrocks in pursuing the advance, and the skill of his trusted commander in capturing Antwerp, were betrayed by the carelessness of the very leaders they sought to serve.

In Antwerp, the conquerors were themselves conquered, carried off by generous and joyful Belgians. As British troops, tanks and trucks had lumbered, almost unopposed, into the city the previous day, citizens leaped crazily aboard, embracing and kissing their liberators, thrusting armloads of flowers at them and freely opening their bistro doors. To the war-weary 11th Armoured Division, the adulation was impossible to resist: it became a day — or several days — "on the house," and the two-day "rest and refit" order from equally captivated officers allowed them to enjoy it to the hilt.

The division ground to a halt, unaware that the German 15th Army could have been cut off and annihilated, and that a thrust of some fifty km more against an enemy on the run would have secured and freed for Allied use the entire Scheldt Estuary that guarded the approaches to the inland port.

Nor did the Allies appear to believe their own intelligence; if they had continued this "pursuit without pause" another 120 km beyond Antwerp to the Rhine, the Germans would have had no defences to stop them.

Many military experts still believe that this double strike would have ended the war by Christmas, and it would have spared the Canadian Army one of the longest and bloodiest battles in northwest Europe: The Battle of the Scheldt.[7]

———•———

Normandy, 5 September, 1944

On this day, *Dolle Dinsdag,* in a remote French villa on the west coast of the Cherbourg Peninsula a full 650 km behind the front lines, the commander-in-chief of the Allied troops lay in bed.

Shifting restlessly to find some comfort for his plaster-encased right knee, General Dwight D. Eisenhower complacently mulled over the successful advances made by all the forces under his command in the three months since the D-Day invasion of France.

It was an uncommonly fine day, better suited to enjoying the vista from his bedroom window of the brilliant sun bouncing off the distant slopes of historic Mont St. Michel, than to adjudicating the various proposals for the "bouncing" of the Rhine.

For the farm boy from Abilene, Kansas, war must have seemed very far away. The supreme commander would find respite in the tranquility of his new headquarters in the sleepy hamlet of Jollouville, a French fishing village that lay just south of Granville on the west coast of the Cherbourg Peninsula. In this peaceful setting, isolated as it was from the battlefields, only the clusters of tents and trailers hastily erected on Normandy's lush apple orchards for the personnel of SHAEF gave an indication that the business of war was being, to some extent anyway, pursued.

And the outlook was as promising as the day. The German 7th Army, Eisenhower's intelligence had reported, had been virtually destroyed in Normandy, "no longer a cohesive force, but a number of fugitive battle groups."[8] Intercepts from enemy signals had indicated that the German 15th Army was now in complete retreat.

Elsewhere, the news was equally electrifying. The Allied invasion of the south of France had been successful. This would offer a new supply base for operations in mid-Europe, as well as prodding Hitler from the "underbellies" of France and Italy. In the east, the Russians had advanced strongly into Yugoslavia; Finland had joined them, becoming part of the Allied side. The Germans had been pushed out of Greece, Rumania and Bulgaria.

Just eleven days before, the liberation of Paris had caused worldwide elation: "The end of the war in Europe [is] within sight," SHAEF had triumphantly informed its military heads.[9] And now a new dispatch informed Eisenhower that Antwerp, western Europe's second greatest seaport, had been captured, its massive docks miraculously undamaged by German sabotage. With Antwerp open and functional, the critical shortages of fuel, ammunition and other supplies that were now crippling the Allied advances would be alleviated. A supply line close to the front would ensure a speedy victory.

But there were problems, as well as pleasures, distracting the supreme commander. A classic tug of war had developed — with Eisenhower uncomfortably in the middle — between Field Marshal Montgomery, commander of the British 21st Army Group, and General George Smith Patton Jr., explosive chief of the 3rd U.S. Army in General Omar Bradley's U.S. 12th Army Group. The gossip at Patton's headquarters, repeated to the supreme commander by an indiscreet aide, was that Eisenhower was "the best general the British have,"[10] a quip reflecting Eisenhower's alleged favouring of Montgomery. It did little to improve shaky Anglo-American relations, or Eisenhower's mood of that morning.

The dissension, fueled by media of both countries, prompted almost continuous bickering between the Americans and British, each demanding credit for their victories. "It seems that so far as the press and the public are concerned," Eisenhower complained, "a resounding victory is not sufficient; the question of 'how' is equally important."[11]

On the 1st of September, Eisenhower had compounded the problem by making a major change of command. With Americans now numbering two-thirds of the fighting troops in northwest Europe, it had become unthinkable that a Briton, Montgomery, could continue to command them. Eisenhower had recently come under intense American pressure to set in motion his long-term plan of taking command of the land forces from Montgomery. Forced to keep one eye on the American voter in this, an important election year in the United States, he allowed political issues to displace strategic ones. The war had to be won quickly, but it also had to be won by an American.

Eisenhower would now carry the responsibility for the tactical management of the Allied armies, as well as for the overall strategic command of the Northwest Europe campaign. This change of command was viewed somewhat cynically in Great Britain, in light of Montgomery's success in this command throughout the Normandy campaign: "The truth is that Americans in an election year must be commanded by an American general so that it can be an American victory…Talk of swapping horses in the middle of the stream!" quipped one wag.[12]

Montgomery himself, eyeing Eisenhower's meagre combat experience with some mistrust, remarked to an associate, "He has never commanded anything in his whole career. Now, for the first time, he has elected to take direct command of very large-scale operations and he does not know how to do it."[13]

Conversely, the Americans were outraged at the effrontery of the British government in promoting Montgomery on the same day to the rank of Field Marshal — a rank that did not exist in the U.S. Army, but which would elevate him to a higher level than even Bradley. The Americans regarded it as a panacea promotion, and something of an insult to the United States. Nor were they impressed by Montgomery's command to date, viewing it as being somewhat stodgy, lacking the flair and daring of General Patton's thrust.

Even Patton, who was generous in his praise of Eisenhower's diplomatic skills in keeping peace within the Allied ranks, was less complimentary about his ability to conduct a war. He felt, his biographer commented, with "almost a physical pain the absence of consistent direction from the top…trying to follow a conductor who did not quite know or failed to comprehend the delicate nuances of a score."[14]

Eisenhower's dual role had necessitated a move from his London headquarters to a position closer to the front. The original intention had been to wait until his armies — and his headquarters — were firmly established on the continent before making this move. As it turned out, the move was committed in such haste as to be retrograde.

Eisenhower had unwittingly removed himself to a post that had radio and telephone linkups with neither his military fronts nor his

SHAEF headquarters in London. "Most Immediate" signals, sent to and from the commander by wireless code, were delayed for as long as three or four days. For some weeks, Eisenhower's communications had to depend on his personal visits by airplane or jeep to the advance headquarters of his commanders.

It was on the return from one of these trips a few days earlier that the fifty-four-year-old general had wrenched his knee so severely that his doctors were compelled to stabilize it in plaster and order him to bed. For several days, the war was to be directed by an invalided commander, working in a state of confusion and silence caused by a primitive communications network that left him far out of touch with the realities of the war.

Hundreds of kilometres away, the man whom he had ousted from the post of land commander, Field Marshal Bernard Law Montgomery, sat in the silence of the map room of the sparsely furnished trailer, one of a pair that served as mobile home and headquarters. Montgomery, the stern, unwavering commander of 21 Army Group, was obsessed on this Mad Tuesday with the vision of delivering an immediate and final blow to Germany. His plan, sent the day before to Eisenhower, seemed to him the only sensible next step. All the Allied strength had to be massed, preferably under his command, for a strike through Holland to the flat industrial Ruhr — or, failing that, under Bradley's through central Germany's hillier Saar area.

Montgomery's resentment that day was directed at his American allies as well as at his German enemy. Patton was stealing petrol from U.S. stores that could be used more profitably by his 21st Army Group. Eisenhower had been wavering for two weeks on strategy, twice changing his mind. He even committed the unthinkable folly of switching commanders in midstream. Montgomery found his superior officer's strategy, as well as his isolation, incomprehensible. The Englishman was to comment acidly: "This [Granville] was possibly a suitable place for a Supreme Commander, but it was useless for a land force commander who had to keep his finger on the pulse of his armies and give quick decisions in rapidly changing situations...In the early days of September he was, in fact, completely out of touch with the land battle."[15]

If only Eisenhower would agree to concentrate the Allied strength in a single thrust, he was thinking, Britain might survive. America had sufficient resources and manpower to last out a lengthy war. Britain had not. After five years of conflict, his country had been virtually drained of resources and was bankrupt of manpower; Britain would be irreversibly crippled if the war was to drag on.

Perhaps mesmerized by these thoughts, Montgomery for once relaxed his rigid attention to the immediate future. His gaze fixed firmly on the Rhine, he forgot to look at Antwerp.

Dieppe, 5 September, 1944

Ironically, many of the Canadians who were to suffer most from this change of command and change of policy were, on that same day, mourning their fallen comrades. The Royal Hamilton Light Infantry (RHLI) marched out of Dieppe on September 5th, having spent five days at the site of their disastrous raid there in 1942 where two-thirds of their number had been killed or captured. This time, the Germans had fled before their advance; there would be no renewed Canadian battle in this French port.

The return to Dieppe was an occasion, too, to take a breather from conflict, to enjoy a moment of peace in the late summer sunshine. There seemed little urgency to get on with the war.

Germany, 5 September, 1944

Adolf Hitler, king and catalyst of the German aggression, had had little sleep in the past twenty-four hours as he sent message after message to his field commanders from the frenzied map room at German headquarters in the East Prussian town of Rastenburg. In a series of incisive moves, he quickly reinstated the old warrior Gerd von Rundstedt as commander-in-chief of the West. The veteran soldier's initial assessment revealed total chaos in the western divisions. The troops, retreating on foot from France, were exhausted and in critical need of food, arms and ammunition. Of the seventy-four divisions that had been sent to beat off the Allied invasion at Normandy, only fifteen weakened divisions were left. Casualties since D-Day now totalled upwards of 400,000.*

But Hitler refused to accept the fact that the great German war machine was running down, and he dismissed the warnings of his commanders. His first priority was to rescue the trapped German 15th Army. By September 6th, units of this force had eluded the British and Canadians and had taken up defensive positions along both sides of the Scheldt Estuary forming the approaches to Antwerp. This tactic enabled the German Naval Group West to proceed immediately with Hitler's command to "mine and obstruct the Scheldt energetically."[16] The remaining units were ferried across the mouth of the river to Walcheren Island and thence back to their own lines. In all, some 86,000 German soldiers were to escape capture.

From a commandeered hotel at Oosterbeek, near Arnhem, new German posts were hastily set up to coordinate the interception and regrouping of forces retreating into that area. Fueled by desperation, Hitler quickly beefed up this makeshift unit with recruits transferred from the air force and navy. He conscripted these forces from the only source left to him — convalescents, men with ulcers, the deaf, the elderly, boys of fifteen and sixteen. There was no bottom line for this miserable mix, except death. Their choices: to be shot by the Allies, or to be shot, along with their families, by their own commanders if they surrendered or deserted. "Fight to the last man and last round," was Hitler's hysterical command.[17]

In England, on Mad Tuesday, the aging prime minister of Great Britain, Winston Churchill, was piped aboard the luxury liner *Queen Mary*, hoping that a week of bracing sea air would shake the last of his bout with pneumonia. The usually bustling map room at 10 Downing Street would be strangely inactive as Churchill and the British chiefs of staff travelled to Quebec for a summit meeting with the American president, Franklin Delano Roosevelt, hosted by

---

* The word "casualty" is used throughout the book in the military sense to mean men killed, wounded or captured.

Canada's prime minister, William Lyon Mackenzie King. Paramount on the agenda of the Joint Chiefs of Staff was discussion of the quick dispatch of Germany. In their mood of optimism, they did not seem to realize that while the mighty *Queen* sailed sedately westward across the Atlantic, the opportunity for a quick end to the war had already been lost.

Lieutenant Colonel W. Denis Whitaker:

In the tranquil English village of Taplow, in Hampshire, I was one of a group of Canadian troops recovering from wounds. We sat in the unseasonably warm September sun watching the calm waters of the Thames, little knowing that in a few weeks our gaze would be locked on the hostile shores of the Scheldt. But on this Crazy Tuesday, the only ire we encountered was from the owner of the impressive estate where the temporary Canadian hospital had been established. Lady Nancy Astor had come upon the officers playing croquet, stripped to the waist in order to get some welcome sun on our backs. Part American by birth, all English by tradition and a tee-totaler by vocation, Lady Astor declared her own personal war on this unseemly state of disarray, and curbed her wrath only when the Canadians offered an amused truce: "We will put on our shirts if you will supply the ward with a case of beer." And she did!

It was a euphoric time for the battered British. The liberation of Paris had marked a kind of "spiritual end of the war."[18] Every day, newspapers and radios carried fresh reports of new advances by the Allies and optimistic utterances by their leaders. The "doodlebug," that devastating V-1 bomb of Hitler's devising, was at long last stilled (the V-2 rocket bomb had yet to be unleashed). There was a partial lifting of the blackout that had so demoralized the British as they groped their way home each night. A new musical at the Palladium, featuring the Happy Gang, had just opened to a full house in London's West End; Ascot's race meeting saw a greater attendance than usual, but transport to the famed race course was as often by pony cart as by Rolls-Royce.

For the wounded soldiers at Taplow, the quest for beer, from stock sadly depleted by the influx of 200,000 thirsty troops before D-Day, was our biggest challenge. Convalescents vied for leaves to lift a pint at Skindles in nearby Maidenhead. And if pub talk got to the war, it was mainly on the theme of "mopping up." The euphoria of *Dolle Dinsdag* had found us, too.

❧ 2 ❧

The Secret Army

"*POUR FRANÇOIS LA LUNE EST CLAIRE.*" THESE INNOCENT WORDS, THE LAST of three successive messages relayed by the BBC on its nightly broadcast to Antwerp, signalled the command to arms for the Belgian Secret Army. On 3 September, in Antwerp alone, 3,500 men of the Resistance responded to the call, taking up their appointed posts in the city.

It was a well-organized and well-commanded fighting unit that rose to help the Allied forces liberate Antwerp. For three years, these men had been waiting — and preparing — for this day of liberation.

The commander-in-chief of the Antwerp Secret Army was a regular officer with the Belgian Army, Lieutenant Urbain Reniers (code-named "Reaumur"). It was this man's task to weld into a cohesive fighting unit the several groups already actively engaged in Resistance work, hiding Jews and Allied escapees from the Germans, and harassing their captors with acts of sabotage. That he could unite these factions, at least for the duration of the war, into a unified and formidable fighting force was a remarkable demonstration of leadership.

Reaumur realized that it was of vital importance to protect Antwerp's dock facilities for the Allies. But the Germans were also well aware of their strategic value. Antwerp was, after the Dutch harbour of Rotterdam, the largest seaport in Europe, a prize so rich that the Allies would place a high priority on its acquisition, and the Germans on its retention. Tucked into a bend in the River Scheldt, eighty km from the mouth of the estuary, Antwerp Harbour offered safe shelter and sufficient draught, even at low tide, to accommodate the world's largest ships.

More than two years before, Hitler had predicted the need to rein-force the defences of the lands bordering the mouth of the Scheldt. But what Reniers was soon to discover, to his great dismay, was that this presentiment had eluded many of the Allied planners, who gave only token acknowledgement to the strategic importance of the Scheldt Estuary. They seemingly did not comprehend the simple fact that whoever controlled the access to the Scheldt controlled the use of the great inland port of Antwerp.

With their capacity of sixty thousand tons daily, the docks of Antwerp could handle all the supplies necessary for a swift and deci-sive Allied victory before the end of 1944. To deny the Allied forces the use of the river and the docks would give the Germans much-needed time for rearmament and reorganization after their defeat in Normandy.

The sprawling dock area was essentially a city unto itself. The warren of docks, five km of them in the immediate port area, pro-truded into the grey waters of the river. These were connected to the harbour by electrically operated lift bridges, and protected by sluice gates that controlled the tidal waters. An additional forty-two km of docks were built into inlets in the northern part of the harbour. Imperiously lining the skyline were over six hundred electric and hydraulic cranes. Sheds and warehouses dotted the quayside scrub-land. Tugs, pilot boats and scores of freighters all contributed to the floating complement of the port. The marshalling yards, huge on- and off-loading areas, were seldom free of controlled chaos. Entire vil-lages, with pubs for thirsty dockworkers and churches for their pious *mevrouw,* were contained in the complex. One could live and die without ever leaving the heart of Antwerp's docks. But in 1944, death was the principal game.

It was on the eastern and northern flanks that the harbour was most vulnerable to attack. The town of Merxem, home to many of Antwerp's seamen, was linked to the port by a series of lift bridges over the Albert Canal. It was this canal, the transport axis, that the city depended on. Major roads and rail lines connected the port by land with Dutch markets to the north such as Bergen op Zoom and Breda. By barge, goods could be transported along the Albert Canal all the way to the German border.

Due south of the docks lay the urban core of Antwerp, with its splendid Central Park where the command post of the German Army was situated (and, unbeknownst to the enemy, in the opposite corner, the HQ of the Secret Army).

Reniers appointed Eugene Colson, a sea captain of fifteen years' service, known only as "Harry" to the men he commanded, as section head responsible for the entire dock area. A chance snowstorm had aborted this firebrand's earlier plan to escape to London and join the Belgian Army. The British Lysander aircraft, bringing agents into the country and taking Resistance men out, had been unable to land.

Go back to Antwerp, Colson had been told. Wait for instructions.

Soon enough, the thirty-year-old Resistance fighter was playing an undercover role, painstakingly building up vital knowledge of the port installations through this gradually expanding espionage network. Each man in his battalion was handpicked for his knowledge of the docks. It was a desperately dangerous business. Many of the early Resistance members who had paved the way for mass recruiting were caught by the German Gestapo and imprisoned in the infamous Breendonck Concentration Camp, which lay south of the city near Boom. Tortured daily, threatened with death, a man would not be censored by his comrades if he talked. "Some came back," Harry remembers, "forever marked, and morally maimed. Many never returned."[1] One hundred and ninety-eight men of the Resistance were killed during the German occupation of Antwerp.

Harry saw his task as twofold: when the liberators came, he had to assist them by preventing the Germans from demolishing the port, and he had to capture and hold the key strategic positions in the port for the Allies.

During these long months of preparation, Harry was careful to live a routine life; even his wife was unaware that the stocky young seaman setting off for work each day could be carrying vital information sewn into the hem of his leather jacket. In spite of the constant danger, Harry couriered messages to his contact in Brussels, favouring crowded thoroughfares for anonymity, each time choosing a different route so that the Gestapo would be unable to trace his activities. The result was that when the police spot-raided the streetcar he was travelling in, looking as they frequently did for contraband butter, coffee, or even potatoes from black-market dealers, they saw only a brawny, hawk-nosed dockworker, pockets void of incriminating evidence, hazel eyes blank to their queries.

In Brussels, Harry would meet the agent responsible for communicating the intelligence back to London. The transmitter was hidden in a small suitcase, carried from place to place for each transmission. Messages had necessarily to be very brief; the alert Gestapo mobile intercepting vehicles could pick up the location of a stationary radio very quickly.

"By 1943 we were ready," he recalls. "I had six hundred skilled men, mostly dockworkers who knew every road, every crane, even every exchange. When I said 'Number 118,' they didn't say 'Where's that?' and look at a map. What I built up was a battalion of technicians, six hundred men who were prepared to fight to protect their city. But they were not mercenary soldiers; they did not have special weapons or training. They were ordinary civilians and volunteers, and they had to fight highly trained German soldiers." [2]

The sluice gates, the hundreds of cranes lining the quay, and indeed all dockside machinery were controlled electrically, an easy target for German sabotage. Harry assembled twenty-one of his best fighters for a mission of vital importance. Eager volunteers were ordered to cross the Albert Canal and man the electrical works on the Merxem side to protect the port's power source from German demolition. Harry assured them that when the Allied forces arrived they would surely provide adequate backup support at the plant.

Harry cited three sections of the port as critical to its defence. The town of Merxem weighed heavily on his mind. It was an area the commander knew well; its streets had been his playground as a lad. Now this tiny hamlet had more sinister importance. It formed the eastern boundary of Antwerp Harbour and straddled the Albert Canal at the south end. Merxem, where the central power supply for the harbour was located, was an essential objective in the battle plan of the Resistance. The capture of Merxem, with its bridges over the Albert Canal intact, would open up a northern route from Antwerp for the anticipated advance of Allied troops into Holland.

But if the suburb remained in the hands of the Germans, they would, without a doubt, defend it strongly: the docks would not be secure as long as the enemy threatened from the flank. Here, too, the Albert Canal, reaching almost due east from Antwerp, could create a grave obstacle to the Allies' thrust north. The Germans were skilled in the use of water for a front-line defence; a strong opposition along the canal could repel any Allied advances to Holland or the Ruhr.

"We will capture the lift bridges and we will keep them in the 'down' position," the determined Maquis leader declared. "The British must get across that canal."[3]

A further vital task that challenged the young freedom fighter was the necessity of capturing the sluice gates intact so that the water level of the port would remain in his control. Of key importance was the Kruisschans Lock, which controlled the ebb and flow of the Scheldt tides at the entrance of the port, and hence the waters of the entire port area. Contriving a visit to the nearby German strongpoint at Stutzpunkt Kruisschans, Harry was able to infiltrate some of his men into this critical point to cut the electrical feed cables that activated, by remote control, flame throwers protecting the lock. He himself would lead the main attack on the Stutzpunkt at the first sign of an Allied advance.

Number 12 Sluiskens Lock, two km farther north along the Scheldt, also had to be defended against German sabotage. This lock controlled the flood levels of the low ground in the villages encompassing the port to the north and east.

At Secret Army headquarters, Reaumur studied the final plans of his section heads. Harry, he thought, had the docks well under control. Resistance groups were consolidated to defend key sectors of the city core. In Hoboken, at the south approach, Resistance Commander Frans De Moor would secure the city approaches for the Allied troops. Others, including Edouard Pilaet (codenamed "François"), would harass German defenders at strategic points in the city. The details could now be passed on by Reaumur to the Comité de Coordination, still in radio communication with London. It was vital that the Allies be alerted to the battle plan of the Secret Army so that they could organize the essential support. The date was 25 August, 1944.

But with plans well on the way to completion, the Resistance movement received a severe setback, threatening the work of years. In a sudden raid, the Gestapo arrested several committee leaders,

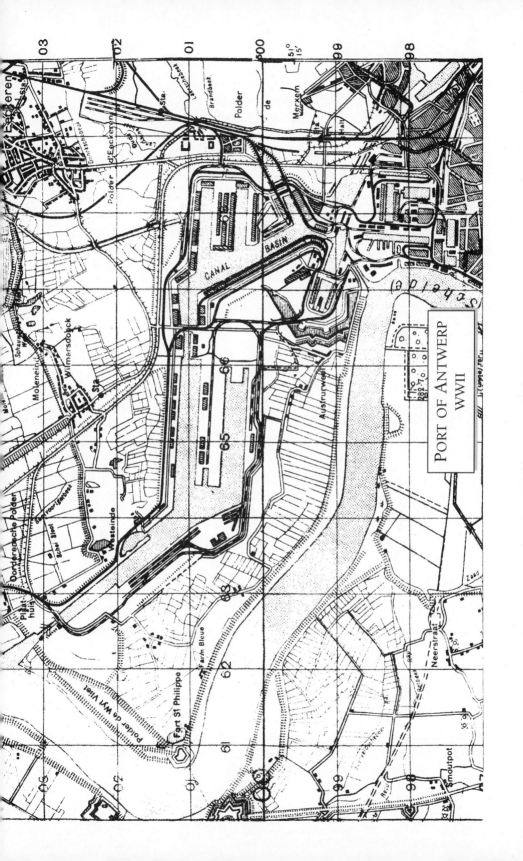

PORT OF ANTWERP
WWII

including the liaison man with the British in London. Reaumur and several of his officers became *brûlé,* and were forced into hiding. At this critical moment all communication with the Allies was cut off.

To Harry's section this was a severe blow. All of his volunteers had pledged their loyalty to the Royalist Movement (MNR) in support of King Leopold III. This had caused a rift with the Belgian government-in-exile in London, which disapproved of the king's wartime actions and therefore questioned the credibility of his supporters.*

As a consequence, the MNR men received no wages, nor even support in the form of food or uniforms. Of greater import, their motives were questioned by their own government and hence the aid they could give was gravely underestimated by both the British and Belgian governments in London.

———•———

The signal to arms, on Sunday, the 3rd of September, found these men of Antwerp prepared for and dedicated to their tasks.

Shortly after dawn on the 4th, the 11th Armoured Division approached the village of Boom, on the River Rupel, a major tributary of the Scheldt that constituted the last water barrier before Antwerp. Some 120 British tanks — all that were left of the original two hundred that had embarked on the pursuit six days before — laboriously churned over those last dusty kilometres toward the bridge across the river.

At a crossroads café not far from the river, a lone Belgian in civilian clothing drank a cup of coffee in quick, nervous gulps, peering restlessly into the half light of dawn for the first glimpse of the armoured column. The Germans, the Belgian patriot had discovered, were preparing an ambush. The British had to be warned.

---

* Enormously popular before World War II, the young king incurred the wrath of his subjects and of the British government and the Belgian government-in-exile when he offered the unconditional surrender of the Belgian Army to the invading German forces on 10 May, 1940. Accused first of collaboration, he was later exonerated. He also fell from favour when, after the death of his popular wife in a car accident, he married a Flemish commoner in 1941, bestowing upon her the title of Princess de Rethy. Many Belgians demanded his abdication following the war; he stepped down from the throne in 1951 and died in 1983.

Just ahead, German 88mm antitank guns lay in wait for the arrival of the British tanks. German demolition troops were poised to detonate the bridges over the river at first sight of the enemy. This demolition would cost the British hours, even days — the infantry would have to be brought up to establish a bridgehead so that sappers could erect another bridge. And the Germans would seize that opportunity to strengthen their defences of Antwerp. For thirty-one-year-old Robert Vekemans, a repatriated lieutenant in the Belgian Army and a member of the Underground, the next few minutes could determine the course not only of his life, but of the outcome of the war.

Since his release from a German prisoner-of-war (POW) camp in 1940, Vekemans, an engineer, had been seconded by Antwerp's public works department to supervise dock and water installations. His papers, therefore, let him move freely through German defence lines at regional water courses. As he crossed the bridges spanning the Rupel, Vekemans had noted the location of demolition wires, mines and defensive guns. Now, alerted by the BBC broadcasts, the engineer had completed his reconnaissance and would relay this information to the first British troops that approached from the south. To his astonishment, he had been there only half an hour when he saw a column of tanks coming up the road.

Now his task would be to convince a wary British unit that his information was accurate and vital. The events of the next moments, which have become known in Belgium as *Le Miracle de Boom,* were documented by a British Intelligence officer from the 3rd Royal Tank Regiment, which led the 11th Armoured Division:

> He stood in the road with his arms raised up, a lonely civilian in a grey mackintosh. The first tank was coming, rumbling up quickly, its turret closed. It was covered by the guns of two more tanks behind it. It refused to stop, bypassing Vekemans, and moving on.
>
> The second tank slowed down, and its commander stuck his head out and pointed back to the fourth in the group. This, in fact, was the squadron leader's tank — that of Major John Dunlop of the 3rd Royal Tanks. Dunlop, dark and

bearded, gestured with his pistol that Vekemans should climb up and say what he had to say.

Standing between two determined armies, in peril of being shot by both, the tall slim Belgian took his solitary stance and delivered his warning. Speaking with quiet determination, in near-perfect English, Vekemans convinced Dunlop to divert his armour to a less well-guarded narrow bridge several hundred metres upriver from the main bridge. The British, suspicious of a trap, insisted that Vekemans take the lead in a scout car. With their tanks camouflaged by nets and hidden behind their own clouds of dust, they rushed this secondary bridge, hoping to cross before the enemy realized that their vehicles were not German.*

The British intelligence officer's narrative continues:

Vekemans wanted to stop in the middle of the bridge; the scout driver didn't. As they passed the middle, Vekemans seized him by the collar, shouting, "Stop, I must destroy the wire to the detonators." The scout car stopped; Vekemans jumped out, carrying a big knife that he had borrowed beforehand from the driver. With machine-gun fire now coming from both sides of the bridge, and with the fear that the bridge would blow up at any moment, Vekemans sliced through the wire in two places.[5]

Having ensured that the secondary bridge was safe from demolition, the Belgian quickly guided the British, now concealed by some houses, to a point behind the main bridge, where they easily subdued

---

* Even then, they might have been too late, but for the second miracle of Boom. One Hauptfeldwebel Berghauser, the German sergeant in charge of the demolition of this smaller bridge, recently came forward with an account of the incident, revealing what a close call it had been for the British: having observed his commander's signal by Verey light to proceed with the demolition, Berghauser had quickly lit the fuse to the prepared charges, checked that it was burning, and ducked for cover. Ten minutes later, when nothing had happened, he realized that the detonator must have been faulty. The German had just started back to his truck for a replacement when the first British tanks nosed onto the bridge.[4]

the German defences. However, at that moment there was a heavy explosion from the south side of the bank. They were too late to prevent the demolition of the great bridge over the Rupel.

But the narrow, ancient wooden bridge they had saved was enough to get the 3rd Royal Tank Regiment across the Rupel. The RTR, supported by infantry, rolled into Antwerp before the Germans had time to organize their defences.

Two hundred and fifty thousand *Anversois* gave these marathon troopers a jubilant welcome, rivalling the near hysteria that had greeted the 11th Armoured's fellow division in the Belgian capital of Brussels the previous day. Later, the Antwerp newspaper *Het Handelsblad van Antwerpen* spoke for all the people with these words: "THE SHOUTS OF JOY, THE SCENES OF WILD ENTHUSIASM — THESE WILL NEVER BE FORGOTTEN, AND SERVED AS FIRST PROOF OF OUR GRATITUDE TO THE HEROES OF THE 11TH ARMOURED DIVISION WHO, COVERED WITH DUST AND HALF DEAD WITH FATIGUE, BROUGHT US LIBERATION WHICH HAD BEEN SO LONG AWAITED AND YET WAS ENTIRELY UNEXPECTED."

Surging crowds, with women offering kisses and men champagne, swarmed onto the main thoroughfares. There were several occasions when the troops found themselves in the curious and awkward position of holding armfuls of flowers as they tried to pick off snipers shooting from upper stories of houses. Despite the BBC's revealing report, the enemy seemed to be taken by surprise, although at several places the Germans offered stubborn resistance, as this British account reveals:

> One [British] armoured column was perturbed to find a German column, similar except it lacked tanks and floral decorations, moving in the opposite direction down a boulevard. The leading British tank, endeavouring to engage, was unable to traverse its gun owing to the people surrounding the tank, so the commander quickly diverted the column down a parallel street, hoping to cut the Germans off. The enemy, however, had the same idea, and there began an intricate and grimly hilarious game of hide-and-seek around the elegant boulevards of Antwerp's most fashionable suburbs.[6]

The King's Shropshire Light Infantry (KSLI) of the 11th Armoured, at that point the only infantry unit in Antwerp, describes the reception given when they entered the city:

> The difficulty of thinking and giving out orders and making oneself heard...amongst this mass of the populace crowding round still cheering, still flag-wagging, still thrusting plums at you, still kissing you, asking you to post letters to America, to give them some petrol, some more arms for the White Brigade,* holding a baby under your nose to be kissed, trying to give you a drink, inviting you to their house, trying to carry you away, offering information about the enemy, etc., had to be seen to be understood...There was the utmost difficulty in preventing groups of people from carrying off whole platoons shoulder high in the midst of operations.[7]

Unsubstantiated but generally accepted accounts circulated that some British soldiers completely disappeared overnight, lost to the drink, the women, and the hysteria of the city. In Horrocks's words, as a result of the sheer headiness of the entire six-day advance, "We were all suffering from 'liberation euphoria'...which made it difficult to get on with the war."[8]

But the business of war had to proceed. At the docks, at 1245 hours, Harry gave the order to commence his attack. He recalls:

> Our first success was the capture of the commanding officer of the Kriegsmarine, Captain Z. Mohr, and his staff of naval personnel securing the docks. These personnel were immediately transferred into the custody of the Intelligence section of the Allied troops who were just then approaching Antwerp from the south. We think the intelligence officer was able to get information about the position of the mines laid all along the River Scheldt by the enemy. It took us from 1315 to 1800 hours to control the whole eastern area of the

---

* A common misnomer for the Belgian Secret Army. Certain of its units wore white cotton coats such as those worn by butchers.

docks. We tried to push on to the north, but in view of our still poor armament (no heavy weapons) we could not get further on. After that we could only wait for the British to arrive with reinforcements.[9]

The British arrived, obedient to General Roberts's mandate to secure the docks, at 1600 hours on Monday the 4th, Liberation Day — but in the form of only a single troop of four tanks from Major Dunlop's C Squadron, supported by a lone infantry company from the 8th Rifle Brigade. With no sense of urgency imparted to them by SHAEF, this token force was all that was sent to control dock installations sprawled over forty square km of land. The officer commanding the troop, Lieutenant Gibson Stubb, describes the brief encounter:

> 4-troop now turned left along the side of the lock, my two other tanks covering the side streets. Here we were joined by a number of the Resistance, some with arms; as we approached the covered wharves which bordered the Scheldt, a number of armed Germans disappeared into a dugout on the lockside. I was on the point of throwing down a hand grenade when the Resistance leader waved me back and he and his comrades winkled the Germans out and took them prisoner, about thirty including several naval officers. We thought all was clear until a tank commanded by Major Wetherall was fired at from a pillbox and from a ground-level slit in the kerbside. His tank was hit but not stopped. My corporal's tank made a direct hit into the kerbside slit and my gunner blew a hole in the pillbox. We had no further trouble here and were pulled back at nightfall, the infantry taking over. And that was Antwerp for C Squadron.[10]

For the tank troops, the approaching darkness demanded withdrawal; the protection of their tanks claimed first priority. These ungainly, near-blind hulks of armour, so vulnerable to night attack, had to be bedded down safely, laagered away from the narrow confines of city streets.

At 1800 hours, one infantry battalion, the 3rd Monmouthshire of the 159th Infantry Brigade, arrived in the centre of Antwerp after a breakneck dash through Belgium. Their orders were to clear the dock area and secure the vital sluices. It took the battalion some twenty hours to cross the city to the docks, their passage impeded first by crowds at near-hysterical pitch, then by a pocket of German opposition, and finally by fatigue. Exhausted men and officers stretched out on the verges of the cobbled roads and slept.

With the infantry slumbering and the tanks withdrawn, the Resistance found it would have to work on its own that night. On the approaches to Antwerp, the Hoboken unit, under Major Frans De Moor, saw action securing key positions until they met the British in front of the Christus Konig Church on Ryswycklaan. De Moor advised the first British officer he encountered of two concerns, the immediate one being information he had about minefields laid by the Germans under the cobbles of the road leading to the city centre. The second expressed the deep anxiety the Secret Army had about saving the port from German demolition. De Moor's alarm sounded the first call for help. Having given that call, De Moor assembled his men at the south end of the harbour to protect the rear flank of the port unit, now engaged in intense fighting.

The German garrison, well-entrenched in underground concrete fortifications near Secret Army Headquarters at Central Park, was captured at 2130 hours. Fighting continued for two hours before the KSLI, with the help of Resistance forces, captured the garrison. It was a moment of intense satisfaction for the Secret Army fighters to participate in the surrender of Major General Christoph Graf Stolberg-zu-Stolberg, the commandant of the garrison. Six thousand prisoners were finally taken. For lack of more suitable quarters for incarceration they were deposited in the local zoo for the night!*

The German town commandant, still holding out in the Burgemeester's offices, was captured by a neat manoeuvre of the KSLI, who entered the building through a rear second-storey window of the

---

* Six months later, the German diplomatic service lodged a protest through the War Office concerning the unsuitability of using lion cages as jails. Responding to the charge, Major Ned Thorburn of the 4th Battalion KSLI asked, "I suppose the War Office realizes that we took the lions out first?"

lavatory. A grenade tossed through the window somewhat startled a lone German using the facilities.

————•◆•————

Crouching at the near-side of the bridge at Groenendaal Laan, bitterly disappointed by the lack of forceful support by the British, Harry rested his gaze steadily on the lift bridge spanning the canal to the suburb of Merxem, a tantalizing few hundred metres away.

During the endless hours of the night, Resistance fighting patrols had captured two key bridges leading to Merxem and had secured both in the down position. Twice, in the early hours of the second day of liberation, Colson had led his men across the bridge at Groenendaal Laan, only to be beaten back by the savage fire of an 88mm antitank gun. The Germans were well dug-in behind the twin barriers of the brick walls of a collegiate and the raised tracks of the main Holland-Antwerp rail line.

The Secret Army fighters, equipped only with small arms, were impotent against the enemy's heavy armament. For now there was no option save withdrawal. Further advances would have to await the arrival of British armoured troops with tanks that could deal with the power of the 88mm on the opposite side of the canal.

"We forced the bridges down," Harry was to recall, "and they stayed down, so the tanks could have got across the Albert Canal. With our bare hands, it was nearly impossible, but we did do that."[11]

The University Squad was beaten back by German fire from a bridge east of the main dock. This was finally blown by the enemy, leaving only the Groenendaal Laan Bridge, the one last artery left over the Albert into Merxem. Harry could only stand by helplessly waiting for reinforcements.

There was another moment of horror awaiting the Resistance commander: he was soon to witness the slaughter of his twenty-one boys, his *wapen breeders,* who were, to a man, shot down by Germans attacking the Merxem power plant.

At the port, the Secret Army had seen almost continuous action throughout the first night and into Tuesday. The ammunition barge *Goro* had been captured and neutralized. The men had gradually pushed their elements forward, until they controlled a wide area of dock facilities. They had seized access roads to Kruisschans Lock and to the villages north of the port. For a short while on the second day of liberation, opposition faltered, possibly under the pressure of determined fighters, possibly because the Germans were in retreat. Resistance men reported to the British that they had seen German troops in force crossing the Scheldt River from the west bank to the east.

"Have we got them on the run?" they wondered. "Are they retreating back to Germany? Or are they going to counterattack and successfully execute the demolition of the port?"

In fact, the next forty-eight hours would see a reinforcement of German resistance as they pounded again and again at the dock fighters and the British infantry defenders, trying to force them back. At Kruisschans Lock, a bitter struggle continued for control of the locks. One of Harry's fears materialized when the enemy opened the floodgates at Number 12 Sluiskens, submerging large areas of low-lying land in the northern suburbs.

But still the dock fighters hung on, a ragged, bleary-eyed, piecemeal army, depleted in ranks but strengthened by their successes. They had on their side a deep-rooted knowledge of their territory, and an advantage of surprise over an enemy who was not expecting civilian resistance of this nature. As well, their morale was incredibly high. So they persevered, doggedly waiting for the British to bring up more reinforcements. Finally, the British did come.

The next morning, September 5th, British tanks rolled up near Groenendaal Laan Bridge, a formidable assembly. Colson, and his commander, Reniers, approached the officer in charge of the tanks and explained that their men were holding intact the last bridge across the Albert Canal to Merxem. They emphasized that these Resistance fighters knew every inch of the dock area and could lead the British to the points where enemy opposition was at a minimum.

"Wipe out that 88mm and there's not much else to stop you from breaking through into Merxem and to the north," Colson told the British officer. "We have been over twice, but we cannot fight a heavy gun with rifles or bare hands. Please," he pleaded, "bring up your tanks and cross the bridge with us."

"I have no orders to advance," was the reply. "Sorry."

The desperate fighters went to 11th Armoured headquarters at Lierre, six km south of the canal. After some considerable wait General Roberts met the men in his caravan. "What do you want?" the Englishman asked.

Colson exploded: "What do we want? We want you to understand that we are men with close knowledge of the harbour, that we are out there holding key positions for you, and that we will help you. But we need the support of your guns!"

Roberts listened courteously to their plea. "Thank you," he replied. "It is noted."

In fact, Roberts's original orders stressed only the importance of capturing the docks, not the canal: "The main task was impressed on me, and I impressed it on my brigadiers, to get the docks intact. The further advance was of secondary importance and for that, in any case, I was not thinking in terms of northeast but east."[12] But soon after he had, as he thought, secured the docks, fresh orders came for the tank regiments to rest and refit for forty-eight hours.

On Crazy Tuesday the simple rules of war had been forgotten, and ally defeated ally. The tough young Resistance fighter did all that was left for him to do. Returning, he pulled his men back from the bridge. And as he watched the British withdrawing their tanks from the port he screamed, "Goddamn you, Britishers, goddamn you."

General Sir Brian Horrocks profoundly regrets those moments of history, blaming his superiors, Montgomery and General M.C. Dempsey, for not stressing the urgency of pursuit: "To my mind, September 4th was the key day in the battle for the Rhine. Had we been able to advance that day we could have smashed through and advanced northward with little or nothing to stop us…but we halted, and even by that same evening the situation was worsening."[13]

The KSLI were indeed to find the situation worsening when at dawn on September 6th they were finally ordered by their brigade commander to advance across the Albert Canal and establish a bridgehead into Merxem.

A reconnaissance unit was deployed to discover the best crossing point. The problem was compounded by the realization that the battalion had no effective maps of the area. There were, of course, local men of the Resistance who would willingly have shared their knowledge of the immediate topography. They could have warned the British of German strongpoints — and they surely would have led them to the undefended locality nearby where they had crossed in a rubber dinghy on two recent occasions. But, perhaps still dogged with misgivings about the MNR, the British did not consult the Resistance. They could hardly be faulted for doubting the MNR when even the Belgian government-in-exile was suspicious. The omission had a profound effect on the division's comprehension of its assigned task to defend the harbour, as the KSLI's battalion history discloses: "It was unfortunate that the division had no maps that went as far as the Albert Canal.* Most officers' knowledge of geography was so scanty that they did not even know where the Albert Canal was. The importance of the bridges over the canal was, therefore, not realized."

The diarist further noted that historian Chester Wilmot, in his book *The Struggle for Europe,* had been "a little hard on General Roberts for not capturing the bridges, but at the time no one mentioned the canal; all that Army and Army Group kept saying was 'You must get the docks, you must get the docks...'"**15

The KSLI's problems escalated. They discovered that few assault boats were available, and the first attempt to cross had to be aborted when they came under extremely heavy fire. A second location was found, and three companies crossed the canal, establishing a small bridgehead by first light on the 6th. As the troops tried to expand their positions, they came under attack from enemy tanks and infantry, which forced them to withdraw into two factory buildings. All through that day, and the next night, heavy fighting continued with the British tenaciously holding on. At noon on the 7th, as no troops were available to reinforce the position in Merxem, the brigade commander decided to withdraw the KSLI. This manoeuvre was

---

* Fighting maps were produced by the graphologist at army headquarters. Owing to the unexpected speed of the advance from the Seine, no up-to-date, large-scale maps of the Antwerp area had been completed by the 4th or 5th of September.

** Wilmot's comment in fact was "Even in the absence of specific orders, however, it is strange that so astute a divisional commander as Roberts did not secure the bridges immediately as part of his general brief to capture Antwerp. The cost of his failure to do so was soon evident."14

accomplished with heavy artillery support. Now, no Allied lodgement existed on the north side of the Albert Canal.

Thus it was that the bizarre events of *Dolle Dinsdag* unfolded in the city of Antwerp. The minds of the British commanders had been seemingly blocked against accepting and trusting the Belgian Secret Army. Had they heeded the pleas of the Resistance, the port of Antwerp could have been opened within days, instead of the months its capture required.

The Secret Army, first rejected by their own government and then by their allies, never adequately reinstated communications in time to be useful for the defence of the port. Years of preparation had been shattered when the Gestapo arrests in August severed their radio link with London. But the bitter taste of frustration did not remain solely with the Resistance.

Brian Horrocks, the prophet who had directed this "most exhilarating period," still smarting at being ordered to halt from after his triumph in Antwerp until the 7th of September, had now to confront the consequences of that halt. The reason he had been given for the "rest-and-refit" was that the 11th Armoured had outrun its administrative resources. It was an explanation that left him seething:

> It was infuriating because we still had 100 litres of petrol per vehicle, plus a further day's supply within reach. If I had ordered Roberts not to liberate Antwerp, but to bypass the town on the east, cross the Albert Canal and advance only fifteen miles northwest towards Woensdrecht, we should have blocked the Beveland Peninsula and cut the main German escape route. The only troops available to bar our passage northward consisted of one German division, the 719th, composed mainly of elderly gentlemen who hitherto had been guarding the north coast of Holland and had never heard a shot fired in anger, plus one battalion of Dutch SS and a few Luftwaffe detachments. This meagre force was strung out on a fifty-mile front along the canal.[16]

Horrocks's observation was not merely idle hindsight. What was perhaps the most incredible piece of madness of all in those mad days had been perpetrated against this respected commander. He subsequently discovered that he had not been given the appropriate intelligence that would probably have spurred him on to give Roberts more incisive instructions.

Although the highest level of British Intelligence had circulated precise accounts of the fact that the German 15th Army was trapped in Flanders and was escaping across the Scheldt and thence through the nearby Beveland Peninsula, Horrocks was never informed of this fact. Every schoolchild in southern Holland, even at that moment lining the roads with flags and flowers to welcome the British liberators, was aware that the Germans were fleeing in the face of an Allied advance.

Colson and his boys knew that the Albert Canal bridges were the key to pursuing the fleeing enemy. But no one told the corps commander, and that was his tragedy: "I suddenly became isolated, without any contact on my flanks and with a complete blackout as to what forces opposed us...Of the Poles and Canadians I had no information at all, and I would have been horrified to learn that 82,000 first-line [German] troops and over 500 guns were being ferried across the estuary and would soon be threatening our left flank. Looking back, it is difficult to understand why this move, which was being observed from the air, was never reported to my HQ.[17]

The 11th Armoured Division, ordered out of Antwerp the following day, would soon encounter the enemy again, this time a waiting enemy with sharp teeth. The division was ordered to advance to Arnhem.

For Colson and his battalion, there would be no sleep for five more days, until the Kruisschans Lock was finally secured. Exhausted and in despair, he and his men were forced to spend seemingly endless nights and days patrolling the ground they had captured, trying to keep the enemy at bay, praying for help, waiting. This time, for the Canadians.

The Great Escape

IN THE EARLY HOURS OF CRAZY TUESDAY, THE PEOPLE OF THE DUTCH region of Zeeland, whose homes bordered the banks of the River Scheldt, were in a state of rising excitement.

The townsfolk gathered on street corners, speculating anxiously about their liberation, for there was no question that the British would come. The people knew full well the strategic importance of their few hectares. In their innocence, however, they believed that the British would also comprehend that it was these lands that controlled shipping access to Antwerp, and it was through these towns and country lanes that the German Army was this minute escaping, with thousands of unarmed, panic-stricken men on the run. One Zeelander noted in his diary: "This spit of land, this South Beveland Peninsula, was the aorta for supply and discharge for the Germans, and for the defence of Zeeland's north shore of the Scheldt. This little strip was for the Germans the only way of escape in the case of possible retreat. Whoever had the approach in his possession was the master."[1]

The Scheldt Estuary had been an important shipping lane for many centuries. This would not be the first time that nations had vied for its possession. The stately Western Scheldt, in peacetime the main waterway to the port for freighters from around the world, coursed briefly north from Antwerp until it reached the neck of the Beveland Peninsula at Woensdrecht. There, the Scheldt's tidal waters hooked westward for the long, seventy-km surge to the North Sea.

Two narrow corridors of Dutch territory straddled the river for most of the distance. On the south bank was the section of Zeeland known as West Flanders, a thin ribbon of Holland orphaned from its mother country by encircling Belgian territory. It had the same flat, featureless terrain found in all of Zeeland — sodden polderland bordered by shores of mud flats and punctuated at precise intervals by a system of dykes built to protect the valuable farmland from the omnipresent threat of flooding by the North Sea.

The Scheldt's northern shore comprised the island of Walcheren at its mouth, and the peninsula of South Beveland, a slender arm of farm country some forty km in length, joined by narrow land-bridges to the island in the west and to the mainland in the east.

The Dutch had used great ingenuity in reclaiming much of Zeeland from the sea; it was the work of countless men and countless years. Yet lying as much as two metres below the level of the sea, the polders were vulnerable to destruction in seconds by man or nature.

At the eastern end of South Beveland, the land narrowed to an area just two km in width connecting the peninsula to the mainland of Holland. Here, for an instant, the unrelenting flatness of Zeeland softened into gentle contours.

At this juncture of peninsula and mainland, enjoying the only rise in land for miles around, were the small farming villages of Woensdrecht and, immediately southeast, Hoogerheide, hamlets of little import until the Allied military planners finally awakened to their strategic importance. When this happened, Woensdrecht and Hoogerheide would have their day on the front pages of the world, and then they would be destroyed.

For the vigilant Zeelanders, the German evacuation was a sign of impending liberation. In the beginning they heard the guns, forty, thirty, then twenty km away. The roar of exploding shells which, in 1940, had heralded the dreaded German invasion, now brought the promise of impending Allied rescue. Telephones were silent, service disrupted. Rumours filled that vacuum.

The most convincing evidence of all that liberation was at hand was the unnerving hush of abandonment. The German occupation force was in full flight. The people awoke, that Mad Tuesday, to an incredible sight: barracks lay empty, with food still on tables, clothes on pegs.

In private homes unmade beds and open drawers attested to the abrupt departure of billeted enemy troops. Trains and roads running north to connect with transport to Germany were jammed with those fleeing from the expected Allied advance.

It was a hybrid mix, this host of escapees: there were members of the Security Service or SD *(Sicherheitsdienst),* the silver skull on their helmets now a symbol of all that there was to hate and fear in men. These special fanatical Nazi corps who served under Heinrich Himmler were the police force of the German-occupied towns and villages of Holland. They staged raids *(razzias)* to kidnap men for forced labour camps, and viciously tortured those who had attempted to elude them. Now, they were arrogantly making off with the few possessions left to the Zeelanders. Some rode stolen bicycles; others were pushing *kinderwaggons* snatched from infants so that they could transport the loot amassed from black marketeering and theft during the years of occupation.

But others of the occupation forces had been men on convalescent leave from the Russian front, content to find roots in the quiet farming communities, grateful, in their loneliness for their own families, for an ambience of home. They had had enough, and too much, of war. On *Dolle Dinsdag,* the sound of the Allied guns at Antwerp triggered panic to escape any further confrontation with death. Joining these men were bedraggled troops bearing the insignia of the once proud German 15th Army, in full retreat from the powerful Allied advance across France and Belgium. Then, too, there were the quislings, entire families who had pledged their loyalties to the NSB *(National Socialistische Beweging),* the Dutch Nazi Organization, and who now were stampeded into flight along with their erstwhile heroes.

German stragglers who had not yet left the town got a boot in the behind from the now-emboldened citizens: "Go home, German. Get out of my house!" they cried.

From a woman of Woensdrecht came this eyewitness account of "Delirious Tuesday":

The big withdrawal of the German Army was in full swing. Wandering soldiers, far from home, looking like vagabonds, trying to find their way to the *Heimat* [native country]. Everything else was lost. The game was finished. No food,

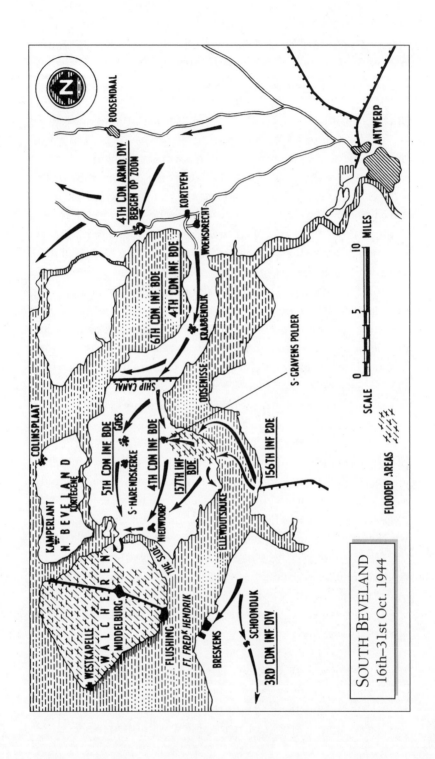

SOUTH BEVELAND
16th–31st Oct. 1944

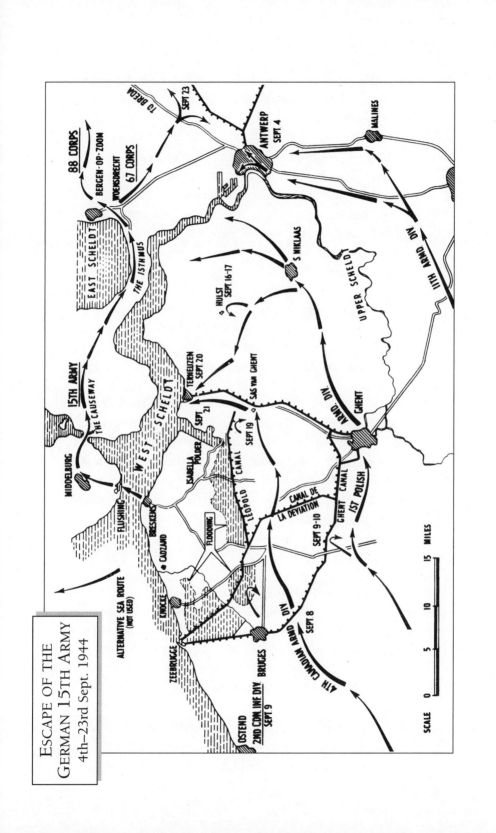

ESCAPE OF THE
GERMAN 15TH ARMY
4th–23rd Sept. 1944

SCALE

0   5   10   15 MILES

88 CORPS

67 CORPS

TO BREDA

SEPT 23

ANTWERP
SEPT. 4

MALINES

BERGEN-OP-ZOOM

WOENSDRECHT

EAST SCHELDT

THE ISTHMUS

11TH ARMD DIV

S NIKLAAS

HULST
SEPT 16-17

UPPER SCHELDT

15TH ARMY

THE CAUSEWAY

MIDDELBURG

WEST SCHELDT

TERNEUZEN
SEPT 20

SAS VAN GHENT

ARMD DIV

GHENT

FLUSHING

ISABELLA
POLDER
SEPT. 21

SEPT 19

BRESKENS

CADZAND

FLOODING

LEOPOLD CANAL

CANAL DE
LA DEVIATION

GHENT CANAL

IST POLISH

ALTERNATIVE SEA ROUTE
(NOT USED)

KNOCKE

SEPT 9-10

ZEEBRUGGE

BRUGES

2ND CDN INF DIV
SEPT 9

OSTEND

4TH CANADIAN ARMD DIV

SEPT 8

no drinks. The very strict leaders from before were also gone. The fanatical discipline was gone like snow before the sun. The urgency of food and peace plagued those soldiers day and night.

In the meantime, the rumour was spreading around that Breda was already in the hands of the British. After that the chaos was total. From all the German positions and depots in this neighbourhood, the Germans were fleeing. The looting of the airbase was taking place. One was celebrating already. The sorrows were over, because tomorrow the Tommies will be here!!![2]

In Bergen op Zoom, where rail terminals connected the main trains to Germany, local men were ordered by the fleeing enemy to carry to the station barrels and casks filled with pure alcohol from the spirits factory, as one celebrant remembers:

Sometimes one of the barrels wandered off the track down into a side street to the great joy of the people of Bergen op Zoom. At the station the Germans were bragging *"und wir fahren gegen Engeland."* They were as drunk as a fiddler's bitch. A bunch of guards, to quench their thirst, were shooting at the barrels. From the so created stream of spirits, they filled their flasks and those who weren't even able to do that dropped themselves with wide open mouths into the stream of the spirits.[3]

Seventeen-year-old Piet Suijkerbuijk, who endured an "expedition through hell," a fifteen-hour marathon through shellfire carrying his severely wounded parents to safety, remembers the dangerous mood of the crowd on *Dolle Dinsdag*:

The Dutch looked with enjoyment at the beaten troops, gloating. Some risked to call nicknames and some hung out the Netherlands' flag, after more than four years. However, this was a dangerous play, because among the Germans there were some fanatics who could not support such insults.

Sometimes they fired on the flags and the result was that the population was more careful, and looked at the retreat from a safe distance. Full of interest we waited for the moment that the Allies came down the street.[4]

For the citizens of Holland, the flight was a sweet sign of victory. "Did you see the Germans running?" they asked each other in high glee. "Do you hear the British coming?" And words that began as a whisper in the dawn of *Dolle Dinsdag* grew and spread across a nation hungry for such news.

—⦁—

The main road just sixteen km north of Antwerp runs through the village of Putte on the Belgian/Dutch border. Putte would have the first sight of the approaching British. So, at Putte, on Crazy Tuesday, crowds waited excitedly for the liberators, arms overflowing with flowers and flags and wine to hail the victors.

In the nearby town of Hoogerheide, an uglier mood prevailed, and the waiting crowd became a mob. Four girls who had bestowed sexual favours on German troops were dragged into the village square, surrounded by angry, vengeful Dutch. "Shave off her hair," one screamed. "Strip her, paint her, shame her vulgar body," shouted others. The women's ultimate betrayal of self and country enraged the traditional morality and honour of their countrymen. Collaborators, Dutchmen who had worked for the enemy or profited by him, were rounded up by their own police force and locked away to protect them from the angry crowd. For many weeks to come, in Holland and in Belgium, the shaving and painting of quisling bodies would continue until the appetite of the mob slackened.

For some, revenge was secondary to the joy of reunion as husband and wife, father and daughter met again after many months of anxious separation. Tentatively at first, men of the Underground, forced into months and even years of hiding to escape German capture, emerged from miserable cellars and airless attics to seek their families.

In the hamlet of Nisse, in the belly of the Beveland Peninsula, Pieter Kloosterman, who was to save so many Canadian and British lives in the coming weeks, snatched a moment from war to put an arm of comfort about his distressed wife. There had been little time for sentiment in Pieter Kloosterman's life. Seven hundred men and women in the Dutch Underground, spread over all of the South Beveland Peninsula, had looked to this man for leadership in their resistance war. Under Kloosterman's command, the Resistance had established a "Pilot Line," an escape route to England for hundreds of Allied airmen who had crash-landed in Zeeland.

Jews, high on the German SS hit list, were hidden in safe houses, sometimes for years, as were their own Resistance comrades who were wanted by the Gestapo. In order to safeguard this burden of extra bodies — and mouths — expert forgers were trained to duplicate identity cards and ration coupon books.

Enemy fortifications were sketched on large-scale maps for Allied Intelligence; strengths of troops and arms were recorded. Guides crossed German lines to take information to the Allies, or to lead friendly reconnaissance patrols into enemy territory. Reports were regularly transmitted to Intelligence links in Britain.

Nor did the Resistance forget the needs of the general population. To counter the mass of distorted information fed to the people through the relentless German propaganda machine, the people listened to Radio Oranje, the BBC's regular Dutch-language news broadcast that was transmitted from London each evening at nine o'clock. For the four years of German occupation, the broadcast had come to represent a few moments each day of truth and hope to be clung to, a lifeline.

Radios had long been forbidden by the occupation forces, who made periodic raids on civilian homes, often discovering these contraband sets. The Underground made simple radio receivers that were passed around freely to the civilians. Even at the risk of execution by the German occupation forces, many Dutch citizens huddled faithfully by these illicit radios each evening at nine. They were never discussed, these secret radios. Not even the children of the household, and certainly not relatives or neighbours, were told where the receivers were hidden.

After four years the bitter lesson had been learned; few could be totally trusted. An innocent word of gossip or a malicious report by collaborators might alert a watchful enemy. They had learned, too, that to save their villages from wholesale destruction, no overt acts of sabotage or violence were to be attempted. They knew all too well that they could be traced to their homes. Gestapo vengeance was swift and cruel.

In these days of oppression, men between the ages of seventeen and forty had to go into hiding to avoid being conscripted into forced labour camps through one of the systematic police raids on entire neighbourhoods and towns. Curfews at night limited the freedom of movement of these "under-divers." The occupation force decreed that special identity cards be carried by all; failure to produce one on demand resulted in a severe penalty.

It was in this environment that Christina Kloosterman waited time and again for her husband to return, always praying that the soft footstep at the door was Pieter's and not the enemy's. In this environment, the couple's only daughter developed diabetes. The disease was fatal, and suddenly their young daughter was gone, taken ill, dead, buried, all while an anguished father lay in hiding, helpless. The SD Police posted a watch at his home and at the cemetery, waiting for Kloosterman to come to his daughter's funeral. Twice they forced their way into his house and brutally interrogated his wife. She submitted to their beatings in silence; the Germans would hear no word of betrayal from Christina Kloosterman. The work of Pieter, her husband, head of the Resistance movement in South Beveland, would go on.

———◆———

A simple concrete cross embedded in the wind-torn dunes on the island of Walcheren offers grim evidence of the terrible risks these Resistance fighters knowingly — and almost daily — took. Throughout the more than five years of Nazi occupation, the Dutch and Belgians operated an underground courier system that led thousands of Allied airmen from behind the German lines to freedom — often just a few steps ahead of the alert German police.

In early September, German SD troops made a surprise raid on two neighbouring farms at Selzaete on the Belgian/Dutch border south of the Scheldt in the Breskens Pocket. They flushed out a

British RAF co-pilot and the Belgians who were helping him (the pilot had escaped through the roof), and ferried the prisoners from the port of Breskens to Flushing on the island of Walcheren where they were imprisoned, the co-pilot separately from the others.

Four days later, the three Belgian Resistance fighters, one of them the farmer who had harboured the fugitives and one his teen-aged son, in addition to two other Dutch civilians, were sentenced to death by Colonel Reinhardt, commandant of Flushing. The five condemned were driven by stealth to the dunes. A firing squad awaited them.

A Polish soldier, who later joined the Allied forces and returned to Walcheren to identify the graves, recounted the next events: "The four men and the youngster were forced to hollow out their own graves in the sand. Then they stood, facing the muzzles of the enemy they despised and the sea that they loved. A German officer spoke to the boy, offering him his life in exchange for information. The lad defiantly refused. The five were tied to stakes and as the order to fire was given, and the volley of shots spit across the dunes, the boy shouted 'Long Live Belgium!' and fell dead."[5]

But still the Pilot Line continued, saving hundreds of lives as the Belgian and Dutch Underground persisted in sharing with their Allies this desperate struggle for freedom.

The story of one of these, a Dutchman, Gerard Alphons Claeys, goes back to a starless night in August when an RAF Lanc streaked across Netherland skies on a bombing mission to the German town of Gelsenkirchen. Suddenly, a Junkers 88 attacked the plane, and with a single burst put out two starboard engines and damaged the tail. Petrol escaping into the hot engines exploded into flames and at 26,000 feet the crew fought their way out of the burning aircraft. Three of the nine men — the pilot, navigator and tail gunner — failed to bail out and went down with her.

The gunner, Flight Sergeant Douglas Jennings, became separated from the crew and landed, wounded and alone, in a Dutch field. Through the final hours of darkness, the young man, a Canadian on loan to the RAF, dodged the main roads, clinging to flooded irrigation ditches as he sought to elude capture. By dawn, feverish, his leg throbbing intensely from the continuous immersion of his shrapnel wounds in the muddy canal ditches, he sought refuge from a local farmer. The choice was unfortunate. The Dutchman, frightened that the nearby German guard would observe the two men together, summoned the local police and turned him in.

Jennings was imprisoned in a Dutch hospital at Rosemalen Lazaret near 's-Hertogenbosch. There were, as he recounts, six wounded Allied airmen in the ward: four British, one American and himself as the only Canadian. There was also a guard stationed at the door each night, and although Jennings was skeptical he later acknowledged that it was the "harebrained plan" of one of these captives — RAF Navigator Ken Forth — that inspired his escape. That it came off without a hitch was a welcome surprise for Jennings:

> I really did not expect the guard in the room to fall asleep, but it turned out there was no danger as he slept an hour later than we needed. I was later told that the poor fellow — he was a Rumanian — was court-martialled for this. Meanwhile, I feigned sleep but then fell asleep myself in spite of taking smuggled wakey-wakey tablets. During our walk period, the bar bolt of the blacked-out hospital window had been prevented from sliding into place. So I had only to take off the blackout cover, tie sheets together for a rope and lower myself to a solarium verandah roof six feet below me. As I was then directly above the compound, I had only to jump over the wall to escape.
>
> At dawn, after whistling the BBC call sign and getting a return whistle, I was able to identify friendly Dutch and they sent men to rescue me from the copse of dense trees where I was hiding. Then I was whisked on foot to a hay stack where they first hid me.[6]

Jennings then was linked up with the Pilot Line. For twenty-six days he was moved slowly towards the Belgian border, sometimes cycling, more often walking, hiding out by day in hidden corners of friendly homes. And he played a silent audience to the remarkable performances of the men and women who helped him in their unceasing defiance of enemy oppression. "There was a constant war of attrition," he recalls. "Germans were stabbed, dumped into the

canals...once a bridge near 's-Hertogenbosch was blown up by ammunition transported in a German staff car by pseudo-German personnel."[7] Risking their lives, and the lives of their families and friends,
the Lowland Resistance workers who guarded the Pilot Line handed
each escapee along to the next secure link in this valiant chain.

As he neared the Belgian border, Jennings met his new courier,
a serious young Dutch school teacher. Real names were never
exchanged during an escape; even the background histories of refugee
and rescuer were falsified to protect them from betrayal if either one
were captured. The Gestapo, these Resistance men and women had
learned, was skilled at eliciting information from their prisoners. It
was only many years later that Jennings discovered that his rescuer
was named Gerard Alphons Claeys. For the moment, they were
forced to share anonymity on this final lap of his treacherous journey. He recalls: "We were on bicycles, with Claeys ahead leading the
way. This was after a previous attempt had been made to take me
across into Belgium at another location on the mainland of Holland,
but there the mounted border guards were very alert. We were seen
— but not arrested and had to turn back from the attempt."

Jennings was impressed at the thick packet of papers that his new
companion guarded with such care. "He was carrying a sheaf of hundreds of onion-skin maps detailing the whole German front at the
Scheldt," the Canadian remembers. "These were in a scale of one-quarter of a mile to the inch, and the work was done with great precision,
giving the disposition of the entire permanent German defence layout
— fortifications, mines, even troop positions. He was trying to get these
to the Canadian forces that were then facing the German armies."[8]

Claeys led Jennings to a small hamlet near the Belgian town of
Eekloo, handing him over to some Belgian freedom fighters. The airman spent nine days in hiding under the noses of the German occupation force, first in a hay stack, later with some members of the
Belgian Underground in a barn. The sudden intrusion of Germans
seeking quarters in which to billet their troops forced the refugees
out. For several days after that, Jennings was a guest in the home of
the chief of police of Eekloo, who was harbouring refugees and clan-
destinely manufacturing arms. Allied troops were approaching; it was
determined that he should stay in this place until rescued by his own

people. However, German officers arrived to bid goodbye to his host, and again, Jennings was over the back fence and away. His final refuge was an attic loft of a building overlooking the German mortar position. It was from here, on the 15th of September, that he saw the welcome spectacle of an advance unit of the Lincoln and Welland Regiment approaching to liberate the town — and himself.

Later, when Allied Intelligence had cleared the airman's identification, Jennings took Claeys down to Canadian headquarters. Both men have brooded over the memory of what transpired as this segment of Jenning's correspondence to his rescuer reveals:

> I was called down to identify you. But because you were not linked in with an established army — you were instead one of the nameless, brave men of the Resistance — you were rejected, along with the valuable maps that might well have saved thousands of lives. I tried, but all my efforts were fruitless. Even though they knew that you had rescued a friendly airman, the Allied officers could not be persuaded to take the risk. I can only guess at the great disappointment to yourself and your people that the Allied forces did not trust the maps. There was no proper liaison between the British Intelligence and these people to instruct them that the maps were real and not a trap to deceive.[9]

On *Dolle Dinsdag*, others, like Nellie van Nispen, were emerging from a different kind of hiding. Nellie was a cheerful twenty-year-old, a pretty girl. She had barely known her parents before they died and had been raised by a sister and brother-in-law who had bought false papers which had changed her age to sixteen. It wasn't very healthy to be female and twenty in German-occupied Holland; the frequent raids scooped up young women as well as men for transport to forced labour camps in Germany.

The road north from Antwerp to Holland, passing Putte, Hoogerheide and Woensdrecht, comes not so many kilometres beyond Woensdrecht to Nellie's home town of Bergen op Zoom, a city of some wartime importance as the staging point for troop trains to and from Germany. On September 5th, the railway station at Bergen was a very busy place.

In the wake of the German flight, Nellie's family and most other townspeople in Bergen raided the stores abandoned by the retreating enemy. "For so long we had so little. Now, everything is for us," the girl thought resentfully. There were sheets and blankets, sugar, shoes, furniture, items that she had almost forgotten, so long had they been missing from Netherlands' shops. For the Dutch, there were also to be spoils of war.[10]

In a German office building, Nellie's little sister found a box of cigars in the drawer of a handsome desk. The youngster paraded home proudly, followed by two Netherlanders carrying her new desk, happily puffing on their stogies. Her younger brother triumphantly produced a sack of boots he had stolen from a German repair shop, only to discover as he proudly emptied them out in the middle of the floor that they were all for the left foot. A bag of sugar, greatly prized, turned out to be salt; they laughed, intoxicated by the day.

The provocative call of freedom had in fact seduced the spirit, and the Dutch citizens now had little trouble in rationalizing their own looting of food and furnishings abandoned by the retreating enemy. In Hoogerheide and Woensdrecht, plundering also became a favorite sport. When the Germans deserted the aerodrome in Hoogerheide, the populace wasted no time getting out to examine the loot. One man who was there tells the story:

> A lot of people were delirious and ridiculous because they plundered a lot of belongings they couldn't use at all, or in limitation, and they had no place to hide it. At the aerodrome, meat, drinks, beds, blankets, furniture from huts and bunkers, all that was left by the Germans was snatched away...My friend said to me: "What is happening over there? I want to go look!" Away he went and after some time he returned with chocolate and other candy that had not been in our shops for such a long time. After half an hour we came back with our plunder. We had a lot of different things: pants, garters, socks, chocolate, toffee, wine, cognac, handkerchiefs,

too much to tell...a great deal of plunder was eaten and drunk in the festivities.[11]

———————•—•———————

In the pre-dawn hours of September 5th, on the lush Dutch island of Walcheren, two young lads crept silently through the familiar streets of their home town of Flushing. Each corner brought a fresh revelation of a wondrous happening: in the German fortifications, guard posts were eerily empty, pillboxes were silent, gun stations unmanned. Cautiously, the boys snaked their way through treacherous minefields laid thickly in the sand and scrub slopes of the steep dykes to their accustomed watching post.

One of the boys was thirteen-year-old Peter Eekman, for whom the sand dunes that encircled much of his small island held no mysteries. His playground in more carefree days, the dunes had become a scouting ground in the serious game of war. In the way of the Dutch in those occupation years, no one spoke of the Resistance. But Peter nevertheless knew that his closest friend's father was deeply involved with this group, and it was tacitly understood that the boys' reconnaissance would be the subject of some discussion behind locked doors.

Since March 1943, the youngsters had observed and chronicled every detail of the eighteen months' extensive construction that had transformed their corner of the "Garden Island of Europe" into a fortress. Now it was one of the most formidably defended enemy positions in northwest Europe. Although it measured a mere fifteen km in any direction, Walcheren's command of the mouth of the Scheldt demanded, and got, a major buildup of fortifications by the Germans. Its encircling rim of dykes, built to keep out the North Sea, now was reinforced to keep out the Allies. The dykes were of imposing stature. Many reached heights of ten metres and were supported in places by concrete bases over one hundred metres in breadth.

Flushing itself had been transformed into a fortress of concrete, isolated against attack by two water-filled antitank ditches, and further protected by barbed wire and hundreds of thousands of mines. Powerful batteries of heavy guns, some with all-round traverse, some sighted only toward invaders from the sea, safeguarded the fortress from invasion. The coastline that once had attracted tourists would now, its seawall bristling with well-concealed armament, repel any aggressor.

The concept of an Atlantic Wall had become the personal brainchild of Adolf Hitler following the ill-fated Canadian raid at Dieppe in 1942. To prevent a recurrence of this landing, the German dictator buttressed the coastline of northern France and Holland with these *stutzpunkt* — virtually impregnable fortifications — that could stave off any invasion from the sea, and that could be defended even from landward attacks for long periods by comparatively few troops. Each commander was required to take a special oath to defend his post to the end.

In Scheldt Fortress South, Hitler's engineers similarly secured the southern entrance of the Scheldt. The ancient moated Fort Frederik Hendrik was reinforced with thousands of tons of concrete poured on its foundations. Heavy guns protruded from concreted crevices built into the fort and in the main harbour of nearby Breskens, creating a formidable potential for crossfire with the guns of Flushing; such crossfire would be able to ward off attack from the North Sea.

In 1942, Flushing had been evacuated of all nonessential personnel prior to the enormous task of building the *stutzpunkt* fortifications. Peter Eekman, who was raised by his grandparents, was grateful that his grandfather's position as director of river pilots gave the family licence to stay in their home. The Eekmans remained, along with less than one-quarter of the city's original sixteen thousand citizens. Their licence to stay would prove to be the entry permit to a living hell.

Those who were ejected could go in only one direction: eastward. Carrying whatever possessions they could manage, they crossed the causeway, a narrow land-bridge linking Walcheren to South Beveland. From here they had to continue their eastward trek. Some families found shelter with friendly farmers along a peninsula rich not only in wheat and barley but also in human kindness. Others had to continue their journey to the end of the peninsula some forty km further on until they reached Woensdrecht at the neck of the isthmus, or, just beyond it, the mainland city of Bergen op Zoom.

The pre-dawn shadows of *Dolle Dinsdag* lifted, revealing a sight that made the boys gasp. Below them, crossing the Scheldt in a confusion of rafts and barges and merchant ships, were thousands of German troops nearing the docks of Flushing. Some units were still equipped with weapons and tanks, trucks and horses; others had the clothes on their backs and little more. Just five km across the mouth of the river, at the small Dutch village of Breskens, the lads saw thousands more troops crowding up to more craft at the embarkation point. It was a pitiful exodus for the once-proud Wehrmacht.

The remnants of the German 15th Army, plus refugees from the experienced 5th Panzer Army and the German 7th Army who had seen their units demolished by the carnage of Normandy, were retreating in confusion and fear, having neither leader nor will to do battle again. With wounds clumsily bandaged, eyes drained of hope, exhausted from days of walking, they crossed to Flushing with only one thought: home.

Fugitives from the German 15th Army formed the greatest part of this shattered force. Most had walked from the Pas de Calais coast of France to Holland, hoping to escape from Breskens, through Walcheren, to Germany. In all, nearly one hundred thousand men were committed to the retreat across the Scheldt in a desperate attempt to elude the Allied net. Many of them were barefoot and filthy, all were hungry and demoralized.

Then another group of disillusioned German soldiers joined their countrymen. These were men from the German occupation force. Frightened by the faces of defeat they saw shuffling by them, terrified by the sound of Allied gunfire drawing nearer, these captors of stolen land, these self-appointed governors of Zeeland, put down their arms and walked away.

So it was that on Tuesday, Mad Tuesday, this veteran force established an escape route that would, in the coming weeks, see 86,100 Germans elude the advancing Allied forces.

Standing at an upstairs window of her home overlooking the harbour of Breskens, Sara de Winde watched this curious flotilla bear the hated enemy on its short journey across the churned-up Scheldt to Flushing. This Dutch *mevrouw,* this most respected citizen of the town of Breskens, who owned with her husband a grocery shop and wholesale food warehouses and resided in a big brick house on

Dorpstraat near the harbour, was playing a dangerous game.

During the past years of the occupation, Sara de Winde's home had hidden dozens of fugitives who were fleeing the Gestapo. This Underground work was camouflaged by a facade daringly contrived by the family. The de Winde home had become a choice billet of the occupying force; there was always one German officer, and sometimes two, living in the best de Winde bedrooms. That was fine with Sara, for the Gestapo wouldn't dream of raiding a house that so hospitably accommodated their own number.

In not so much comfort, but sharing the same roof and hospitality, there might be as many as a dozen fugitives. Most of these were "under-divers," Dutch Resistance men who were on the German hit list and had been forced to "dive" underground to escape the relentless searches. Sometimes, the de Winde house sheltered Allied airmen shot down over Dutch territory. A well-organized underground escape route would pass the flyers from one safe house to the next until they crossed the German line. Burrowed into airless corners of the rambling de Winde storerooms, often hungry, always afraid, these men could be betrayed by a single creaking floorboard or a sudden cough.

For the Allied escapees, capture would mean spending the duration of the war in POW camps. For the family de Winde and their Resistance comrades, death was the single certain consequence. There would be no trial, no appeal; the cold muzzle of a pistol would give instant retribution. But individually and collectively, every member of the family was determined to fight by whatever means necessary and available to protect the men and women whose continuing work against the Germans would help free their country.

Fifteen-year-old Hannie de Winde, a girl of much vivacity and charm, was fully committed to smuggling contraband papers and arms. Her slim waist was frequently camouflaged under thick multi-pocketed corsets that concealed forged identification cards, stolen ration coupons and weapons for escapees. She thought it terribly amusing that the German soldiers loitering on street corners, imagining her pregnant, would step back respectfully. False papers adjusted her age to her condition, and the disguise had the further benefit of protecting her from soldiers' advances.

Sara worked with her daughter smuggling arms and documents.

But she also had to forage for food and clothing for her clandestine guests. Always adhering to her normal routine of caring for her younger children, of operating the shop for her ailing husband, always under the vigilant eye of the enemy, she played her role with the consummate skill of an actress.

Fear was the single emotion that she would not permit. On one occasion, a German officer newly posted to Breskens decided to conduct an impromptu inspection of the de Winde house: "But you can't see the rooms until they are properly cleaned and tidied for you," Sara protested gaily. He agreed to return in two hours, which just gave her time to shift two of her illicit guests to other quarters.[12]

Sara's son, Peter, had spent many dangerous months in active sabotage. War had picked up schoolboys like Peter and taught them the street-skills of a common thief. Now, this nineteen-year-old led armed raids on German posts, stealing bulk lots of ration coupons or freeing imprisoned comrades.

But in these dangerous days, Peter de Winde had himself been forced underground to wait out the war in the damp gloom of an anonymous cellar. It was only by night, and then rarely, that he could visit his family, lest he be recognized by the occupation force and sent to a concentration camp.

So the family de Winde had survived these perilous wartime years, waiting for Allied rescue. But now Sara de Winde coolly weighed the events occurring before her observant eyes. Years when danger had been her constant companion had honed the perceptions of the woman. The abrupt German departure spelled bad news for the Dutch compatriots. Absently, she smoothed out a crumpled notice that had been handed over to her by one of the Resistance. Dated the 3rd of September, it read:

SOLDIERS OF THE WESTERN ARMY! WITH THE ENEMY ADVANCE AND THE WITHDRAWAL OF OUR FRONT, A GREAT STREAM OF TROOPS HAS BEEN SET IN MOTION. SEVERAL HUNDRED THOUSAND SOLDIERS ARE MOVING BACK-WARD...WE HAVE LOST A BATTLE, BUT I TELL YOU, WE WILL WIN THIS WAR!...AT THIS MOMENT EVERYTHING ADDS UP TO THE NECESSITY TO GAIN THE TIME WHICH

THE FUHRER NEEDS TO BRING INTO OPERATION NEW
TROOPS AND NEW WEAPONS. THEY WILL COME. SOLDIERS,
WE MUST GAIN THIS TIME FOR THE FUHRER!

Field-Marshal Model[13]

"Having the Germans here is bad," she mused, "but having them leave is even more dangerous. Why have they not blown up any of their fortifications? What is the plan of this Model that he begs for time from his soldiers? We will see: the Germans will be back — and things will be much worse for us."[14]

Indeed, the Germans were soon to fulfil this grim prediction. In defence of the Fuhrer's Fortress of West Flanders, soon to be known to thousands of Canadian troops as "Breskens Pocket," a vastly more powerful enemy did return to the Scheldt in the days following *Dolle Dinsdag*. And hundreds of Canadian and Dutch lives were wasted on its shores.

❧ 4 ❦

The Adversaries

O N THE FIFTH OF SEPTEMBER, THE SUPREME COMMANDER, GENERAL
Dwight D. Eisenhower, eyed with distaste the correspondence
he could no longer ignore, noting wearily that his two temperamental commanders were at each other's throats again.

The controversy had been stirred up by a developing crisis in the
war that Eisenhower had predicted some weeks before: the Allied
forces, he had told General Marshall in August, were advancing so
rapidly that supply lines were becoming seriously strained: "Further
movement in large parts of the front, even against very weak opposition, is almost impossible. The potential danger is that while we are
temporarily stalled the enemy will be able to pick up bits and pieces
of forces everywhere and reorganize them swiftly for defending the
Siegfried Line or the Rhine."[1]

Eisenhower had also confided to his chief that there was no point
in reaching the German border unless the armies could exploit that
position when they got there.

Clearly, success was creating its special set of problems. Before
D-Day, Supreme Headquarters military planners had predicted that
twelve Allied divisions would cross the Seine at D plus 120. Instead,
at D plus 90, an entire month ahead of schedule, sixteen Allied divisions were already 240 km beyond the Seine. With the supply structure already severely strained by the speed of the latest advance, the
risk was that it would collapse under its own momentum. By encouraging the hectic advance of the armies of the Allied Expeditionary
Force across France and Belgium in late August and early September,

Eisenhower had created a monster that had an insatiable appetite for fuel and other supplies.

The demands were staggering. On any given day, the thirty-six reinforced divisions in action, serving the armies of Britain, the United States, Canada and other Allied nations, required a total supply allotment of twenty-five thousand tons — all this to maintain two million fighting men on foreign soil. These men had to be armed, supplied with ammunition, and transported. Their vehicles and equipment had to be replaced, their numbers reinforced, their wounded evacuated. They required food, clothing and lodging, and always at an ever-increasing distance from their single docking facility on the Normandy beachhead. It had become essential to establish advance supply depots in order to permit Allied thrusts into Germany.

It was not only the military that created supply demands. SHAEF (Supreme Headquarters Allied Expeditionary Force) was under pressure from the commander of the Free French Army, General Charles de Gaulle, to look after the liberated French civilians. There were five million civilians in Paris alone who required enormous quantities of food, clothing and medical supplies.

The problem lay not so much in getting the essential supplies to Europe as in moving them forward from Normandy to the troop positions. Allied bombing had effectively destroyed much of the French rail network. Materials, therefore, had to be off-loaded onto trucks, and then transported over roads that were often badly damaged. The Red Ball Express, the longest one-way truck artery in the world, was set up to operate twenty-four hours a day over a circuit of 1100 km. Over five thousand tons a day were moved by this ingenious system, but it was an amount well short of the required tonnage. Masses of materiel lay uselessly on the docks; eight entire divisions of troops, about 120,000 men, were grounded at the port, their trucks commandeered for transporting supplies. Infantry were rationed in rounds per rifle. Tanks and armoured vehicles were ditched wholesale because of lack of parts.

Antwerp, and only Antwerp, with its ability to handle as much as sixty thousand tons of supplies a day, could satisfy the demands of the Allied armies. Not to be ignored was the city's proximity to the front line and, with the coming of autumn storms, the protection offered by its inland harbour. For combatants on both sides of this war, Antwerp was an unparalleled prize.

But now, Eisenhower's prediction had become a grim fact. His armies were seriously overextended and were on the brink of immobilization because of lack of supply. Patton had been virtually forced to a standstill for the first four days of September, his petrol ration reduced in one day from 400,000 to 38,000 gallons. Then Montgomery's 11th Armoured Division, down to a single day's fuel supply for its tanks, was abruptly halted after its bold capture of Antwerp for a three-day "refit, refuel and rest."

The critical shortage of petrol had severely curtailed the Allied advances. Now it became a factor in unleashing even more intense rivalries, catapulting Eisenhower into the middle of an acrid controversy with his field commanders. The tug of war was gaining momentum.

Montgomery and Patton were each convinced that they had surefire plans to a quick victory, plans that they had submitted to the supreme commander. Patton, with the verve of the dashing cavalry officer he had been, wanted to charge the enemy relentlessly until he pushed him over the Rhine and back to Berlin. Montgomery, too, was insistent that the only way to finish off Germany was with one immediate, powerful, concerted deathblow, preferably delivered by his army toward the Ruhr, or, otherwise, by Patton's toward the Saar. But not, he stressed, by both. "There is only supply enough to feed one of us," Montgomery said briskly to Eisenhower, "so take your pick — but be quick about it!"

In those early days of September, however, Eisenhower wavered between the two, juggling petrol supplies between the Union Jack and the Stars and Stripes so clumsily that in the end both Montgomery and Patton became furious at each other and at their boss. And, as one historian noted, in fretting about the weaknesses of his two commanders, the supreme commander lost sight of their strengths: "Eisenhower had under him two absolutely magnificent commanders — one [Montgomery] for the methodically planned out 'set piece' attack, the other, Patton, for the flowing battle."[2]

On the 2nd of September, Eisenhower flew from his HQ in Granville to Versailles for a meeting with Patton's boss, General Omar Bradley. Patton was outstripping his supply lines again, Eisenhower complained, and gave orders to halt him. Brought to an abrupt stop in his flamboyant sweep just fifty km short of the German border, Patton defiantly pushed ahead, hijacking petrol from the 1st U.S. Army to get his tanks rolling again. "Continue until the tanks stop," he bellowed at his armoured divisions, "and then get out and walk, goddammit!"[3]

With his tanks finally drained of the last drop of petrol, Patton became apoplectic with rage. By diverting Patton's petrol to "appease Monty's insatiable appetite," the fiery commander complained that Eisenhower had put "harmony before strategy," sacrificing their best chance of an early victory. Patton was convinced that his own advance could have "bounced" the Rhine and bulldozed straight into Berlin. In stopping him, Patton raged, Ike was causing "a momentous error."[4]

But even as he spoke, a decision was in the making at Granville that would abruptly alleviate Patton's fuel famine. Instead of unleashing either one of his bickering commanders for a deathblow, Eisenhower laid down a conciliatory policy, stringing his armies along a so-called broad front on the Rhine. On the 5th of September Eisenhower wrote, "I now deem it important, while supporting his [Montgomery's] advance eastward through Belgium, to get Patton moving once again."[5] So Montgomery would have his thrust through the Arnhem corridor of Holland, but only a limited one, without the massed support he had demanded. Patton would have his petrol supply reinstated to regain his momentum.

It was a decision that would please the politicians and dismay the military. But in formulating this decision, Eisenhower was fulfilling his mandate. His job was essentially a diplomat's job, demanding all his mediatorial skills to cement the interests of all nations into one Allied force. Many believe that in discarding the "deathblow" strategy and spreading his supply ration so thinly as to weaken all its elements, Eisenhower missed the opportunity to end the war.

For now the Germans had been given badly needed time to toughen up their defences. Now those buoyant romps across the map of Europe would become an agonized inching against a determined enemy in the final struggle to reach the Rhine.

But there was still good reason for optimism, Eisenhower knew. The Allies had one definitive advantage over the Germans. The Allies had Ultra.

Never in the history of warring mankind has one antagonist had the overwhelming advantage of a regular forewarning of his opponent's plans. Yet this is precisely what the British, aided considerably by the Poles, were able to gain from the beginning of World War II.

When the Nazis had come into power in the 1930s, they had bought up the patent on the Enigma machine to provide a system of enciphering secret information within the party organization. Polish mathematicians made the first strides in breaking the powerful German coding device. Fearing Nazi military intentions, the Polish government gave their discovery to the British just before the outbreak of the war, and the French and English scientists continued the investigation until Enigma was completely broken. The resulting deciphered messages were designated by the name "Ultra," signifying the ultimate in secrecy.

As early as 1940, every coded wireless communication between German command posts, air bases and even submarines at sea could be intercepted and the resulting decodes, labelled Ultra, were put into the hands of Allied strategists and high-ranking field commanders.

At Bletchley Park in Buckinghamshire, batteries of cryptographers, many drawn from civilian circles, worked out of the now famed Hut 3 to interpret these intercepts to the maximum benefit of the Allies. Translation required a highly precise and technical knowledge of the German language to ensure that shading of intent was not lost. It required, too, a precision of mental process; the fact that most of its decipherers were master chess players was no coincidence. Piecing together various bits of information flowing from Enigma, these men and women could essentially reconstruct a major troop movement or the enemy's plan of attack. Occasionally, there were communiqués directly from Hitler to a member of the German High Command, and these offered a unique glimpse into the mind of the enemy leader.

Security was so tight that only a tiny, handpicked group of senior military commanders — sworn to secrecy — could be trusted with the Ultra secret. Commanders on Ultra's elite roster rarely ranked below the position of army commander. Senior men, such as Britain's General Dempsey or Canada's Crerar, were expected to contrive a plausible rationale, based perhaps on prisoner interrogation and/or aerial photographs, for disseminating top secret information to corps or division commanders such as Horrocks.

The biggest danger accompanying the use of Ultra intelligence was the possibility of inadvertently betraying the source by acting too blatantly on its information. Awkward, occasionally ambivalent, and even dangerous incidents occurred because of the restrictions on the material. Elaborate deceptions were contrived to camouflage from the enemy any question that his communications had been infiltrated by British Intelligence.

In the supreme commander's hand, then, was Ultra's continuing story of the rout of the Wehrmacht. The German 7th Army had been physically crushed and was demoralized to the point that it was no longer considered an effective defensive force. Divisions were down to a fraction of their former strengths. The Panzer Lehr and 9th SS Panzer Divisions of the 7th Army, front-line formations each with some 20,000 Normandy veterans, had now ceased to exist. The 1,400 tanks of the German Army were reduced now to a reserve of fewer than one hundred — a twentieth of the Allied holdings. The Luftwaffe was a token force; to combat more than 14,000 Allied planes, the Germans had 573.

To Eisenhower's certain knowledge, six divisions of the German 15th Army, comprising almost one hundred thousand men, were retreating in disarray to the mouth of the Scheldt, crossing the river to Walcheren in commandeered ferry boats. The locations and strengths of each unit as it retreated up the coast towards the estuary were faithfully reported within the German High Command, and simultaneously intercepted at Bletchley Park.

The ingredients of victory were on hand. The enemy was on the run. The supply problem would be solved with the opening of the port of Antwerp. Eisenhower's most experienced commanders, Montgomery, Bradley and Patton, had submitted plans that they insisted would put an early end to the war. But nowhere did any of those proposals emphasize the priority of securing Antwerp's approaches.

On 5 September, 1944, neither his chief, Dempsey, nor Montgomery, nor Eisenhower thought to tell the one man who could have immediately intercepted them that the Germans were trapped: "I suddenly became isolated...with a complete blackout as to what forces opposed us," Horrocks said.[6] And that was the essence of the Antwerp tragedy.

Instead, on *Dolle Dinsdag*, General Dwight Eisenhower penned a note of some four paragraphs to Bernard Montgomery. Poor lines of communication caused the last half of the letter to reach command headquarters in Brussels first and two days later the beginning paragraphs arrived: "While agreeing with your conception of a powerful and full-blooded thrust toward Berlin I do not agree that it should be initiated at this moment to the exclusion of all other manoeuvres. The bulk of the German Army that was in the West has now been destroyed. Must immediately exploit our success by promptly breaching the Siegfried Line, crossing the Rhine on a wide front, and seizing the Saar and the Ruhr."

The last half of the message finally broached the subject of the great need for ports: "While we are advancing we will be opening the ports of Havre and Antwerp, which are essential to sustain a powerful thrust deep into Germany."[7]

Thus did the absentee landlord of war irresolutely address the twin challenges of an enemy army trapped within a few kilometres of his forward line and the need of a port whose use was mandatory to the successful conclusion of hostilities. Missing were the conviction of purpose and the urgency of command that would have allowed his slumbering armies to take decisive action.

On *Dolle Dinsdag*, three men alone shared alarm for the outcome of these issues: the Chancellor of Germany and supreme commander of the Wehrmacht, Adolf Hitler; Admiral Sir Bertram H. Ramsay, commander-in-chief of Allied naval forces; and one fairly obscure Canadian general.

At the concrete fortress *Wolfschanze*, Hitler's "Wolf's Lair" in an East Prussian forest, the German dictator worked far into the night in his heavily guarded map room. There, he exhorted his commanders to station their troops in strong positions on both banks of the River Scheldt.

Antwerp, the dictator emphasized, was of extreme strategic importance to Germany. He stressed the decisive need of holding "Walcheren Island, the bridgehead around Antwerp and the Albert Canal positions as far as Maastricht."[8]

Adolf Hitler thus spelled out his strategic defence plans to obedient German commanders who immediately stabilized their retreating forces and consolidated them with such speed and force that the next few days would come to be called the "Miracle of the West." And within a few hours, the Allied military commanders had been informed through Ultra of Hitler's plans.

The next day, the day Antwerp was captured, Admiral Sir Bertram Ramsay sounded an alert to the dangers inherent in not acting quickly to secure the seaward approaches to Antwerp. His directive, sent to SHAEF and to Montgomery's 21st Army Group, contained a stern warning: the Germans, Ramsay predicted, would mine the Scheldt River to block the Allies from using the port unless the river were immediately seized under Allied control. He noted: "If the enemy succeeds in these operations the time it will take to open the ports cannot be estimated."

Then on the following day, Mad Tuesday, Bertram Ramsay made a forlorn — and prophetic — entry in his diary: "Antwerp is useless unless the Scheldt Estuary is cleared of the enemy."[9] The third man to realize fully the vital need for immediate action in securing Antwerp was a comparative new boy to high command, and in the pecking order of international importance, well down the list.

Lieutenant General Guy Granville Simonds, at forty-one the youngest general ever to command a Canadian corps in battle, had been spending some contemplative hours in the map room of the HQ at Moyenville in northern France. He was disturbed by the current emphasis on capturing the Channel ports.

Simonds was in a unique situation. As commander of the 2nd Canadian Corps, he would not ordinarily have had access to Ultra signals. However, at General Crerar's special request (possibly because Crerar's illness on occasion interfered with the regular conduct of his duties), General Simonds was fed "raw" instead of "pre-digested" Ultra intelligence: "He [Simonds] was to prove not only a brilliant commander, but an enthusiastic Ultra customer," reported the guardian of Ultra, F.W. Winterbotham.[10]

Simonds was, therefore, aware from the intercepts that the German Army was trapped. An idea was germinating in his mind. Why, he mused, was he being diverted to lay siege on the chain of Pas de Calais ports on the French coast when they were almost as far back from the front as Cherbourg? Why not, instead, clear Antwerp's approaches immediately and nab the escaping German Army at the same time?

Outlining his thoughts in a memo to his immediate superior, General Harry Crerar, commander-in-chief of the 1st Canadian Army, the young officer brashly proposed reversing Montgomery's orders to attack the Channel ports, and instead giving full chase to the fleeing enemy: "I suggest, sir," General Simonds wrote to his chief, "that the 2nd Canadian Corps push up the coastal sector, behind the coastal defences, simply masking the fortresses with light forces."[11]

But Crerar, fearing the strong fortifications of these ports, had planned to capture each fortress, one at a time, in a carefully staged "set piece" attack. This could involve lengthy delays as it required careful reconnaissance, planning and execution in each case.

Anticipating this argument, Simonds countered that it was his opinion that while the fortresses had great defensive capabilities, "They are not an offensive threat on our flanks. By making for Breskens and sweeping eastwards from there along the south bank of the Scheldt toward Antwerp, we could catch the German 15th Army and the refugees from the 7th Army and the 5th Panzer Armies in a second pocket. To hook around the Scheldt first would delay the attacks on the Channel ports by only a few days'; their capture would contribute nothing [to the supply shortages] at that juncture."[12]

Recollecting the delays caused by shortages of bridging equipment and petrol during the Italian campaign, Simonds urged that preloaded landing craft should beach these essentials at intervals along the Channel coast, to be picked up as needed by the advancing troops.

It was unfortunate for Simonds, and of tragic consequence for the army he was soon to command, that a series of dismal little occurrences should have ruptured, for the moment, friendly relations between his commanding officer, Crerar, and the latter's boss, Field Marshal Montgomery.

The rift had caused tension enough in 1st Canadian Army headquarters. Crerar was loathe to inflame it further by questioning directives from Montgomery at 21 Army Group. As a result, Simonds's suggestion never even got off the ground, and a war that might have been rapidly concluded was instead reheated to a point far more intense than the military minds at SHAEF could have imagined.

For Guy Simonds, it was a time of total frustration. He was convinced that his "hook around the Scheldt" would have effectively stopped the German retreat. But he deemed it impossible to go to Montgomery and so over the head of his superior officer at this time of strained relationship between the two men. He felt powerless to pursue the idea: "I would have given anything to have had ten minutes with Monty at the time. He would have seen at once the chance of entrapping the German 15th Army and the veteran [Panzer] refugees. Crerar could not, and simply passed on the orders from Army Group. Relations were not very good between Monty and Crerar at the time, and though I protested the order to give priority to the capture of the Channel ports, Crerar refused to raise the issue with Monty."[13]

General Crerar had, in fact, recently had ten minutes or so with Montgomery — and it had been a very unpleasant confrontation that had ruffled the Canadian considerably, and had irritated the Briton even more than usual. At a time when smooth communication between these three men — Crerar, Simonds and Montgomery — was of very great importance to the progress of the war, a silly sequence of nationalistic bickering disrupted harmony in the Allied camp.

It had all begun at Dieppe, at the graveside of eight hundred Canadians. On the first day of September, a Friday, the 2nd Canadian Division was, by Crerar's orders, given forty-eight hours for rest and refit. The stated reason for the halt was the need to assimilate one thousand reinforcements into division ranks, depleted by more than a third of their regular strength following the Normandy campaign.

When Montgomery heard about this the next day he fired off a strong signal of countermand: "it is very necessary that your two armoured divisions push forward with all speed towards St. Omer and beyond. NOT repeat NOT consider this the time for any division to halt for maintenance."[14]

Montgomery also requested Crerar's presence at a meeting at Tactical HQ of the Second Army the following day, Sunday, at one o'clock.

What obviously had not occurred to the Field Marshal, nor if it had would he have countenanced it, was the possibility that in fact Crerar had a second and to him much more important reason for declaring a time-out from war: Crerar was determined to honour the Canadian dead who had fallen on the beaches of Dieppe.

In 1942, in an operation created and jointly run by the top military leaders of Britain and Canada, seven battalions from 2 Canadian Infantry Division staged a seven-hour raid on the shores of France. This reconnaissance in force subsequently turned out to be primarily an appeasement to the Russians for the lack of action in the West — although valuable lessons were also learned on invasion tactics. The Canadians were ordered to assault the port area that was heavily defended both by infantry and by batteries of German guns entrenched above and in the surrounding sheer cliffs. It was a badly conceived operation. Many survivors believe security was so lax that the Germans were waiting to ambush and slaughter the unsuspecting Canadians. Casualties were tragically high. Of the five thousand attacking troops, a mere sixteen hundred returned to England.

Twenty-five months later, the men from those same battalions, some mourners, some survivors, were again poised to attack the picturesque French seaport. But this time there was no German opposition. Hitler's wireless command to the Dieppe garrison to fight to the last man had been delayed by twenty-four hours. The Germans had already fled or surrendered, and the Canadians returned to a tumultuous welcome from the liberated Dieppoise.

All this was on the mind of Harry Crerar that Saturday, the 2nd of September, as he weighed the two options open to him. With the next day falling on a Sunday, it had seemed appropriate to hold back the men for a formal religious service followed by a ceremonial parade at which he was to take the salute. But obeying Montgomery's command for the division to continue the advance would automatically cancel the ceremonies.

Harry Crerar regarded himself as the protector of Canadian nationalism, as well as commander-in-chief of Canada's army. It was his mandate, laid on him by the government of Canada, to ensure that his country would not suffer any slights of colonialism. Hence, in Crerar's mind, two wars were being waged: the physical, violent one against the Germans, and the more subtle, subjective one against any ally who might threaten Canada's autonomy or prestige.

Consequently, Crerar sent back a friendly note to Montgomery, requesting that their meeting, if possible, be postponed by a few hours to allow for the service. As for the order to get going, he coolly replied, "in my opinion a forty-eight-hour halt [is] quite essential."[15]

The Calgary Highlanders had not participated in the Dieppe raid, but a member of the regiment, enjoying the unexpected respite from battle, commented:

> Moving into the suburb of Neuville les Dieppe, the men were treated to the good news that they would have two days' rest with no duties other than a march past to commemorate the re-entry of Canadian troops into the city. Those who had taken part in the famous raid attended a memorial service at the Canadian cemetery on September 3rd, exactly five years after the mobilization of the battalion in Calgary. An impressive parade of the entire division marched past General Crerar in columns of sixes in the afternoon. Although it was a long march on a hot day and had involved considerable effort in "smartening-up," the troops must have felt proud and triumphant as they marched past the saluting base between large crowds of cheering Frenchmen.[16]

A livid Montgomery, unimpressed by ceremony or display of emotion, confronted Crerar the next day when the Canadian finally arrived at 21 Army Group headquarters. Crerar rather testily responded that according to the Statute of Westminster, the Canadian Army was under the direct control of the Canadian Parliament, and hence he, its appointed representative, had a definite responsibility to his government and country which at times might run counter to his [Montgomery's] own wishes.

This "Canada first" attitude was to cause misunderstanding fairly often, both with Montgomery's 21 Army Group, and even within his own ranks. Crerar's insistence on allowing or even creating distractions from an all-out war effort for the sake of a measure of nationalistic pride was even to confuse the younger Simonds, who failed to understand the political pressures resting on his superior's shoulders.

Crerar could hardly be faulted for pursuing his mandate. He was in an untenable role laid on him by a shortsighted government apparently more obsessed with protecting its precious autonomy than in liberating Europe.

Harry Crerar was fifty-five years of age when he took over command of the 1st Canadian Corps in Italy in 1943, his first experience in a major military command position. An artillery officer in World War I, he had followed the long, arduous peacetime climb up the rungs of promotion of the permanent force until 1940 when he was appointed Chief of the General Staff with the rank of major general. During these years, Crerar was known by his associates as a commander of great discipline, a highly intelligent student of military history, a man wedded to his job and country. Lieutenant General W.A.B. Anderson (then Lieutenant Colonel, GSO 1 Operations, 1st Canadian Army) sums up the challenges Crerar encountered:

> He knew what General Currie had to put up with in World War I to establish a Canadian Corps and a real Canadian identity. He knew perfectly well that one of his missions was to make sure that the Canadian Army was identifiable and not just part of a "glorious British enterprise." And he had to put up with a very opinionated, single-minded fellow, Monty. And he was a match for Monty. When Montgomery, for battlefield reasons, didn't think the 2nd Division should waste time marching into Dieppe, going though a Canadian kind of catharsis there, Harry Crerar determined they would. He was the right man in the right place to look after the Canadian interest.[17]

And Lieutenant Colonel Walter Reynolds, GSO 1 Air, 1st Canadian Army, admired the finesse with which the Canadian handled pressure:

> The whole thing [for Crerar] was to try and keep eight balls in the air at once. He had not only to get along with Eisenhower and the staff at SHAEF, but with Monty and the 21st Army Group. In addition he had to keep the [Canadian] minister of national defence and the war office happy. And there were all those troops he commanded under the 1st Canadian Army: Canadian, British, Belgian, Polish, Dutch, Norwegian, Czechoslovakian, American…he wasn't a popular figure, not

an egocentric bird like Montgomery, but he was a very good diplomat and he never got his just due for what he did.[18]

In September, 1944, Crerar faced two other challenges that he plainly found difficult to come to grips with. One of these was his physical health; the other was Lieutenant General Guy Granville Simonds. Continuing anaemia made it increasingly miserable for Crerar to carry his heavy responsibilities, often prompting him to hand over the shop to his corps commander. Finally, advised to seek further tests in hospital, he relinquished command temporarily, freely nominating Simonds to command the 1st Canadian Army at the time of the Battle of the Scheldt.

For Simonds, the command opportunity was like opening a door to a smouldering fire. His feverishly active mind exploded in flashes of fiery brilliance that marked him, even in those first few weeks, as the most tactically innovative general ever to emerge from a Canadian army.

Fortunately, most senior commanders were not required to be political animals — that Simonds might have handled miserably. Instead, they could indulge the luxury of single-mindedness, a quality for which Simonds, as well as Horrocks and Montgomery, were often, but not always, admired. Because these three were of a type, they shot ahead in concert, impatiently shaking off the restraining influences of their more politically oriented bosses. "Simonds saw things only from a military point of view," his friend of many years, Major General H.A. Sparling, remarked. "He didn't recognize that the political side had problems too."[19]

Another prominent Canadian military leader remarked thoughtfully, "Harry Crerar was really too much of a gentleman to be a completely successful army commander. To be really good, you had to be a bit of a bastard."[20] That Guy Simonds was "a bit of a bastard" is often enough acknowledged, occasionally in distaste for his ruthlessness, but more frequently in admiration for his unerring command on the battlefield.

In his early days as a student at the Royal Military College, and during eighteen years of peacetime service as a gunner in the permanent army, the British-born Simonds was called "The Count." To some, the name was a slightly sardonic acknowledgment of his immaculate appearance and manner. Just under six feet tall, straight of stance and spare of build, dark hair slickly combed back behind a carefully coiffed widow's peak, moustache meticulously trimmed, uniform impeccably tailored, Simonds was the "compleat officer," as one senior officer termed him. His dark good looks were not lost on the ladies, who found the renowned icy blue eyes somewhat more melting in their effect.

But men who worked up through peacetime ranks in his wake recall best his perseverance in mastering his profession, putting all else aside to concentrate his entire effort on achieving his objective. When war came, these attributes merely intensified. He developed an educated approach to battle — flexible and probing — the very antithesis of the old-guard traditionalism that marked many of his seniors when he first began his mercurial ascent. And all the while he was, it was often suspected, terribly ambitious.

War had culled much deadwood from the army; a ruthless purge, initiated by Montgomery and continued to an extent by Simonds, had produced an army that was tough and smart — and young. Every major over forty was removed from the fighting units.

Simonds himself was forty-one years old when he took temporary command of the 1st Canadian Army in late September, 1944. Exactly two years earlier, his first command appointment involved a unit of just over one thousand men. Eight months after that he was promoted to the rank of major general, commanding the fifteen thousand men of 2nd Canadian Division.

Then, in 1943, after the tragic air crash that killed Major General Harry Salmon, Simonds took over Salmon's command of the 1st Canadian Division just before the invasion of Sicily. This was to be his first experience of leading troops into battle.

Simonds took on the task with such tactical brilliance that in November, 1943, he was given an even more challenging task: to command the 5th Canadian Armoured Division which had arrived in Italy in a dangerous state of battle unreadiness. Again with determination and vigour he transformed the division into a battle-ready unit that was ultimately to distinguish itself in the Italian theatre. But Simonds, now a lieutenant general, had been moved on to yet another fresh challenge: to lead the 2nd Canadian Corps in the invasion of Normandy in June, 1944. In those constantly shifting battle situations provided by difficult terrain and a fierce and determined enemy, Simonds demonstrated an ability to improvise, and a distinctive imagination that prompted this appreciation by British Major K.J. Macksey:

> Of all the Allied corps commanders, Simonds was among the most versatile and best equipped to deal with the wide variety of operations posed to his 2nd Canadian Corps. He had commanded in action an infantry division in Sicily and an armoured division in Italy, was young, ruthless and aggressively intolerant. Yet his educated approach to battle made use of every possible modern aid to help reduce casualties and still achieve striking penetrations of the enemy line. No Canadian field commander had greater experience or acquired more respect from friend or foe.[21]

"Guy was so involved with soldiering that nothing else mattered," recalls Brigadier J.M. Rockingham (later Major General), commander of the 9th Canadian Infantry Brigade, who served under Simonds during the Battle of the Scheldt: "He was a brilliant fellow and he came up with a wonderful plan in Caen, going into Falaise [Operation Totalize]. We were ordered to advance our tanks and troop-carrying vehicles at night. But navigation was nearly impossible in the dark. Guy said we had to use direction finders to keep the armour on direction. 'You know perfectly well you can't put compasses in tanks,' we told him, 'there's just too much metal around them.' But Simonds just said he'd figure a way, and he did."[22]

What Simonds did was create a beacon. He ordered a stream of phosphorescent tracer fire to be fired along the route from Caen to Falaise, leading the armour to its destination.

Moving several thousand fighting men with their equipment through unfamiliar territory by night invited chaos. But Simonds's fertile mind lit upon another dazzlingly imaginative concept: by bouncing the rays of searchlights off low cloud cover, Simonds created "artificial moonlight" to guide his men.

It was the corps commander's idea, too, to take the turrets and guns off a type of armoured gun carrier called Priests in order to convert them into troop-carrying vehicles. Instead of lagging well behind their armoured battle-mates, infantry could now advance, securely protected, toward the enemy, and at the same pace as the tanks. So forceful was Simonds's determination to create these troop carriers that, in a matter of three days, mechanical engineers of Royal Canadian Electrical and Mechanical Engineers (RCEME) had transformed some seventy-six Priests into troop-carrying "Kangaroos." They were ready for the Falaise attack, each capable of transporting a dozen men into battle.

But there remained still another problem of concern to the commander. This attack centred on a narrow front, leaving the flanks of the troops completely vulnerable to enemy encroachment. In a daring and unprecedented move, he arranged for the Royal Air Force to lay on a night attack of heavy bombers that would hang a dense curtain of explosives along the flanks of the advancing Canadians.

Even his staunchest friends and associates recall the aloofness of Guy Simonds. Sometimes they forgave it as shyness, often they labelled it coldness. Clearly, Simonds did not have Montgomery's ability, so well remembered by Lieutenant General Frank Fleury, "of unbending, getting down to the lowest echelon and talking to the men." But, Fleury said firmly, "He was unquestionably Canada's finest senior commander. I don't think anyone would argue with that. However, that didn't make him well liked."[23]

The major discernible flaws of this man were a hot temper, generally held under tight rein, and a tendency towards impulsiveness which was not quite so successfully harnessed.

In Italy, Montgomery finally had to intervene behind the scenes when Simonds flew off verbally at a highly regarded brigadier during a large staff meeting. Brigadier Richard Malone, who was attached to Montgomery's staff at the time, described the meeting with Montgomery:

> Monty called General Simonds up for a fatherly talk. He cautioned Simonds, who was very young for a general and who was commanding his first real battle, to take things a little more easily. He suggested to him that he should give his

subordinates their heads a little more and not try to personally direct every battalion in action...This lesson was possibly the hardest one Simonds had to learn in the fighting
ahead. After issuing his own order it was almost impossible
for him to refrain from taking a hand in the detailing of
orders to smaller formations.[24]

Occasional lapses such as these are considered to have held
Simonds back from even more rapid advancement both during and
after the war.

"People sometimes speak of Guy as a cold, cold fish," recalls
Major General Chris Vokes, a divisional commander in Italy and
northwest Europe, and Simonds's lifelong friend. "But if you command in wartime you've got to be pretty damned cold. One thing
about Guy — you always knew where you stood with him. He was a
straight shooter."[25]

But if you command in wartime, you have also to be highly
skilled. "The men knew that Guy Simonds was more professional
than any officer they'd run into since World War I," General Anderson recalls. "They knew they were dealing with a real pro. Troops
sometimes like fellows who are backslappers and jokers, but when
the chips are down they really respect a fellow who knows what
he's doing."[26]

A classmate from the Royal Military College who commanded in
a different theatre remembers Simonds's reputation as that of an
implacable leader who would never hesitate to remove any of his
subordinates if he felt that they were not competent in their jobs.
Simonds himself issued this tough-minded directive to his officers:

> I fully appreciate that the removal of officers who may have
> given long and faithful service, particularly when they may
> be personal friends with whom one has been associated in
> the same regiment, is a most distasteful duty. Nevertheless,
> it is a duty that must be faced, and a commander who shirks
> it is unlikely to possess the resolution to drive through a dif-
> ficult situation in battle. Consideration of its effect on an offi-
> cer's family has occasionally resulted in dilatory action in

dealing with those who are believed to be ineffective. Such matters must not receive consideration.[27]

That he took his own advice is evidenced by the fact that on a single day, in Normandy, he fired a brigade commander and two of his battalion COs, and in another instance he removed one of his best friends from a senior command position.

Brigadier John Rockingham remembers sitting in an orchard with Simonds one steamy August afternoon in Normandy:

> It was the first day I had taken over the 9th Brigade; Guy had fired my predecessor for failing to make his objective or something. And that same day, he'd fired two battalion commanders too. It wasn't a very happy atmosphere, so Guy called a meeting of the officers and said, 'If any officer has anything to say, now's your chance.' Some clown stepped forward and said, 'I object.' Guy looked at this guy with his icy blue eyes and replied: 'Men are fired in war because they think they need only make a partial commitment. In war you are fully committed.' The officer quickly stepped back into the ranks and nothing more was ever said.[28]

"He surrounded himself with people who were highly competent and very well qualified," notes Brigadier General (then Major) W.K. Lye, RCE: "If Guy wasn't getting what he wanted, he would immediately replace the individuals concerned until he had a team that was working as a well-oiled machine, exactly the way he wanted it to operate."[29]

Simonds's ruthlessness inspired admiration from many of his commanders. Major Elliot Dalton, of the Queen's Own Rifles, reflects: "One of the biggest factors in an infantry unit is whether the men can relate to the officers, the higher command particularly. Then you've got a good team. Simonds was a fine tactician and he was a winner. Men like to go with a winner."[30]

But there were others who could only resent this all too frequent rolling of heads, and the manner in which the execution was effected. One senior officer recalls a chance encounter with Simonds in Normandy: "I was sitting in a jeep at the side of the road, having just done a recce to find our next battalion headquarters, when Simonds came up. He was in that Staghound armoured car of his, complete with dispatch riders, and he asked me (we had been friends for years), 'Where is the headquarters of 4 Armoured Division?' I said, 'Sir, I don't even know where the headquarters of 3 Division is and I'm in 3 Division.' He said, 'That's why you're still a major. Drive on!'"[31]

A painful fact of command, and one of the most difficult for men who must lead troops into battle, is that the consequences of their decisions must be measured in terms of human life. Elliot Dalton remembers when a company of his men was cut off from the rest of the battalion by German paratroopers:

> I was just about to order an operation to rescue them when Guy Simonds came into my caravan HQ. "You leave those men in there and send in your other company to reinforce them at first light," Simonds told me. "That way you will take fewer casualties than you would by withdrawing them and then having to attack again."
>
> These were men I had fought with since D-Day. They had had so many casualties they were well below strength; I hated to leave them trapped behind enemy lines all night.
>
> Simonds said to me, "That's an order." I thought he was a ruthless s.o.b., but he turned out to be 160 percent right. The men hung in there for the night. They held their position although it got pretty uncomfortable, and next morning we sent in the other company to consolidate it.
>
> I got the impression that this man saved lives by being a hell of a tough guy on the surface. He would make a very cold-blooded mathematical calculation. He would send his men through their own artillery barrage if he thought fewer of them would be killed than by not putting down any barrage and having them go against enemy machine guns. He would make his troops do things that would lose people, but always the very least number possible.[32]

But this professional soldier was running into political obstacles that for all his abilities he was helpless to circumvent. The change of command "mid-battle" from Montgomery to Eisenhower on the 1st of September, Montgomery's apparent and baffling loss of his sense of direction in the management of the war following Antwerp's capture, the distraught attitude of his immediate commander, Crerar, all served to keep Simonds from the obvious next step of defying the command hierarchy and going over the head of his chief to promote his plan to cut off the German 15th Army.

"He had a pipeline to Monty," General Anderson recalls, "but he couldn't overuse it."[33]

If, in fact, Simonds had bypassed ordinary channels and presented his plan directly to Montgomery, he would probably have received an attentive hearing. Simonds's enormous respect for the British Field Marshal was not one-sided. Montgomery had recently told a senior Canadian official that his young protegé was "the best straight tactical and operational commander the Canadians had."[34] Simonds alone, with his far-reaching plan to intercept the escaping Germans, might have jolted Montgomery back to reality.

"For a very brief period, the German command structure collapsed," Simonds was to muse ruefully. "The opportunity was fleeting but it was there, and against an army which had many many times shown its ability to react quickly it was a folly to let the opportunity slip."[35]

If, during those critical days in early September, Guy Simonds demonstrated an uncanny perception of his enemy, so also did Adolf Hitler anticipate a major Allied offensive on his wavering western front. The only thing he did not, could not, foresee was the inconceivable crumbling of the Allied thrust at the eleventh hour.

In his sparse headquarters in East Prussia, Hitler flew into frenzied action. His office was a dank, airless, concrete fortress, buttressed by his own paranoia against the military leaders he had ceased to trust since the July 20th assassination plot. SS guards stopped and searched everyone who entered the shelter, even those in uniform, the most trusted of his military leaders who had now been imperiously summoned in this crisis. The signals room punched out Hitler's frantic directives to his field commanders, messages urging, exhorting, even threatening his armies to retrench staunchly against the enemy. Adolf Hitler needed time to rebuild his western defences, time to complete his new rocket weapons.

And thus was created, in a matter of less than three weeks, the "Miracle of the West," the rebuilding by the Germans not only of a beaten army, but even its fighting spirit. It was this that Guy Simonds had forecast in August, this "amazing German ability to recover from a reverse."[36] But in those heady days, few would heed such gloomy pronouncements.

In the early days of September, Hitler's own maps told their story of the impending German defeat. The Battle of Normandy, concluded in the third week of August, had been a telling blow to the Wehrmacht. As the tattered remains of once-powerful SS troops struggled eastward towards Germany, exhausted and in total disarray, their minds turned from war to the forlorn hope of seeing their families again. They had had little sleep or food and had not even commanders to guide them home or comrades to soothe their terror. One German soldier spoke for many when he wrote this letter home: "We have no vehicles or guns left, and whoever is still alive will have to fight as an infantryman. But I won't stay with them very long. I really don't know what we are still fighting for. Very soon I shall run over to the Tommies if I am not killed before I get there."[37]

General Simonds recorded the final tally after the Normandy victory:

> The scale of the German disaster can be judged by recalling that on D-Day the 12th SS Panzer Division had a strength of over 20,000 men and 150 tanks. After their defeat, some sixty officers, NCOs and men escaped from the Pocket [Falaise], being led through the woods by a French peasant, and later joined some other bands of stragglers from the division. The unit was then down to three hundred men, ten tanks and no artillery. The route [advancing through France] was littered with abandoned German equipment. Though there would seem little doubt that additional personnel were probably collected from bands of stragglers as

the retreat progressed, most of the equipment had to be abandoned.

Simonds noted with surprise the unprecedented sight of a German 88 battery, well-sited and concealed, still with ammunition stacked by the guns: "I had never before seen the Germans abandon such a position without a fight. Further on we found Panther and Tiger tanks, undamaged and with fuel in their tanks, abandoned by their crews.

"I turned to Foster [Major General Harry Foster, GOC 4th Canadian Armoured Division] and I said, 'This is a rout!'"[38]

A rout it was, as the fleeing troops withdrew in confusion, some through Belgium, escaping just ahead of Horrocks's armoured divisions, others to Breskens to cross the Scheldt to safety. Many fled across Holland until they were stopped, often at gunpoint, by German officers stationed at all important crosspoints, and at special posts along the escape routes. These were military police, with orders to capture the fugitives and shoot them if necessary. They were empowered, too, to commandeer returning vehicles. The now-deposed commandant of the German garrison in Paris, grown portly with years of occupation spoils, found himself on foot, summarily dismissed from his luxurious, custom-fitted black Mercedes.

The troops were sent to collecting depots for eventual transport to Germany for regrouping and refitting. First priority was given to the rehabilitation of the veteran fighters with SS insignia on their collars who had fought with fanatical determination in Normandy.

In his book, *Defeat in the West,* Milton Shulman quoted German Chief of Staff General Blumentritt as exclaiming: "The only instructions that came from Berlin were 'Hold! Hold! Hold!' Since it was impossible to carry out this order, we advised units to report any retreat they were forced to make in the following words: 'Thrown back or fought back. Counter-steps are being taken.' These are the only terms that would satisfy Berlin that a withdrawal had been necessary and thus save the commander involved from severe punishment for having disobeyed orders."[39]

One of these commanders was Lieutenant Colonel Friedrich Augustus von der Heydte, commanding officer of the crack 6th

Parachute Regiment. It was the misfortune of the Allied armies to have numbered in their opposition a veteran professional military man with the training and intelligence of this aristocratic German. Sixteen generations and seven hundred years of family tradition pre-destined the young Bavarian to the military.

There were many of his class in the Wehrmacht, but von der Heydte had two other traits that marked him for a brilliant career: he was intelligent and he was tough. His intellectual abilities were first recognized by the Carnegie Institute before the war, which had twice honoured him with prestigious awards for his work in International Law. In military fields, he cannily managed to remain enough in favour with the Nazi regime to be spared the purge of high-ranking German officers following the assassination attempt on Hitler's life in July of 1944, while at the same time managing to avoid being tagged a Nazi.

On the battlefield, he used his wits to analyze the thought processes as well as the tactics of his enemy. It was his standing order that the first prisoners taken were to be brought directly to him for interrogation: "When I spoke to the prisoners, I always asked them if they trusted their commanding officers. I could find out a lot about a unit if I could assess the morale of its fighting men."[40]

But he was not merely a pedagogue in battle dress, this Bavarian baron; von der Heydte was also a front-line warrior of no small daring. When Germany attacked Crete in 1940, he was the first paratrooper to jump, leading his men to capture the capital city. A plane crash in Italy left him with such extensive injuries that he was never again able to raise his left arm or have full use of one hand. And even after that, when the Luftwaffe had ceased to exist, von der Heydte retrained his men as front-line infantrymen who fought proudly in Normandy and later in Holland and Germany. An Allied intelligence report described von der Heydte's infantry as follows:

In these young, indoctrinated Nazis, fresh from a Luftwaffe that had ceased to exist, their faith in their Fuhrer and in their cause had not died...none of them had felt the sickening impact of defeat. They had not given way to despair and hopelessness that now gripped most Germans. Parachutists they were in name only. They had never been taught to jump from an aeroplane. The bulk of them had received no more than three months' [infantry] training. But they possessed two other compensating virtues — youth and faith.[41]

It was while fighting the American troops in the Normandy marshes of Carentan that von der Heydte, then thirty-seven years of age, devised an ingenious plan to salvage his men from the Fuhrer's interdict, and then created an even more inventive scheme to recruit a whole new division into his decimated ranks. He emphasized the difficult position the Wehrmacht was in:

> *Halten sie, halten sie…*'Defend to the last man'…that is all we heard from Hitler. It was impossible but I found a way. I established an aid post for the wounded a safe distance behind the lines, and every day I sent men back, wounded or not.
>
> Then, when we couldn't defend any more and were planning our retreat, an SS Division arrived. They were too late, but they insisted on making one last attack. When that failed, they started to run. I had a table set out at a crossroads, manned by a staff NCO and two men armed with Schmeissers. When the SS came to this point, they were given the choice of volunteering for the paratroops — or being court-martialled. Not surprisingly, they all joined up.

So, bolstered by his "volunteer" SS Division and the salvaged veterans of his paratroopers, von der Heydte firmly led his defeated troops around the American lines to safety:

> When I reached Germany, I was told that the German Army was not in the control of its commanders. The whole command organization had broken down. Nobody knew to which corps or army he belonged.
>
> Most regiments had been sent back to Germany to rebuild. The whole front was quite open, completely unprotected except by local police who were not able to defend. The Germans even had the crazy idea of forming the Volkssturm with old men and young boys of less than sixteen who were

to fight Allied tanks with shotguns! But you couldn't meet a real soldier anywhere. If Eisenhower, in the beginning of September, had decided to continue the attack into Germany, then the war would have been over.[42]

At about this same time, the German 15th Army, which had remained largely uncommitted on the French coast near the Pas de Calais, had also started to withdraw. One hundred thousand men, mainly on horse-drawn vehicles or on foot, thus began their escape northward. Here, too, the commanders had lost their influence over the men. It was retreat in chaos.

Their commander, General Gustav von Zangen, was ordered by Hitler to cross the Leopold Canal, an east-west artery close to the Belgian/Dutch border, and make for the small port of Breskens on the south bank of the Scheldt. From there, they were to cross the river to Walcheren, proceeding east along the isthmus of South Beveland through its narrow neck at Woensdrecht to the safety of the Dutch mainland.

On the 5th of September, the day after Horrocks's 11th Armoured Division liberated Antwerp, Hitler responded with a directive to the aristocratic Gerd von Rundstedt, the newly appointed Commander-in-Chief West. The dictator reiterated the urgency of holding the banks of the Scheldt Estuary, not only as an escape route for his armies, but also as a way of keeping the Allies from having the use of Antwerp's port facilities. He therefore ordered that the defences of Walcheren and both sides of the Scheldt leading to Antwerp be strengthened. The positions, he stressed, were to be defended to the last man.

Briefly, the German troops wavered, for once oblivious to the messianic utterances of their Fuhrer. Defeat seemed imminent. And so, on 5 September, *Dolle Dinsdag,* many of the men ordered to take defensive positions on the Scheldt Estuary put down their arms and walked away.

It was more a convulsion of fear, a response of blind panic, than an organized, bona fide rebellion. By 6 September, many of the guns were again manned at key fortress positions; the River Scheldt, as predicted two days earlier by Admiral Ramsay, was being heavily mined against Allied invasion.

Hitler's greatest fear was that the Allies would push northward over the Albert Canal towards Holland, cutting off his trapped 15th Army as it emerged from the Beveland Peninsula. He therefore concentrated those troops that he could muster in a line along two critical waterways that would stave off encirclement by the enemy.

Along the Albert Canal from Antwerp, he employed every available battalion to reinforce the faltering defensive position. Gradually, fresh paratroops bolstered the few men that Lieutenant General Kurt Chill had positioned there on his own initiative on 2 September, following the emergency order from Hitler to all commanders to defend strategically important positions. Reacting swiftly to the pending crisis, Chill had fattened his slim ranks with German police, security troops, naval and airforce personnel, anyone he could lay hands on. When Antwerp fell on September 4th, this makeshift line was all that opposed the British steamroller. But it was enough, because the British had run out of steam.

On the 5th of September, this ragtag assortment held off the Belgian Resistance men who, despite not having the necessary heavy guns to challenge even a force as weak as this, had managed to hold the Groenendaal Laan Bridge for the entire night, crossing it twice. On the same day, the British tanks that could easily have dealt with the 88mm gun that opposed them at this last intact bridge over the Albert Canal at Merxem were pulled out of the line for a "rest-and-refit."

"I have no orders," Secret Army commander Harry had been told truthfully enough by the British commander.

The following day, buttressed by additional infantry from elements of 88 Corps, Chill's line repelled General "Pip" Roberts's assault across the Albert by the 4th KSLI, an assault which had had to be postponed for some hours when few of the battalion boats were available. In the coming days, while Horrocks's armoured divisions caught their breath after their dash across France and Belgium, the German line was stiffening with regrouped 15th Army soldiers and eager young paratroopers rushed into action. And when a permanent system of defence under normal division and army group commanders was established in mid-September, Chill's emergency force was supplanted. It had done its work well.

———•———

Meanwhile, on the 4th of September, General Eugen-Felix Schwalbe, whose girth and florid complexion gave evidence of his enthusiastic enjoyment of his nation's renowned brew, began an operation he was to remember as "one of the most satisfactory achievements of my military career."[43]

Hard of hearing, Schwalbe compensated for his deafness with an incongruously high-pitched voice that could be heard day and night at the Breskens docks, haranguing troops to board one of the patchy assortment of craft he had scraped up for the brash escape. The distance across the mouth of the Scheldt, from Breskens to Flushing, although only five km, required sturdy vessels to handle the tidal currents and to withstand harassment by Royal Air Force fighter bombers.

With the help of naval personnel, Schwalbe unearthed two large Dutch civilian vessels, three capacious rafts capable of carrying eighteen vehicles each, sixteen small Rhine boats, each capable of holding 250 men, and a Siebel ferry.

Setting up guard posts on the road to Breskens, Schwalbe intercepted those men who were retreating in panic and ordered them to stay well camouflaged and hidden in positions near the quay, awaiting transport. Pamphlets were dropped urging deserters to rejoin their units.

On the night of 4 September, the first crossings in this audacious exodus were launched. Incredibly, Allied Intelligence was aware of every move of the enemy. The Ultra intercepts coming in daily by the hundreds during the retreat and the evacuation spelled out the precise locations, and even the exact strengths, of German forces.

Once again the alarm was sounded by an Ultra message. Hitler would never let the Allies gain the use of Antwerp Harbour. That had been made clear in several intercepts. Now the Germans were unwittingly advertising the fact that their armies were trapped. Eisenhower had the information immediately, as did Montgomery, Crerar and Simonds, and SHAEF Intelligence, which on the 9th of September, several lacklustre days after first being apprised of the evacuation, disseminated the following harvest of errors for the benefit of its fighting units: "In the main battle area, the 15th Army is now isolated and its divisions are cut off on the Flanders coast, though some may escape by ferry or by sea. The approaches to Holland ahead of the British advances are meantime only blocked by natural water obstacles and by the meagre resources of Commander-in-Chief Netherlands, amounting to one division and some oddments."[44]

Within four days — by the 8th of September — ten thousand of these "oddments" had made the crossing. These were marched forthwith along the Beveland Peninsula to Woensdrecht where some of them were diverted south to join Battle Group Chill in reinforcing the German line along the Albert Canal.

For Schwalbe it was a time for holding his breath. He was in constant dread that he would be cut off at the Beveland Peninsula by British troops moving north from Antwerp. An alternative plan was set in readiness should this occur: the evacuation would take place through the canals running north to Rotterdam. But such a trip would be difficult and slow, and would take twelve hours instead of the three-quarters of an hour for the crossing from Breskens to Flushing. And the alternative plan meant that he would certainly have to abandon all his heavy equipment.

From almost the start of the evacuation, 84 Group of the RAF, well briefed on the situation, offered continuous harassment to the escapees, sometimes staging as many as six raids a day until increasingly poor weather reduced the number of sorties. Schwalbe stuck as much as possible to night crossings, but as the weather deteriorated, day crossings were attempted.

It was the survivors of voyages such as these that young Peter Eekman saw from his dugout in the dunes. On the 16th of September, one hundred British Marauder fighter bombers attacked the miserable convoy, killing one hundred and seventy-five Germans with a single direct hit. Few Zeelanders who watched the German exodus would ever forget the cries of the escapees, helpless before the double onslaught of gales and RAF bombs.

To protect the army from a rear-guard attack while the evacuation was going on, Hitler ordered heavy reinforcement of the Leopold Canal, an east-west artery eighteen km south of the Scheldt coastline. The 70th German Division, commanded by Lieutenant General Wilhelm Daser, was brought over from Flushing for this task. Their first action was to destroy all bridges, making the entire canal an impregnable anti-tank ditch.

The evacuation originally used the docks of Breskens for the movement of heavy equipment, and of Terneuzen for personnel. But on the latter's capture by the Polish Armoured Division, Schwalbe funnelled everything through Breskens. The enemy was closing in, he was thinking, but still the rear-guard line, entrenched along the Leopold, held.

In nineteen days, the stocky German estimated he had brought to safety 86,100 troops along with their 616 guns, 6,200 horses and 6,000 vehicles. Only the 64th Infantry Division was left behind to carry out its sacrificial stand south of the Scheldt in the Breskens region. Of the evacuees, a number would defend the Walcheren fortress. The rest would traverse the South Beveland Peninsula. There they would join Battle Group Chill, still holding the line from Antwerp eastward to the German border.

From the 4th of September, and for a period of some three weeks thereafter, the British and Canadian armies had these escaping Germans trapped between them. Yet not a single serious effort was made by the Allies in all that time to drive those few dozen kilometres northward to Woensdrecht to intercept the German Army. Instead, the British were halted at Antwerp and then redirected eastward to Arnhem, turning their backs on a hapless enemy. By failing to take strong action, Eisenhower permitted this large force to retreat and rearm. To a man, they would all turn and fight again, this time against troops of the 1st Canadian Army.

Hitler had prayed for time to patch his western defences and launch his new weapons. The Allies were very generously giving him what he wanted. The Canadians, too, were inadvertently cooperating with the Fuhrer's wishes. On the 9th of September, Crerar issued the order that Guy Simonds had so desperately disputed. The command reiterated Montgomery's wish that the 1st Canadian Army give first priority to the capture of the Channel ports. There was to be no offensive action against the enemy escaping across the River Scheldt, although "close contact" was to be maintained.

Only the two armoured divisions under Canadian command, the

4th Canadian Armoured and the 1st Polish Armoured, could take up the chase. But in the apathy of the moment, even these had been halted for a two-day rest. Nor had they the infantry strength to penetrate the now more heavily reinforced enemy defences on the Leopold. The Poles did succeed later in capturing Terneuzen, a secondary evacuation port some twenty km east of Breskens, sinking and capturing many of the enemy's escape craft. But it was clearly a case of too little, too late.

Another Ultra signal was picked up at Bletchley Park that was to bear directly on the situation confronting Canadian troops. On the 3rd of September, Hitler ordered Colonel General Kurt Student to create a new army. The 1st Parachute Army came into being, and in time to dispatch some units to bolster defences on the Albert Canal. The events that followed were yet another manifestation of the "Miracle of the West" that saw Hitler pluck an entire army out of thin air at a time when any other country less obsessed with power would have been on its knees.

Thirty thousand men were recruited for this "instant army" under its commander-in-chief, Student, who had commanded the paratroopers to victories since 1938. From Luftwaffe air crews and ground staff, now out of action with virtually no aircraft left in Germany, from convalescent paratroopers who were proud survivors of prestigious combat airborne units, from remnants of the Hermann Goering and SS Regiments, this powerful new force was created. Now these men would be retrained into first-line land soldiers. They brought with them the high morale, the dogged and courageous fighting skills, and the political passion that came to mark them as the elite of German fighting men.

Of note in this unit was the German Reinforced 6th Paratroop Regiment, Lieutenant Colonel von der Heydte's highly trained and motivated fighting organization. Germany's most experienced and famed paraleader now had under his command four thousand infantry, retrained and refitted into a viable unit. Included in this number were skilled paratroop veterans that he had rescued from the Normandy carnage, salvaging an incredible sixty percent of the unit.

What made this force of von der Heydte's unique, at that time of looming defeat and demoralization in Nazi Germany, was the high morale of the paratroopers, a state that the thirty-seven-year-old commander worked energetically to promote:

> All my men were volunteers, and that insured good morale. Then, too, I had a very good relationship with my soldiers, a camaraderie. There was no attack in which I did not participate myself, no order that I didn't give from the front. In the paratroop tradition of modern war, it is essential to observe and command from a forward position. It is impossible to command from the rear. When we parachuted, I jumped with my men. When they patrolled, I patrolled too. If a soldier knows his commander is out there with him, he will attack in a different way. He will have a different attitude, be more aggressive.

Von der Heydte noted that commanding a paratroop regiment was complicated by the fact that under the Nazi regime there were three different types of men attracted to the paratroopers: "The first had a love of adventure. The second was the type of soldier who wished to be bound in teamwork. He was looking for comradeship. The third was the idealistic type, the convinced young Nazi who wanted to fight for the Fuhrer and for Germany."[45]

Later, the front-line Canadians would have no trouble distinguishing the sting of this force. In the wake of the veterans, quickly emulating their heroes, were newly recruited boys with youth and vigour on their sides, as well as an idealism for the game of war and for the leader who played it with such courage and drive.

Alexander Schmidt was seventeen years old when he was invited to "volunteer" for the 1st Parachute Army. Alex and his brother had been sent by their parents to wireless school some months before in the hopes that the youngsters could escape conscription into the German Army. And now here was this officer with a chest full of campaign ribbons persuasively depicting to thousands of young Germans the glories of serving the Fuhrer in the elite Paratroop Corps.

Those who did not volunteer for service were assured that they would be conscripted for the eastern front. Thus it was that on a sweltering afternoon late in August, 1944, young Schmidt obediently signed up with the stern Luftwaffe major. In just eight weeks, huddled in a damp woods in the drab Dutch village of Esschen, he would have Canadian troops in his gunsights.

Those lads who were not already fanatical Nazis when they joined the unit were intimidated by threats of death to fight with similar passion. Fight to the end, Hitler had screamed, and few dared oppose him. Mad he may have seemed, this dictator who had destroyed so many millions. But Adolf Hitler knew his people; he could reach out and touch the pulse of fear in every German. He was quick to capitalize on every error made by his enemy.

Some three thousand miles away, in the United States Congress, a colossal blunder was in the making. On the 24th of September, the American press leaked the story of the Morgenthau Plan. Named for the U.S. Secretary of the Treasury, and initially endorsed by both American and British heads of state, the plan offered a postwar solution for a defeated Germany that would see that country dismembered and reduced to a pastoral nation.

"A potato patch!" thundered Propaganda Chief Joseph Goebbels, delighted to have such inflammatory material at hand to fire the will of the faltering Germans. The fact that its author was a Jew only intensified German indignation. Although the plan was dropped, the damage had been done. German manhood, threatened with the emasculation of the homeland and the enslavement of the people, rose in fury to battle, now wholly committed to Hitler's orders to fight to the death.

On *Dolle Dinsdag,* the 5th of September, the disintegration and imminent surrender of the German forces seemed a certainty. On the 13th of September, in Washington, General George Marshall, chief of staff of the army, sent a message to all his commanders predicting the end of the war against Germany before the 1st of November, 1944, although, he warned, "cessation of hostilities may occur at any time."[46]

A week after this pronouncement, its armies dramatically increased in strength, and infused with fresh determination, Germany had been revitalized into a powerful and dangerous enemy. The critical importance of the port of Antwerp to the outcome of the war was imparted to the German troops fighting in the Battle of the Scheldt in this directive:

FROM THE COMMANDER-IN-CHIEF, 15TH ARMY

The defence of the approaches to Antwerp represents a task which is decisive for the further conduct of the war. Therefore, every last man in the fortress is to know why he must devote himself to this task with the utmost strength...After overrunning the Scheldt fortresses, the English would finally be in a position to land great masses of materiel in a large and completely protected harbour. With this materiel they might deliver a death blow to the North German plateau and to Berlin before the onset of winter...and for this reason we must hold the Scheldt fortresses to the end. The German people are watching us. In this hour, the fortresses along the Scheldt occupy a role which is decisive for the future of our people.[47]

VON ZANGEN

From the lofty pronouncements of Hitler and Goebbels, von Zangen and Student and Schwalbe, to the thoughtless mouthings of German youth such as Alexander Schmidt, the word was absolute: Germany must hold the Scheldt fortresses to the end.

❧ 5 ❧

Groundwork of Errors

BY THE THIRTEENTH OF SEPTEMBER, AFTER VACILLATING FOR TWO weeks on the issue, Eisenhower formally authorized the postponement of an assault to free the approaches to Antwerp until after the conclusion of Montgomery's proposed breakthrough to the Rhine (Operation Market Garden).

Indeed, even while the liberation bouquets were still fading in Antwerp's bars and bistros, the 1st Canadian Army was ordered to give first priority to capturing the Channel ports. Crerar obediently instructed Simonds: "The capture or destruction of the enemy remaining north and east of the Ghent-Bruges Canal becomes secondary in importance. While constant pressure and close contact with the army, now withdrawing north of the Scheldt, will be maintained, important forces will not be committed to offensive action."[1]

That the Allies were fully aware of the mass escape of the German 15th Army was clearly evident. By the middle of the month, 21 Army Group maps existed that actually charted the path of the escapees. On the 19th of September, Crerar instructed 84 Group of the RAF to make every effort to "interfere with, and destroy, the enemy now in process of ferrying himself across River Scheldt."[2]

But General Schwalbe, despite the harassment, had already ferried the first ten thousand infantry of the beleaguered German 15th Army from Breskens to Walcheren. The remainder, some fifty thousand in the Breskens area alone, were positioned near the port awaiting transport. Hitler's directive, intercepted by Ultra on September 7th and promptly reported to the Allied commanders, had emphasized the need to "obstinately defend" the Scheldt approaches, at both Walcheren and Breskens.[3] Three German units, the crack 64th Infantry Division and elements of the 245th and 70th, were then positioned on the Leopold Canal, which now served as a natural defensive line. Running roughly parallel to and eighteen km south of the Scheldt, the canal would effectively ward off any attempts by Allied armour to break across the rear of the German line and intercept the escape.

In fact, the Germans had little to fear. The Allies, although alerted in full detail to the enemy plan to protect the evacuation of their one hundred thousand troops, showed little interest in thwarting it. The strength of the 2nd Canadian Corps had been, in General Simonds's words, "dissipated." Crerar had been forced to deploy his divisions along a line stretching over 240 km from the Channel ports across northern Belgium as far as Antwerp, finally provoking a protest from Simonds that the front was getting unmanageably long.

"What really killed the pursuit and [resulted in the loss of] a great opportunity to fully exploit the Normandy victory was the order to capture the Channel ports, coupled with the order to take over the defence of Antwerp," Simonds recollected regretfully. The corps was brought to a "grinding halt."[4]

With the 2nd and 3rd Canadian Infantry Divisions sidetracked, the 4th Canadian Armoured and the Polish Armoured Divisions (under Canadian command) were given the job of clearing out the enemy from the south bank of the Scheldt from Antwerp to the North Sea. It was an assignment that Simonds was understandably reluctant to give. Polder warfare was an infantry-slogging job; armour would be of little effect.

Tanks would have extreme difficulty in making any sort of dent in the strongly defended German line along the Leopold. The enemy had blown all bridges across the canal. Strong infantry action would therefore be required to form a bridgehead and allow the sappers (engineers) to construct bridges, thus allowing the armour to cross. Even if the tanks could secure a holding on the enemy banks, yet another problem would confront them.

An AEF intelligence report in early September had predicted that the enemy, using the polders to their advantage, could expect to keep the Canadian tanks at a standstill. Simonds had been alerted to the dismal news that the ground, which lay almost at sea level, would likely be flooded by the Germans. It was, the report stated dolefully, "a honeycomb of polders fringed on the coast by dunes and dykes, its entire area liable to saturation or flooding."[5] Simonds knew this polder country of Breskens Pocket would be completely unsuitable for the deployment of armour, but what else did he have available?

An infantry division had three brigades, each of which had three battalions. These nine divisional battalions comprised some 7,500 men. An armoured division, however, had just a third of that number in infantry strength. In this case, the 10th Infantry Brigade had three battalions: the Lincoln and Welland Regiment, the Algonquin Regiment and the Argyll and Sutherland Highlanders of Canada, all Ontario-based units.

On the 8th of September, the Argylls, supported the next day by the Lincs and Winks (Lincoln and Welland Regiment), drew first blood in a successful assault over the Ghent Canal, five km south of the Leopold, at the pretty hamlet of Moerbrugge. Although surprised that neither assault boats for crossing the canal nor artillery support had been laid on for the attack, the battalion launched the assault, anticipating negligible opposition on the other side.

They were stunned by the ferocity of the enemy's resistance. During much of the following day the riflemen clung to their precarious foothold in the town, beating off counterattacks in close street fighting.

Captain William Whiteside, antitank platoon commander with the Argylls, manned gun positions on the near side of the canal and for a time manhandled essential supplies under heavy fire to the beleaguered troops. Whiteside relates a grisly tale in which a house of God became a German fortification: "There was a church on the road leading from the canal. The Germans had been using it for their snipers. In the afternoon one [Argyll] company reached the eight-foot stone wall around the churchyard, and dug slit trenches in the river side of the wall. But the Germans got all the pews out of the church and leaned them against their side of the wall. Then they climbed up and started throwing grenades over. Potato mashers were raining down on our guys' heads."[6]

At 1900 hours, the strongest counterattack, and mercifully the last, was beaten off by the weary Canadians, and by early morning of 10 September the sappers had completed a bridge. During the two days of fighting, one hundred and fifty Germans, including several officers, were captured.

———•———

Five days later, it became the turn of the Algonquin Regiment to launch a midnight attack across the Leopold Canal, this time with orders to establish a bridgehead at the tiny Belgian village of Moerkerke. The regiment was ordered first to cross the thirty-metre-wide Canal Derivation de la Lys, then clamber up its steep banks and across an exposed, elevated dyke about the width of an express motorway before sliding down the next bank and across the Leopold Canal. On the 13th of September, the War Ops Log recorded the order: "At zero hr [2200] tonight, Alq Rgt will force a crossing of the Canal Derivation de la Lys and the Canal Leopold in the area Moerkerke...4 Cdn Armd Div will then fan out in both directions to clear the north bank of the Canal Leopold pushing on as fast as possible to Fort Frederik Hendrik."[7]

Nothing in those few lines could reveal the extent of the slaughter that awaited the Algonquins during the next fifteen hours. Canadian military historian Colonel C.P. Stacey observes that "could these orders have been as fully and speedily carried out as written, a good part of the Battle of the Scheldt would have been won."[8] In fact, had these orders been carried out, the fleeing German 15th Army would finally have been cornered in the water-encircled "island" of West Flanders, now dubbed by the Canadians as Breskens Pocket.

But the operation was fated for disaster from its inception, founded as it was on the "groundwork of errors" that Major George L. Cassidy, author of *Warpath*, the battalion history, bitterly recounts.[9] In the next fifteen hours, the muddy Leopold and its murky banks would claim the lives of many Canadians.

Right from the start, the attack was checkered with mistakes. The initial errors, on which many tactical blunders were pyramided, were contained in the intelligence reports that seriously underestimated German strength. The Algonquins were told to expect an enemy weak and demoralized, with little equipment, who would show little or no fight if attacked in force. These would number only four thousand, spread across the entire Pocket. Instead, 350 Canadians were pitted against a large, well-equipped force, many times their number, with ample reserves to draw on from the fifty thousand troops deployed around the Breskens area awaiting transport over the Scheldt.

Recce patrols trying to add to this information were hampered by snipers shooting at them, even in the village streets. Air photographs proved very misleading, at one point indicating an area of inundation where there was none.

Urgently needed reinforcements were rushed up to fill out the depleted ranks of the regiment. The new troops, many with little infantry training, were scheduled to have a short indoctrination course before setting forth. This had to be cancelled when they were late in arriving. "It was barely possible to take down their names, assign them to companies, give them the briefest of briefings, and show them what an assault boat looked like, and then it was time to move off," Cassidy noted.[10]

The assault began in the late evening, with all four companies taking part under a heavy covering barrage. The Lincoln and Welland Regiment was to be used for the boat-ferrying party, but in the confusion of darkness few of the assigned paddlers managed to make contact with the assault troops.

So the first obstacle the Algonquins encountered was in man-handling the forty heavy, awkward, eighteen-seater wood-and-canvas boats. Groping blindly down Moerkerke's narrow alleys leading to the canal, the riflemen had to heave the craft up and over the first steep bank, then paddle across the Derivation Canal and up again on the near-vertical climb to reach the slit-trench-covered island between the two dykes. These bramble-covered banks rose sharply to nearly eight metres. Now in plain sight of the Germans, and soon in their gunsights as well, the Canadian troops had to quickly drag the craft over the island, haul it down the next bank, paddle across the second canal to the enemy side and scramble up the final bank.

The men had not yet entered battle, but already they were exhausted. Nor were there personnel to return the boats to the near side of the canal to be put into service ferrying ammunition. This was to prove a costly omission. "One by one," Cassidy recalls, "the little errors were piling up, laying the groundwork for catastrophe."[11]

The crossing was made under intense enemy fire. B Company immediately suffered a number of casualties, amounting to more than one platoon of men. C Company, under Major A.K. Stirling, was dismayed to discover that the company's wireless set was out of order.

By 2300 hours, however, all four companies were across and working towards their objectives. The enemy was relatively quiet. The sappers had even begun to build a bridge across the two waterways so that the division's tanks could cross in support. (This effort had to be abandoned later because of heavy enemy shelling.)

However, the two companies on the right were in danger. In the confusion of darkness and thick smoke from the enemy artillery and mortar fire, both C and D companies had gone wide of their objectives. Two of Major Stirling's platoons, commanded by Lieutenants Butler and Hunter, had silenced an enemy mortar crew and then had pushed their way inland about two hundred metres. But now they found out that, with the wireless set out of commission, they were completely cut off from communication and contact with company headquarters.

At 0200 hours, the battalion first aid post in Moerkerke suddenly came under intense enemy fire, and a direct hit killed the R.C. padre, Father Tom Mooney. A number of other Algonquins, including the Protestant padre and medical officer, were wounded.

"A few minutes later," Cassidy reported, "after the wounded had been brought into the battalion HQ shelter, this house too received a succession of direct hits, finally catching fire. It was decided to evacuate to another headquarters. Shortly, this one also became the centre of a well-aimed barrage."[12]

It was later discovered that a vicious act of espionage was compounding the already troubled operation. A German sympathizer with a wireless set was discovered to be calling down enemy fire from behind Canadian lines.

Dawn brought a renewal of ferocious German attack. Several enemy snipers who had eluded capture earlier by hiding out in dark hallways and cellars of village cottages posed severe problems.

It had been a night of frenzied action for the German defenders as well, as a subsequent enemy account indicated:

The Canadians succeeded in forcing a bridgehead at Moerkerke. If it had been allowed to develop it would not only
have cut short any further evacuation through Breskens, but
would have secured the vital grounds south of the Scheldt.
When news reached the corps commander of 89 Corps,
General Freiherr von und zu Gilsa, he came down personally to see Lieutenant General Erwin Sander, commander of
the 245th Infantry Division at Lapscheure. There he gave the
strictest instructions that the bridgehead must at all cost be
eliminated, promising him the Corps reserve to help him
achieve the task.[13]

This was the weak and demoralized enemy that the Canadians
had been told to expect.

It was a morning of unmitigated hell for the Algonquins. The
engineers were forced by continuous heavy shellfire to abandon
attempts at bridging. The Germans had infiltrated all sides of the battalion, even to the extent of manning a gunpost in their rear, on the
island between the canals. In fact, they had penetrated so close to the
forward positions of the Canadians that artillery fire was almost useless against an enemy now fewer than twenty yards away.

"Snipers had to be cleared out of one house no less than three
times, and a minor battle had to be fought to extricate Lieutenant Dan
McDonald and Sergeant Marshall from a chicken coop in which they
had been surrounded, but not by chickens," Cassidy recalls. McDonald related how he had an egg two inches from his nose, and couldn't
make up his mind whether to eat it there or take it with him when he
went — if he went.

Company commander Major A.K. Stirling reported grimly: "Just
before daybreak the enemy started counterattacking the position and
under cover of darkness succeeded in infiltrating between the forward platoons and the one on the bank. These counterattacks continued throughout the morning, accompanied by heavy mortar and
artillery fire. Attempts were made to contact the forward platoons by
shouting, but this had no results."[14] Finally, Lieutenant Butler was
brought back, wounded, to the bank; Lieutenant Hunter and his platoon could not be contacted.

Ammunition ran out, and although no less than twelve attempts were made it was clearly impossible for ammo parties to cross the canal under the now vicious German fire. Several men ran around picking up ammunition from the wounded and dead, even German dead.

At 1100 hours, they had exhausted their supply of two-inch mortar and Piat ammunition. With just a few rounds of small arms ammunition, the order came forward: "One round, one German."

"Enemy attacks reached a new crescendo," Cassidy continues. "It was evident they had been ordered to smash the bridgehead at once, before we could exploit it further. So he sent wave after wave of men, heedless of casualties, against our battered forward positions."[15]

Finally, at noon, lacking any fresh reserves, its forward platoons overrun and with casualties as high as 75 percent, the battered Algonquins were ordered to withdraw. Under cover of a smoke-screen and a heavy artillery barrage, the survivors struggled to safety, fighting their way out from house to house, crawling through ditches.

At the bridge site, the shortage of boats took its toll. Four or five German prisoners volunteered to row wounded Canadians back to safety, returning several times for more men. Many, too late for boats, swam back, abandoning clothes and weapons.

Still unable to reach his lost platoon, Major Stirling was forced to abandon it, hoping the smoke would tip them off to the withdrawal. "We know now that it did not," Cassidy stated. "Lieutenant Hunter and his brave little crew fought to the very end, the last giving in only after their commander had been killed."[16]

Forty-two percent of the Algonquin Regiment were the casualties of this groundwork of errors. Sixty-six men were taken prisoner, including those in Stirling's lost platoon. Fifty-eight were wounded. Of the twenty-nine killed, three were officers, including Father Mooney, the first Roman Catholic padre to be killed in action in the Northwest European campaign and the fourth of any denomination since D-Day.

From the conclusion of this battle until the middle of October, General Simonds ordained that the 4th Canadian Armoured Division make no further attempt to cross the canal in force. Instead, it was ordered merely to clear and patrol the area south of the Leopold from the North Sea to the Terneuzen Canal. Unquestionably, Simonds realized the futility of committing the meagre infantry resources of the division against an enemy that had now declared itself as so obviously overpowering in numbers and strongly motivated to defend.

George Cassidy, who by a miracle was only slightly injured when his jeep ran over a Teller mine and was blown up on the 18th of September, remembers those next weeks as a "nightmare period" for the Algonquins. The battalion skirmished with but could not dent the defences of an enemy less than one hundred yards away on the opposite bank of the Leopold.

It was in these circumstances that the forward platoon of the Algonquin's D Company, 17 Platoon, was lost:

War Diary, Algonquin Regiment, 22 September

At 1030 hrs D Company was ordered to move west of Philippine to work patrols out from this area. The company deployed and went to battle in order to gain control of the dykes and 17 Platoon was successful in crossing the obstacle under heavy fire. They were seen consolidating in buildings on the enemy side and were engaged in a hand-to-hand fight.

It was Private Ted Gale's first real day at battle. It became his last. For twelve hours the thirty men of his platoon witnessed every horror that war could fling at man, until finally there was no recourse left but to submit to capture.

Gale was an early victim of the Canadian reinforcement travesty that was to kill and maim so many troops on the Scheldt. Originally with a tank unit, the twenty-year-old was one of countless thousands of troops transferred abruptly into the infantry at the onset of the campaign. It was a last-ditch attempt by the Canadian government to bolster the dwindling infantry reserves of the 1st Canadian Army. Training was often cursory; men were sent into action ill-equipped to survive. Gale records his nightmare experience: "There was a farmhouse with a couple of outbuildings, a milk shed and a smokehouse, where we dug in. We captured half a dozen Germans there; one of the men thought we should shoot them but our officer wouldn't let him. We were in there all day, firing small arms at the Germans. Then they brought up an 88 gun along the road and started to knock the house down. They blew the roof off. Soon they were dropping hand grenades through the windows."[17]

Patrols from time to time were sent out to contact the forward platoon but due to enemy machine-gun fire and heavy shelling these attempts were unsuccessful.

During the afternoon, fresh troops arrived at Algonquin head-quarters, in the form of an officer, Lieutenant T.C.W. Byres, and fifteen ORs (Other Ranks). They were sent immediately to join the forward company and half an hour after he arrived, Byres was ordered to lead a patrol to make contact with 17 Platoon. The patrol advanced warily across the enemy line under cover of darkness. It never returned. Byres' body was found eleven days later, hopelessly entangled in barbed wire, a mute testimony to the loneliness of death on patrol.

Meanwhile, the men of 17 Platoon fought on, ammunition nearly gone, the hopelessness of their position now apparent. "We fought right up until it got dark," remembers Private Ray Perry, Gale's clos-est friend on the mission: "We ran out of ammunition and then the Germans came in at us under darkness and took us. We were all pretty banged up. Ted was wounded and unconscious; he had twenty-two wounds in his leg. Another boy lost his leg. I was hurt a little bit in the hand. Our officer, when I first saw him I thought for sure he had lost his eyesight, blood was just streaming down his face."[18]

When Ted Gale came to, he was on a barge with the German wounded, being ferried across the River Scheldt to Flushing. Perry was taken behind the lines to a barn where the German command headquarters was set up: "They were really good to us, the front-line Germans; they gave us their supper. But then things got pretty rough. We were in boxcars for seven days and they did nothing for our wounds until we reached the POW camp."[19]

The Battle of the Scheldt was over for the men of 17 Platoon. But for the rest, the men on the dyke, "It was already clear that operations here would always be extremely sticky ones," George Cassidy summed up. "The enemy knew the ground, whereas we could see only our own side of the fence. The surrounding country was inun-dated, forcing us to make any large effort right up a dyke road, or in the words of the CO, 'Up the bloody funnel.' The enemy were dug in solidly in concrete bunkers underneath the dykes."[20]

So it went on, a battle that was less a battle than merely a dismal succession of patrols. One of these, however, is vividly remembered by Lincoln and Welland Major James L. Dandy as somewhat more colourful than usual. It was called "Operation Styx." And it was "a piece of cake," as its gleeful commander reported.

Late in September, Dandy was ordered to lead his company on a fighting patrol across the Leopold to capture German prisoners in order to obtain vitally needed information about enemy units, positions and strengths for the pending October assault by the 3rd Division. A full-scale rehearsal simulating the exact battle conditions was staged to ensure success for the raid. The operation, which became a classic among fighting patrols on a company scale, was highlighted by a tactically skilful plan, conceived and coordinated by Brigadier R.W. Moncel, commander of the 4th Canadian Armoured Brigade, and further highlighted by a daring execution by Dandy.

Before dawn, at 0515 hours on 27 September, Dandy's three platoons, totaling ninety men, silently boarded boats and crossed the canal undetected as their sister company provided diversionary fire.

"I left one platoon to protect my bridgehead and sent another to cover my right flank," Dandy reported. "I was to go in with the last platoon. We still had an hour of darkness, and I told them, 'The whole thing here is speed. Don't give them time to get set or you're going to get shot up.'

"The Germans had dug into the backs of the dykes and had bunkers there too. I told the guys to grab a bunker and get the prisoners out quickly." In fact, one of his men disobeyed long enough to demolish a bacon sandwich that a surprised German had just prepared for his breakfast.

At 0615 hours, Major Dandy informed Moncel, "'I am gathering in the harvest. Ten POWs so far.'

"The brigadier radioed back that we had enough and should clear out, but by the time we did we had fifteen prisoners for interrogation," Dandy continued. "The funny thing is that while we had no casualties, Brigadier Moncel's forward headquarters on the Canadian side of the canal was hit and he had to get out because the house was on fire!"[21]

Occasionally, though, a patrol would backfire. On one occasion cited by the Algonquins two members of the Belgian Secret Army who had volunteered as guides on a patrol were found shot. They had been stripped and thrown into the canal. The Germans, who refused to recognize these Resistance fighters as anything but terrorists, would not offer the ordinary protection of the Geneva Convention, nor even the dignity of a soldier's death.

Meanwhile, to the east of the Leopold line, the 1st Polish Armoured Division, under the command of the 1st Canadian Army, was handed a task of formidable proportions. On the 12th of September, General Simonds ordered the Poles to clear the Germans out of the south bank of the Scheldt River from Terneuzen to Antwerp. The area was firmly held by units of the German 712 Infantry Division determined to stop any Allied movement that might threaten the rear of their escaping 15th Army.

Since 1939 the Polish division had been facing no-win situations. When the Germans invaded Poland in September, 1939, the unit, under Colonel Stanislaw Maczek, fought a brilliant holding action against the Germans in the south of Poland until it was forced to withdraw to a position near the Hungarian border. Here it kept the border open for other escaping Polish troops before having to withdraw into Hungary.

For a short period, the members of the brigade were interned by the Hungarians. When released in 1940, they moved to France where once more as a brigade they faced the overwhelming strength of the German Army.

With the fall of France in 1940, about 25,000 Polish troops escaped to Britain where they were reorganized and formed into the 1st Polish Armoured Division under the skilled command of Maczek, now a general.

After intensive training for the invasion, the division moved to Normandy early in August, becoming an integral part of the 2nd Canadian Corps for most of the war. It was a welcome alliance. The Polish advance to close the Falaise Gap earned them great fame, marred only by the slaughter of hundreds of their troops when they were bombed accidentally by the RAF. Total casualties from this and other operations, which often the Poles would spearhead, mounted finally to almost 6,000 men or more than thirty percent of the division strength.

Their morale, however, remained high, probably because of the speed and success of their advance and the concrete yardstick of captured prisoners credited to them. As did their Canadian allies, they held on to the dangerous and erroneous assumption that German morale was as low as theirs was high.

The ground itself posed many obstacles, and as General Simonds had projected when he protested the diversion of his infantry divisions to other battle arenas, it was quite unsuitable for armour.

The Ghent and Hulst canals themselves were obstacle enough, but it was the roads that plagued the Poles, too narrow for tracked vehicles to turn and too exposed, raised as they were along the tops of dykes. The ground below the roads, much of it inundated, was impassable, so the division was forced into the role of sitting duck for a well-armed and camouflaged hunter.

The Poles operated against this enemy principally with infantry well supported by artillery. It was necessary to have bridging equipment close-up so that operations could commence at the earliest opportunity, allowing the armour to cross over in the wake of their infantry comrades, and to exploit their success.

This tactic was instrumental in driving a firm wedge across the Hulst Canal on the 18th of September, and allowed Polish sappers to complete a bridge next morning. For the first time, the Canadian Army had manoeuvred into a threatening position, just a little over ten km behind the actual German evacuation ports of Terneuzen and Breskens.

This the enemy was determined to stop. Counterattacking viciously, the Germans broke up the first attempt on September 17th, inflicting heavy losses on the hapless Poles. Seventy-nine men of the division were listed as casualties from that attack, but the Germans were finally driven off.

By the 20th, the Polish Division had reached the banks of the Scheldt Estuary, finding and sinking some of the German evacuation fleet along the river. In human life, the price was high. During the twelve days of fighting, seventy-five Poles were killed, one hundred and ninety-one wounded and sixty-three were missing. But they had at least compelled the last evacuees of General Schwalbe's escaping 15th Army to consolidate into the town of Breskens, giving up hope of using the Terneuzen port as an embarkation area.

By the evening of 21 September, the Poles had successfully completed their assigned task of "mopping up" the south bank of the Scheldt to the eastern juncture of the Terneuzen and Leopold canals.[22]

With the 1st Canadian Army entangled in a morass of misinformation and error and, despite the Polish successes, "Round One" of the Scheldt battle clearly belonged to the Germans.

⇻ 6 ⇺

Sinking of an Island

LIEUTENANT COLONEL BILL ANDERSON, GENERAL STAFF OFFICER IN charge of Operations (GSO 1 Operations) for the 1st Canadian Army and an integral part of the army team, was to ask, "How many generals, in the height of a major conflict, are the authors of so many great innovations?"[1]

But, after artificial moonlight, phosphorescent path-finding and Kangaroos, there was still one more innovation to come, of such brilliance that it made possible the freeing of the approaches to the port of Antwerp.

Cursed by some, praised by many, Lieutenant General Guy Simonds was to make his lasting imprint with a single decision of unprecedented boldness. What ultimately earmarked him for greatness was his decision to sink the island of Walcheren.

In mid-September, the Plans Section at 1st Canadian Army headquarters formulated a scheme to capture South Beveland and the island of Walcheren. Ignoring the weight of evidence confirming that the Germans were well entrenched in the Breskens area, the Plans Section had based its proposal on the incredible assumption that this area of Flanders, lying south of the river, would somehow change hands and be occupied by Allied troops when the offensive resumed early in October.

But even as pen touched paper at army headquarters, Allied Intelligence was aware that the mass exodus of the German 15th Army through that very territory at Breskens was well underway. Bletchley Park was kept busy deciphering Ultra decodes about the progress of the evacuation, and was passing on a running account to the army commanders.

Moreover, the 4th Canadian Armoured Division had reported that after its costly defeat at Moerkerke the enemy was strongly massed on a defensive line at the dual canal fortifications of the Leopold and the Canal de Derivation de la Lys, protecting the German rear-guard. The Algonquin Regiment had been determinedly beaten back by this tough defensive force, with one hundred and fifty-three casualties. Many had survived only by swimming for their lives across the chilling canal waters.

At 1600 hours on the 21st of September, Simonds shot back with his own appreciation of the task. Masking his contempt for the ill-conceived proposal from Plans Section, and coolly dismissing it as "based upon too many hypothetical considerations," Simonds refuted the Plans Section's assumption that the area of Flanders between the Leopold Canal and the Scheldt, the Breskens Pocket, would tumble easily into their hands.

"The clearing of this area may be a major operation," he predicted tersely. As well, he pointed out that even if the pocket of land was cleared of the enemy, it had already been flooded to some extent by the Germans, and might be further saturated to the extent that the area would be useless for the gun positions necessary in the final attack on Walcheren.

It was this continuing problem of the enemy's tactical use of water that most absorbed Simonds's attention as he sought a solution to a seemingly impossible task. Not only did the Germans continue to cling to the canals, fortifying their banks with pillboxes and camouflaged weaponry and thereby defending against any infiltration; they were also letting in the North Sea to confound the Canadian advance.

From a report obtained from a prisoner of war, Simonds had learned that the Germans, controlling the sluice gates of all the land below sea level, intended to use "ground saturation" rather than total flooding: "This denies to us the use of the ground for movement to exactly the same extent as if it were completely flooded, but allows the enemy the use of his roads, [and] avoids the flooding of buildings, stores and many works which must be of importance to him,"

Simonds explained. "Attacking across a 'saturated' area, movement is possible only on top of dyked roads," the corps commander pointed out. "We sacrifice every advantage which we normally possess in the offensive."[2]

By forcing the Canadian troops to fight across flooded polder country, the German defender provided himself with a vastly superior advantage. For it was the defenders who controlled the dyked roads, all of which lay above water level. They needed only to sit back and concentrate their fire upon key intersections of the roads to have total command over any moving object in those sodden, treeless lowlands. Effectively, they denied the Canadians freedom of movement anywhere but on those vulnerable roads, making them, in the process, an easy target for well-protected and well-hidden German guns, well-dug-in German infantry and well-placed German minefields.

Even the isthmus to South Beveland, although on slightly higher ground, might well funnel the Canadians onto a long narrow stretch of road, making them vulnerable to any concentration of enemy fire. It would, as Simonds forecast, be a battle fought over ground "highly unsuitable for an armoured division," and in some areas even impassable for infantry.

But it was the diamond-shaped island of Walcheren, guarding the mouth of the Scheldt, that posed the greatest problem. The land approaches to the island, either from the Breskens Pocket to the south or from South Beveland in the east, or both, could only be captured by tough, metre-by-metre slogging by foot soldiers. This would be a costly and formidable task for the Canadian infantry. It was a task that Simonds realized would require all the resources available to the 1st Canadian Army.

The 2nd Canadian Infantry Division, now in a defensive role in Antwerp, was therefore ordered to proceed north across the Dutch border, clear out German resistance and finally seal off the South Beveland Peninsula. The division would then continue west along the peninsula as far as the German fortress of Walcheren. The 4th Canadian Armoured Division and the Polish Armoured were to provide this force with right flank protection by driving north to Bergen op Zoom and Breda respectively. The task of clearing the Breskens Pocket was given to the 3rd Canadian Infantry Division, as soon as it could be freed from clearing the Channel ports.

But even this combined weight of two infantry divisions, vulnerable as they were to enemy artillery, might find it impossible to force their way through the mired polderlands to Walcheren Island. Simonds believed that an amphibious attack must also be planned: "I consider that the project of an assault across water cannot be ruled out if Walcheren Island must be taken," he stated. "It may be the only way of taking it." But this was to be "a last resort and a most uninviting task."[3] Additional troops, perhaps commandos, would likely be needed for this demanding assignment.

Simonds was deeply concerned by the terrible cost in lives, Canadian and British, that could occur if the invading troops were given no protection against the more than sixty German coastal guns embedded in concrete along the shores of Walcheren. These gun batteries had to be destroyed. Otherwise the invasion would in all likelihood be a suicidal failure, with the resultant loss to the Allies of an unparalleled opportunity to shorten the war.

Lieutenant Colonel Anderson recalls an earlier moment in the map room when Simonds looked up from overlays of Walcheren's defences and said, "If we've got to do this, there's only one way. We've got to have an element that isn't orthodox or we'll never make it. We will have to let in the sea."

"His unorthodox element was the breaching of the dykes by heavy bombers," Anderson remembers. "And it was absolutely stupendous."[4]

It was a moment unique in military history when Simonds revealed his dramatic plan. The handful of Canadians who witnessed the evolution of the concept will not soon forget the impact of his words: "Bombing operations should be undertaken to break the dykes and completely flood all parts of the island below high water level. Those parts of the island which remain above water should then be systematically attacked, day and night, to destroy defences and wear out the garrison by attrition."[5]

Labelled "crazy" right from the start by almost everyone in the astonished group around the conference table, the plan made the point that by creating large gaps in the dykes and allowing the sea water to rush in through the breaches, new, undefended beaches would be established for safe landing of the invasion force.

Simonds proposed that commandos could then steal through the gaps in assault boats just before first light. Once on the island, they could attack from behind the German positions, which were on the dykes pointing to the sea. Most of the guns were embedded in concrete and could not be turned inland, making them impotent against an attack from behind.

"It was Guy's idea that the movement back and forth of the tide would create beaches that never existed before, that the enemy would never have heard of," Anderson recalls. "So the Germans would be defending every known bloody beach, but now we were going to create two new beaches, one at either end of the breach. This would enable us to move along the dyke, attacking the enemy defences from behind, which would create a whole new tactical problem for him, one he wasn't ready for. That was Guy's basic concept."[6]

Coupled with his strategy to flood the low-lying areas of the island, thus forcing the Germans to cling to isolated outposts of defence, unable to maintain supply communication, Simonds emphasized the importance of a "softening" of the island by heavy air bombardment. The bombing would reduce the number of enemy fortifications that had escaped damage from the floods, particularly those on the high dykes that rimmed the island. It would also threaten the morale of the German troops. Simonds's plan noted: "When it is considered that the morale of the garrison has sufficiently deteriorated, waterborne patrols may be sent to determine the situation. If found to be ripe, airborne, followed by waterborne troops, should be landed."[7]

Simonds's Walcheren solution electrified army and corps headquarters. "The advice that he was getting from his staff ranged from, this is a brainstorm, to this is a wild idea," Bill Anderson remembers. "Some were saying, 'Forget it. We'll never get the air force. He'll never persuade Bomber Command to go in by day.'

"Others, the technical types, were saying that 'they wouldn't be able to breach the dykes: the whole thing is half-baked, it will never work.'"[8]

For a few perilous days the fate of the plan wavered.

On the 23rd of September, despite Eisenhower's assurance of

complete support, U.S. Lieutenant General Lewis Brereton flatly
turned down the request for the use of his airborne troops to smooth
the way for a naval invasion of Walcheren, terming the proposed use
of the paratroop units "improper employment."[9]

There was some encouragement at first in the supreme commander's promise to provide massive air support to the Canadians.
Eisenhower had told Montgomery that he would give him whatever
he needed to open Antwerp, "including all the air forces and anything
else that you can support."[10] But this was to prove as empty an assurance as were his previous promises.

The next day, the chief engineer of the 1st Canadian Army,
Brigadier Geoffrey Walsh, informed General Crerar that Simonds's
proposal was impractical. Basing his recommendation on the combined opinions of a number of hydrographic engineers, intelligence
personnel, residents, and seamen, Walsh appeared to have done his
homework. The effect was devastating. His discouraging memo noted
that: "The Westkapelle Dyke is the largest on the island and one of
the oldest in Holland. It is composed of heavy clay and because of its
age will be very thoroughly compacted. At Mean High Water Level it
is between 200 feet and 250 feet in width with very flat side slopes.
To make a gap 100 feet long requires the removal of some 10,000 tons
of clay. It is very improbable that even the most accurate bombing
could produce a clear channel."[11]

Crerar, already skeptical and perhaps preoccupied with the illness that would soon send him to hospital, accepted the judgement.
The War Diary of the 2nd Canadian Corps sets out the situation:

> ### 25 Sept. 1944:
> Brig GE Beament, First Cdn Army, brought to corps com-
> mander [Simonds] an appreciation prepared by chief engi-
> neer's office on the possibility of flooding Walcheren. In this
> it was argued that the island would not flood adequately
> even if the dykes were breached and that it would be next
> to impossible to breach the dykes by bombing. Army com-
> mander [General Crerar] minuted his appreciation that
> unless the corps commander adduced other arguments,
> the proposition be dropped and consideration given to

what other methods should be adopted to open the door
to Antwerp.

To these objections, Simonds replied: "It is a fact that the great
proportion of the island is several feet below sea level. To breach the
dykes *cannot* be said to be impossible no matter how large the quantity of earth is to be shifted by bombs."

Furthermore, Simonds went on, bombing alone could not
destroy defenders and defences sufficiently to pave the way for a
seaborne assault. The dykes had to be breached: "Operationally, there
is nothing to lose and much to gain."[12]

Crerar acceded, but the dissenters, and there were many, still persisted, and the controversy dragged on. The sinking of an island had
consequences not only for the Canadian Army that had conceived
the plan, but also for the RAF Bomber Command, British Navy,
Marine commandos and, of course, the thousands of Dutch citizens
who lived on Walcheren and would see their homes, their farmlands,
and perhaps their very lives threatened by a single bombing raid.

Brigadier Ted Beament still remembers the confusion at army
headquarters during those final weeks in September while General
Crerar struggled with his illness: "We'd been having a lot of confer-
ences on this problem of attacking Walcheren — it was really the
main stumbling block at the time — but none were very conclusive.
I can only conclude that Crerar was a very sick man."[13]

But with the urgency to capture the Scheldt now seemingly fully
appreciated by SHAEF and the army commanders, this vacillation in
deciding upon a course of action was threatening to cause dangerous
long-term delays. Fate, at this moment, intervened. On the 26th of
September, General Crerar flew to Montgomery's headquarters,
reporting the physicians' findings that a severe case of anaemia
required him to be hospitalized in England for further tests and treatment. Crerar then summoned Simonds to army HQ in Ghent. The
meeting was recorded in the corps War Diary:

27 Sept. 1944:
Gen Simonds went to army HQ and returned in mid-afternoon. He is temporarily to command 1st Canadian Army

during General Crerar's absence. Maj-Gen Foulkes arrived at 1800 hours to similarly take command of 2 Cdn Corps.

Now Simonds, armed with the authority that only Canada's commander-in-chief could wield, lost no time in resuming the argument. He called a special meeting on the 29th of September, assembling all pertinent high-level Allied commanders — his own corps commanders, his senior staff officers, as well as representatives from the air force, navy, SHAEF and the 21st Army Group. Ted Beament relates the events of that meeting: "When Guy came up to army, he had had all the facts put before him, made his own appreciation, called a conference, and this of course involved the navy and air force. He gave them his plan, and that was it. Everybody was dumbfounded to have somebody to tell them what the hell to do in no uncertain terms."[14]

"That was a very dramatic moment," remembers Bill Anderson who was also at the meeting. "Guy called a conference and said, 'My intention is...' and they all realized that here was a whole new force to be reckoned with."[15]

"We had a deputation from Bomber Command up," Brigadier Beament recalls. "Guy explained the importance of breaching the dykes from the army point of view, that because the island was constructed rather like a saucer, flooding would impede the movement of the enemy mobile reserves and therefore greatly facilitate Walcheren's successful capture.

"The Bomber Command fellows went and conferred among themselves and came back and said, 'It's just not possible.'

"I can remember Guy looking them in the eye with those steely blue eyes of his, saying, 'Well, gentlemen, that's pretty disappointing. Had you been able to take that on as a task it would undoubtedly have saved many lives in the assault.' And he said it in such a way that it shook them a bit and they went and conferred again and came back and said that they could not guarantee success, but by God they'd try."[16]

At this point, a deceptively lethargic-seeming western Canadian answering to the curious name of "Spot" offered a reprieve. Major Bill Lye recounts the incident.

"I can remember the night that Brigadier Walsh, the chief engineer,

sent for 'Spot' West, 'Spot' being Captain West, RCE, and a staff officer of the Royal Canadian Engineers.

"Walsh asked West if it were possible to breach the dykes at
Walcheren by bombing them in any special way. West said he didn't
know but that he would like an opportunity to study it. He then went
back and requisitioned air photographs that seemed to fill the office
tent we were operating in. I'll always remember this tall fellow sitting
at his table, a six-foot-long table, and he had a pile of air photographs
beside him about four feet high and a stereo instrument.

"He would take stereo pairs, pair after pair. He had an overlay on
one side and he would mark certain things on his overlay. He was a
sleepy-looking character and I had the impression several times during the operation that he was really fast asleep with his head on the
stereo instrument rather than looking at the photographs. For two days
and nights he did nothing but study all the stereo pairs, and in the end
he came up with an overlay of a map, and I can recall his words.

"Pointing to his map, 'Spot' said: 'Bearing in mind the conditions
of the tides, it is my opinion that if the dykes are bombed here, here,
and here, between the dates and hours of such and such, the island
will be flooded in X number of days.' The plan was relayed up to
Bomber Command and became the basis for sinking Walcheren."[17]

A Canadian Military Operation Report describes the ensuing
events:

> General Simonds had not long to wait for a decision on his
> argument in favour of this terrible experiment. The chances
> of its practicality were accepted by the experts at the grim
> calculus of cost-for-cost, determined on behalf of the men
> who would soon be ordered to make the assault by land or
> water, in the teeth of the enemy's fire.
>
> Considerations of strategy prevailed over those of eco-
> nomics; the saving of life had a stronger case than the avoid-
> ance of dire hardship and of the loss of land and stock for our
> helpless friends, the Dutch. Too much depended on silenc-
> ing the German guns for these unhappy alternatives to be
> avoided, and Walcheren's rich acres were condemned to the
> spoilation of the sea.

Quoting Air Marshal Sir Arthur Harris, the report concluded with this uncompromising summation: "The wholesale destruction of property is always justified if it is calculated to save casualties."[18]

The final proposal was referred on to Eisenhower at SHAEF headquarters for top-level approval. On 1 October, Simonds had his answer:

1 Oct., 1150 hours:
Re Operation Infatuate
The Supreme Commander has approved the project to flood the island of Walcheren.[19]

The man who was closest to Simonds during those eventful days, his aide (ADC), Captain Marshal Stearns, remembers vividly the anguish of finally making the decision to order out the bombers:

It was a very tough decision to be made. Queen Wilhelmina was aware of this plan; in fact, there is no question that everybody in Holland and on Walcheren Island knew that there was going to be an attack, and just what form it was going to take. The RAF had dropped leaflets over Walcheren telling people to get out because there could be a bombing. Every possible effort was made to get the people off the island. Queen Wilhelmina obviously would have been alarmed and she decided to contact Winston Churchill, saying did he realize the great harm the bombing would cause to her population and please not to allow the operation to take place.

Winston Churchill felt that he had to advise Monty of this call from Queen Wilhelmina and that she was disturbed, but I don't think he took any positive position on it. He left it entirely up to Monty.

I have a picture which is in the records where Monty, Bertie Ramsay, who was head of the navy at that time, and Guy Simonds, the three of them are standing at army HQ and the three of them together are deciding whether, after being in touch with Winston and knowing what Wilhelmina's feelings were, whether they were going to bomb that island or not.

There was not the slightest doubt what Guy Simonds wanted — and also Bertie Ramsay. I'm sure Monty thought it was the smart thing to do; Winston was not going to interfere although he couldn't completely disregard her wishes and not pass on her feelings to his army commanders. So they decided to bomb it.[20]

On the 2nd of October, in accordance with instructions from 21st Army Group, two B-17 bombers of 406 Squadron, USAF, flew low over the islands at the mouth of the River Scheldt, releasing thousands of leaflets printed in the Dutch language. Twice that day, Radio Oranje repeated the words to the people of the islands:

Voice of SHAEF No. 37

Here is a message from Supreme Headquarters.

There is every likelihood that a severe and prolonged aerial bombardment will be carried out shortly against enemy troops and installations on your islands.

It is the earnest desire of the Supreme Allied Command that the civil population shall be spared the effects of this necessary military action to the greatest extent possible. Not only aerial bombardment, but the danger of flooding also threatens your lives and the lives of your families. For your protection, leave the islands. If that is not possible, if it is necessary for you to remain on the islands, remove yourselves and your families *immediately* to a place of safety.

All military objectives — roads, canals, transport lines, power stations, railway yards or sheds, warehouses and depots, enemy concentration of all kinds — are the centres of danger. Leave their vicinity *immediately*.

Travel only by foot. Take nothing with you that you cannot easily carry. Keep off highways and move only across fields. Do not travel in large groups which may be mistaken for enemy formations. Keep away from low-lying ground and from military objectives until the enemy has been driven from your islands.[21]

In Flushing, on that day, the youngster, thirteen-year-old Peter Eekman, stood with his grandparents watching the drop, scrambling with the others for a copy of this curious missive. At first they were puzzled. There had been plenty of heavy bombing before; why would their liberators-to-be trouble to deliver a warning now? Then the significance of the message sank in: Everyone knew that our liberation would bring sacrifices, they thought, but no one had ever thought of flooding! But they have to do it, the British. No matter what damage it does to us, the dykes have to be breached. It is our only hope of freedom.

And in bewildered clusters, the people shared their anxiety: "Where will they attack first? How soon is this to happen? Where can we go?" And Peter Eekman has vivid memories of the turmoil brought onto his neighbours by that cascade of paper:

> The island was sealed off by the Germans. The causeway [the only land-link between Walcheren and South Beveland] was open to military traffic only. Quite a large number of Flushing families left for the town of Middelburg, but most decided to stay. Among those who went there were many employees of the shipyard. The German naval commander was afraid that not enough workingmen would be available to repair the naval ships. He had a meeting with the garrison commander of Flushing, Colonel Reinhardt, and other officials. They decided to pay extra money to these employees.
>
> My grandparents also decided to stay in Flushing. My grandfather said, "It will be dangerous any place, so it's better to stay in our own home. We can only wait and see."[22]

And so, on Tuesday, the 3rd of October, just a brief month since the bizarre events of *Dolle Dinsdag,* a new horror touched the Zeelanders. It came down in the form of 4,000, one-thousand-and-five-hundred-pound-armour piercing, delayed-action bombs, 1,270 tons of explosive failing from an armada of 247 Lancaster bombers.

Their target was the Westkapelle Dyke, fourteen km northwest of Flushing. In a brilliant demonstration of precision bombing, the RAF attacked the venerable 15th-century dyke that rose ten metres above the sea, and was in some places one hundred metres wide at the base. The bombardment lasted two hours. When it was done, the work of five hundred years holding back the North Sea had been erased by a series of explosions that had penetrated the guts of the dyke, spewing forth ten thousand tons of clay. A breach over one hundred metres long had been made, and now the sea was rushing in to flood the land. Walcheren was sinking.

So successful was the mission that ten planes carrying the potent 12,000-pound "tallboy" bombs were called back as they reached the approaches of Walcheren.

To the terrified people on the streets, the awesome sight, to become a continuing nightmare, was of the black bellies of the monster aircraft shuddering over their heads as they dropped their screaming cargo.

The pilot of one of these aircraft, RAF Flying Officer Thomas Clayton, was flying four thousand feet above the frightened crowd when he began experiencing some difficulty. "Seventy Lancasters in my group went in that first day," Clayton recalls. "I was flight engineer with 514 Squadron based in Cambridge, flying with a partly Canadian crew.

"I remember that we sort of made a mess of our first run. Although the weather was excellent, we had the bad luck to run into a puff of cloud that caused the bomb aimer to lose his target. We had to go around again and this put us literally on our own. The other sixty-nine aircraft had actually left the site by the time we got back. High tide was 2:15 P.M. and we were there at 1:03 the first time around and 1:08 the second. The original intent was to have us all out in five minutes.

"This was special precision bombing. We were supposed to let all eight bombs go at once, salvo bombing. The delayed-action, armour-piercing technique was developed to avoid explosion on impact. We wanted the bombs to go to the base of the dykes where the explosion would have the greatest effect. It would also ensure that we got out of the way before the explosion.

"Of course, the Jerries were trigger-happy, which was commonplace. They were really after us and they didn't need radar to assist them because they could see us well enough to fire at us over open sights. They didn't use any heavy ack-ack on us because at 4,000 feet the range was too short. So they used light anti-aircraft guns, and what we commonly refer to as 'Flaming Onions' that come up in threes. We only suffered slight damage but the aircraft smelled a lot of cordite. We got back in one piece."[23]

And Pilot Officer Sidney Aldridge inadvertently took back a souvenir of Walcheren that earned him a reprimand for low-flying: "As I circled over the target area I was at such a low altitude that I saw a frightened civilian fall from his bicycle after seeing our plane heading towards him. On return to base, we discovered that a number of German telephone wires were wrapped around the Lancaster."[24]

Aerial reconnaissance later in the day showed water spreading well into the fields below Westkapelle. In the next forty-eight hours the strong tides surged through the gap twice a day, widening the breach each time, and building, grain by grain, Guy Simonds's new landing beaches.

On the 3rd of October, word of the first mission came back to Canadian Army headquarters. Marshal Stearns recalls the moment: "I remember Geoff Walsh coming into the Mess at lunch the day they breached the dyke, and saying to Guy Simonds, 'Walcheren is starting to fill up.' We knew we'd made hits on the dyke, that the water was getting in and I remember those exact words: Walcheren is starting to fill up. I guess Wilhelmina's appeal did stop a lot of the heavy bombing, the additional bombing. She said it would ruin the island for agricultural purposes."[25]

To Bill Anderson, it was an impressive moment too: "The simple truth is that those damned planes came over by day and bombed the dykes, all according to plan. They came a second time and widened the breach and it bloody well worked, just like the man said it would. I just can't say enough about Guy Simonds as a commander, who had an innovative idea and then had the sort of forceful personality and power command that pulled it through."[26]

Four days later, the RAF struck again, this time at Flushing. Young Peter Eekman made sure he had a grandstand seat:

> It was a Saturday, quite warm and clear, and I was waiting in
> my backyard for my friend. At one-thirty P.M. there came an

air raid warning, but as this was common practice to us throughout the past years of occupation, I did not pay much attention to the alarm. From the northwest and east I heard the monotonous drone of hundreds of aircraft. They were invisible as I could not look out over the rooftops of the houses surrounding our garden. But even at our age we were already experienced in recognising different aircraft types by the sound of the engines.

"Probably Lancasters on their way to some target in Germany," I thought. Suddenly, the earth started shaking and some explosions could be heard.

It is amazing how fast rumours spread. People in the street knew already that the dykes were being bombed. At two o'clock my friend came and we decided to go down to the esplanade and have a look. The attack was still on, but we slipped away and hoped my grandparents would not notice us. In just five minutes we were at the stairway leading to the esplanade. Although civilians were not permitted to enter the boulevard, we gathered all our courage and went up the stairs — and landed in the midst of some German officers. They were probably too preoccupied to send us away.

We saw the Lancasters circling over the dyke area. Flying one after the other, they dropped their bombs, turned away and then returned again for a second run. Nearby, at a distance of fifty yards from where we stood, a four-barrelled gun fired its 20mm shells in the direction of the Lancasters, deafening our ears. At a certain moment, eight to ten Germans came running down the dyke from their gun position which lay amidst falling bombs.

At about five P.M. we returned home. I got a severe punishment from my grandfather, but I did not care about that. My friend and I had been one of the few of our town to watch the air attack from so close.[27]

A total of four raids, all successful, were made on the Walcheren dykes: two at Flushing and one on the east coast at Veere in addition to the pioneer thrust at Westkapelle. Air photographs showed most of the island flooded, with only the perimeter dykes and dunes and the towns of Middelburg (in the island's centre), and part of Flushing on the south, still above water.

The attacks had caused little disruption of the German batteries and concrete bunkers built into the rim of high ground on the periphery of the island. These were earmarked by Simonds for attack in subsequent weeks in the promised daily pounding of Walcheren that Eisenhower had endorsed. But inside the island, German bunkers were filling up. Fortifications, supply caches and ammunition dumps were destroyed. Roads were inundated, cutting off the beleaguered German garrisons from reinforcements or supplies.

The few towns that were above sea level were crowded with refugees. The main water system was destroyed; there was no drinking water, only salt water that the people tried unsuccessfully to distil and, for the lucky ones, rainwater from the well. All the trees were killed, and the crops devastated.

In Westkapelle, 125 civilians died during the bombardment of the dyke. Forty-seven persons had fled to a windmill during the bombardment; the mill received a hit and collapsed while the water came pouring in from the breach in the dyke. Many were trapped under heavy beams, with the water rising around them. Help arrived and efforts were made to dig them out. Three were eventually saved; the others drowned miserably in the ruins of the mill.[28] German propaganda reports claimed that five thousand civilians had been killed. The people scoffed. It had been a heavy sacrifice, but a necessary one. Better, they said, to spill water than to spill blood.

A Canadian Military Operations Report summed up the impact of the bombing on the enemy garrison:

> The fantastic flooding mesmerised the Germans into fatal inactivity, destroyed their communications, and sapped their morale to an incredible extent. Prisoners, and particularly the more senior officers, repeatedly cried "The water! Without that terrible water you would never have beaten us" in accents of despair and frustration, and there could have been no better or more eloquent tribute to the higher planning of the operation than that paid to it by the Germans themselves.

It is comforting to conclude that neither General Simonds planned nor the stricken Dutch civilians suffered, in vain.[29]

But as successful as the first part of Simonds's proposal had been, the second part, the prolonged heavy bombing of Walcheren intended to destroy those concreted fortifications on the island's rim, was floundering in yet another Allied paroxysm of uncertainty.

It was widely agreed that only an exceptional weight of bombs could penetrate the reinforced concrete. In his initial enthusiasm for the proposed attack of Walcheren, the supreme commander had wholeheartedly supported Simonds's urgent plea for "day and night systematic prolonged heavy bombing" of German gun batteries menacing an Allied invasion. The 1st Canadian Army, he had insisted, was to have priority claim on Bomber Command for the complete saturation of the targets selected.

Indeed, for the final weeks of September after Eisenhower's endorsement of this "vital operation," several bomber attacks were made, dropping some six hundred tons of bombs. The citizens of Flushing noted gratefully that in this "fine example of precision bombing by Lancasters, no civilian targets were hit."[30] In early October, the air force had concentrated on breaching the dykes. It was toward the middle of that month that Eisenhower's abandonment of his written promise of support began to cause its mischief. Again, controversy threatened the Canadian operation, again with Eisenhower square in the middle of another tug of war.

The first blow was the flat refusal of General Brereton, commander of the 1st Airborne Army (backed by Air Chief Marshal Sir Trafford Leigh-Mallory), to commit his men to an airborne landing at the Walcheren Causeway, the land-bridge from the South Beveland Peninsula to the island.

Then the promised bomber support for the Canadian Army assault began to sputter out. In an abrupt move by the senior officers of the Strategic Air Force, spearheaded first by Leigh-Mallory, commander of the Allied Expeditionary Air Force, and then by Eisenhower's deputy supreme commander, Air Chief Marshal Lord Tedder, another policy was declared which would give top priority to German industrial plants as Allied bomber targets.

On the 28th of September, Leigh-Mallory maintained that heavy bomber support would only be useful to the Canadian operation immediately before the attack on Walcheren, when the enemy would have no opportunity to repair the damage to his batteries. He seemed not to have considered that although it would require a massive drop of bombs to damage a casemented battery, the damage, once achieved, could not quickly be repaired.

Eisenhower, who now no longer had direct control of the air forces, gave in to the persuasive pair. Montgomery, still recoiling from his Market Garden disappointment at Arnhem, and possibly more upset than was generally realized, also gave his general agreement to the rationale. He did, however, insist that three or four days before Walcheren's "D-Day" invasion the air force should give the island "everything we have got" in the way of heavy bombing.[31] On October 24th, Tedder, acting with the approval of Eisenhower, forbade further heavy bomber attacks on Walcheren.

This dual concurrence of the two leaders was all the encouragement that Bomber Command needed to begin promulgating what must be one of the most spiteful and damaging pronouncements to arise in any war from ally to ally: from his lofty perch, and facing no imminent personal danger of war, Tedder had decided that the infantrymen — Canadians in particular, it would seem — had become too dependent for support on the bombers. The troops might, he felt, become reluctant to fight on their own if too much back-up aid from the bombers was offered. "The repeated calls by the Canadian Army for heavy bomber effort to deal with a part-worn battery on Walcheren...is in my opinion only too clear an example [of army demoralization]...The army has been drugged with bombs; it is going to be a difficult process to cure the drug-addicts," he said.[32] Tedder's weaning process of the "drug-addict" Canadians by refusing them vital support was ultimately responsible for the deaths of many Allied soldiers and sailors.

84 Group RAF was then assigned the responsibility of preparing and executing a pre-invasion air plan. Again, the Grand Hotel in Bruges became the planning centre for meeting after meeting as the myriad of details were worked out for D-Day.

The RAF, working with the Canadians, drew up a schedule and

priority list of targets, the four foremost being that deadly quartet of batteries already earmarked as intensely dangerous to assaulting crafts or troops: W15, embedded in the seawall at Westkapelle, W13 and W11 in the sand dunes below the town and W17 flanking it from the north. They pointed out, however, that these were concrete-and-steel gun emplacements that could not be put out of action by the weight of attack that 84 Group was able to deliver. Only Bomber Command could make a dent through those tons of reinforced concrete.

But no one, it would seem, was listening to the repeated Canadian requests for heavy bomber support, nor even to the frequent warnings about the notoriously bad weather that was usual in that season and indeed already evident in the constant, driving rain these planners were now experiencing.

D-Day was scheduled for the 1st of November. A much paler version of Bomber Command's mandate from Montgomery to drop "everything we've got" was initiated on the 28th of October. Two hundred and sixty-one heavy bombers made a strong daylight raid on Walcheren, dropping 1,189 tons of high explosive. On that day, Flight Lieutenant Bill Walker, a twenty-one-year-old Canadian pilot in 4 Group, RAF, had a taste of the threatening North Sea weather:

> It was overcast all the way across the Channel. The weather was dreadful. Finally we broke through the clouds to get our bearing and found ourselves in the gun sights of a British cruiser. Those British ships used to shoot at everything so we got back up in a hurry. We came into Westkapelle and dropped our bombs at about five thousand feet — there were about one hundred planes in my group, each carrying fourteen five-hundred pounders — and I even had time to get around again and give my gunner a chance to spray them again. They said in our briefing that we were flying "army support" at the Scheldt, but that was my only run at it. The next day, and the day after, I flew bombing missions to Germany.[33]

The next day, 358 bombers dropped 1,562 tons more. And on the third day, the 30th of October, eighty-nine aircraft unloaded 555 tons at the enemy batteries. The final day before the invasion, the weather, as the Canadians had feared, closed in. All bomber attacks on Walcheren were cancelled.

The total number of tons of high explosives dropped over Walcheren in those last three pre-invasion days added up to just over 3,300. In a similar period, Bomber Command dropped almost ten thousand tons over Germany, far in excess of the tonnage dropped on Eisenhower's "vital" objective of Walcheren.*

So the Canadian Army was slipping back to its low priority position, on the one hand being instructed to get on with opening the port of Antwerp, on the other, being denied first the paratroop support and then the bomber support that it needed to do the job. Furthermore, the Canadians were instructed on the 2nd of October that the British and American operations against the Ruhr were to have first call on essential supply.

But, on the 9th of October, Eisenhower, for the first time, added a sense of urgency to his memo to Montgomery: "Unless we have Antwerp producing by middle of November entire operations will come to a standstill." And, on the 10th and again on the 13th, the supreme commander continued to give token acknowledgement to the situation, albeit withdrawing support at the same time.[35]

The failure of Market Garden to catch the Germans off balance, possibly even finishing off the war, and the worsening supply problems, seemed finally to have made their points.

On the 16th of October — ironically, the very day that the Royal Hamilton Light Infantry was making its desperate bid to drive the Germans out of Beveland — Montgomery finally acknowledged the importance of the operation: "I have given Antwerp top priority in all operations in 21 Army Group and all energies and efforts will be now devoted towards opening up that place."[36]

To the staff at 1st Canadian Army, this meant that they could expect some relief from the supply famine. It also meant, as Lieutenant Colonel Anderson recalls, some disruption of routine at headquarters:

---

* Colonel C.P. Stacey, Canadian military historian, who did considerable research on these statistics, and whose figures we quote, wrote: "The fact is that even in the final period before the assault Walcheren was not being given the highest priority among Bomber Command targets."[34]

"The Supreme Command had a change of heart. They decided that the clearing of the Scheldt should be given No. I priority. The result was that the authorities all came around to visit us, and I have never seen so many senior officers come in to one army headquarters. They all wanted to know when Walcheren could be captured."[37]

The battle of words was finally to wind down; the bastard Battle of the Scheldt, for so long denied by all, was now legitimized.

A routine encounter between an over-age Canadian artillery officer and a one-eyed British Guardsman on the blustery plains of Salisbury resulted in a partnership that would play a minor but unique role in the Walcheren battle. If the Goliaths of Bomber Command would not release their powerful "tallboys" to smash the German concrete-protected guns, this unusual pair of Davids at least produced a sling-shot of remarkable sting. It was called Land Mattress.

On a frigid mid-winter evening in 1944, a lone Canadian, distinguished by a shock of snow-white hair, checked in for dinner at the Officers' Mess at Larkhill, the British School of Artillery near Stonehenge. Lieutenant Colonel W.E. Harris, veteran Canadian gunner who had commanded a regiment until senior artillery officers decided he was too old for active duty, was now, to his great distaste, relegated to staff work at Canadian Military Headquarters in London.

The artilleryman noted a single familiar face in the room. The young British colonel who had conducted the artillery demonstration Harris had witnessed that morning was sitting dejectedly in the corner of the Mess.

"That was an imposing demonstration today, Colonel Wardell," Harris commented.

Mike Wardell looked up. "Much good that will do!" he answered, and then added, "Oh! You're the Canadian!"

As the two shook hands, Eric Harris recalled their earlier meeting: "I first saw him when our small group went out on the ranges to see the demonstration. An English colonel, in Guards battle-dress, looking somewhat out of place on an artillery range, and wearing a black patch over one eye, was standing beside a contraption which certainly did not look like a gun. The weapon, if it could be taken to be one, seemed nothing more than four rows of narrow stove-pipe, each of six pieces, tied together and mounted on a two-wheeled twenty-hundredweight trailer."[38]

Wardell introduced the curious weapon. It was, he explained, a rocket-firing gun, capable of firing up to eight thousand yards, the same range as heavy mortars, yet considerably lighter and more mobile. Harris's skepticism turned to enthusiasm when he saw from his observation post the designated target enveloped in what he would always remember as "one of the most accurate, concentrated, vicious mass explosions" he had ever seen. Suddenly, within a very short period of some five seconds, all twenty-four shells seemed to come together directly in the target area and to reinforce each other with a tremendously devastating effect.

"Damned good!" said one of the War Office observers next to him. And then the same man uttered the words that would become the anathema of Harris and Wardell, "Too bad it's too late!"

During dinner, Harris heard the story of how the infantry officer, a publisher in peacetime, had become so obsessed by rockets.

In 1942, fighting Rommel's Afrika Corps at El Alamein, Wardell's position was being overrun by enemy troops. In desperation he seized an anti-aircraft weapon ordinarily used for shooting rockets at German planes, and turned the fire on the attacking German infantry. The result was electric; the enemy was demoralized by the devastating impact of the rockets and subsequently withdrew. Mike Wardell was himself wounded and lost an eye in the action but he never forgot the usefulness against troops of a weapon designed to fight planes. Back in England, he determined to design a rocket gun specifically for this purpose. Wardell took on another war, this time against mule-headed British authorities who were convinced that the war would be over before the weapon could be properly designed and tested.

At this point, Eric Harris stepped into the fray. The pair decided to approach Canadian officials, although without a great deal of optimism. Historically, Canada seldom took the lead over Britain in such matters, but perhaps this time, they thought, the Canadians would do something on their own initiative. To their surprise, back came the decision, supported by General Crerar and Brigadier H.O.N.

Brownfield, head of all Canadian artillery, to make the undertaking a wholly Canadian venture.

So, on the 15th of September, 1944, the 1st Canadian Rocket Unit, informally known as Land Service Mattress, was formed. Two weeks later, the unit was anchored off the coast of France at Arromanche, where they were compelled to sit out an eight-day storm before rejoining Harris and Wardell at Bruges, preparatory to training for the Walcheren assault.

Colonel Wardell, now formally attached to the Canadian Army, and Harris flew directly to army headquarters. "We were a pretty jaunty pair," Colonel Harris remembered; "Mike had been invalided out of the Guards, and because of age I had been relegated to duty in England only. Now we were back at the front, and with our own battery to fight with.

"In the damp little tent where we found quite acceptable quarters we drank a quiet and thoughtful toast for what the months, and this day, had brought us."[39]

⇒ 7 ⇐

Streetcar War

O N THE TENTH OF SEPTEMBER, LEG STILL ENCASED IN PLASTER, EISEN-
hower flew to Brussels airport where, in a meeting with Montgomery, he agreed that the opening of Antwerp should be postponed
until after Operation Market Garden (the codename for the Arnhem
breakthrough now in intensive preparation for its September 17th
launching). Once again, the tug of war between Montgomery and
Patton received conciliatory treatment from the referee. Monty
would have priority, but not *all* the priority; Patton was to get a generous portion of the available petrol. "Monty's suggestion is simply
[to] give him everything. This is crazy," the supreme commander
said in exasperation.[1]

However intense the drama of the dockside days in Antwerp was
to become, it would inspire little attention or support from high command. As a result, only minimal and ill-equipped defensive forces
were spared to hold Antwerp's city and port facilities. The 2nd British
Army, assigned to defend the port after the liberation, had neither the
orders nor the strength to attack the Merxem Bridge or Kruisschans
Lock, the operations for which the Secret Army had pleaded.

Now it was the turn of the 4th Canadian Infantry Brigade to hold
Antwerp Harbour, but it had no broader mandate; it was simply to sit
tight and consolidate the gains that had been made largely by Harry's
dock fighters on the 4th and 5th of September. Lieutenant Colonel
W.A.B. Anderson observed that the Canadian Army was "lower in priority for resources than all other armies in this operation."[2] The 2nd
Canadian Corps, he concluded, could do very little more than sharpen

their pencils on the planning board. The plans themselves could only become operative when supplies were freed.

By now, the shortness of supplies was being keenly felt by all the battalions. The Canadian flank was "allowed to languish," wrote historian Chester Wilmot.[3] And citing the Scheldt battle as "one of the grimmest and longest" of the Northwest Europe campaign, British historian Eversley Belfield echoed the thought: "The Canadian Army…was treated as a kind of odd-job organization, and thus given a very low claim to supplies."[4]

On the 16th of September, the War Diary of the Royal Hamilton Light Infantry, 4th Canadian Infantry Brigade, duly noted the battalion's new assignment: "RHLI took over from the Royal Welsh Fusiliers in Antwerp Harbour. Our role was to guard the docks and port facilities of the port of Antwerp. Strength of the battalion thirty-five officers and 724 ORs. Lieutenant Colonel W.D. Whitaker returned to the unit and took over command after several weeks of convalescing in England from wounds received at Verson."

The five thousand men of the 4th Canadian Infantry Brigade comprised three regiments (all from the province of Ontario): the Royal Hamilton Light Infantry (RHLI), based in Hamilton and known more familiarly as the Rileys, was alone on the docks, spread thinly on a line of some twelve km from Groenendaal Laan Bridge through Kruisschans Lock to a point just south of the village of Oorderen; the Essex Scottish Regiment, from Windsor, overlooked the suburbs of Merxem and Eekeren where the Germans were still strongly entrenched; and, nearby, the Royal Regiment of Canada, from Toronto, was defending the Albert Canal to the east.

Sergeant Pete Bolus of the RHLI was one individual who decided to do something about these shortages. His wartime friend, Corporal Arthur Kelly, remembered Bolus's enterprise: "Pete was the toughest little guy in the Rileys. He fought, lived, gambled and loved the same way he drove a tracked Bren carrier — wide open and straight ahead. His father owned the Royal Fruit Store in downtown Hamilton, Ontario, across from the Royal Connaught Hotel. Pete was kiddingly referred to as the 'Royal Greek Banana.' He had been on the Dieppe raid and he was a hell-raiser."[5]

So no one was surprised in Antwerp to hear Bolus, senior sergeant of the RHLI Carrier Platoon patrolling the harbour, say he was damned if he was going to see his Bren gun carriers ditched through a lack of parts, even if he had to resort to a little deception. Bolus remembers one such experience he had in the carrier platoon: "We couldn't maintain the vehicles. I had been all over the country trying to find bogey carrier wheels. Parts just weren't available; we only had makeshift wheels. So one day I drove over one hundred miles and I came back with four new wheels. We only got three at the depot, but on the way back, we stole one. We stopped another carrier, and while I was talking to the driver, my buddy Elmer Brian was stealing the spare bogey wheel from back of his carrier."[6]

The 5th Canadian Infantry Brigade, holding the line at the Albert Canal to the east of the city, was similarly affected by the supply famine. One of its battalions, the Calgary Highlanders, recalls severe artillery ammunition rationing: "At this period the Calgary High-landers, sorely depleted in strength, were covering an enormous area. Most of the division's supplies were still being brought up the long route from Arromanches in Normandy. The standard firing ration at that time was three rounds per field gun per day and five rounds for heavy mortars. We were at that time down to a strength of 400 men."[7]

So, under-strength and under-armed, the 2nd Canadian Division leaped into a sparring match with a strongly reinforced and determined enemy. The result was essentially a two-week standoff. Only at the end of a fortnight were the Canadians able to obtain the supplies necessary to get back on the offensive.

During the standoff over the last half of September, as Market Garden reached its grim conclusion, the "odd-job" Canadians waited for ammunition for their guns, and wheels for their carriers, and experienced some of the most bizarre circumstances of the entire campaign. They called it the "Streetcar War."

The baroque city of Antwerp that in happier years attracted tourists from around the world was now, in September, 1944, to host a new kind of visitor: the Liberator. The survivors of the heat and stench of war in Normandy were to savour the elegance and glitter of this diamond centre of the world.

The RHLI War Diary for 20 September, at 2100 hours, notes with relish that Antwerp's diversions are both delightful and abundant:

"The CO granted six-hour passes on a basis of seven and one-half percent [of strength], permitting the troops to visit Antwerp, which was apparently well stocked with ice cream, beautiful girls and beer."

In macabre contrast to the unrelenting grimness of the docks, where warehouse walls were pockmarked with bullet holes, roads pitted by mortar shells, and streets still stained with the lifeblood of the defenders, the city of Antwerp sparkled like the gems for which it was famed. Only a short streetcar ride separated death from life. The Royal Regiment was to reminisce that "Ordinary urban life went on in Antwerp much as in peacetime. The trams continued to run, nightclubs remained open, and the shops sold a reasonable assortment of goods. Two bands played each night at the Century Hotel — 'J'attendrai' and 'La Vie en Rose' were probably the most popular numbers — and the Belgian girls in their elegant evening dresses were certainly [or did it, after all, only seem so?] the most beautiful in the world."[8]

A historical officer at 2nd Division HQ, Captain T. Murray Hunter, was struck by the variety of goods in the shop windows, in direct contrast with the scarcities in the United Kingdom: "After the 'lean' years in Britain — where fruit such as grapes, when obtainable, sold for seventeen shillings and sixpence a pound — it was a great treat to be able to buy a kilogram of grapes for approximately two francs in Antwerp."[9]

For the Canadians, it was a few weeks "on the house." There seemed no limit to the generosity of the Belgians. Even two weeks after the liberation, it was almost impossible for a Canadian to buy his own drink at a bar; there was usually a bountiful Belgian waiting to pick up the tab. Occasionally, though, the hospitality backfired, and then some fancy footwork was required, as one Italian-Canadian soldier roguishly discovered:

> Some of the cafés were run by Italians. We came into one and I started talking Italian to them and they couldn't do enough for me, just because I was the first Italian they had seen from Canada that spoke to them in their own language. They went out in the backyard of this one café, a family café. The old man produced a case of chianti that had been buried before the war. Then I started running up a tab on them. I ran up about fifty thousand francs in these different places and one

of my buddies had to go back and tell them that I'd been captured and that the Germans had torn up all the tabs.[10]

In the language of war, luxury commodities such as money, food,
drink and women existed mainly in the present tense, and the fun of
pursuing them gave almost as much pleasure as their acquisition.
There wasn't much point in worrying about the delicate points of possession when, in all likelihood, the owner or the borrower would soon
be dead. And often the antics of the pillage were amusing enough for
the pillagers to shrug off any elements of legality. If you captured a
German, his money, watch, rings and boots and by definition "anything that wasn't attached to his body" logically belonged to the captor. *"Haben sie gelt?"* was war lingo for "You're under arrest!"

"We left their personal pictures and such and we always returned
their wallets," one soldier, who chose not to be named, remembers
virtuously. "But we took their money. No one called that stealing."

Nor was petty pilfering from army stock considered robbery. One
platoon had an "at home" at the best brothel on Schipperstrasse,
financed by an impromptu sidewalk sale of leather army boots — all
of Canadian manufacture.

One particularly notorious truck driver subsidized his crap games
with a full billfold that was frequently replenished by an ingenious
and quite illegal scheme: visiting a neighbouring town, he would sell
his vehicle to a local citizen for however many francs he could get.
The deal completed, the driver exited with the money, whereupon
his accomplice, a military policeman, promptly turned up, accusing
the gullible burgher of conducting an illicit transaction. The truck
was returned to his friend, who was not only enriched by several
thousand francs by the scheme but also was provided with an escape
from the realities of the front.

Humour was a quality highly prized by front-line troops who
needed the absurd, the foolish, the genuinely funny to balance the
day-to-day horror of their lives.

The Century Hotel was the popular watering hole for officers;
now and again, though, the hospitable Anversois would invite the
men to their homes. In at least one case, an intense love affair developed between a young lieutenant and a Belgian woman. The officer

dutifully brought along army rations when he was invited to the family home; the husband would as perfunctorily produce black-market beefsteak — purchased, no doubt, from his profitable dealings in black-market diamonds. The relationship might have wilted at the dining table had not the V-1 buzz bombs fired the affair. When the staccato roar of the bombs announced an imminent raid, the lady's fearful husband went skittering into the garden air-raid shelter. The young lovers, thankful for their privacy and unmindful of the danger, stayed on in the house. The relationship was as brief as it was passionate; two weeks later, the lieutenant was killed on patrol.

More often, affairs were casual on both sides, conducted matter-of-factly and with little concern for the luxury of propriety or moral standards. In wartime, such things were reserved for more important issues like loyalty to one's battlefield comrades and survival in the field.

One highlight in a soldier's life was payday. Two days after the Rileys marched into Antwerp, they had a welcome visit from the RHLI paymaster, Captain Maurice Gervais of the Royal Canadian Army Pay Corps.

Pay parades were staged whenever the battalion was at rest, or was issuing leaves to the men. But payday involved a lot more than just handing over a few francs; Gervais frequently found himself in the role of father confessor and marriage counsellor as well as financial advisor. He also became the equalizer at the crap games.

A private soldier received $1.30 a day, augmented, for the married men, by the $35.00 a month that was sent directly to their wives. The scale escalated with rank; a lieutenant colonel was paid a lordly $11.00 a day. Paradoxically, the private soldier usually had a much fatter roll of franc notes than did his colonel, a curious phenomenon that Gervais well understood:

Our guys had a lot of money.* Everyone got an advance of
two hundred French francs before we went to Normandy. We

---

* The sale of victory bonds was always very brisk at the front, even when the action was heaviest. At the end of the Scheldt campaign, the South Saskatchewan Regiment had purchased $47,000 worth of bonds, more than any other battalion in the 2nd Canadian Infantry Division.

had pay parades every time there was a rest period but some guys never drew a penny; they just kept accumulating money. Then there was the "loot route." Every time a German put up his hand to surrender, he had his wallet in it.

One lad that was killed had fifty thousand Belgian francs. I don't know if his wife got it or not. The authorities could be difficult to deal with in those days. They questioned how a private could come by that much money — it would be in excess of ten thousand dollars — but we said he had won it gambling.

Gervais was often to champion the men he paid: "We were supposed to look after their best interests, and sometimes that meant breaking a few rules. But you couldn't forget that many of them wouldn't be around next week or next month; I figured I'd give them everything I could."

Gervais's "everything" included dodging enemy bullets when he took the payroll to the forward platoons at Antwerp dock. And once, it nearly cost him one hundred and twenty-five thousand dollars, and his job:

I would estimate what I would require and then I would give a voucher to the field cash office which was at rear div headquarters. They would give me the money. The same thing happened when we would move into another country and I took back money in exchange for the currency of the country we were working in. This is where I got in serious trouble. Theoretically, the men couldn't exchange any funds greater than they had drawn from their paybook. But the men had an awful lot of French money they wanted to exchange for Belgian currency. What they did, of course, was get the fellows who didn't have any money to sign for them and then hand it over. When we arrived in Belgium there had just been a new issue of French francs at even money. So after I exchanged their money for Belgique I wound up with about half a million worthless old francs that I couldn't get rid of.

I took them to the field cashier at rear division and the bastard said, "This isn't all out of paybooks. I won't take it." That was a fair amount of money to be stuck with; my heart sank in my boots. I went down to the Bank de Commerce on the rue d'Hôpital and had a few words with one of their officials. We exchanged cigarettes; that is, I exchanged my cigarettes for his goodwill and I walked out with my new money.

But it was not just men on leave that the paymaster helped out:

The top brass took a very moral view in those days of sending the marriage allowance of thirty-five dollars a month to a wife who was not being strictly faithful. We had lots of letters cutting off allowances because the wives were playing around. I had a whole pile of them. When I left the regiment, I took every one of those letters and burned them. They weren't mine to burn, but I burned them anyway. There was so much heartbreak in those letters.

I got word one day to interview a guy and tell him his wife's allowance had been cut off. He could continue sending her an assignment of pay if he wanted, but she had got herself pregnant. He came over and said, "I know why you want to see me." In this letter — he handed it to me to read — she said, "I went to this party and I was having a good time with this fellow who didn't go to war. I agreed to go home with him. All the time I was doing it, I was thinking of you." Then there was another guy who hadn't had any sex for two years. He wrote home and asked his wife if it would be all right. She wrote back and said, "Sure, it's all right, dear, but don't you pay more than five dollars because that's all I'm getting for it!"

I saw more guys with problems than the padre. Just before D-Day, a soldier went on leave to the north of England. He came over to see me when he came back. He said, "I had a strange experience. I went into this pub and there were some air force fellows there. They said, 'Come on over here, Canada. You can't buy a drink tonight,' and I thought,

'Why not?' They said, 'We just came back from Canada, and boy they treated us right.'"

So they bought this soldier a drink and then another. Then one flying officer said, "There's one chick that really looked after me." He takes out his wallet and it's this guy's wife. So he said to me, "I don't know what I'm going to do about it."

About two weeks later, I got a letter from headquarters saying that I should interview this man, that I should tell him his wife is pregnant. So I had the guy over, very privately of course, and asked him what he intended to do. "I'll tell you what I'm going to do," he answered. "I want to continue sending my assignment of pay to her. I know what human nature is. I haven't been running around much but I have certainly had girls over here. As soon as I get home, I want to adopt that baby." So after getting a sworn statement from him that he would adopt the child, they reinstated her allowances and dated them back.[11]

Even with these diversions the troops did not always, or easily, find it possible to turn off the war. Men on leave sometimes drank with desperation, or because, as one soldier put it, "It wasn't possible to stop fighting suddenly. All of us were over-tense. We drank with a grim determination to get drunk."[12] When they were very drunk they brought their war into the barroom, brawling and bloodying their comrades. And when they were even more drunk, finally they could sleep. Soon enough, they would catch a streetcar back to the hell at the end of the line.

These troops (some really just boys of seventeen or eighteen) were strung helplessly between a seductive sweetness of life at one end of a streetcar line and a life that was no life at the other end. One private remembered clearly that the worst times were when he was sent on leave, when, just briefly, the pressure eased. Then, of course, he would have to go back. "It was better to stay in there and put up with the hell you had to put up with. I wish they'd left me up there."[13]

Each respite made going back a little bit tougher. The momentum of the war was faltering; the troops were finding it more and

Soldiers of the Fusiliers de Mont-Royal celebrate the liberation of the Dutch village of Hansweert.

Woensdrecht priest flees burning village following heavy shelling.

RHLI Bren carrier knocked out by Germans in Woensdrecht battle.

Lieutenant Colonel Friederich von der Heydte, German paratroop commander defending Woensdrecht.

Major William Ewing saluting the fifty-five graves of his Black Watch battalion following Black Friday, at Ossendrecht, 26 October 1944.

Colonel Eugene Colson (alias "Harry")
of the Belgian Secret Army, defender of
the port of Antwerp.

Field Marshal Bernard Montgomery awards
an almost unprecedented Military Cross
to Belgian Resistance fighter Lieutenant
Robert Vekemans.

Retreating German troops demolished Albert Canal bridge, 28 September 1944.

A strategy conference: General Harry Crerar (left) with Supreme Commander General Dwight D. Eisenhower.

Major General "Pip" Roberts (right) and Lieutenant General Brian Horrocks plan the dramatic tank drive north of the Seine.

Antwerp liberated.

The final decision to sink the island. Left to right: Guy Simonds, Bertram Ramsay and Bernard Montgomery.

(left) General Eugen-Felix Schwalbe: saviour of the German 15th army.

(right) Hannie de Winde, young Dutch Resistance fighter.

Algonquin Regiment attacking across Leopold Canal.

Belgian Resistance fighters revere fallen Canadians at Moerkerke.

more difficult to maintain any kind of fighting trim. And when a man got too drunk, or too scared, he just didn't turn up for a few extra hours or even days. This was seldom charged as desertion. Officers who had shared the front line with their men for three continuous months could usually find compassion for minor disciplinary offences of this kind.

As one officer noted, "People slack off. You just give them one opportunity and all of them slack. It's just human nature, if you're not under pressure or being driven or pushed. Keeping them up is the whole problem. It's awfully hard to rev people up after they've had a little touch of it.

"That's why at Antwerp we were going to seed fast, sitting around on our asses, going to a pub across the road from our battalion head-quarters, drinking beer or liqueurs. That was a strange world we lived in. That's the 'Streetcar War.' Crazy!"[14]

Yet, in the midst of all this, there was the war. Every corner of the city where weapons could be dug in saw field guns and mortars in position to provide defensive fire for the Allied troops and harassing fire against the enemy. Almost every night fighting patrols crossed the Albert Canal to get information or to raid the enemy and bring back prisoners.

The officers and men who occasionally went out on pass to Antwerp went fully armed, the pistols in their pockets and the knives strapped to their persons "providing a strange contrast to the plush and gilt decor, the sweet music, and the soft lights of the cabarets."[15]

The RHLI lost several men in these peculiar circumstances, as its adjutant, Captain Osborne Avery, recalls:

One night we sent a couple of men out to patrol the bridges, Jim Telfer, a corporal, and Private Elliott. They ran into a guy who pretended he was a member of the Belgian Resistance. They were lost and he said he'd take them back and they were never seen again until right after the war. They were taken prisoner.

It happened on leaves, too. The guys would catch a tram at the end of the dock area and go downtown for the night. It was always assumed that they were probably rubbing shoulders with the Germans who were in civvy clothes. Possibly Jerry was sitting right next to you at the bar. Get a little high and it wasn't too hard to take a wrong turn coming home, and you were gone for the duration. You had to be very careful. We lost several people this way.[16]

———•———

Thirteen days after the liberation of Antwerp, and even when the 2nd Canadian Division had taken over the responsibility of guarding the docks the Germans still threatened the city. With the advent of the Canadians, hope rose for Colson that his long and harrowing defence of the Antwerp docks would end. These new allies would surely have the tanks and artillery support for which he had so passionately begged, first on the 5th of September from the British 11th Armoured Division, and later from the Welsh Fusiliers.

During those thirteen days, the men of the Secret Army's dock force had doggedly pursued their objective of helping the Allied forces prevent the Germans from demolishing the port installations. They had slept only in snatches, patrolling around the clock, relying heavily on their one advantage of familiarity with every inch of the ground they defended.

"The area was vast, our men few; we were continually harassed by the Germans who were trying to regain hold of the port and destroy whatever equipment they could get their hands on," Colson recalled.[17] Belgian citizens, hesitant at the beginning, now swelled the Secret Army ranks until Harry had three thousand men under his command. But it was still virtually impossible, even with the combined strength of the Rileys and the Resistance fighters, to enlist enough troops and arms to patrol every shadowy corner of that vital strip of dock facilities that stretched along the Scheldt. Infiltration was inevitable. Even so, the achievements of the Secret Army forces were stunning, particularly against an enemy whose strength was rapidly increasing with the influx of escaping 15th Army troops.

The German forces were obsessed with the urgency of breaking through and destroying the harbour. Fresh waves of assault had continued to pound the port defenders during those two weeks. The undermanned Allied defenders and their inexperienced Resistance supporters somehow hung on, repelling an enemy perilously close to sweeping into the key northern dock area.

The Germans attacked Allied defences at the village of Oorderen, northwest of the harbour, setting off many fires in the hapless town and forcing the Allies back. It was see-saw skirmishing — even to the extent of seeing Germans and Canadians swap slit trenches and bar stools by day and night. Patrols from both sides moved in and out of Oorderen and Wilmarsdonck for days until they finally collided — a confrontation that the Rileys still remember: "We would be there usually in the daytime," Gordie Booker recalled. "The Germans were generally there at night. In fact, we both drank at the same tavern. The innkeeper thought it was a great joke, but the Germans crossed us up one day and came in when we weren't exactly looking and we were driven out for a while." [18]

The action was recounted somewhat more tersely in the Riley War Diary:

21 Sept., 0600 hours

A fighting patrol in Oorderen was attacked by two platoons of enemy infantry who had infiltrated from the area of the railway immediately north of the town. The enemy were successful in entering the platoon HQ located in a large house, and bitter hand-to-hand fighting followed. Both sides suffered casualties. Corporal Kelly, J.C., was killed in this action. The carrier platoon was immediately dispatched and was successful in covering a withdrawal.

"We got all the smoke bombs we could from the rest of the battalion," Carrier Platoon Sergeant Peter Bolus reported gleefully. "We could usually put about fifteen bombs in the air in one minute and we straddled the position with them. As it happened, the wind was just right and the smoke came out beautiful. Next thing you knew, the company that had been stranded comes marching through the smoke and we got them out. Then we started dropping high explosive shells right on top of the Germans. We were having a field day!" [19]

Gradually the Allied line consolidated and strengthened, but the villages surrounding the docks — Wilmarsdonck, Oorderen, Eekeren and Merxem — still remained in enemy hands awaiting a Canadian offensive. On September 20th, the dock fighters requested and received artillery support from a battery of the 4th Field Regiment RCA in support of the RHLI, resulting in a successful attack on Wilmarsdonck.

But each day casualties mounted for the Belgians. One fighting patrol ran into a very strong enemy contingent and had to pull back, leaving two dead, three severely wounded and twelve prisoners. This pariah of the Allied fighting force still was given little support by the British liberators, and it still went without recognition from its own government. "In this action," Colson observed, "as it happened in all previous actions, our casualties were taken care of by ourselves."[20]

It would be some weeks — actually the 5th of October — before the Belgian government-in-exile finally recognized these royalist volunteers as an official armed Resistance unit. Until then, the wives and dependants — and widows — of casualties received no financial help; the fighters had to forage for their own food, uniforms and arms, and, often, tend their own wounded.

But finally a link had been made between Secret Army men and an Allied force, a link that was to grow in strength and resolution as the Resistance and the Canadians worked together towards the goal that had become paramount to both. For Colson's men, exhausted but tenaciously clinging to their positions, there was a glimmer of hope. Their docks, after three years of intensive underground planning and three weeks of vicious fighting, could now be considered secure — as long as the defenders could continue to hold on.

———————◆————————

In this most curious few weeks of war, one officer found himself briefly heading up a mini-army. The RHLI War Diary has this unusual entry for 18 September:

> *0900 hours:*
> The CO, Lieutenant Colonel W.D. Whitaker, and the IO, Lieutenant L.H. Doering, visited "Lock Force" area to coordinate the defences of the positions occupied by D and A

Companies. The enemy shelled this area with 88mm air bursts. No cas [casualties] were sustained. "Lock Force" was the most important part of the battalion area as the locks and bridges which "Lock Force" guarded controlled the water level in the whole of the Antwerp Harbour.

Major Louis Froggett looked as if he would be more at home, glasses perched on nose, instructing a grade four mathematics class, than commanding an infantry company at the front line. Men who mistook his amiable round-faced countenance and pudgy physique for softness learned very quickly that there was in this man a core of tempered steel. Once, a group of raw recruits newly arrived at the front hesitated when ordered to advance towards the German line. Froggett, brandishing his Sten gun directly at the men, said grimly that while they might get killed going forward, they sure as hell would get shot if they went back.

Froggett hated war, more than most men, but he was prepared to dedicate every shred of energy, courage and resourcefulness to do what he had to do. And in Antwerp Harbour in September, Froggett was having an exuberant experience commanding Lock Force.

This battle group was created to prevent the Germans from penetrating the vital Kruisschans Lock at the western entrance to the docks, a strategic defensive point where many of Colson's men had fallen in the fierce battle for its control. The Germans showed no signs of letting up on their constant counterattacks designed to demolish the locks. A further hazard confronting Lock Force was the very real possibility that the enemy would blow up Kruisschans using their new one-man midget submarines.

To meet these threats, a number of specialized units were uniquely married up under Froggett's command to provide the technical skills and diversity of weapons necessary to repel assault whether from amphibious craft, land attack or air offensive.

Froggett's Lock Force comprised some two hundred and fifty Rileys, not only from the RHLI D Company normally under his command, but also from A Company from the same battalion. In addition, this mini-battle group had specialized naval forces, searchlight batteries and ack-ack units, all serving under infantry command.

For a brief period in this zany Streetcar War, the myopic major from Brantford had his own personal army.

———•———

On the 23rd of September, the RHLI was finally ordered to extend its line to prevent enemy infiltration into the villages of Wilmarsdonck and Oorderen. Although greeted by considerable mortar and machine-gun fire, there were only four casualties, none fatal.

With the floodgates of 12 Sluiskens finally in Allied hands, steps could at last be taken to close the gates opened by the retreating Germans in the first days of the Liberation Battle. Many of the low-lying lands in the northern suburbs around Wilmarsdonck and Oorderen were badly flooded. Oorderen, too, was still smouldering from the fires.

The Germans, however, were still strongly established at the line of the railway tracks in the marshalling yards north of Oorderen, even to entrenching weapon pits under the freight cars. But there was little the Canadians could do about it at this juncture, at least until their supply crisis eased.

The battalion War Diary restated the problem that had plagued the Secret Army and the British battalions and was now, with its line extended, to become the paramount headache for the Rileys: "*23 Sept.*: The battalion position was extremely large and very difficult to defend from infiltration."

As a rule of thumb, one battalion could defend adequately only one square kilometre of ground against enemy infiltration. In Antwerp, the four hundred riflemen of the RHLI, even with the effective support of the Resistance, had been spread thinly over forty square km, rendering their task nearly impossible.

———•———

In civilian circles, life took on a strange unreality as people continued to go to work, sometimes changing trams as they crossed the canal into enemy-held territory, sometimes driving their own cars. Children played around crater holes in the streets as they walked to school.

A Merxem woman, whose husband became very ill, set out by

foot to find medicine, hugging the back lanes to avoid the sporadic street fighting. She arrived back late that night, having taken twelve hours to cover six km.

One man left the house in the morning to buy his wife a package of coffee and returned home a month later. He had run into a German police raid and had been sent into the country to dig antitank ditches where he remained until he escaped.

No one paid any particular attention, therefore, when Karl Six set off for work at the same time every day. A tall, lean man, conservatively dressed, Six kissed his wife and children goodbye each morning in German-held Eekeren, climbed on a passing tram and got off at the canal. Crossing quickly on foot, he would make his way to the modern Ford Motor Company plant near Albertdok in Antwerp Harbour. Occasionally, he would drive out of the plant in his shining red and black La Salle sedan, his great pride.

Later, leaving his car behind, he would retrace his route home, often stopping for a pint at a pub or two and for a chat with one of the German officers relaxing at the end of a day. In his excellent German, Mr. Six would commiserate with the fellow who would be assigned for patrol duty that rainy night.

Certainly no one was aware that the Ford building was the battalion headquarters of the RHLI, and that the man, Six, was a lieutenant in the Secret Army, assigned by Harry to work in liaison with the RHLI. The information he was to provide each day on activity behind the enemy lines was invaluable to Allied Intelligence.

This espionage work conducted by Secret Army men attached to each Canadian battalion was an important factor in keeping the port from the German grasp. Another was the sheer courage of the Canadian and Resistance men acting on this information to harass the enemy night after night on fighting and reconnaissance patrols.

Soon after the battalion's arrival at Antwerp's docks, an order was issued by 4th Brigade Commander, Brigadier Frederick Cabeldu, that extensive patrolling behind enemy lines be initiated. Few assignments would be less welcome to the "streetcar warriors."

While patrol warfare traditionally heightened during those lacklustre periods when the offensive had stalled, as was the case in Antwerp, it was always an essential part of battle tactics. It was also the most dangerous and disagreeable. As their War Diaries chronicle, the men of the 2nd Canadian Division had a bellyful of patrolling in the Streetcar War. Night after night, small bands of infantrymen would crawl through enemy territory seeking prisoners and information. Many never returned.

War Diary, RHLI, 19 Sept., 0800 hours:
A recce patrol under Lieutenant D.T. Knight of A Company was sent out and Knight was killed by an enemy LMG [light machine gun] located in a house. There was a very heavy fog which permitted the enemy patrol to work up close to our area.

And in the days that followed:

War Diary, RHLI, 20 Sept., 2100 hours:
The scout platoon including Lieutenant J.A. Williamson and Corporal H.A. Sams was successful in reaching the outskirts of Merxem, where they obtained valuable information on enemy locations.

24 Sept., 1500 hours:
A fighting patrol of Lieutenant A. H. Cairn's platoon went forward to the area of the railway tracks and were fired on by enemy snipers and suffered two casualties.

25 Sept., 2200 hours:
During the night the scout platoon sent out two recce patrols.

26 Sept., 2100 hours:
B Company sent out a fighting patrol under Lieutenant D.A. Bonnallie and guided by Private Trussler, W.A., of the scout platoon, who located an enemy soldier in a slit trench and successfully brought him back. The POW was a marine who had been on sentry duty when captured.

27 Sept., 1700 hours:
A fighting patrol under Lieutenant Cairns attacked a pillbox

on the railway north of Oorderen. Covered by the fire of his platoon, Lieutenant Cairns single-handedly attacked the pillbox with grenades and rifle. He brought back four POWs all of whom were from 711 Inf Div from the 15th Army. Lieutenant Cairns was burned on hands and face by a 77 phosphorus grenade which exploded prematurely, and was evacuated.

The RHLI Regimental History has its own description of this heroic action: "While his men supplied covering fire Cairns crawled close enough to lob several phosphorus grenades onto the roof. One of the grenades exploded prematurely, burning his hand and face, but he nevertheless rushed forward and began firing a rifle through the weapon-slits at point-blank range. Four Germans promptly surrendered."[21]

With both sides playing a defensive role, each would send out patrols by night to plant minefields ahead of their front lines. And demolition experts would spend many hours clearing the mines:

28 Sept., 1700 hours:

A fighting patrol under Lieutenant E.L. Garinger of A Company consisting of one platoon took up an ambush position. An enemy advance guard of four was permitted to infiltrate past the leading section of our patrol where they were all killed by our fire. This was followed by an attack on our position by approximately thirty enemy and unfortunately the Bren guns of our two leading sections jammed and our platoon was forced to withdraw under heavy enemy mortar fire. One of our patrol, Private Robinson, was killed and four ORs injured when the patrol encountered a mine field which had evidently been laid several nights previously and was located about one hundred yards forward of our own mine field.

The War Diary had this final, terse entry the following morning: "A Company sent forward a stretcher-bearer party and picked up the body of Private Robinson."

The scout platoon was the principal means by which a battalion commander could peer into the heart of the German defences, and the only way he could assess the strength and location of the enemy. The scout platoon became his eyes and ears, the elite unit of any regiment, with tasks of such priority and importance that its commander worked directly under the commanding officer of the battalion.

There were three seven-man sections in a scout platoon, each section commanded by a corporal. Overall there was a platoon sergeant and a lieutenant — the latter chosen for his qualities of leadership, initiative and courage. Lieutenant John Williamson was such a man. Enlisting as a private soldier in C Company of the RHLI, Williamson's skills quickly identified him as officer material. After officer training in Britain and Canada, he rejoined his regiment in Normandy, taking command first of a rifle platoon and later of an entire company. A quiet man, thoughtful, he was superbly trained, fearless and absolutely confident.

When the leader of the scouts, Lieutenant Hughie Hinton, was killed in Normandy, John Williamson was the logical choice as successor. Within a few weeks, he was committed to the most dangerous task in any army, during one of the most dangerous periods of the war for any scout unit.

A scout had to have an intimate knowledge of field craft and map reading, and a finely tuned ability to use the land so as to be able to crawl undetected to within a few feet of the enemy. He had to be essentially a loner, confident in handling, on his own, any situation that might come up. But most of all, a scout had to know how to handle his weapons. Williamson recalls:

My men were all good soldiers. They knew how to get around and how to be inconspicuous. They were all good marksmen, the best ones working as snipers. I equipped them all with captured German weapons — Schmeissers and Barettas and even an MG42 machine gun. Our theory was that any fighting we would have to do would be very close to the German defence positions. Weapons have a very distinctive sound. If we opened up with our own weapons, they would immediately recognize us. If we opened up with one of their guns, they could be lulled for a few seconds into the security that it was one of their own people shooting at someone else.

I was told I could have the pick of any man in the battalion and I had excellent men. They always believed they
were the elite. I believed it, too. We had a good mix, a couple
of German-speaking soldiers, which was important in getting
enemy information. Some Italians, Chinese, Indians…they
probably wouldn't win any prizes on the parade square, but
that wasn't what they were being paid for.[22]

What they were paid for was to infiltrate enemy territory. In
groups of two or three, scouts would be sent out, usually at night, on
reconnaissance patrols to gain information about enemy positions
and strengths in men and weaponry.

Faces blackened, knitted caps pulled low on their heads, they
would often lay-up in German territory for two or three days, watching, listening to, and taking note of the enemy. At night they might
move on to a new location to gather additional intelligence before
returning to their own lines.

Another type of patrol was the fighting patrol. This comprised
an entirely different formation with, usually, a very different mission,
though one that was just as dangerous for the men. Using men from
the rifle companies with perhaps one or two scouts as guides, these
fighting patrols might comprise a section of seven men, a platoon of
thirty or even a company of close to one hundred. They could be sent
out by day or by night.

Fighting patrols were useful in knocking out a single strongpoint
or probing the strength of a position. But their most dreaded assignment was one that required them to take prisoners in order to gain
information. This was exceedingly difficult and hazardous and this
work was universally despised.

The assignment, by definition, required the men to establish very
close contact with the enemy, who would strongly resist any efforts
to capture him. In the confusion and violence of the moment, either
the captor or his prey could be killed.

Some outfits demonstrated a somewhat casual regard for the riflemen's lives, sending out fighting patrols just to keep their men in top
condition, or in the vain hope that they might bump into some Germans. But it was the policy of the RHLI that their fighting-patrol

objectives were always carefully and clearly defined, and that their orders were concise and understandable.

Planning in detail was the prerequisite for success, and for safety. If time permitted, a sand table model of enemy positions would be constructed and would be studied by each man assigned to the fighting patrol: whenever possible, the RHLI staged rehearsals over ground similar to that of the operation.

The task of recce patrols could not be as specific because more latitude and flexibility were required. However, as with the fighting patrols, every man was put clearly in the picture.

Another scout officer, Lieutenant Joe Nixon, learned very quickly to develop a built-in antenna for danger. He had to. When, on the 15th of August, 1944, Nixon was given command of the scout platoon of the Black Watch (Royal Highland Regiment) of Canada, he became the seventh officer appointed to the job in a little over a month. One by one, in the bitter fighting of Normandy, the previous six had fallen, either killed or seriously wounded. Nixon relates,

> Colonel Frank Mitchell was our CO then, and he coached me. I'd be up at the front with Frank, and I'd hear the report of those mortars going off. I'd duck under the colonel's van and he'd say, "For God's sake, get up here. I'll tell you when to duck. I know when they're coming and where and how close they're going to land." He'd be there with his Balmoral tam on; he didn't even wear a tin hat.
>
> We had a fair number of casualties but the scouts were very independent people and learned very quickly to tell where enemy fire was coming from. We were pretty careful. We didn't have any special protection, but we were very crafty and wary of what was going on. They were all good soldiers.
>
> I had my pick of all of the sergeants in the battalion. The sergeant was the most important. Then, between the two of us, we handpicked our men from within the battalion. We were using the ones that nobody else could handle anyway. They were very undisciplined men and had to be led; they couldn't be told what to do. I remember the day when I was introduced to the scout platoon — it was about two o'clock

in the morning when I finally got to them — they were the most bedraggled bunch I had ever seen in my life. Rather than wearing their packs they had a couple of bands of bandoliers around their shoulders, grenades stuck in their belts, and old straw hats on.

The only trouble we had was that those that were very good we put a tremendous amount of pressure on. They were working all the time, day and night. You didn't find the men that were qualified for that job very easily. It was very difficult because you didn't have the replacements for them.[23]

The agony of patrol is intensified when the skills of survival have not been taught or developed. *Toronto Telegram* war correspondent Allan Kent described the experiences of two raw young Canadians of the Royal Regiment:

A CANADIAN PATROL
MEN DIE TO SHOW WAY FOR ANTWERP ATTACK
By ALLAN KENT
Toronto Telegram War Correspondent

Antwerp, Sept. 27 —

Young Alvin Waddell, whose home is on a farm between Barrie and Collingwood, returned to his platoon headquarters at noon yesterday after the worst morning he has ever known. Waddell was the first man to come back from a fourteen-man fighting patrol that crossed the Albert Canal in the Flemish city's dock area at first light this morning and probed into the German positions in the Antwerp suburb of Merxem. He was wet from head to foot, his face was covered with mud and his uniform was torn and filthy.

Kent related the stories of Waddell and a second man, Charlie Luther, from Montreal, both of the Royal Regiment.

They took off their wet clothes in front of a stove in a pokey second-storey cafe at the dockside and rolled themselves in blankets on the floor. By three o'clock these two were the only men back at platoon headquarters. The Hamilton lieutenant who led the patrol and a Toronto private were in hospital. Of the seven other Canadians, two were known to be dead and the rest by tonight would have been picked up either by the Germans or by our own stretcher-bearers. Three Belgian patriots who volunteered to help them lost their lives.

The armies are so close that they are actually throwing grenades by hand into their opponent's positions. All bridges but one have been blown up by the Germans, and that one is under constant watch, so the patrol had to set off in a rubber dinghy and one assault boat. At the canal's edge they were joined by three Belgian Resistance, who asked permission to accompany the patrol and show the way (two were brothers).

They set out slowly and cautiously for what they had come to know as the "Green Road" in Merxem.

"Then, just as we got near a tenement house where dock workers used to live, we saw a German soldier," Waddell said. "He was wearing a soft hat, but when he saw us he darted into a doorway and started to yell like mad.

"The call aroused other Germans. Two of them came out of a building fully equipped with machine guns and steel helmets. One of the Belgians shot at them and they jumped back into the building again.

"The enemy did not venture to leave the house again but started throwing stick grenades on the patrol from the second- and third-storey windows.

"It was getting too hot and a boy from Toronto had a knee knocked out by shrapnel," Waddell continued. "The officer told us to climb over the railway embankment and hide behind it. When we were doing this, the Jerries really let us have it, peppering us with a machine gun.

"A few of the boys got hit then. One of them, a corporal, was lying at the base of the embankment with his arm almost off at the shoulder."

Luther cut in to say it was at this stage, too, he saw one of the Resistance volunteers get it full in the mouth. The

other two Belgians ran to his aid — it was one of the brothers — and helped him toward a tunnel. But they never got
there. They were mowed down before they made it.

But meanwhile, Waddell and a companion were setting
forth across the flooded area. They, too, were raked by
machine-gun fire and dropped into a water-filled slit trench.
The companion stood up for a moment to throw a smoke
grenade behind them, under cover of which they could move
forward, but as he stood he was shot full of bullets.

"I lay beside him for two hours there in the water. We
were joined by another wounded man whose face was covered with blood from a mortar burst. He was in terrible agony
but there was nothing I could do."

It was the youth's first experience at the front. Kent chronicles
his long effort to escape German detection, as he finally crossed the
canal to safety: "That's my first time really up there with the Jerries,"
Waddell said. "Never really fired at one before."[24]

The most poignant description of life on patrol came from a
British infantry officer:

There was first the problem of finding your way in the dark,
of not making a noise, of not showing up against the moon
or the skyline, and of distinguishing between bushes and
enemy sentries. There was much creeping forward, much
stopping to listen, many false alarms. And then, when something was found, there was a further reconnaissance, the little
tactical plan, to gain more information or to try to grab a prisoner. On the return there was still a chance of being lost, of
meeting an enemy patrol, of stepping on a mine, or of the
coughers and stone-kickers giving away the path of the patrol,
and then when our lines were reached there was always the
chance that some trigger-happy sentry of our own might fire
off into the darkness into the patrol. It was often after a hard
day's fighting that an officer would be called upon to take
out a patrol to harass the enemy or destroy an abandoned
tank or (and this was the hardest of all) for a prisoner, or

just to find out how far the enemy had gone. Riflemen were sometimes so tired that they would fall asleep at each pause of the patrol.[25]

The greatest danger, beyond being shot or captured, was of setting off a mine or booby trap. The Germans were masters of this defensive art; their imagination and cunning were limitless. They would connect explosives to a corpse — theirs or ours — so that when it was moved, the explosive would be detonated. This stratagem was applied to a myriad of seemingly innocent household objects: doors, windows, even wine bottles left invitingly on bar shelves could become instruments of death. A can of golden syrup was found to be rigged…cigarette tins exploded when opened. Trip wires were another lethal enemy device, making night patrols the more dangerous.

But the greatest fear was founded on man's age-old terror of the dark; it was of lying, wounded, separated from friends, alone in the blackness of night. Abandoned.

But if you didn't get taken prisoner or fall on a mine and blow a leg off, if you made it back, there was always the streetcar at the end of the docks waiting to take you to the bright lights and soft women of Antwerp.

<hr />

Lieutenant Colonel W. Denis Whitaker:

For two weeks, the RHLI was on the defensive, having neither supplies nor orders to push ahead. Finally, on the 2nd of October, I received the instruction to strike north of the port towards the village of Oorderen. Riley patrols probing the enemy line throughout September were now concentrated on one enemy position, heavily dug in at the marshalling yards north of Oorderen, which was harassing the Canadian line. This obstacle had to be eliminated before the battalion could move north to the Dutch border. Reconnaissance reports indicated that this would be no easy task.

The Germans had fortified the entire area of the marshalling yard, a strip of high ground almost twice the length of a football field that blocked the Canadian advance. The place was bristling with machine guns entrenched under the freight cars, and in concrete pillboxes interspersed along the position. Every gun was pointing directly south towards Oorderen, where the Canadians were located.

Shortly before midnight on the 1st of October, a scout platoon patrol of two men was sent to observe enemy strength. It estimated the Germans to number about two hundred, clearly prepared and waiting. For the RHLI, a frontal attack would be suicidal. The only hope was that the Germans, having concentrated all their fire power towards the south, might be wide open from the flank. The battalion War Diary describes my battle plan as I disclosed it at a planning meeting of key personnel, known as an Orders or "O" Group:

2 Oct., 1630 hours:

A battalion "O" Group was held. The CO, Lieutenant Colonel Whitaker, presented a plan to attack the enemy positions in the area of the right flank of two railway sidings, with C Company under Major Pigott, supported by one platoon from B Company. H-Hour* was set at 0545 hours, 3 Oct.

I realized that this attack would fail unless I could catch the Germans off guard. The element of surprise was critical. Basically, my battle plan was to feint a frontal attack while Joe Pigott's men moved up in stealth to the unguarded west flank.

It was our fire plan that made the attack somewhat unusual. I had in support a number of different units. There were two platoons of the Toronto Scottish MMG — that's eight medium machine guns — as well as two troops from the 2nd Canadian Anti-Aircraft Regiment firing 40mm Bofors guns. In addition, we had four 17-pounder anti-tank guns, twenty-four field guns from the 4th Field Regiment firing 25-pound shells and sixteen 3.7-inch anti-aircraft guns. Utilization of all this power firing directly into the German positions would provide a devastating fire plan and would, I was certain, assure the success of Joe's attack.

---

* H-Hour is the military designation of the time an operation is to commence.

All our weapons were directed at right angles to our line of advance, starting at the west end of the German defences and gradually sweeping in a line from west to east as C Company moved forward. The fire plan called for the barrage to move at the rate of one hundred yards every four minutes, with Pigott's troops advancing forward at the same rate behind its protective cover.

Half an hour before H-Hour, Major Jack Drewry and I went to the old red-brick church in Oorderen with the object of viewing the attack from its steeple. In those days, church steeples offered one of the few high observation posts in the dead-flat landscape. Both sides used them for observing and sniping; both sides blasted holes in them with antitank guns to discourage their use. As a result, few of these venerable steeples survived the Battle of the Scheldt.

Jack Drewry, who clambered up this steeple with me, was a very knowledgeable gunner from the 4th Field Regiment, Royal Canadian Artillery. In his present role, he was officially known as the "CO's Rep." Theoretically, Jack's job was to stick close to me, advise me on the use of the guns, and relay artillery orders to the gunners. In reality, we worked so closely and were together so long that he became an extension of me and a close friend. As, indeed, I was to him. No twins ever second-guessed each other as accurately and often as we did during the Scheldt campaign. This symbiosis of ours was to spare many Canadian lives in the coming weeks.

At H-Hour, a deafening barrage went up and C Company began its advance. To our horror, we observed that one of our own field guns was firing short, right into the path of my advancing men. I had a terrible decision to make — and it had to be made instantly. If I aborted the operation at this point many lives would be lost, more than if I risked some of the troops being hit by fragments from our own shellfire. I had little choice but to carry on. The gamble paid off. The enemy was taken by surprise and at 0630 hours, just forty-five minutes from the initial barrage, the success signal was given. Thirty Germans were killed or wounded and eighty prisoners from the 711 Division of the 15th Army were captured. Of Joe Pigott's men, four were killed and twenty-one wounded, all from German small arms fire. Fortunately, the recalcitrant 25-pounder did no damage to the Canadians.

No one was more surprised — or relieved — at the result than company commander Major Pigott: "I didn't think it was going to work," the Hamilton man recounted. "If Jerry ever looked to his right and saw us coming down between the rows of boxcars...well, he'd have us like pins in a bowling alley." [26]

While the port area was being secured, the Royals and Essex Scottish were trading daily skirmishes, often at eyeball-to-eyeball distance, with an enemy well consolidated at Merxem and along the Albert Canal.

The Germans, as General Simonds had anticipated, were skillfully using water as their defensive line. The Lowland canals provided ample water barriers that gave the Germans a tactical advantage over the Allies.

Water, even a narrow and placid canal, is a natural and effective antitank, and even antipersonnel, ditch. The attacker, forced to cross the water by small boats and rubber dinghies, would immediately become vulnerable to crossfire from well-entrenched machine guns on the opposite bank. The resulting carnage was to be repeated countless times throughout the Scheldt campaign during the Canadian offensive. The Germans, essentially, retreated or were shoved back, canal by seemingly endless canal, until their backs were finally to the sea.

In September, the 4th Canadian Armoured Division had clashed against the defences of the Leopold Canal head on, but had been unable to overcome the tenacious German hold on this water barrier encircling much of the Breskens Pocket. The next canal, hastily converted into an enemy defence line, was the Albert Canal, which coursed in an eastward direction from Antwerp. At the outset, there was only a shaky, makeshift force pulled together expeditiously by Lieutenant General Kurt Chill in the early days of September to prevent the British from crossing the Albert and advancing northward to Holland. This meagre force had only twenty-five tanks and thirty-five batteries of 88mm anti-aircraft guns defending a fifty-km front.

By the end of the month, however, the line was fortified with fresh and determined paratroopers as well as with troops of the escaped 15th Army. And so it became, as the Royal Regiment remembered,

> a time for tricks and ingenuity, for the silent attack upon the German sentry, for the patient watch of the sniper, and sometimes for more ambitious schemes.
>
> There was, for instance, a street in Merxem running perpendicular to the canal, lined on both sides with houses except for one vacant lot on the west side. Since this street had a greenish hue because of the grass growing between the cobblestones, it was known as "Green Street." Now, on Green Street lived a platoon of Germans whose habits were very regular. They billeted on the west side of the street and every day, sharp on the stroke of noon, they would all issue forth with mess tins, cross the street, pass the vacant lot, and disappear into a house on the other side to dine. One day Captain George Blackburn, a FOO [Forward Observation Officer] from the 4th Field Regiment, RCA, very casually began to register his guns on the gap the Germans crossed. The following day, just before noon, he called for the target. When the unsuspecting Germans appeared in Green Street, Blackburn shouted "Fire!" and eight guns pumped shells into the midst of the unfortunate enemy platoon.[27]

———•———

At 0300 hours on the 2nd of October, the Royal Regiment of Canada, supported by a Secret Army battalion under Colson's command, sent two companies across the canal at Merxem. Later on that morning, the Essex Scottish entered Merxem from the west across the contentious Groenendaal Laan Bridge. More than 153 prisoners were taken, and by evening all four companies were consolidated in the northern outskirts of the suburb, having incurred only light casualties. The Resistance, however, ran into enemy mortar fire, and suffered heavy losses, with thirteen of their number killed and ten severely wounded, including one fighter who lost both an arm and a leg. After evacuating their wounded, the force then occupied the power plant and other strategic buildings. In a nearby warehouse, a bonanza of enemy loot, piles of long white fur coats and jackets, was taken and redistributed.*

The population of Merxem was extremely glad to see the Canadians. Their liberation had been delayed nearly a month after Antwerp, lying just across the canal, had gained its freedom — nearly a month since Colson had heard the damning words, "We have no orders." It had been a period of intense stress and extreme shortages.

The 4th of October saw the Essex Scottish push through Eekeren and then north some ten km to the village of Starboeck, almost at the Dutch border. Here they captured a bridge over a canal. The Essex War Diary entry does not disguise their jubilation:

> *4 Oct., 1944:*
>
> This was a most successful day for the battalion as we finally succeeded in getting off our backsides and pushing the enemy out of a strong position. On more than one occasion the Jerries had been seen hot-footing down the road trying to keep ahead of our advance.

Meanwhile, the 5th and 6th Infantry Brigades had the important task of clearing the east and northeast sectors around Antwerp before they could forge ahead to Holland. Two canals barred their advance: the Albert Canal, still stubbornly defended by a wary enemy, and the secondary German defence line on the Turnhout Canal.

Camped by the leafy banks of the Albert on the 26th of September, men of the 5th Brigade's Black Watch observed the enemy on the north bank at eyeball distance: "The Germans have more snipers in the trees and hedges around this area," the battalion war diary reported. "No casualties have resulted, however, as the men keep well

---

* A number of these were to warm Canadian troops as well during the cold autumn months. A letter unearthed at the Centre de Recherches et d'Etudes historiques de la Seconde Guerre Mondiale in Brussels, dated 7 Oct. 1944, read: "Dear Harry: Thank you for the kind and excellent cooperation given us by your unit during the operations around Antwerp. If you have any to spare, could Lieutenant Six bring some of those white fur jackets to us?"

The letter was signed W.D. Whitaker, Lieutenant Colonel, RHLI.

under cover." But somehow the canal had to be crossed. The following night, after an unsuccessful attempt by the Black Watch to find an unopposed crossing, her sister battalion, the Calgary Highlanders, was ordered to form a bridgehead over a semi-demolished footbridge at the damaged lock gates at Wommelghem, seven km east of the docks.

Eight men volunteered to make a daring raid across the bridge. Led by Sergeant G.R. Crockett, the fighting patrol edged furtively across the footbridge, swinging hand-over-hand from rusty, twisted pipes as they neared the north bank. Suddenly, they were challenged by a German sentry. Crockett silenced the man with his knife. Two machine guns opened fire on the band. Furiously, Crockett swung his Piat on one of the guns, knocking it out before turning on the second one with equal success.

A slender bridgehead had been forced, but the enemy responded fiercely. As the Calgaries quickly bolstered the position with their remaining men and their engineers began building a bridge across the canal, the Germans launched two fierce counterattacks and a "terrific" battle developed in the black pre-dawn hours.

For his courageous role in this successful operation, Sergeant Crockett was recommended for the Victoria Cross but received instead the highly regarded DCM (Distinguished Conduct Medal). Major Bruce MacKenzie received the DSO for his efforts in leading D Company to repel the counterattack.

The crossing opened up a way for the 2nd Division to push forward towards the Dutch border. Now the 6th Brigade would be faced with the task of crossing the Turnhout Canal.

———— • ————

Troops of the South Saskatchewan Regiment, who had also found the diversions of a standstill war pleasant, had been enjoying a three-day rest in mid-September in Contich, a small town south of Antwerp. "Many lasting friendships were made," recalled their diarist. "Two regimental dances were held, and although the floor was rough and the orchestra not the best, the gaiety of the entire crowd compensated for these deficiencies."[28]

The SSRs left Contich on the 23rd of September and were then ordered to establish a bridgehead across yet another of the damnable canals — this time, it was to be the Antwerp-Turnhout Canal, flowing northeast of the port. It was to prove as stubborn as its precursors.

The 6th Brigade's assault was begun on the 24th of September near Lochtenberg, some twelve km northeast of Antwerp. With the Fusiliers de Mont-Royal (FMR) crossing on their right, the SSRs were to cross a small secondary canal to the southeast of Lochtenberg before coming to the main one.

Between the canals, however, they were pinned down by machine-gun fire. Artillery fire was brought down on the enemy positions but it did not silence all their weapons. Smoke was then used to mask both flanks, and at 1300 hours a successful crossing was made and the unit continued on to establish a bridgehead over the main canal at Lochtenberg.

At the outskirts of town, they were held up by two German light tanks firing machine gun and high-explosive shells. Casualties were severe. Two SSR men crept forward with a Piat and managed to damage one of the tanks and force it to withdraw; Major Harry Williams was killed crawling down a ditch to direct the action against the tanks.

Meanwhile, the FMR was being counterattacked and was forced back across the canal by two hundred German infantrymen and twelve tanks. In this action they incurred one hundred and thirty casualties, twenty-seven of them men of the Secret Army who had assisted in the assault.

The brigade commander, realizing that the SSR was now overexposed, ordered it also to withdraw across the canal. Divisional HQ then made the decision to renew the assault on a two-brigade front. The 6th Brigade was to make a diversionary attack at their present location while the three regiments of the 5th Canadian Infantry Brigade, the Calgary Highlanders, the Régiment de Maisonneuve and the Black Watch were to launch a new attack a few kilometres to the east.

On the 28th of September, the SSR put in this diversionary attack for the 5th Brigade, again crossing the Antwerp-Turnhout Canal, this time with good effect. The Régiment de Maisonneuve was then able to form a bridgehead on the enemy side of the canal near the town of St. Leonard.

From this bridgehead the Black Watch launched a successful

action, taking the town. It was then on toward Brecht, where the Calgary Highlanders established another firm base from which the Black Watch attacked Brecht itself. This battle on the 1st of October was most successful as the Black Watch jumped over their start line at 0800 hours and had the town firmly in their hands by noon.

While many Germans were killed, and some two hundred prisoners taken in these encounters, Canadian casualties were also high. During the three days of fighting, the Black Watch alone sustained one hundred and nineteen casualties.

Now it was the 5th Brigade's job to provide a firm base for the 6th Brigade, backtracking southwest and parallel to the canal to clear the enemy from the bank. But first, the Queen's Own Cameron Highlanders of Canada had been assigned the task of taking the village of Sternhoven. This being accomplished, the advance along the Antwerp-Turnhout Canal commenced at 0615 hours on the 2nd of October, with the Camerons on the right and the SSR on the left. The FMR took over the Camerons' positions.

For the French-Canadian troops there was a special greeting from the ever-efficient German propaganda machine, trying to provoke rivalry and dissatisfaction between French- and English-speaking Canadians:

FRENCH CANADIANS
SOLDIERS OF THE REGT OF MONT ROYAL

This is the second time we meet. Of the 5000 comrades of the 2nd Div who came to Dieppe in 1942, 3500 were killed or taken PW.

WHY?

"To gain important experience," as Churchill calls it. You are facing today German troops on the canal, Antwerp to Turnhout, and, besides the Poles and the poorly equipped Belgians, your losses become heavier every day.

We are sure you never wanted the war, any more than we.

Your hearts are in your homes. You are thinking of your provinces of Quebec and Montreal, but you so far from your own country. They told you to liberate some countries which you don't even know. They put you in the front line while the British are having an easy life, without risks, in Paris, Brussels and Antwerp, made possible by a victory for which your blood flowed. They are plundering the shops, they drink beyond any limits, they enjoy themselves with the French girls. But you; you are obliged to fight for them.

You are in a country where there is nothing but rivers and canals. The English were clever enough to send you to the most difficult battlefield. The war is *not* yet finished. Approaching the frontier of the "REICH" the German resistance becomes stiffer and stiffer. Be sure, Hell is waiting for you with new German weapons.

Think of your wife, your fiance, your parents and children. You must save your life for them. One can recover from a sickness. If you manage to get some civilian clothes, nobody will recognize you. You are *not* obliged to fight — come to us until the end of the war. Lay down your arms, helmet and belt, desert, stick your hands up, put up the white flag and you are saved.[29]

An intermediate objective of the South Saskatchewans was their old nemesis Lochtenberg. In this they were supported by the 6th Field Artillery which was directed by the CO's Rep Major R.B. Dale Harris, firing pink smoke shells to identify known enemy positions so that the RAF could attack these positions.

Four times that day the RAF Typhoons attacked enemy concentrations and strongpoints across the canal, directing their rockets with deadly accuracy.

The rocketing was a sight that never failed to thrill infantry onlookers who were grateful recipients of Typhoon support on many occasions during the Scheldt campaign. "Typhies," as they were affectionately known, would make a steep dive to their targets and would seemingly come to a full stop as each released its eight rockets.

The effect was devastating, both to the enemy fortifications and in particular to his morale. After releasing their rockets, the Typhoons would continue their dives while firing their cannon at the targets. Then, at about five hundred feet, they would pull out, just in time to avoid disaster.

After clearing the Albert Canal, the 6th Brigade with the SSR on the left and the Cameron Highlanders of Canada on the right, passed through the 5th Brigade position, moving southwest, parallel to the Turnhout Canal. Their final objectives were the town of Brasschaet, ten km north of Antwerp on the Breda Road, and the nearby Camp de Brasschaet. At one point, the newly appointed SSR commanding officer, Lieutenant Colonel Vern Stott, until just a few weeks ago 2/I-C of the Calgary Highlanders, was experiencing a long roadside wait for some TCVs (troop-carrying vehicles) in the move up into Holland. With wry humour Stott declared, "If I stand on these crossroads much longer, I'll be picked up for vagrancy."[30]

By the 3rd of October, both objectives of the 6th Brigade had been captured. The South Saskatchewans recall the triumphant reception vividly: "Rarely have troops been received so warmly with flowers, kisses, apples, kisses, beer, kisses, and much handclasping and smiles. The Belgians were crying with emotion."[31]

Now a different sort of pamphlet was circulated by the community of Brasschaet:

TO OUR GOOD POPULATION
LIBERATED! LIBERATED!
LIBERATED!
BY THE SOUTH SASKATCHEWAN
REGIMENT OF CANADA

At last the hour of liberation has struck.

The four years of oppression, and the terror during the last month, which has no comparison in human history, are finally over.

With a strong determination and cunningness did our people oppose the invader to the end.

Therefore our people may be proud of its behaviour.

Therefore Belgians will be proud of you.

Finally all our sufferings are over.

We call upon volunteers to remove the roadblocks in order to open the main highways for the Canadians and the Belgian Resistance. The secretary will personally guide the first group. It is dangerous for anyone to proceed without guides since those places are mined.[32]

Brasschaet, 3 Oct. 1944

———•———

After the Oorderen success on October 4th, the RHLI finally was ordered to advance north from Antwerp Harbour. Their course paralleled that of their sister battalions, the Royals and the Essex, when the latter had completed the breaching of the last German water defences in northern Belgium. The 5th Brigade was concentrated just slightly to the east.

With Operation Market Garden finished, the supply crunch had eased enough to allow the 2nd Canadian Division to resume the offensive, although rations in ammunition were still noted by battalions well into October.

At the Dutch border, the Resistance fighters were ordered home by their commanders. For some, the war was over. Others, like Colson, would rejoin Canadian units fighting through the Dutch polderlands to free the approaches of the Scheldt. Their victory was a bitter one. In the months of September and October, eighty-seven of their number had been killed, 114 wounded.

So, a single day short of the one-month anniversary of Antwerp's liberation, the way was finally cleared to advance toward Holland.

Thus were massed, by the 5th of October, the 4th, 5th and 6th Canadian Infantry Brigades, poised to plunge across the border into Holland to seal off the South Beveland Peninsula at Woensdrecht, and to force the enemy off the peninsula and into the North Sea.

Now, at last, the men of the 2nd Canadian Division were, in their words, "off their backsides" and back in the war.

8

Black Friday

ON THE SIXTH OF OCTOBER, THE RHLI LED THE 4TH CANADIAN Infantry Brigade north on the main road to Holland, passing through the Essex Scottish at the town of Putte which straddled the Netherlands-Belgium border. The now-familiar scene of rejoicing by liberated Belgians greeted the soldiers on the approaches to the town, but as they crossed the railway tracks that marked the frontier it was a wary and impassive Netherlander who observed their approach.

The joyful Dutch burghers who had lined the streets on *Dolle Dinsdag,* the 5th of September, bearing welcoming flowers and wine for their liberators, had endured one month more of captivity. A new German had returned after Mad Tuesday, Nazi thugs from Himmler's notorious *Sicherheitsdienst* police, who had none of the compassion and tolerance of the earlier captors, or the cool professionalism of the Wehrmacht.

In these oppressed days, the Dutch witnessed, in their words, half-drunk Germans, filthy and abusive, crashing into their homes, taking all that there was. The cars and bicycles went, then the horses. Livestock was slaughtered, food requisitioned. Citizens were rounded up for forced labour, digging antitank ditches, gun emplacements and slit trenches as the Germans hastily amassed defences against the expected Allied invasion. Others were hauled out to repair roads and rail lines that transported enemy troops and supplies.[1]

Hundreds of the German V-1 and V-2 rocket bombs, falling short of their intended target of Antwerp's docks, rained mercilessly on these helpless people, forcing them into the makeshift backyard air-raid shelters. And a new prayer was born: "Dear Lord, send that bomb another few metres, please; let it fall into the Scheldt."

This farming community had already witnessed the destruction of its fields and crops as the waters of the Scheldt were deliberately let in when the Germans opened the sluice gates in August. On *Dolle Dinsdag*, it had waited anxiously for the liberator who never appeared.

Now, on October 6th, disillusionment and frustration had dampened their faith. Was this to be another day of folly for the Dutch? Would this new liberator desert them, leave them to endure the retaliation of a spiteful enemy? Better it was to watch and wait.

But there was a number of men and women of the Dutch Resistance, some of whom had been forced underground to escape SD purges, who eagerly offered to work as guides and interpreters for the Canadians. So it was that a Dutchman, codenamed "Charles," joined the RHLI. Charles eventually became an honorary active lieutenant during this service with the battalion throughout the remaining months of the war.*

As the Rileys advanced toward the town of Hoogerheide, they met a roadblock of huge poplars felled by the enemy across the main access road. This was a predictable delaying defence measure of the enemy, who would then register mortars on that point in the road. More strongpoints at intervals along the route offered spirited but sporadic opposition, and some twenty-five casualties resulted, including one man killed. But this was, as the Canadians would discover, only the preliminary baring of teeth.

The main objective of the 2nd Division was to seal off the South Beveland Peninsula from the mainland, thus severing the German communications line over what was called "the land-bridge to South Beveland." This strategic point was controlled by the small town of Woensdrecht, in ordinary times a simple farming village.

Now, in October 1944, the town and the isthmus that it dominated had become essential targets. It was through this isthmus, a

---

* Shortly after the war, several members of the regiment were surprised to receive an invitation to the wedding of one Leo Muysken. Learning of Charles's true identity for the first time, they determined to give the newlyweds an enthusiastic Canadian send-off — complete with a generous sampling of Canadian rations for the banquet table!

funnel little more than a single, sodden kilometre in width, that the railway line and road passed. Through here, from supply depots in Germany, passed the essential reinforcements of troops, arms and supplies, the lifeline for the defenders of South Beveland and Walcheren. It fell to the Canadians to sever this line of communication.

The rail line had become a powerful enemy strongpoint, as men from the 70th Infantry Division were rushed from Walcheren to reinforce the position. Machine-gun posts were dug in securely on the enemy side of the dyke, with only their muzzles poking ominously through the near slope.

Woensdrecht, too, offered a supreme vantage position to the Germans. Five hundred years before, the Scheldt's waters had encroached right up to the perimeters of what were to become Woensdrecht and its neighbouring towns of Hoogerheide and Ossendrecht. Over the ages, tidal waters had created great dunes of sand. When, eventually, the Dutch had dyked off these areas of the sea into neat rectangular polders, and had then pumped them dry, there was left a curious formation some twelve metres in height known as the "Brabant Wall," a ridge of gentle pastureland curving behind the villages.

It was on the reverse side of this modest elevation, the only high, dry land to be found in South Beveland, that the guns of Woensdrecht were firmly embedded and sighted on the flat fields below. These guns would fell hundreds of Canadians in the grim days ahead.

For five days, the Royal Regiment of Canada, along with the Calgary Highlanders and the Black Watch (Royal Highland Regiment) of Canada, mounted attack after attack, pounding at the resolute enemy holding on to the approaches to the isthmus. To the infantry in the field, the endless rain and mud and icy water that was now their environment became almost as formidable an enemy as were the German troops.

On the 7th of October, the Royals advanced on Ossendrecht, establishing a firm base for future attacks on the main objective of Woensdrecht, now only five km to the north. A German report on that day confirmed the growing seriousness of the confrontation: "The fighting at the isthmus very soon bore the stamp of a big battle. With very heavy material support (artillery, air and armoured) the enemy tried to take and block the Woensdrecht Isthmus by frontal attack. On this day, after some fighting, Ossendrecht was lost. The situation was becoming continually more dangerous. Reserves to counter further enemy advances were no longer available. The general command had to direct the request for immediate help to the army, from where the speedy dispatch of the Battle Group Chill was promised."[2]

So in the second week of October, the German High Command, alarmed at the Canadian advance, rushed this emergency force to Woensdrecht to protect their communications line. Its orders were to defend to the last.

The meagre unit that Lieutenant General Kurt Chill had frantically pulled together on the 2nd of September, as a desperate measure to hold the line of the Albert Canal, had burgeoned into a force powerful enough to ward off a strong Allied thrust during the September crisis. Its principal bite had at first come from the skilled 6th Parachute Regiment, commanded by Lieutenant Colonel Friedrich von der Heydte. As the formidable reputation of Battle Group Chill spread quickly through the Allied lines, enemy propagandists were quick to exploit the fact.

A tidy little deception was generated by skilled German strategists. The name of the now-defunct Battle Group Chill, that had long generated great respect in its enemies, was to serve a new and fruitful purpose as a ghost battalion. Von der Heydte made this recent admission:

> Chill's Battle Group had done its job in the first weeks of September. It was gradually replaced by normal divisions although he still commanded 85 Division. But the army decided to keep the name alive, to intimidate the enemy. When I fought at Woensdrecht, Battle Group Chill was merely a camouflage name to disguise the strength and location of my battalion.
>
> My real task was to move quickly from one trouble spot to the next. [Colonel General Kurt] Student called me his *"Feuerwehr,"* or "Fire Brigade." For me it was a good assignment. I had only to attack — and I got everything I wished. If I said, I can't attack without this and this, the next day I got it.
>
> To attack is more interesting, and it is not so difficult as to defend. Our poor infantry had to come in after me to

defend the position that we had taken, and I would be sent to another trouble spot.[3]

During the 8th of October, German reports continued the deception by citing the arrival of the first combat units of Battle Group Chill, hastily brought in by truck to Bergen op Zoom: "First of all were the two battalions of 6 Parachute Regiment under the commander, Lieutenant Colonel von der Heydte. Both command and troops were excellent, the cadres were experienced and battle-seasoned. Active parachutist rank and file were very good replacement troops. That same afternoon Lieutenant Colonel von der Heydte received the order to form a combat group from his two battalions and to start immediately and reoccupy Hoogerheide and then to push on later southwards to Ossendrecht.[4]

The same day marked Canada's first encounter with polder fighting as the Royal Regiment of Canada advanced under cover of thick ground mist across exposed enemy territory to gain an important position on the near side of the isthmus neck. The conditions the Royals faced, as all Canadian battalions were to find in the coming weeks, rewrote the rules of war. Private Al Butler of the Royals describes the feelings of the men on the polders: "We had a job to do, but we had to make our own rules, improvise. The old book just didn't work any more. Too many men were getting killed. When you came down to the nitty-gritty, it was the poor guy in the slit trench trying to go from dyke to dyke that did most of it."[5]

There was little dry land left in that morass of inundated polder country. The roads and rails, all running along the tops of the dykes that neatly bisected these fields of reclaimed polderland, were the exception. Dead straight, ten or twelve feet in height, these dykes had become ready-made defensive lines for the Germans. For the attacking Canadians, the only other approach was across the sunken fields between the dykes, "flat as the local beer" as one artillery punster put it. There was really no protection at all.

It was a battleground heavily weighted on the side of the defender, who could dig in his guns and troops along the sides of the dykes and at their intersections and set up a crossfire that would destroy any foe approaching either up the dykes or across the polders. Struggling through flooded fields at times up to two metres deep, totally vulnerable to enemy fire, the Canadians fought hard under near-impossible conditions against a well-entrenched opposition.

Although the Royals stubbornly held on to a narrow toehold on the near side of the peninsula against fierce German counterattacks, they had heavy casualties and were unable to advance that final kilometre to seal off the narrow neck of the isthmus from the mainland. Determined attempts to broaden their position had met with utter failure: "The Germans opened up with a murderous fire," their regiment historian noted, "which practically annihilated one of the assaulting platoons and caused heavy casualties among the remainder."[6]

Major Tim Beatty, commander of D Company, encountered and dealt smartly with some canny enemy tactics in this fashion: "Some Germans came out from behind the dyke opposite us with their hands up. As they got nearer, they broke into a run, evidently trying to outflank and capture our machine guns. I got Jack Maden, the Toronto Scottish Mortar guy, to let her go, and that finished that."[7]

On the same Sunday, the Black Watch on the right mounted an assault against opposition so heavy that two days of see-saw fighting netted them not a single centimetre of gain from the enemy. They incurred eighty-one casualties.

Then it was the turn of the Calgary Highlanders, with orders to capture Hoogerheide. From the 7th of October through the 10th, the Highlanders fought one of their most courageous actions against the same enemy guns, now firmly lodged on the Brabant Wall. The Calgaries called it the "grim road to Hoogerheide."

After reaching their objective by literally clawing their way into the town, they were counterattacked again and again by the fanatical German paratroops. Every company, at one time or another, was on the verge of being overrun.

Even battalion HQ was not inviolate. One officer and nineteen men, with flame-throwing Wasps and tanks, captured a German concrete pillbox in the field close to the Canadian headquarters. Lieutenant Sandy Pearson actually grabbed one of the German weapons as it protruded through the slits.

Before dawn on October 9th, German fighting patrols infiltrated between two of the forward companies and later surrounded one. In a night of confused fighting, the survivors of this company finally succeeded in breaking out of the enemy encirclement and reaching battalion lines. Incredibly, the Canadian line held.

Major Mark Tennant led his rifle company to their objective of the church in Hoogerheide, where he was wounded by heavy mortar and machine-gun fire. His vivid impression was of the high fighting morale of the men: "At least five officers and many other ranks refused to be evacuated when wounded," he noted proudly. "Brave men died and others jumped to take their place."[8]

Still, a sense of humour never truly deserted the men. Major F.H. Clarke of the Calgary Highlanders recalled one of several characters who populated the ranks of the Calgaries:

> I had a friend, a fellow named Win Lasher, a captain. He and I were very close. I went over on the boat with him and we had a riot going across. He had a good voice and he used to sing "Road to the Isles"; that was his favourite.
>
> At Hoogerheide, Win went out with me to find out what in hell was happening. Just as we came around the corner of an old barn, we saw two Germans plucking chickens. Our Bren gunner was going to go and take these guys prisoner but Win said, "Don't be a bloody idiot. Wait until they finish plucking the chickens." So we got the two Germans, and the plucked chickens too.[9]

In fact, the official estimate of German prisoners bagged in the action by the Calgaries was five hundred and eighty.

That there was frustration for the enemy in this see-saw action is evidenced by this German account of the battle:

> In the two following days attack and counterattack alternated. Three times the vanguard unit, Combat Group v.d. Heydte, succeeded in thrusting through the southern edge of Hoogerheide. Every time, the position gained had to be given up again for lack of force against the enemy counterattack.
>
> In a vigorous attack the paratrooper combat groups succeeded, in spite of stubborn resistance of Canadian troops,

in pushing through to the edge of Hoogerheide. By counter-attacking, the enemy regained, in the late evening hours, part of the village.

On 9 October several enemy armoured vehicles driving up on the embankment west of Hoogerheide, pushed onto the Woensdrecht-Flushing railway line. They were beaten back. The connection with the 70 Infantry Division along the railway embankment continued to exist.[10]

Now, after three days, the three battalions had inched their way, dyke by bitter dyke, towards Woensdrecht. The battle lines were drawn for the epochal confrontation to come; only a few thousand metres separated the Germans and the Canadians. The task of sealing this isthmus was given to the Black Watch.

* * *

On Friday, the 13th of October, a day that has become infamous in the memories of all Canadian infantrymen as "Black Friday," the Black Watch of Canada was slaughtered. At 0615 hours on that day of horror, Operation Angus committed this venerable Canadian regiment into a battle that was to inflict 183 casualties, including the wounding of all of its company commanders.

"Black Friday" can also be recorded as a day of betrayal of the "citizen soldier," the young volunteer of the Black Watch who had eagerly joined the Canadian Army. They had been committed to a no-win battle.

There were many adverse factors at large on that black day; their sum was inevitable disaster. The plan of attack seemed to be poorly conceived. Intelligence was bad. Supporting arms were inappropriate. And the troops were ill prepared. It was a formula for failure, and all of us from the RHLI who watched it unfold hour by hour were horrified.

Essentially, the brigade battle plan called for the battalion to make a frontal assault in daylight against an enemy of proven strength and resourcefulness. It was an uneven match. The Black Watch had been a troubled regiment for some weeks, continually hampered by their heavy losses of experienced men and the inadequate training of their replacements. In a single week of fighting in July, at St. André-sur-Orne in Normandy, there were 324 casualties, with more than one-third of that number killed. Whole sectors of the regiment were wiped out, the attack companies virtually destroyed. The remaining nucleus of six officers and approximately 350 other ranks never really had a chance to reestablish the strength and experience of the battalion.

In August, 124 more casualties were incurred. In September, fighting around Antwerp, ninety-four. In October, even before Black Friday had taken its terrible toll, the guns of Woensdrecht had accounted for 190 more casualties.

The week before the battle, 104 ORs arrived as replacements. In simple mathematics, then, the strength of trained Black Watch men had been depleted by one-half through casualties, and then augmented by only a quarter with men who were mainly untrained as infantry.

Lieutenant Colonel Bruce Ritchie, who had just taken command of the Black Watch at the end of the third week of September, 1944, describes his desperate efforts to rebuild a battalion left tattered by ceaseless poundings:

> When the battalion went into action after D-Day, the guys had had three or four years' training. But after the first big slap in the ass at St. André, we were never able to get organized with trained troops.
>
> Even when we got replacements, the battalion had been knocked down with such strength that they weren't a fighting entity any more. Right after St. André, we got some guys who were S/2s; in other words they were of questionable stability. Then the poor buggers had to sit there their first day and watch the heavies bomb the front end of the Polish Armoured advance lines. That didn't do much to cheer up those guys that had just arrived, watching that deal.*

---

* On 14 August, in Normandy, RAF bombers, misjudging their target, dropped their bombs on I Canadian Army positions, killing or wounding over four hundred men. Worst hit were troops from the Polish Armoured Division and Le Régiment de la Chaudière.

When I took command just before the Scheldt, I was assured by the division commander that we would not be thrown into the thick of things until we could get organized a little more. But almost immediately we got a movement order to proceed up to Merxem and to move northwards there. I objected very strenuously. The remnants of the battalion had suffered a pretty bloody nose at some previous battles. The remaining officers and NCOs were more or less a collection of reinforcements. We needed more time; I bought a few more days, that was all.[11]

Ritchie's time-out paid off. The Black Watch scored two successive victories with few casualties at St. Leonard and Brecht: "Morale was very high after Brecht. We had an objective and we'd grabbed it. One of the companies had been cut off and, instead of just folding up, which we might have expected with untrained troops, we held that and regained it. We didn't have too many casualties that time."[12]

The lamed battalion was struggling to its feet again. But even then, the shortage of well-trained and experienced riflemen was inevitably causing problems. "We were sent reinforcements," Colonel Ritchie recalled, "and they were keen. Most of them had joined up after D-Day. But some of them had fired maybe one Bren gun burst in their whole training."

Colonel Ritchie remembered one instance when the battalion was seriously threatened because of the raw recruits:

When we were regaining position in Brecht, part of the scheme was to shoot up this street, where the Jerries had established strong defensive positions in the houses. A platoon went up the street to reestablish contact with a company that was held up. At that moment, our Bren guns fired from upper windows over their heads. One whole platoon went to ground. They were so green that they couldn't distinguish our fire from the enemy's. This was a pretty critical moment until we got them on their feet again. That was the first time they had heard at close quarters the sound of guns fired in anger.[13]

Then, at Hoogerheide, the fragile confidence of the battalion was shattered. On October 6th, 119 casualties were recorded. A subsequent battle on October 8th took a further toll of eighty-one.

Finally, without the opportunity to regroup into a viable fighting force, the Black Watch was thrown against the proven weight of the paratroops, the toughest soldiers that Germany could produce.

Lieutenant Colonel W. Denis Whitaker:

Two ultimatums were issued as a result of the battle plan for Operation Angus. The first was made by me as commander of the RHLI.

My battalion's role in this pending attack was to protect the Black Watch start line by forming a firm base for its attack. I was therefore required to attend the Orders Group on the day before the attack.

When the briefing was over, I walked out of the 5th Brigade headquarters tent near Hoogerheide, and absently strolled through the rubble of this once tranquil farming town. My thoughts were in a turmoil. Nothing about the battle plan made sense.

Why make the attack in broad daylight over open and saturated polders against a strongly defended enemy position?

And why, I pondered, adopt this complicated plan of attack? An infantry assault should always be as simple as possible. A highly complex operation is difficult to carry out and even more difficult when you are trying to coordinate the use of supporting arms and tie them into the actual plan with green troops.

Confusion was inevitable, I thought. It would be almost impossible to control one company of perhaps eighty men, many inexperienced, moving through another of the same size, with both under heavy shelling and small arms fire. It would certainly be confusing to the supporting arms, such as the artillery, air force, mortars, armoured corps, and so on. The more complex an attack, the more difficult it is to achieve success.

This was the Black Friday plan that prompted my ultimatum. After the conference, I went to see Brigadier Fred Cabeldu, my brigade commander, and said with some force that I thought the plan would fail, that there would be heavy losses, and that I could not allow my men in the RHLI to be ordered into this debacle.

Brigadier Cabeldu agreed with my stand and changed our orders. As it turned out, my assessment was correct. The Black Watch did not take their objectives; they did not even get beyond their start line. Lieutenant Colonel Ritchie, the Black Watch CO, well remembers its outcome:

> When we were out on the dykes on that October 13th, morale wasn't too good in some of those poor guys that were out there. They didn't know whether to advance or stay down...Jerry had us pinned over open sites with heavy machine guns.
>
> The calibre of the enemy was completely misjudged at brigade HQ. I never got a good briefing on the enemy. We were misinformed; we had no idea the Germans would be so good. We really were up against the créme de la créme.
>
> They taunted our guys. They would jump out of the slits on the dykes, taunt our guys, and as soon as we started to fire, they'd get down. They had the situation in complete control.
>
> It was a funny sort of battle plan — crazy. We were instructed to take four posts, four areas roughly in the form of a square with a 1,000-yard side.
>
> We went in with a dawn attack supported by tanks, which were completely useless at the time except for general covering fire owing to the flooding and heavy ground fog. We were pinned down by heavy machine-gun fire right from the beginning; our forward troops had to fight their way to the start line.
>
> We retook the start line, as it were, but we only managed to get the near corner areas of the so-called square. We were devastated by fire from the many strongpoints. We'd bring down fire, put down smoke to try to move the men up but the Germans had our positions taped and they countered with mortar fire.[14]

Two companies led the attack. In less than two and one-half hours, they were both pushed back, leaderless, to the start line. Their commanders were wounded, their companies reduced to mere remnants. Still they fought on. The twenty-five men left in one of the companies struggled to within fifty metres of their objective, but at 1110 hours the enemy was reported to be crawling up to the Canadian position. German sniper fire and machine guns peppered the lead platoons.

Captain W.J. Shea, intelligence officer of the Black Watch, witnessed from the top of a barn the capture of sixteen Canadians, some of them officers, who were marched off down the railway embankment. "The companies are being annihilated," he reported.[15]

At 1500 hours, another "O" Group was held and the battalion's remaining two companies were ordered to remount the attack. The plan was identical to that of the morning, although this time it saw the use of flame throwers in support.

Major William Ewing, commander of one of these companies, was outraged:

> The concept of the attack was fundamentally cockeyed. We had to cross something like 1,200 yards of beet fields with no cover other than beets. Then there was a water course that crossed our front; we couldn't get over that except on a narrow bridge which was under enemy machine-gun fire.
>
> We'd have been delayed only two or three hours if we had gone in later in the dark. As it was, the Germans had a very easy position to defend. There were two dykes that intersected and they were more or less on our objective. The fire was coming from two machine guns on the dyke that faced us. Then there were a couple more of those killing machines operating from the right dyke, the dyke that led from our start line to the enemy dyke. The enemy held the other intersecting dyke at their end of it. When we got into the intersection of these two dykes, we were in a cross fire and there wasn't a hell of a lot we could do. Actually, we were trying to grenade the buggers. We were throwing grenades onto the dykes which were coming back onto us. They were rolling back down.
>
> The only reason we got anywhere near the objective was

because we took casualties from our own artillery. But when we got there, we simply couldn't hang on.

We had a bad time. My company strength initially was in the order of ninety men and there were only four who weren't either killed or wounded in the bloody thing. It was pretty rough, and it was bad for the morale of the battalion. When you lose all your key people, all your senior NCOs, even down to corporal, which is really what happened…you never really recover from it.[16]

The records show that in this grim episode the Black Watch lost a total of 183 all ranks, fifty-six of them killed.

There were men, officers, who objected to dying for what seemed to be a "cockeyed" idea. Several withdrew, a rare circumstance in the Canadian Army, and one that Colonel Ritchie recalled with compassion: "We had a number of walking wounded who walked out of battle. Under other circumstances they wouldn't have done this."[17]

So ended this black day in Canada's military history, formally documented in these words:

All through the hours of darkness the troops had been evacuating their many wounded from their exposed positions in the soggy fields. One company had been virtually wiped out, and losses generally left the exhausted battalion completely unfit to take any further part in the fighting until it had been rested and reinforced.

In this grim episode among the polders, such costly failure was charged not only to the nature of the ground, the eligibility of the objective itself as a target for the enemy's artillery and the fighting quality of the defenders, but also to the lack of experience and even of elementary training among the more recent arrivals in the battalion itself.[18]

The battalion War Diary records a macabre postscript to Black Friday:

At 0100 hours, on 14 October, the brigadier ordered that the battalion should withdraw. The weary men rode back in carriers and jeeps to the positions they had left barely twenty hours earlier, though to them it had seemed days. Typical of their condition was one man lying atop a pile of accoutrements on a carrier, sound asleep with the earphones from his disconnected set, awry, upon his head.

The men were given a hot meal immediately upon their return and then they slept the sleep of the exhausted. It was thought best to have them forego lunch and sleep right through until 1600 hours when supper was served. The Knights of Columbus showed a movie tonight. That originally scheduled was entitled *We Die at Dawn* but this was hurriedly changed and the film substituted therefore was in a much lighter vein.

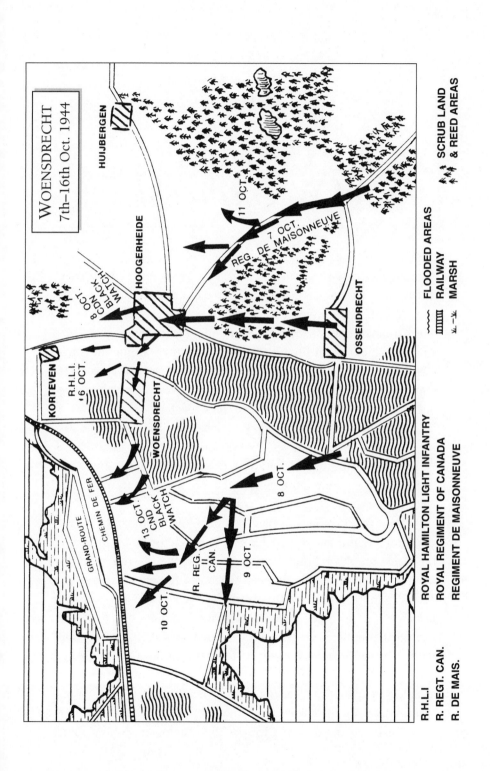

WOENSDRECHT
7th–16th Oct. 1944

HUIJBERGEN

HOOGERHEIDE

KORTEVEN

R.H.L.I.
6 OCT.

WOENSDRECHT

OSSENDRECHT

11 OCT.

7 OCT.
REG. DE MAISONNEUVE

8 OCT.
CDN.
BLACK
WATCH

8 OCT.

9 OCT.

10 OCT.

13 OCT.
CND.
BLACK
WATCH

R. REG.
II
CAN.

GRAND-ROUTE

CHEMIN DE FER

FLOODED AREAS

RAILWAY

MARSH

SCRUB LAND
& REED AREAS

R.H.L.I.   ROYAL HAMILTON LIGHT INFANTRY
R. REGT. CAN.   ROYAL REGIMENT OF CANADA
R. DE MAIS.   REGIMENT DE MAISONNEUVE

The Guns
of Woensdrecht

BY OCTOBER 1944, AN INFANTRY OFFICER REACHING THE AGE OF twenty-three or -four was considered old. Mostly, the ones that got killed off were the young men, the recent replacements or transferees from other units, men whose training, whose experience and whose coolness under fire became the unnerving wartime yardstick that measured their chances of staying alive. In that sense, a man was born on the battlefield, and if he didn't know very much about the business of infantry survival he died there too.

Joe Pigott was one of those seasoned old infantrymen. He was twenty-three. Louis Froggett (of Antwerp dock fame) and Huck Welch, all-star football player, were two more of the wartime "old boys." The fourth man, the senior officer of the quartet, was a survivor too, until the crisis at Woensdrecht.

These were my four company commanders, majors in the Royal Hamilton Light Infantry, who led off the attack for Woensdrecht in the black, pre-dawn hours of Monday, the 16th of October. For by now, the backlash of Black Friday had had its effect on the Rileys, too. The second ultimatum arising from the Black Watch debacle had been issued. This time, it was not from me but to me. The dead and wounded from Black Friday were still being carried off the Beveland polders when Brigadier Cabeldu called a 4th Brigade Orders Group.

The RHLI was given forty-eight hours to plan and execute an assault; those guns of Woensdrecht had to be silenced once and for all. Within the hour, the wheels were in motion to formulate a winning plan. I held a battalion "O" Group with my company commanders and supporting arms to fill them in on the broad objectives. Maps and aerial photographs were distributed, and the men were given time to study them.

We needed more information about the enemy numbers and positions, and we needed specifics about the terrain. Recce patrols were sent out on missions that night to get this essential intelligence.

The Rileys were proud of their battalion's reputation during the Northwest Europe campaign of never failing to take an objective and of never being driven off by counterattack. We were determined we would succeed again. We were angry at the terrible waste of life we had witnessed when the Black Watch lost almost half their strength — futilely, without wresting a foot of ground from the enemy.

There was no point in reinforcing their mistakes; we had seen too well how badly the strength and skill of the enemy forces we faced had been underestimated. He was tough, this enemy, professional and brave, skilled in use of weaponry, canny in battlefield intrigue. Looking down from rain-soaked slit trenches in the shelter of Woensdrecht Hill, he could see virtually every living being that breathed on the flats below. All civilians were being evacuated; the Red Cross had informed us of that. The Germans were dug in and fortified, waiting for the attack they knew would come. The Black Watch's daylight attack had met a well-organized and battle-ready enemy.

To achieve some element of surprise, one that could give us an immediate advantage in the engagement as well as limit the number of casualties, we hoped to catch the Germans off balance with a night attack. The major "catch 22" built into all night attacks is that assault troops lose their sense of direction in the darkness and often miss their objectives. In Normandy, General Guy Simonds came up with an innovative solution to this problem by firing phosphorescent tracers overhead at fifteen-second intervals from Bofors guns to direct the forward advance of the infantry. Theoretically, the men had only to follow the fireworks to find their targets. Even adopting this idea at Woensdrecht, I reckoned the darkness of the Scheldt might make the task a little more difficult. I couldn't imagine just how serious a hazard the darkness would become.

Strong artillery support was essential. My fire plan, probably the most extravagant I'd ever put together, involved 168 guns. Seventy-two of these were field guns (25-pounders) from the 4th, 5th, and 6th Field Regiments, RCA, which normally supported the 2nd Canadian Infantry Division. Forty-eight medium guns (100-pounders) were with Canadian Medium Regiments, RCA. The remainder were 3.7-inch guns of the British Royal Artillery — normally an anti-aircraft weapon, they had been adapted for use in a ground role. Additional support was provided by medium machine guns and heavy mortars from the Toronto Scottish Regiment, as well as a section of Royal Canadian Engineers and a squadron of the 10th Armoured Regiment.

The three regiments of 25-pounder guns fired their high explosive shells at a maximum rate of five shells per gun per minute. Each shell was loaded manually by the gun crew of five men. These regiments formed an integral part of each infantry division and provided the major supporting fire for the infantry both in offence and defence. The mediums were 4.5-inch guns firing a 100-pound shell. The heavy anti-aircraft 3.7-inch calibre guns fired shells which burst in the air just above their target.*

Before the RHLI put a foot over the start line, I intended to lay on a dense concentration of shellfire on the German positions to allow our men to close with the enemy under its protective cover. Troops had been taught to get up to within twenty-five yards of where the shells were falling and stay there until the moment the fire was lifted. The object was to be upon the enemy defences before he could recover from the traumatic effects of the shellfire.

So the three essential components in my battle plan were there: determined men, fire and movement, and the element of surprise ensured by a night attack. That fourth component, luck, would determine the winner.

On Sunday afternoon, at 1600 hours, I called an Orders Group to give a final briefing. The shell-battered town hall of Hoogerheide served as RHLI headquarters, its carved, oaken door hanging crazily from its hinges. It was through this door that the dozens of personnel involved in mounting and supporting the attack — infantry, artillery and other supporting arms — entered for the briefing.

---

* The Toronto Scottish account of their part in the bombardment noted: "Two thousand mortar bombs, the biggest show since the Caen breakout."[1]

"O" Groups were an essential element in the function of a battalion in any military operation. The success of the action would depend upon the efficacy of the plan, and the confidence it instilled in the participants; so, certainly, would the survival of the men who were to execute the battle plan.

At the first battalion "O" Group, the four company commanders and other officers from the supporting arms were instructed in detail about the coming operation. They were given pertinent information about enemy strength and disposition, and a general overview of Canadian action and strength in the area. The all-important intention or objective of the action was clearly defined; then the method of achieving the goal was explained in full detail. Finally, administrative and communication tasks were assigned, and questions and discussion were encouraged.

This nucleus of command would then hold "O" Groups for their own subordinates until every man involved in the battle had been thoroughly briefed on his area of responsibility and activity, however large or small this might be.

The general plan was a simple one, a night attack on a double axis, with the whole unit, including battalion headquarters, moving forward as one onto the objectives. The start line was a track which was halfway between Hoogerheide and Woensdrecht. The rate of advance was one hundred yards in four minutes. The intention: to capture the Woensdrecht feature. H-Hour was 0330, Monday, the 16th of October.

Carefully examining the sandbox contour model prepared by our Intelligence Section to represent the area topography and the enemy dispositions of Woensdrecht, the four company commanders studied their tasks.

The commanders of A and C companies would lead their men to forward positions approximately 1,500 yards distant to the hill that rimmed the northern edge of the town. They had reconnoitred the area with me that morning in the small, single-engine Austers which were piloted by officers of the Royal Artillery for low-level observation of the enemy. These gave us a very good view of the land and allowed us to make definite plans as to the best way to attack.

The remaining companies, under the command of Joe Pigott and

Huck Welch, were designated as "mopping up" units, to stay 150 yards behind.

Signallers were instructed to link up all companies by land lines when the objective was reached, so that we would have an alternative to our frequently unreliable radio net. This was a task often made extremely hazardous by enemy shell and mortar fire. The RHLI Intelligence Section under Captain Lyle Doering had the task of laying lines of white tape to mark the start line and the FUP (forming-up position). Never was the procedure more important than on this night, when men would have to grope for their positions in total darkness.

Again, Major Jack Drewry, CO's rep, artillery advisor, and my close friend, would have a key role in the coming hours.

Another intrepid individual, Captain Steve Stevenson, an artillery FOO (Forward Observation Officer) was ordered, with his section, to positions with the front-line troops. Steve's job was to register defensive fire tasks and to pinpoint gunnery targets from the highest point of observation. In normal warfare, this would be a tall tree, a steeple, any high building. In Beveland the loft of a barn or house was often the best — or only — observation point the FOO could manage. At Woensdrecht, Steve discovered, this was to prove more dangerous than usual when the Germans were counterattacking: "I was spotting from the bedroom of this funny little red house when a shell hit the wall just below me, just a few feet below the window where I was looking out. Well, next thing I knew, I was crashing through the floor, me, my batman, my radio pack...the house just collapsed on me. And we didn't even get scratched."[2]

As orders filtering out of the "O" Group descended down the line, each man silently weighed his chances of still being alive at the end of that day. Of their objectives, the ranks had been well briefed. Of the strategy, the understanding of why the hamlet that waited darkly ahead of them should be worth the lives it was about to claim, nobody knew. Or cared. These five hundred Canadians were concerned with two things: survival and success. If the commanding officer had demonstrated an understanding of the task and consideration of the men who would achieve it, and if he had then developed a sound plan, he would win the confidence of the officers and, through them, of the troops.

The morale in the RHLI was high; I think success had brought a good deal of that about. We had seen others fail where we had succeeded. And our officers were strong; that made quite a difference. Through their own qualities of leadership, they could instil confidence in the other ranks.

Air reconnaissance photos had shown German slit trenches and concrete bunkers dug into the slopes, dykes and houses of the town. The intelligence report also told a grim tale: Dutch Resistance and the Red Cross had reported spotting two thousand German paratroopers in the woods north of Woensdrecht. If this information was correct, we would have to face a formidable counterattack force, five times our number. In reality, it was a military rule of thumb that, to ensure success, the ratio should favour the attacker by five to one. Facing us was the ratio in reverse. It made the hope of winning a long shot.

But H-Hour was crowding in on us and there were still several administrative tasks to assign: cages for prisoners of war, for instance, and dumps for ammunition and petrol, each with map references.

The trenching tool was of particular importance. In this bizarre war, digging in when objectives were reached had almost more immediate priority for assault troops than firing back. His trenching shovel, as one survivor extolled, had become "a mighty weapon of war, a treasure to be hoarded carefully, lest it be snatched up by some pilferer; being without a shovel left one feeling as naked as a man in Piccadilly without his trousers."[3]

Finally, a hot meal and a substantial four-ounce tot of rum were ordered for all troops at 2359 hours, in the dying moments of Sunday, the 15th of October.

———•———

From his headquarters in a large white-brick country estate in the densely wooded ridge bordering the northern outskirts of Woensdrecht, Lieutenant Colonel Friedrich Augustus von der Heydte, nineteen years a career officer in the Wehrmacht, studied intently the last drops of wine in his glass. However excellent the vintage, however liberally he had dispatched the bulk of the absentee Dutch owner's cellar to his Bavarian home, it could not distract him long from the business at hand. His "fire brigade" had been rushed to this new trouble spot; he must ensure that it would not fail in its assignment.

On the 5th of October, a runner had brought an urgent message from Chief of Staff General Student to von der Heydte's central Holland HQ in Alphen. A strong force of Canadians had been observed moving forward north of the Scheldt Estuary in the direction of Woensdrecht. Von der Heydte was to break off the attack against the Polish Armoured Division and leave immediately for Woensdrecht. The paratroop commander recalls the anxiety at German headquarters:

> I was told that it was of extreme importance that we defend Woensdrecht. General Student advised me that there were three reasons for this: first, to secure the 15th Army retreat; then, it was important to hold open communication from Walcheren through the neck of South Beveland and through to Germany. Finally, the Germans had expected that, after the Arnhem experience, the Allies would attack up the coast in a pincer movement through Rotterdam and east to Germany. That had to be stopped. I realized the urgency of the mission: it was the first time in the whole war I had been ordered to break off a successful attack mid-battle.[4]

That night, four thousand German troops advanced westward toward Bergen op Zoom, some in trucks, most marching on foot through the bitter, rainy night to their newly established headquarters on the main Bergen-Antwerp road just north of Woensdrecht. It was an ideal defensive position. Part of the property of the estate contained a brickyard, an excellent observation post for von der Heydte's paratroops. From the comfortable quarters of his command post, the commander could easily observe all troop action in the vicinity, as he recounts: "I would take my customary evening stroll, and could walk just a thousand metres away, to the houses over at the top end of the ridge overlooking Woensdrecht. Or, if I wished, I could easily get to the first cluster of farmhouses at Hoogerheide."

The commander could also observe the German occupation force in those towns, and was highly displeased at their undisciplined actions: "We found German troops who were just elements of our occupation forces, and other dispersed groups of German soldiers who were on the march to the north. But we found no German troops able to fight."[5]

However, the 6th Parachute Regiment was independent of these itinerant soldiers. Von der Heydte believed that his trouble-shooting troops had all the skill and ability needed for their new task. They needed no help from this dubious police force to stop the Canadians from sealing off the mouth of the isthmus.

In all, the "fire brigade" comprised a force of over 4,000 men, including support staff. In terms of battlefield effectiveness, it had 2,600 experienced, well-trained fighting men, four times the number of any Canadian infantry battalion. His companies were at 75 percent of normal strength (Canadian companies at that time averaged about 45 percent strength), numbering 156 soldiers in each of the regiment's seventeen companies. These were divided into three light battalions and one special battalion of engineers, infantry guns, mortars and anti-aircraft guns. These elite troops had been given high priority from the German High Command for all the supplies of arms and ammunition they might need.

As soon as his men were established, von der Heydte received orders to attack the advancing Canadians. But then a new obstacle — evidence of the confusion in the ranks of German occupation troops — delayed the German attack. As von der Heydte explained: "The execution of this order turned out to be impossible because of the supposed existence of unknown minefields which had to be cleared before an attack could be undertaken. No maps could be found in which the mines had been indicated.

"However, during the week that followed, the two villages of Woensdrecht and Hoogerheide were fought for very heavily. Some houses changed occupants nearly every day."[6]

During this second week of October, the Canadians were in contact with this force. The Royal Regiment captured the village of Ossendrecht, just a few kilometres south of Hoogerheide. Then the Calgaries fought for three days on the "grim road to Hoogerheide," a bitter, see-saw conflict where Canadian and German met head on in hand-to-hand fighting. On Black Friday, the 13th, the Black Watch met the fury of these paratroopers, and few survived.

Von der Heydte had never commanded his regiment against Canadian troops. Now, fighting alongside his men in the front line, he could observe and evaluate this new enemy. He personally interrogated prisoners from the Canadian regiments, probing for weaknesses he could exploit. It was the outcome of these interrogations that he was pondering in the dying hours of Sunday October 15th:

> I talked to many Canadian prisoners in the past few days. I always asked, "Who do you trust?" I could find out a lot about their units if I could assess their morale. No American, except Patton's men, ever said he trusted his general. The Americans had a great mass of material and they trusted that, not their generals. The British had a more sportsmanlike spirit; they trusted their commanders. The Canadians are loyal to their command. And they have the strong artillery, where we have almost none. But they are volunteers. What can they know of battle tactics?[7]

At 0230 hours on the morning of the 16th of October, a disturbing report reached von der Heydte:

> A young lieutenant, one of my company commanders, reported that the scouts had observed some unusual movements in the Canadian position five or six hundred metres south of our front line. There was no indication of any attack at that moment, just a "change of attitude." It was essential to find out just what was happening.
>
> I jumped into the sidecar of my motorcycle and ordered my driver to proceed quickly through the town to the forward observation outpost. My intention was to assess this change and, if it appeared to be an attack forming up, to withdraw my men to the pre-established rear line of resistance. The troops had been briefed on the position on which they were to fall back in the event of attack; from there we could launch strong counterattacks to regain our main line of resistance.
>
> This was the tactic I intended to follow. When I gave an

order to defend a certain line, I always gave a second line as
a retreat line. The best way to withstand an attack was to
withdraw from the position known to the enemy without his
being aware of it, and build up a new defence line in a position not known to him.

Looking from behind some bushes, I saw that I was too
late. The Canadians had begun their attack. I gave the order
to retreat to those of my men that I could find; my duty was
to bring as many as possible back to the prepared positions.[8]

H-Hour minus 30

The period just before a battle begins can be the most agonizing of
an infantryman's life. Your comrades are all around you, and that's
reassuring, but still you are completely alone. You want to run, to
scream, to pray, to do anything but cross that start line. But you continue to stand there, sweating, praying, hating war, hating yourself
for being afraid. One rifleman recalls that the waiting was far worse
than the battle ever could be: "When we were on the start line, waiting, I never knew that I could pee so many times, nervous pees. I was
that scared. Once you got moving, then it was all right. We would
settle down and just block out all the extraneous nonsense so you
could concentrate on what you had to do."[9]

Seeing these men cross the line into battle was a very moving
experience, as one Canadian padre remembered: "My boys move
in tonight...new boys with fears and nerves and anxiety hidden
under quick smiles and quick seriousness. Old campaigners with
a faraway look. It is the hardest thing to watch without breaking
into tears."[10]

And when the battle begins, with an ear-bursting barrage, you
determine not to let the men you lead see how frightened you are. If
you're in the ranks, you hope like hell your bosses know what they're
doing. You hope they value human life — especially yours.

Demolition Platoon Corporal Arthur Kelly most clearly recalled
"that moment when you put in that attack, when you climb out of
that slit trench...if you were to look around and find that you didn't
have an officer, boy, that would have a tremendous effect on you
psychologically."[11]

Minutes before H-Hour, an urgent call came through my Tac headquarters. It was the second-in-command of A Company, a young captain named Lyn Hegelheimer.

"Sir, something very strange is happening here. The company commander fell asleep some time ago and we've been trying for an hour without success to wake him."

As 2/I-C, Hegelheimer had on this occasion been posted as LOB (Left Out of Battle), one of several veterans kept back to ensure that the battalion, despite losses, would have an ongoing cadre of seasoned officers and men. He had therefore not attended the battalion "O" Group, although he had later seen some aerial photographs of the position. However, there was no option but to order him to take command, with only a quick briefing on his tasks. His senior officer's bizarre sleep would have to be dealt with at a later time; for now, the battle for Woensdrecht had begun.

H-Hour: 0330 hours

One hundred and sixty-eight guns opened fire in one massive, ear-splitting, earth-shattering barrage. And five hundred Riley rifle-men rose as one, hugging the awesome fire curtain, advancing over the start line under its fearful cover. The sky screamed, its blackness ruptured.

It was a night of intense darkness. The phosphorescent tracer fire marked its trail in space to guide the men to their objectives. Its splashes of light spilled eerily onto the fields where they advanced.

The carrier platoon, having begun the attack as foot soldiers guarding the start line, suffered the first casualties of the assault. We were upset to discover that one section had got too far forward when the opening artillery barrage began, and, tragically, had incurred seven casualties from our own guns.

Normally, hugging the bombardment was a hazard the veteran troops could understand. Casualties from enemy fire would have been very much greater had they not learned to lean into the barrage. But they were not all seasoned veterans that marched on Woensdrecht that raw October morning. Several were young, ill-trained reinforcements in battle for the first time, as Carrier Platoon Sergeant Pete Bolus recalls:

We were told at what time the barrage was coming down and that we were to get out and not get caught in it. My section pulled out about a minute before the barrage started, but even then, we had one hell of a time trying to find our way back in the darkness. But Jimmy Ratcliffe's section took a real beating. Seven of the men got hit. They didn't get out in time.

We had had a few reinforcements come up; I didn't even get to know these guys' names that were hit. The older fellows were all in one piece practically; they knew how to look after themselves.

The thing about it was you got a feeling for it; you knew when things were going to go bad and you went under cover. It was a skill that you seemed to develop. The reinforcements would see us walking around but when we went under cover, they thought we were chicken. They were scared but they wouldn't listen. They would say, "There's nothing to it."

We lost a lot of good kids that way. Some of them didn't have more than their basic training. Some of them hadn't even had that. I had a kid who came from the ack-ack regiment, who didn't know how to detonate a grenade.[12]

0500 Hours

The silent night closed in again on the village. So far, there had been no resistance; Woensdrecht was as a ghost town. Froggett of D Company was the first to report in. "Balmy Beach," flashed the success signal. Thirty minutes later came "Argos," Hegelheimer's A Company salute. Then "Rough Riders"…"Tigers"…the four companies were on their objectives. Or so they thought.

The commanding officer of C Company, Major Joe Pigott, paced restlessly in the farm cottage, now his headquarters, just above the main road into Woensdrecht. The silence, he thought, was disquieting:

I remembered from fighting in North Africa that a favourite tactic of the Germans, and one of their greatest strengths, was to pull out of strategic positions when the heat was on, and then lay on a well-planned, well-executed counterattack.

I warned the men that the present quiet was unnatural and was not to be believed and that we were going to catch hell first thing in the morning.

I had positioned my three platoons the best I could, but it was so black we dug in mainly by feel. We couldn't see Hegelheimer's A Company; there was a rise of high ground between us.

When dawn broke, I discovered to my horror that I had positioned one platoon so far out of line it couldn't even support the other two. We were desperately trying to adjust the thing so that we could put up a reasonable defence when the counterattack came.[13]

0615 Hours

Pigott wasn't the only company commander running into problems in those pre-dawn hours. Daybreak had some disquieting shocks for all the forward RHLI companies. Like Pigott, the other company commanders found their platoons too dispersed to form a cohesive defence. That was one of the problems of the night attack; it was very hard to site good defensive positions because it was very difficult to see anything, and the things one did see did not look the same at night as they did in the daytime. Now they were frantically moving their men up to ensure that they were all in slits defensively positioned to repel the expected counterattack. All four companies were now under continuous artillery and mortar fire.

Major Louis Froggett discovered he was a hundred and fifty yards short of his objective, but he soon managed to correct and consolidate his position. He had driven back the Germans so quickly that their candles still burned in their dugouts.

Behind Froggett, Major Welch reported from the centre of the village that B Company was getting a lot of casualties from snipers hiding out in the shadows of houses and barns near the main crossroad of the tidy cottage-lined streets. He was working feverishly to try to clear up the situation.

He was surprised to see emerging from behind the church three of his own men, grinning through soot-streaked faces. They had been sent on recce patrol into the village three nights ago and found themselves trapped. As Sergeant Harold Hall, then nineteen years old, still clearly recalls: "I had a patrol out and I didn't get back before daylight. There was a church in the square and I had to hide behind it. The Germans started coming into the square from all directions; we were cut off. I took two men in through the back door of this little church; I remember standing there with my back against the wall just about ten feet away from the Jerries. Then we hid in the coal bin for about three days. I was missing in action for four days."[14]

The carrier platoon by this time had picked up their vehicles and were being led by their commander, Captain Bill Whiteside, across an open field toward the village. An incident occurred that has Sergeant Bolus still chuckling: "They were shelling the hell out of us, but this was one of the comical things: there were pigs running around and a pig got hit. Whiteside stops the whole convoy of carriers, jumps out and slits its throat. Then he says, 'We'll bleed this one and come back for him later,' and away we went. A day or two later, he held a lecture in the barn while he dissected it; the guy had been to vet school."[15]

Up above, on the northern end of the slope closest of all to the German defensive line, Captain Lyn Hegelheimer was in command of a company for the first time. Few assignments would ever be tougher than this literal baptism of fire. Along with his fellow company commanders, he had slightly misjudged his positions in the intense darkness and had lost communication with his scattered platoons. But, as he sadly recalls, his troubles really started on his initial approach when he overshot his objective and had to backtrack down the road to reach it:

> We still hadn't seen a damn soul since we left the start line. Nobody had fired a round at us. Suddenly we saw a couple of German troopers walking up the road talking to one another. Why they didn't hear us, I don't know. I was at the head of the company so I whipped out my pistol and we took them prisoner. They thought we were Germans because we were coming from the wrong direction. Finally we arrived at our objective. Then just at daybreak I got the three platoon commanders together to coordinate our defence.

At daylight, my senior officer of A Company comes riding up in a carrier driven by the sergeant major. He got out and I said, "Well sir, here's your company." But I don't know what the hell happened to him after that. Later, I could see him standing in front of the carrier and the CSM driving. He had sort of an odd look on his face. Then he just disappeared from my view.[16]

At 0615 hours, while the commanders were consolidating their positions, I moved battalion headquarters forward into Woensdrecht. The white-stuccoed farmhouse, for decades the home of Cornelis van Beek, was now to become my home for some days ahead. The house was on Dorpstraat, the main east-west road through town. Welch was in a house a few blocks west on the same street, with Froggett on the rise above him.

Captain Bob Wight's demolition platoon had been ordered to barricade themselves in a house on the northwest corner of the street a few hundred yards west. Their job was to hold, a defensive position guarding that western flank. Meanwhile, my two advance companies, with Pigott and Hegelheimer, were just over the slope to the north of us, out of our sight.

The Scout Platoon had followed the lead companies in, clearing some two dozen Germans from houses and farm buildings around the crossroads where my HQ was to be established.

Six Germans hiding in the van Beek cellar were rooted out, and then four more from a dugout in the yard. These prisoners, plus another fifty or so sent back from the forward companies, were taken to the POW cage, and then transported as quickly as possible to divisional headquarters for interrogation.

Even within Geneva Convention restrictions, we had discovered that trained intelligence interrogators could ferret out information about the strength and disposition of the enemy forces. It was information that could save many Canadian lives and in Woensdrecht we were in urgent need of this help.

I was deeply concerned to note that all our prisoners bore insignia of the 6th Paratroop Division, whom I knew to be specially trained and skilled infantrymen. They already had the reputation of being an elite, hard-fighting battle group who were only committed to major trouble areas.

As I leaned over one wounded prisoner to question him, he glared up at me and spat in my face. Even in captivity, the beast could snarl.

1000 Hours

Shortly before ten o'clock in the morning a private soldier, a young recruit, was squatting at his gun position beside a barn window. It was his first day of war. He peered through the narrow dormer and commented cheerfully to the man next him: "Hey, I didn't know the Americans were fighting here!" The novice, confusing American steel helmets with German "coal skuttles," thus became the first RHLI man to spot the enemy counterattack.[17]

Minutes later, a runner brought the alarming news that Hegelheimer's company was being overrun by German paratroopers with Mark IV tanks and self-propelled guns. Our Piats and antitank guns had been knocked out. Fierce hand-to-hand fighting had ensued. One of our antitank men, Sergeant Alf Southern, fired point-blank at the enemy until finally his 6-pounder was hit by the powerful 75mm weapon and put out of action. Then the FOO, Captain Stevenson of 4 Field Regiment, radioed in that his carrier had been hit and was burning.

It was at about this point that the senior A Company commander turned and left the field. (It was later suggested that he suffered from battle fatigue, having been in continuous action and under heavy pressure since early July.) Unfortunately, when men see their own leaders turn away from battle, it becomes a very natural choice that they shall follow, and that is what happened on Woensdrecht Hill. Pigott and I both had to watch this horrible sight, those wretched men running panic-stricken down the hill toward us.

I pulled out my revolver and stopped some of them at gunpoint. Further over, Joe stopped the others the same way. We ordered them back to Pigott's C Company to take up additional defensive positions.

We had just minutes to wait for the German offensive to reach Joe's company. Pigott describes the action around him:

> The company in front of me was attacked in force by German paratroops, excellent troops, first-class troops who

knew how to handle their weapons and the ground. They overran the A Company men and in the process killed and wounded a lot of them.

Unfortunately, communications between myself and A Company, because of the confusion, were virtually nonexistent and I wasn't aware of the extent of the disaster forward until the first wave of German paratroops accompanied by tanks came into sight about fifty metres away.[18]

Pigott's driver, Private Harry Gram, had been wounded by shrapnel and Joe had been trying to get him to walk down to the Regimental Aid Post. Just as a German SP (self-propelled) gun pulled up, Gram pulled out — in the wrong direction, as Pigott later recalled:

Instead of walking out the back door and down the street like he should have, Harry decided to take the jeep, which was parked in front of the house — it had about forty holes in it and wouldn't run. He got in and tried to start it. It wasn't going anywhere. Cursing...I never heard such language in all my life. Here's this tank sitting there with a self-propelled gun, not twenty-five yards away. All of a sudden the turret opened, an officer stood up, gestured to Harry to move on, and poor old Harry got out and walked away down the road. Seconds later, the German was dead. He got a direct hit.

There was no time to organize our own counterattack; the enemy was almost on top of us. My only chance was to contact my commanding officer and through him order a concentration of artillery to bring all our fire power directly on our position. At the same time I was yelling and shouting at my troops to get down in their slit trenches and pray when our shells started to fall.[19]

Joe's position was desperate; so was his appeal. Our only hope was to direct on his headquarters all of our available artillery strength — a "Victor Target" — a concentration of fire which gunnery men maintain even today was seldom if ever duplicated in World War II.

There was too much at stake to indulge the thought that this man, my friend, was inviting death, and was asking me to be his executioner. Jack Drewry, CO's Rep, was at my elbow. I yelled: "REFERENCE 'C' HEADQUARTERS, VICTOR TARGET, SCALE TEN."*

Within seconds, Drewry was on the radio net and brought down a massive concentration of shellfire, almost beyond conception in intensity. It was directed with pinpoint precision on Pigott's own headquarters.

We had pulled off a target of opportunity, a bombardment of four thousand shells, about fifty tons of high explosives, which completely knocked out the enemy tanks and killed, wounded or dispersed the paratroops involved in the Germans' counterattack. Incredibly, because they were down in their slits, just one of our men was slightly wounded. The Rileys sprang from their trenches and drove off the rest.

Joe Pigott's Citation for the DSO reads in part:

> At this point Major Pigott was wounded by fire from the gun which was still in action. Despite his wound, and with no regard for his own personal safety, he proceeded across one hundred yards of open ground, under heavy machine-gun and shell fire, and personally directed an antitank gun forward into a position from which it was able to destroy the self-propelled gun. The enemy were then forced to withdraw.
>
> Throughout the whole encounter Major Pigott moved from one platoon to another under constant fire, encouraging his men and directing their fire. He was personally responsible for beating off a fierce enemy counterattack which threatened the whole battalion position, and was an inspiration and example to all ranks.[20]

---

* The target was the map reference for C Company headquarters. A Victor Target is one which brings to bear as many guns as are available in the army — in this case, three divisional artillery regiments (each of seventy-two 25-pounder guns), three medium regiments (each of sixteen 4.5-inch guns), and three regiments of heavy anti-aircraft regiments (each of sixteen 3.7-inch guns). This makes a total of 312 guns, firing at ten rounds per gun.

For some of the Rileys, the war was now over. Signaller Jimmy Bulmer was captured in the root cellar of A Company headquarters, where he had dived for cover when the counterattack began. Piecing together the kaleidoscopic recollections of his capture, Bulmer tells of his final moments on the battlefield:

The German tanks were coming down the long road from Bergen op Zoom. I asked my senior officer what we were going to do and he said, "Dig in and fight them off." The Germans started mortaring. One shell hit the jeep; the horn stuck and the noise went on and on. Then one hit the house and I got into the root cellar.

There were three of us down there, waiting: the interpreter — young Cyril, the Belgian kid — was down there with this old stretcher-bearer called Pop. (We called him Pop because he was so old to us. He must have been thirty.)

Finally, we heard German voices upstairs. I said to Pop: "When that door opens, put the white flag up with the Red Cross." The door opened and two enemy stood looking at us. One had a Schmeisser. He was sweating. Standing right behind him was a guy with a flame thrower. They took us out with our hands up and on the way the watch went, the cigarettes went, and everything else went. I'm glad they didn't look at the watch because I'd got it off a German a couple of weeks before. They got us out into this clearing.

This German lieutenant colonel came over and said (his English was perfect, better than mine), "What are you? American or British?" I said, "Canadian, sir," and he said, "Good. We fought you before. You're good soldiers." Then they pulled out. They were a special hit-and-run outfit.

There were about thirty of us taken prisoner. On the way back we came under shellfire, our own Canadian 25-pounders. Later, we were interrogated, one at a time, about who we were and what our codes were. I pretended I didn't know. That walk started there on the Woensdrecht Hill and ended up at a prison camp near Hanover in Germany.[21]

1410 Hours

Twelve hours had passed. Although the immediate crisis had been averted, the Germans showed no inclination to back down; the battle was far from won. We had gained, by incredible effort, the narrowest of fingerholds on Woensdrecht Hill. In this brief time the cost had already been appalling. Rifle companies generally numbered over one hundred; we had been reduced by one-half. I contacted Brigadier Cabeldu's 4th Brigade HQ by wireless about our thinness on the ground: "Estimated strengths at the present time are: A Company, one officer, eighteen ORs; B Company, two officers, thirty-nine ORs: C Company, two officers, forty ORs; D Company, one officer, sixty ORs." [22]

Twice that afternoon, help came from the skies. A large force of Spitfires dropped fifty tons of bombs on enemy positions. Later, our friends the "Typhies" joined the fray.

Heavy mortaring and shelling and sniper action continued to harass the Rileys, particularly in the west end of Dorpstraat where Welch was taking a lot of fire. Although I knew he was in agony with a painful knee injury from his football days with the Hamilton Tigers, Huck fought furiously to maintain his position.

We were feeling the almost overpowering strength of three columns of paratroops, some two thousand men, as we later learned from von der Heydte. With the professional skill that had already won him a reputation for tenacious fighting, von der Heydte had recovered from the surprise of our assault and had organized a powerful counterattack. He was, as he later told me, as determined to recover his position as we were to hang on to it:

> At first light, soon after the surprise Canadian attack, I gave the respective orders to counterattack. Our aim was to restore our main line of combat. We attacked in three columns: one over the railway embankment west of Woensdrecht; another — with which I fought personally — over a smaller railway embankment northwest of Woensdrecht, and

a third smaller one northeast of the town. The first two columns succeeded in joining up in the northwest part of Woensdrecht. We managed to recover some of our old positions, and my men dug in to their old holes.[23]

In fact, it was this strong force of counterattacking paratroopers that converged near the lead companies' positions. It was under von der Heydte's personal command that his men overran A Company and threatened to overrun Joe's. And it was von der Heydte himself who spoke a few sympathetic words to Signaller Jimmy Bulmer when he was taken prisoner. Many decades later, meeting for the first time, we recreated the events of a battle that we both still remember with horror. I had the last word in 1944; he was to have it forty years later: "It was very close fighting. When you attacked, we missed each other by only ten minutes, you and I. I was just above the road on which you began your advance. And our two sides were only a hundred yards apart when we came back in the counterattack. Once," he added with an odd look, "my men shot at you."*[24]

The guns of Woensdrecht were not to be silenced for five more days of agonizing effort when the battered Rileys were finally relieved by the Queen's Own Cameron Highlanders of Canada on the 21st of October.

After the first eighteen hours of fighting, ninety-one casualties had been evacuated. In just two days, we had managed to hang on to the narrowest of holds, measuring a single kilometre in width and 500 metres in depth. The cost: 167 casualties, twenty-one of them killed. But nothing would ever duplicate that brief moment of horror when men, hysterical with fear, had to be forced at gunpoint to return to battle.

---

* This surprising recollection is substantiated in the RHLI War Diary, 18 October, 1600 hours: "The CO [Lieutenant Colonel Whitaker] and IO [Captain Doering] visited D Company and looked over the company defensive position, then to B Company. By error, the CO, driving the carrier, went beyond the FDLs [forward defence lines] and an enemy sniper hit the carrier several times. A hasty retreat was made.

Still, the Germans pummelled the thinning line of Rileys. Froggett's company was infiltrated on several occasions, and one whole platoon was overrun; only six men returned. Nor did the situation ease much during the next day. Thirty-nine reinforcements, almost none with any infantry experience, were sent in. However, one company from the Essex Scottish Regiment took some of the heat off Pigott's position.

Sniping was still heavy in Froggett's area, and infiltration of the enemy was becoming so serious that Lieutenant Bob Wight was ordered to lay trip wires in front of Froggett's line. "We were told not to wait for the dark," Wight later explained. "I was to send men up the ridge in broad daylight, and that would mean that they would be within sight of enemy snipers. Joe Hoonan said, 'I'll go by myself. There's no point in having three or four of us milling around there.' It was a brave act."[25]

There were so many brave acts in those treacherous days. On the third day of the action, German infiltration brought the enemy perilously close to the forward lines of the Rileys. Lieutenant Williamson of the scout platoon sent out three snipers to try to relieve the pressure — Corporal Joe Friyia, Privates Heinz Kunzelman and J.S. Whitehead — with startling results, as Williamson recounts: "They noticed that there were some Germans within fairly close distance, about 100 yards or less, in slit trenches, and so they decided to assault them on their own. They dropped right into the slit trenches with the Germans. Each of them had pistols which they used. They killed several and routed the rest."[26]

Corporal Friyia, who was subsequently awarded the Military Medal, was shot in the foot. With Froggett's help, he managed to get back, as did Whitehead. But Kunzelman was lost, believed killed, and was never heard of again.

Days and nights ran into one another, seemingly endless hours of mud and cold and exhaustion. Those who lived fought. Even when their vision blurred and their hands shook, when fatigue and fear threatened to engulf them, there was always someone to set a new pace.

One night, Major Froggett requested that a section from the carrier platoon set up machine-gun posts in front of his line to prevent further infiltration during the nights. Sergeant Pete Bolus was one of three men who volunteered to dig in on the ridge:

> We were up quite a bit in front of Froggett's position in a sort
> of a draw, sweeping the area all night with pretty continuous
> fire so the Germans couldn't come up through it. We used to
> take up three boxes of ammunition, which is a lot, and we
> used that much each night. We took all the magazines that
> we could possibly carry. We must have had about twenty
> magazines up there, always loaded. You'd let off a magazine
> and then you'd load it right away. We'd come back there each
> night and would have to dig in and set up new positions. It
> was good to get out of there in the mornings.[27]

Night after night, the three men went forward into the silent fields
toward the German lines and took up their desperately dangerous task.
And the other Rileys, watching, found that the impossible was within
reach for them too: "You see these guys, all night long firing their Bren
guns, never stopping, and you think, 'If this bloody little Bolus can do
this, why can't I?' And that's what kept a lot of us going."[28]

A short distance away, just where the road dipped into a hollow, Bob
Wight's demolition platoon was also being clobbered by heavy
sniper activity.

Taking a couple of men, Wight ducked down the street and into
a house where he suspected a sniper was hiding. They burst into the
kitchen. Wight stopped short at a scene of domesticity totally incongruous amidst the armed conflict going on around it: a family sat
around the table, father and mother and two children, one a toddler.
Before them, on a table festive with freshly cut fall flowers and delft
china, were plates of food, the morning meal, untouched. Then he
realized that the entire family was dead. There were no bullet wounds,
no blood, no signs of violence. They just sat on, and on, lifeless.[29]

On the 21st of October, the weary 4th Canadian Infantry Brigade was
given a twenty-four hour rest, and with it the opportunity to plan the

next phase of its advance. The 4th Brigade was relieved by the three battalions of the 6th: the South Saskatchewan Regiment, Les Fusiliers de Mont-Royal and the Queen's Own Cameron Highlanders of Canada — the last taking over the Riley positions.

Since early in October, the 6th Canadian Infantry Brigade had been given the task of forming right-flank protection for the remainder of the 2nd Division. This seemingly easy assignment had evolved into a series of unpleasant skirmishes. The enemy patrolled aggressively and counterattacked with both infantry and tanks. The ever-present mortars and shellfire made these next two weeks particularly hazardous as the casualty rate steadily mounted. If the action was low key, it still could kill and wound the combatants.

Captain Guy Levesque, carrier platoon commander with Les Fusiliers de Mont-Royal, was hit in the elbow by an armour-piercing shell while quietly enjoying a cup of tea outside his headquarters at Kalmthout, in northern Belgium. His driver and dispatch rider were killed; Levesque lost an arm: "When I was wounded, there was no fighting. It was just a shell that came in; I don't even know where it came from, if it was the enemy's or one of ours. But we knew the enemy was all around us."[30]

In Kalmthout, one of the courageous fighters of Antwerp's Secret Army, Lieutenant Edouard Pilaet, offered the services of his two-hundred-man unit to the FMR commanding officer, Major Jimmy Dextraze. The FMR history enthusiastically records the contribution of these men of the Resistance who fought with the battalion for six weeks: "Lieutenant Pilaet is a brave man who never backed down before the enemy. He always volunteered for the most dangerous tasks."[31]

Once, during those days, the FMR had advanced to its objective late at night, digging their slit trenches in inky blackness. Captain Robert Beauvin, who led an FMR company throughout the Scheldt battle, recalls a very bad moment. "When we woke up in the morning, there was one trench with our troops, but in the next trench there were Germans and we were all mixed up. Fortunately, they surrendered."[32]

The MO of the Queen's Own Cameron Highlanders of Canada had a similar escapade. Heavy casualties had made it necessary to move the Regimental Aid Post up to the forward positions. Captain

J.R. Scratch had the weird experience of being awakened from a deep sleep of utter weariness by five German soldiers carrying a white flag, demanding some attention for their wounded comrades. "'Doc' Scratch was our favourite jazz pianist and quite a character," recalls Major Kenneth Smith. "He insisted on sampling the rum issue for 'my boys.' He got a lot of mileage out of the story of the Germans waking him!"[33]

"The new front was so long that it was necessary to use all available troops," the Camerons' history recounts. "Field artillerymen, tankmen, antitank gunners and members of ack-ack batteries, all found themselves performing the unfamiliar and uncomfortable infantry tasks. In addition, the Camerons had under their command about 150 Belgian volunteers who set a fine example of courageous and unstinting service."[34] This force was led by Colonel Colson of Antwerp docks' renown.

It was in this period of confused fighting in the first two weeks of October that the brigade was issued explicit warnings to be on guard against an extremely cunning enemy. The Germans were masters of great ingenuity. In one instance, the CO of 108 Antitank Battery RCA, Major Dalton McCarthy, had gone forward to drop off one of his captains at his new battery position. Sergeant Major R. Adams relates the story: "On the way back the major was attracted by some soldiers waving from a nearby field. Thinking they were in need of assistance he left his driver in the jeep and proceeded alone to where the soldiers were. The next thing his driver saw was the major with his hands up in the air being rushed off in an easterly direction. The driver immediately drove to BHQ and reported the incident. RHQ was immediately notified and plans were made to send in a raid but it was called off at the last minute. The big flap that resulted was from the fact that the major had in his possession the codes for the day."[35] Another enemy ploy was to lure a Canadian unit into ambush by waving the white flag of surrender. On one occasion, an SSR platoon exchanged fire with the enemy. Two Germans stood up, shouting "*Kamerad!*" Two Canadians got up to wave them in and enemy 20mm fire swept the Saskatchewan position, causing nine casualties; fortunately, none of them was serious.

Now, after these bizarre days of skirmishing, the 5th and 6th Brigades were ordered on the 23rd of October to clear out all German-held outposts to the north and east of Woensdrecht that were still resisting the final mopping-up. There was still fight left in the enemy, as the brigade discovered when it put in an attack to clear out the last pockets of opposition: "With the village of Woensdrecht as the jumping off point the attack went in as planned at 0700 hrs., 23 October," records the regimental history of the Camerons. "The SSRs came up against stiff opposition and were pinned down. A Company of the Camerons went to their assistance and were also forced back after a bruising scrap in which Lieutenant Hayman was killed. Forty prisoners of the German 6th Parachute Regiment were captured."[36] The battle continued into the following day.

The FMR, then in the centre of the 6th Brigade attack, had a very sticky time. Under the command of 2/I-C Major Jimmy Dextraze, the battalion had advanced on the village of Nederheide, just a thousand metres east of Woensdrecht, when it ran into a vicious German defensive strongpoint. The FMR was pinned to the ground. Several platoon attacks were launched to unseat the German paratroopers, but none of these was successful. The FMR Regimental History describes the grim tenacity of the battalion in pursuing its objective, despite heavy casualties:

> The enemy stopped all progress. It was now eleven o'clock and the furious resistance of the enemy had broken up all the assaults of the FMR. Finally, in the middle of the afternoon the battalion received the necessary aid. Two companies of the Régiment de Maisonneuve came to assist and the South Saskatchewans and the Camerons launched a violent attack on the enemy's flank. The Germans appeared to be wavering but they didn't give in yet. At dawn their retreat was reported. Thus ended, on Tuesday morning the 24th of October, the engagement of the FMR called the Battle of Woensdrecht, although this village had been taken a week earlier. The battalion lost six officers of whom three were killed, (one a company commander), and about ninety NCOs and men of whom thirty were killed.[37]

While this was going on, the Calgary Highlanders began an action that was finally to seal off the road and railroad line which ran between

Bergen op Zoom and Walcheren. Confronted by an unyielding enemy, it took four days of heavy slugging before the task was completed.

While the neck of the South Beveland Peninsula was thus being firmly closed, plans were finalized for the next step in the Scheldt operation: the 2nd Canadian Division had now to do an about-turn and advance westward along the Beveland Peninsula as far as the Walcheren Causeway. This was to be the division's final action in the Scheldt campaign. But soon the rumour was flashing around to war-weary men that Brigadier H. Keefler, Acting Commander of the 2nd Canadian Infantry Division, had challenged his brigade command-ers to a macabre sort of race: the first brigade to establish contact at the causeway linking the western end of the Beveland Peninsula to the island of Walcheren would be spared the assignment of attack-ing it...and perhaps the agony of dying on it.

Obviously, the division could not turn its back on a dangerous enemy. It was apparent that the westward advance could not be ini-tiated while the rear or eastern approaches to the peninsula were still vulnerable to attack.

Dubbed Operation Suitcase, this important task of protecting 2nd Division's rear line was being pursued by divisions from four differ-ent countries: Great Britain, Poland, the United States and Canada, all temporarily under the command of the 1st Canadian Army.

The decision of SHAEF in mid-October to give the opening of Antwerp harbour top priority was to have a strong and immediate impact on the direction of the Scheldt battle. Now, instead of the right flank of the Canadian Army having to support the British, the situa-tion was reversed. The 1st British Corps, under General Crocker, received orders to "prevent the enemy interfering with 2 Canadian Infantry Division during its ops to capture South Beveland."[38]

The 2nd British Army and 1st British Corps, also part of the international team, guarded the most easterly flank of the Canadian line. 84 Group of the RAF supported the Canadian Army through-out. (Curiously, it comprised mainly British airmen, while 83 Group, largely Canadian in numbers, supported the British Army.)

In its first time in action, the "Timberwolves," the 104th U.S. Infantry Division, was given the assignment of protecting the Canadian right flank to the west of the British — a job they handled with "great dash," as General Simonds was to comment.[39] This was the first time that an American unit had ever served under Canadian command.

The 1st Polish Armoured Division and the 4th Canadian Armoured Division, both of whose infantry battalions had endured severe punishment from the enemy while clearing the south bank of the Leopold Canal in September, would now avenge their fallen comrades. Their determined fighting to protect the immediate rear of the 2nd Canadian Division would be a key factor in allowing the division to advance out the South Beveland Peninsula.

Intelligence gathered from POWs and captured documents identified enemy troops in this area as 15th Army. These units, although somewhat diminished in numbers, were equipped with many extra automatic weapons, making them particularly strong in fire power. The operations became even more intense when von der Heydte's 6th Paratroop Regiment was sent in its "fire brigade" role to stop the Allied advance.

Because of the excessive casualties suffered in the fighting on the Leopold Canal, the Poles had been experiencing the same problems that were plaguing other units under Canadian command. Replacements were scarce, and those that did trickle through were poorly trained. However, they had persevered in their advance, fighting to the east of the 4th Armoured along the axis Oostmalle-Merxplas-Baarle Nassau during the final week of September, and completing its task of providing added depth for the right flank protection of the Canadian Army.

The Poles had fought a series of strenuous infantry and tank attacks, using mixed brigade formations. Each armoured brigade would have attached to it some infantry elements, and to each infantry brigade were attached some armoured elements, with the artillery ready to supply maximum support on call.

The low standard of training in the infantry, the scarcity of Polish replacements, and the stubborn German defence resulted in high casualties as well as greater losses in tanks supporting the infantry. The Polish commander believed that to restore their fighting capabilities would require from six to eight weeks of intensive training away from any action. Obviously, this was not practical because the Allies had too few bodies on the ground to spare them.

The division launched an assault on the 29th of September where, after a sharp fight, they captured first the town of Oostmalle and the following day Merxplas. Continuing their advance, they encountered strong resistance from the paratroopers in the area south of Baarle Nassau. Von der Heydte recalls the unusual tactics that incurred heavy losses for the Poles:

> The Poles attacked in a strange way, first with their tanks and then with their infantry. I ordered my men to stay in their holes and let the tanks roll by them, so I had nearly no losses. The nearer the tanks came to the holes, the more difficult it became for them to shoot our men. There were some trees 100 metres away. Within these I camouflaged my four 88s and when the Polish tanks approached to 500 metres or so, then the 88s had a direct shot. The rest of the Polish tanks that were still able to move turned around and went away. When the Polish tanks retreated the Polish infantry attacked. But the poor Polish soldier didn't understand the world anymore. He had no supporting fire — nothing. For my infantry it was easy.[40]

Relief for the battle-weary Poles came on the 6th of October when units of the 49 British Division took over their responsibilities, allowing them to assume a defensive position and take advantage of a few days' rest and refit. With this change, the I Polish Armoured Division came under command of I British Corps where they remained for their next action, the capture of Breda and Moerdijk.

This phase commenced on 27 October and by 1400 hours the main road Breda-Tilburg had been cut. Breda itself was taken by a gallant action of the Polish 3rd Rifle Brigade three days later, when they captured seven enemy officers and 569 ORs.[41]

In the final step before the 2nd Division could safely turn its back on its enemy, the 4th Canadian Armoured Division was to unleash an assault to free up pressure in the "back yard" of the Canadian line.

On the 21st of October, the 10th Infantry Brigade of the 4th Armoured launched a two-pronged surprise assault on the Belgian town of Esschen, fifteen km northeast of Woensdrecht. Moving up stealthily by night, the Lincoln and Welland and the Algonquin Regiments advanced cross-country in single file. So complete was the surprise that during the next day twenty-two enemy vehicles drove into town, unaware that it was in Canadian hands.

The next big objective for the Armoured Division was Bergen op Zoom. Seven km east of that city, the Canadians ran into a German strongpoint in the woods that cost them many casualties. Supported by flame throwers, a task force comprising a company of Algonquins and the British Columbia Tank Regiment launched an attack on this strongpoint. Advancing several hundred yards, the two lead tanks were suddenly knocked out.

Observing the Canadian advance was an infantry soldier from the 6th German Paratroop Regiment, Private Alexander Schmidt. It was he who had been instructed to mine the road. And, with another rifleman, he had been told to take up machine-gun positions nearby for the night. The seventeen-year-old boy who, just two months before, had sought to avoid war by enrolling in Wireless School, had spent his first night of combat manning a machine gun on the dykes of Woensdrecht. Now he was experiencing his second frightening encounter with warfare. The event is still vividly recalled by Schmidt:

A Canadian tank which had broken through the day before blew up on the mines. Later on, two more tanks came, with infantry troops. The first one stopped about five meters from where I was dug in. For several seconds I just stared at this Canadian fellow.

If he sees me, I thought, I am done for. I had one of these Panzerfausts [short-range antitank weapon] but in order to shoot it I would have to get up. As I was trying to figure what to do, the other guy with me shot and hit the tank with his Panzerfaust. I started to shoot with my machine gun and the last tank retreated along with the infantry back toward the village.

Now we had these two tanks and the crew from the first one got out. They were wounded; they were lying there on the ground. And from the second one they came out too; they were a little bit burnt. We didn't know what to do with them. We were all alone; our lines were much further back. My comrade went back to his own company and said that we had four wounded but they replied they couldn't do anything. So we decided to take them back to the Canadians.

We took a Red Cross flag that was in the tank and went to the village where the Canadians were. We told them we had some of their wounded and that we couldn't do anything with them because we didn't have transportation and if they wanted them, they could come and get them. It gave some risk for the Canadians to go back because they didn't know how many of our troops were there; they didn't know that we were alone. However, an ambulance took the wounded. When we left, we shook hands and they gave us a package of cigarettes.

This turned out to be very dangerous for young Schmidt.

The next day, as the Algonquins were poised to make a decisive assault on the bazooka nest, the Germans abandoned their position. Terrified, and deserted by his own company, Schmidt recounts his capture:

It had gotten dark, and I was alone. The others had left but it was forbidden for me to leave without orders. Finally, someone from my company told me to come back. I had two machine guns, so I buried the one that didn't work and took my gun that was working and went back to where the company was waiting for me. An officer said, "Where's the second machine gun?" I said, "I couldn't carry two!" And that was a very serious incident, to leave ammunition and weapons. So he ordered me back to get this machine gun.

That took me about half an hour because the Canadians had advanced and I had to be very careful not to make any noise, so by the time I returned my company had left. I started to march a little bit and a corporal joined me. He said, "I know the way, but don't make any fuss." I didn't know then what he meant but I understood afterwards: he was going to give himself up. As we marched the way which he directed, in the night, all of a sudden we heard, "Hands up!" We had marched right into the Canadian lines!

I was frisked and that's when I got into serious trouble with those cigarettes. I also had a Canadian pistol that I had taken from one of the wounded the day before, and I had my pockets full of Canadian cigarettes. The guards said, "Where did you get all this from?" I related my story to them and after a while they checked it out. Then I could go inside and have coffee. In the morning we were transported to a camp for the rest of the war.[42]

On the 27th of October, the war ended for Alexander Schmidt. Also on this date, a German propaganda leaflet was picked up by the Algonquins:

WHY DIE FOR STALIN?

In dying for Stalin your soldiers are not dying for democracy or the preservation of the democratic form of government — they are dying for the establishment of Communism and a form of Stalinist tyranny throughout the world. Furthermore, they are dying for the preservation of the integrity of small nations (England's old war cry) but are dying so that Poland shall be a Soviet State; so that the Baltic States shall be incorporated in the Soviet Union and so that Soviet influence shall extend from the Baltics to the Balkans...

Every British soldier who dies for Stalin is another nail in the coffin of Britain's hopes of maintaining a balance of power in Europe.

Should the equilibrium pass to Stalin then the equilibrium of the world is at an end.

THOSE WHO ARE ABOUT TO DIE...
THINK IT OVER!![43]

The push along the sandy road to Bergen op Zoom was to take the 4th Division four more days. The polders had been replaced by a different terrain, equally dangerous. As usual, the Germans had made the most of it. Captain Bill Whiteside, antitank platoon commander with the Argyll and Sutherland Highlanders of Canada, recalls:

> The land that we went through was very sandy with hillocks and mounds of sand, and for armour it was terribly difficult going because if they got off the road they just spun their wheels. They weren't going anywhere. There were a lot of woods and the Germans were well supplied with mortars plus mines of all kinds. I remember one spot where there were not many defending troops but they had mined it with those little Schu-mines, and also with antipersonnel mines — the ones that pop up and clip you.
>
> We had our carriers just doing a scouting operation back and forth on our flanks on each sideroad. I don't think I remember seeing that done anyplace else.[44]

And to Major Jim Swayze, mortar platoon commander of the Lincoln and Welland Regiment, those four days cutting a path through the endless succession of mines and obstacles the Germans had strewn in their path "felt like four weeks": "The battalion was married up to Dave Currie's South Alberta Regiment, but tanks were monumentally unsuccessful there. All the approaches were mined — even to the point where, when you got off the road, they had trip wires of piano wire strung to 88mm shells on the trees. And at one point they had a 500-pound aerial bomb in the middle of the road that went off and got one of the flame-throwing crocodiles. It went up higher than the trees and killed all the English chaps in it."[45]

On the afternoon of the 27th of October, word was received that the 29th Reconnaissance Regiment of the 4th Canadian Armoured Division had reached the key city of Bergen op Zoom, just ten km from Woensdrecht. The Germans had withdrawn to a strongpoint just north of the town where a canal formed an antitank obstacle running east to west. This had to be crossed and the enemy eliminated.

But getting into Bergen was a lot easier than getting out the other end of it, Captain Whiteside remembers. The first attempt to cross the canal, a frontal attack in daylight by the Argyll and Sutherland Highlanders and the Lincoln and Wellands invited violent retaliation from German mortars, machine guns and snipers. For thirty-six hours the enemy hurled all available fire on the attackers, beating them back and inflicting many casualties.

A second attempt was made, this time at a narrow crossing west of the town near the Scheldt. A recce patrol actually managed to cross and advance on the enemy side of the canal for several hundred yards without any response from the Germans. Unwittingly, they had crossed a heavily mined field, but by a miracle, they had avoided all the mines. The company that followed was not as lucky. A platoon commander stepped on a Schu-mine, seriously injuring himself and alerting the enemy to the company position. At once, German machine gunners opened up, forcing the Canadians back.

At dawn, a third attack went in, following the line of the previous one across the end of the canal, through the minefields and then back along the steep bank on the opposite side of the canal. The Argylls had almost reached the start of the houses in town when the enemy stopped them, as Bill Whiteside remembers all too clearly: "The Germans were in slit trenches at the top edge of the bank. They just stayed in their trenches tossing grenades down the bank at our men. They never even had to lift up their heads. For a while, it stopped us completely. Major Gordon Armstrong got a DSO for this operation. Probably the Lincolns took a worse beating than we did, but we lost, killed and wounded, sixty men."[46]

The battle raged through the day, finally abating in the late afternoon when the Algonquins made the crossing as well. But still the enemy would not be silenced. Shell and machine-gun fire continued through the night.

The exhausted men were pulled out the next morning, the 31st, for a deserved rest and recreation break. They had established a bridgehead, and the 4th Canadian Armoured Division could now advance across the canal to dominate the main road north. The battalion War Diary describes its Hallowe'en banquet and dance held that night in Bergen's Hotel de Draak: "Pretty Dutch girls and members of the local young ladies Bible class were invited and a joyous evening of entertainment was had by all."[47]

The Battle of the Scheidt was over for the 4th Canadian Armoured Division, but on the 31st of October the 2nd Canadian Infantry Division had only just reached the Walcheren Causeway — now a blackened, bomb-cratered corridor of fire — and the loser of that grotesque race was then calculating his chances, collectively in a brigade, and individually as a rifleman, of surviving its crossing.

10

Johnny...Which One Was That?

IN THOSE VIOLENT WEEKS OF FIGHTING DURING THE BATTLE OF THE Scheldt, the men at the front soon witnessed what they came to acknowledge as Canada's blackest disgrace. Political games were being played with human stakes on Europe's battlefields in October, 1944, and Canadian soldiers were the losers.

Although much has been written and said about the Conscription Crisis of Canada in the fall of 1944, few historians have asked the fighting men what to them was the real crisis.

The real crisis did not take place on the floor of the House of Commons, or behind locked doors at a fiery meeting of the War Cabinet. The real crisis declared itself on the battlefields of northwest Europe, when we commanding officers came to realize that Canadian volunteers were being rushed, almost totally untrained, to the front lines to relieve infantry deficits.

The need for reinforcements was desperate.* When the government woke up to the shocking facts of the acute infantry shortages, it was estimated that 16,000 men would be required to see the war into 1945. As early as the end of August, 1944, Canadian infantry units were reporting a deficiency of 4,318 soldiers.

Ironically, by the fall of 1944 when these shortages existed, there were nearly half a million men and women enlisted in the Canadian

---

* The word "reinforcement" was the term generally used by the British to mean replacements for casualties. In the United States, the term was "replacement" or "repple-depple."

Army. Of these, 85,000 were men in fighting formations of all services. The problem lay in the fact that although there was a surplus
of some 390,000 men available for general service, none were infantry
trained. Some were on administrative staffs; under bureaucratic army
methods — in which Canada excelled — it took seven non-combat-
ants to keep one infantryman in the field. The remaining reservoir of
volunteers were men who had become redundant in the services to
which they had originally been assigned (primarily the engineers,
artillery, army service corps, ordnance corps, armoured corps, and
even air force ground crew) and who now could be remustered into
infantry ranks. But these men lacked the necessary skills to be effective in front-line combat, and setting up an infantry retraining programme would take time.

Now Woensdrecht's dead and wounded would have one last
voice, one final contribution to make. The terrible numbers of casualties sustained by the 4th and 5th Brigades in their struggle to drive
the Germans back from the neck of the Beveland Peninsula provided
statistics that unmasked the truth about the critical shortage of trained
reinforcements available for front-line service in the infantry. When
the facts could no longer be suppressed, it became very clear that
Canadian lives were being sacrificed and the supreme efforts of the
troops eroded for the sake of gratifying political ambition and con-
cealing personal incompetence. The potage of misinformation and
mistruth that had been fed to the Canadian Parliament and public
through the long summer and fall of 1944 was to have a spiralling
impact on the government of Canada. Its Liberal prime minister,
Mackenzie King, would barely avoid being Woensdrecht's final victim.

The Canadian Army overseas, unlike most of the Allied forces,
was composed solely of volunteers. Whether or not there should have
been enforced military service — conscription — during World War
II, such as existed in Great Britain and the United States, was a political issue of some complexity that cannot be debated on these pages.
Rightly or wrongly, a certain proportion of Canadians, both in Quebec and within some ethnic groups of the prairie provinces and the
west, did not wish to fight a war for King George VI of England.

Early in the hostilities, in June, 1940, the National Resources
Mobilization Act was passed, authorizing conscription of NRMA men

for home defence only. Then in April, 1942, following a national plebiscite, Bill 80 was passed. This released the government from its promise not to expand the Act to include overseas service — thus clearing the way to send NRMA men to war. Quebecers, who strongly opposed this, were not appeased by King's slogan: "Not necessarily conscription but conscription if necessary."[1] By now, in Canada, there were some 70,000 conscripts, many with extensive infantry training, whom King steadfastly refused to send overseas.

Preparation for D-Day in the spring of 1944 brought the issue to the fore again. In March, concern about the supply of trained reinforcements, particularly for the infantry, was raised by Canadian Army officials, and even by Montgomery. The issue was as quickly suppressed.

The man responsible for camouflaging the facts was Lieutenant General Kenneth Stuart, Chief of Staff at CMHQ (Canadian Military Headquarters) in London. Stuart was the direct appointee of, and directly accountable to, Canada's Defence Minister, the Honourable J.L. Ralston. In March, Stuart issued an order to his staff that no important communication regarding the reinforcement situation was to be submitted to National Defence Headquarters, 21st Army Group or elsewhere that had not been seen and approved by himself. On the 13th of May, Stuart wrote Ralston that they were making "considerable progress in respect to the CMHQ viewpoint, and in respect to the tendency to write 'alarmist cables.'"[2]

It is surprising, however, that Ralston would condone, by silent acquiescence at any rate, this suppression of the facts from his own London representative. Canadian historian Colonel C.P. Stacey writes: "The actual fact is that, in part at least with Ralston's knowledge, the officer whom he had placed in charge in England after McNaughton's removal enforced a policy of soft-pedalling on this question and saw to it that communications which he considered 'alarmist' were not sent to Ottawa."[3] From that date onward, Stuart issued, and Ralston received, only the most optimistic of reports on the reinforcement issue.

Even Field Marshal Montgomery was misled. In March he had underlined the potential seriousness of the infantry deficiencies to Stuart, pointing out that since the reinforcements would comprise remustered men switched over from other services, "rigorous training" was

essential before they could be "fit to take the field as [infantry] reinforcements." Stuart reassured him: "Action," Stuart replied, "is being
taken regarding absorption of surpluses to assist in meeting deficiencies. Every effort will be made by this means and by direct ship-
ment of reinforcements from Canada to make good deficiencies in
the infantry arm by target date."[4]

In fact, it would be another five months before energetic remustering began, and before a retraining scheme of any scope was put
into effect to teach men from other services the skills of the foot soldier. But by then, the deficiencies in infantry strength were reaching
crisis proportion. CMHQ had seriously underestimated the anticipated number of infantry casualties, adopting as they had an apples-
and-oranges yardstick based on the light British casualties of the
North African campaign.

By early August, heavy casualties from the Normandy campaign
— the 3rd Canadian Infantry Division had the highest of all of 21st
Army Group's fifteen divisions in action and the 2nd Canadian
Infantry Division was close behind — brought the infantry losses to
a startling 75 percent of the total army casualties, and escalated the
deficiency figure of trained riflemen to almost two thousand. Still,
Stuart doggedly clung to his stance, informing the Cabinet War Committee on the 3rd of August that there were, as a relieved Prime Minister Mackenzie King confided in his diary, "plenty of reserves."[5] It
is possible that King, a civilian, did not understand (or wish to understand) the explosive potential of the casualty report.

A strongly worded warning from General Crerar at about that
time, stressing the infantry shortages as "the most serious problem
of the Canadian Army at the moment," presumably never got any farther than London, where an obedient CMHQ staff officer would have
suppressed it for its "alarmist" content. To bridge the emergency,
Crerar, seemingly convinced (as were Stuart, Montgomery and even
Eisenhower in this era of victory euphoria) that the war was winding
down, suggested looking into shortening the conversion training
period: "It is quite clear that the only solution lies in vigorous remustering and strenuous conversion training. Request careful study of
possibility of shortening conversion training by grading on entry and
so securing a prospect in four weeks…

"In view [of the] distinct possibility that operation of next four weeks may prove turning point remustering policy should be based on that view. It is vital that our offensive power be maintained and long-term futures must be risked to produce early."[6]

Although a remustering program was finally instituted, the situation continued to ferment throughout the month of heavy casualties in August, with a mid-month deficiency of 2,644 general duty infantrymen. So serious did it become that reinforcements were being supplied on a day-to-day basis. Stuart was counting on an Allied victory before the end of the year. The replacements, he was convinced, could be eked out to span that period. But by late August, with the deficit in infantry manpower increasing alarmingly to 4,318 men, he could no longer avoid confronting the issue. In a top secret cable to Ralston on the 26th of August, he acknowledged for the first time that he had erred in failing to establish realistic casualty rates for the Canadian troops. The deficit, he now maintained, could not be met for the next few weeks. He made an emergency proposal that the so-called infantry tradesmen, men such as cooks, shoemakers, lorry drivers and clerks, who had never received training as fighting troops, be transferred to front-line duty on a "temporary" basis. Ralston, possibly not comprehending or not wanting to comprehend the implications of the request, approved it without referring it to Cabinet. "It was a Sunday morning," he was later to explain. "I simply initialed the telegram and handed it back to the chief of the General Staff."[7]

This was the first bare hint in Ottawa of the fact that untrained men were being sent into battle, but no one stirred in response. However, commanders in the field, and in the training depots, were well aware of this travesty. And they were angry.

The enemy infantrymen were well-trained soldiers. It was later discovered that the Germans, facing — somewhat more realistically than the Canadians — similar infantry shortages, pulled battle-experienced officers and NCOs back into the training conversion camps to give simplified but highly concentrated instruction courses.

But the Canadian volunteer did not have the benefit of this kind of insight. A senior administrative officer at one of the four CITRs (Canadian Infantry Training Regiments) near Aldershot, England, reveals that the CITR as a training unit was really a misnomer: "They were really just transient camps for administration and documentation of the reinforcement stream. There were so many routine administrative jobs to get done, so much paperwork, that there wasn't time for any training. Men were moving in and out all the time; they were only sent there for a matter of weeks — certainly no longer than a month."

To his consternation, he discovered that any training that was done was supposed to have already been done in Canada. There simply wasn't the opportunity once they were sent overseas, as he noted:

> At that point in the war, from August '44 on, there was no time to give any instruction and there were no instructors to give it. And I wasn't aware of any pressure brought on the CITRs to give training. The reinforcements, mainly remustered from Canada, had no sooner arrived than they were drafted over to the continent to replace the casualties. The men got the occasional route march, but not much more.
>
> We also had men posted with us who had been wounded, and not just once or even twice. They would be hospitalized, and then returned to active duty — just pushed right back into the mill again.[8]

Company commanders raged at those who forced them to send these troops into action: "We had only feelings of disgust, of contempt for the prime minister and the politicians who were not facing the realities of the crisis, and most of all we felt anger. The feeling was becoming very deep-seated in all the troops that they were being used and being sacrificed by their government in order not to face public opinion"[9] was the reaction of Major Joe Pigott.

Lieutenant Colonel Roger Rowley voiced the anger of all of the Canadian troops who saw volunteers pounded relentlessly in the field with no relief while some 70,000 conscripted soldiers waited in Canada: "We had five divisions, or the equivalent, of trained men sitting back there in Canada, and that s.o.b. Mackenzie King just wouldn't send them overseas. It took me all winter to get my battalion into adequate shape to break out on the Rhine. If we had really got involved in another long-drawn-out, head-knocking operation again, we'd have been in big trouble."[10]

The crisis began for the Royal Hamilton Light Infantry in a singularly undramatic way. Rain and high winds swept the cratered slopes of Woensdrecht Hill the morning after the RHLI attack, and the exhausted survivors, now pitifully few, braced themselves for fresh counterattacks.

Ninety-one of my men became casualties before dusk on that first long day of battle; we were soon to lose that number again as the enemy pummelled the thinning line of Rileys. We had not enough bodies on the ground to probe forward against the German line of defence, nor even to control our position.

It was into this havoc that thirty-nine reinforcements reported for duty that foul morning. Two days later, 150 more were sent up. And bit by bit, reports and comments filtered into my headquarters until they finally revealed the travesty: 189 men, most of them untrained, had been ordered to battle against some of Germany's finest soldiers.

The reinforcements were nearly all men who had been remustered from other arms of the service. It was evident that they had been shunted over to infantry units with only the most rudimentary training. Tragically, they did not know how to look after their weapons — or themselves. They didn't, for example, know how to load or fire their weapons, as one puzzled sergeant major told me later: "I held up a Piat gun and said, 'How many of you guys recognize this?' But nobody had ever seen one. It was crazy! Then I brought up a case of Bren guns, still packed in grease, and explained that their first job was to wash them. But they didn't even know how to take one apart."[11]

"We were detonating grenades," added his sergeant, "and this one young guy took the detonators and dumped six or seven into his hand. I kicked them out of his hand and he said, 'What the hell are you doing?' So I asked, 'Maybe you want your hand blown off?'"[12]

It was then that we first fully realized that as soldiers we were being placed in jeopardy by our own Canadian military and government leaders. A mere handful of self-serving men was exposed as having protected their political necks by ruthlessly exploiting the volunteers, many of whom had never seen a gun fired in anger, pitting them head on into one of the bloodiest infantry battles of the war.

We fighting men at the front had not only the task of waging war, but we had now, at the same time, to grapple with this monstrous handicap forced upon us, not by foe but by so-called friends…not by those we strove to conquer but by those we strove to save.

After breakfast I went back by request to A Echelon HQ to speak to the newly arrived replacements. Something was terribly wrong, I felt, when you had people arriving at the front who could not recognize a Bren gun and had never thrown a grenade. I tried, in a bare half hour, to instil in these men some essential knowledge for survival, but it was a pretty futile exercise, as all of us at Tac headquarters realized. It would take a minimum of at least three months to get a team that was even starting to pull together.

Nevertheless, I tried to give them confidence by instructing them about the regiment, its history, and, especially, its successes in never having failed to achieve and hold an objective in the Northwest Europe campaign. I told them they should feel honoured to have the opportunity to serve with the RHLI. I said we realized they had had very little training, and that we wanted to help them to become acclimatized to battle conditions.

The first thing I stressed was that all tactics were based on the principle of fire and movement: in other words, infantrymen should move in attack only when supported by fire of sufficient volume to keep the heads of the enemy down. I emphasized the importance of keeping close to our artillery fire in the attack so as to close with the enemy at the earliest possible moment when the fire lifted. They were introduced to the all-important trenching tool. Most of all, I advised them to rely on help from the old sweats.

I described how they should hug the ground for the greatest protection, how to use "dead" ground out of sight of the enemy. I stressed a few truths, such as that the enemy shell that they could hear for a long time was safe enough; you only heard the dangerously close ones for a couple of seconds — and if you didn't hear them at all, it was game over.

What I didn't say, couldn't say to those men, was that their country stood behind them. It seemed no longer true. We had always believed that we had an implied contract with Canada. We were willing to risk our lives for our country, but we expected our country to back us up, with adequate weapons and tactical support, and trained manpower. These poor transferees they sent us had been betrayed — and so had we.

A corporal from transport was looking on: "Those lads are so inexperienced, the cost will not only be their own lives but the lives of many of the older fellows who will inevitably try to guide and protect them," he predicted sadly. He was to experience just how accurate his warning was. In the days to come, he would drive the reinforcements up to the front first thing in the morning, and often pick up some of the same men, dead, that evening.

"The sun never set on those poor buggers," the transport men would say to one other. "No one even got to know their names, what they looked like, their likes and dislikes.

"'Johnny…which one was that?' they'd ask."[13]

Most of us had become battle-wise through experience in Normandy and during several years of training in England before D-Day. We had endured the toughest sort of training — tougher, in many instances, than conditions encountered in actual battle. Even in training we were blooded; live ammunition was used, and there were casualties.

And we were fit. Part of our training on the Isle of Wight for the Dieppe raid included frequent fifteen-mile march-and-runs in full battle order. Eleven-mile forced marches, also with full packs, had to be completed in two hours. One man from the battalion who was badly wounded in the Dieppe raid was told in hospital that there would have been many more deaths if the men had not been in such excellent physical condition. Shock alone, he was informed, would have finished off a lot more of them.

This toughness was missing now in some of these reinforcements — and so was basic discipline. "A lot of them had six quick weeks spent mostly in documentation and equipping," one lieutenant observed. "The major lack of training was in weapons handling, but weapons training is part of instilling discipline, automatically doing this and that at the right moment, and the standard of discipline was terrible as well. The mystery to us was how some NCOs remustered from other services had not even learned to handle a personal weapon."[14]

One Riley company commander watched with dismay as morale tumbled, in direct proportion to escalating casualties and consequent replacements: "The troops we still had who had survived Normandy and the advance through Belgium and Holland were becoming increasingly exhausted. They were in constant exposure to battle. We were seriously undermanned and we were badly off for satisfactory reinforcements, both in numbers and in terms of training. Keeping morale at a high level became terribly difficult."[15]

The RHLI was not unique in having to set up classrooms on the battlefields. Woensdrecht had taken its toll on all the battalions of the 2nd Canadian Infantry Division. A private soldier from the Royal Regiment recalls:

> Some of those kids could tell me what was playing just a week ago at Shea's Theatre on Bay Street. I had left Toronto four years before, but these boys are telling me what was featured at the movies last week. They didn't even stay at a holding unit in England or go on manoeuvres like we did. They were young, from all over the country. They had never seen anything like what was going on at the front, with the Moanin' Minnies and the mortars and all. They were just whistled right into battle.
>
> I would give them a little help, advise them to get into their bloody hole and stay there or get under a truck, "For heaven's sake, don't run," that sort of stuff. There were even officers that didn't know what kind of warfare was going on. There were some we called "one-pip wonders," expecting their batmen to dig their slit trenches![16]

The Royals figured that the reinforcements sent them were so badly trained there was just no sense in putting them in the way they were. "They didn't know anything, poor fellows," noted one officer whose company strength was down from over one hundred to a mere forty-five men. "So we had to send them back and train them ourselves. Then we gradually brought them up under fire as they were required. But you couldn't, in a few fast lessons, hope to teach all the tricks."[17]

An officer in the Essex Scottish recalls his concern over the calibre of men that came up as platoon commanders: "The new men were not experienced, and the men underneath them were equally inexperienced." The officer found it pretty tough sending them out on patrol: "If it was a fighting patrol that you'd have to send them on, then you were practically condemning the poor bastard to a no-win situation. The best that could be said of some of these reinforcements was that they were bodies, and they did fill out platoon and company strength. You just couldn't keep on grinding out your same old NCOs."[18]

One lieutenant, although reasonably well trained, arrived too late to fight in the battle. He had this indignant account of his activities during those critical weeks of September and October:

> In late August I was a gunnery officer stationed at a holding unit in England when a staff officer appeared one day. He asked all the junior officers to volunteer to switch to the infantry. About two dozen of us did volunteer, and we were amazed to be immediately given two weeks' leave. When we returned, we were sent on an Infantry Conversion Course. To our surprise, the other non-volunteers were there too. There was a great deal of complaining about this arbitrary method of operation by the officers who hadn't volunteered. Although the training on the course was very intensive and useful, the weeks of delay were such that by the time we were posted to infantry units we all missed the fighting around the Scheldt.[19]

The Black Watch, the most sorely wounded of all the battalions, was therefore most heavily inundated with remustered reinforcements, having received 182 men since just before Black Friday. The ill-trained group had no surprises for Colonel Bruce Ritchie, whose battalion had been force-fed with raw reinforcements since the initial disaster at St. André-sur-Orne in Normandy and who then had gone on to see the battalion's successes at Brecht threatened by a whole platoon of confused and frightened novices.

On the 19th of October, Major Allan Stevenson, 2/I-C of the

battalion, soberly handed his commanding officer a slip of paper that would stun the population of Canada. Analyzing the training background of 379 all ranks in the four rifle companies of the Black Watch, Stevenson discovered that 174, or 45 percent of the men, had had one month's training or less as infantrymen before joining the battalion. Stevenson's damning summation: "It is unnecessary to point out to you, sir, that the previous training of a man listed as for instance 'one month' on paper, probably represents considerably less time actual training. This assumption is borne out by the fact that very few men arrive with knowledge of the Piat or elementary section and platoon tactics. Some reinforcements have never fired the Bren l.m.g. or handled grenades."[20]

"The report was handed over to the Canadian defence minister," Ritchie recalled, "but the other important issue was that we had to take time out from battle to establish training for our reinforcements. We taught them the simplest battle formation such as fire and movement, which was brand new to most of these people and to their officers. Brand new."[21]

But the cadre that most keenly felt the reinforcement crunch was the French Canadian battalions. One basic reason for this was that many French Canadians resented Canada's participation in a war they regarded as having been generated by England and its king, rather than as a war to defend Canada. Consequently, although there were originally 55,000 French Canadian volunteers in the Canadian Army, overwhelming opposition grew throughout Quebec to any attempt to conscript French Canadian men for overseas duty.

In the national Canadian media, Blair Fraser made this harsh assessment: "French Canadians feel their sons in uniform are treated unjustly. They say their soldiers are told to 'speak white.' They are aware that the navy and air force use only English."[22]

With few men to replace casualties, inevitably the three French Canadian battalions fighting so valiantly at the Scheldt became the scapegoats for these "back home" sentiments. "French reinforcements weren't plentiful," acknowledges a senior gunnery officer, "so they were coming up pretty fast, with no break-in period. These poor buggers were being sent up and popped into a slit trench in the evening, and they were attacking the next morning. They never got to know their neighbour or the other guys in the platoon. I always felt they had the worst of anyone."[23]

A platoon commander of the Régiment de Maisonneuve confirms this: "Morale was affected. It was difficult for the men to fight every day, without the support of reinforcements. We had almost no one left. And we had a lot of problems getting officers, too. My whole company was down to about twenty-seven men. It was very bad. Those poor kids didn't know what to do. They had no training. They joined the army, were sent overseas and came up to the front line. It was very, very fast."[24]

Just sixty km west of us, the 3rd Canadian Infantry Division was waging its vicious battle for the Scheldt under conditions equally as appalling as those endured by their 2nd Division comrades. High casualties on the flooded polders of Breskens Pocket had resulted in critical shortages of manpower. The 9th Brigade alone, in the first week of the offensive, lost 111 of all ranks killed and 422 wounded. Lieutenant Colonel Roger Rowley, commanding officer of the 9th Brigade's Stormont, Dundas and Glengarry Regiment, recalls bitterly that his battalion had reached the point that its performance was jeopardized:

> I was down to three stripped-down companies. Let's face it, there are four rifle companies in an infantry battalion because they each have a tactical function to perform; you simply can't operate without your four elements of manoeuvre. You get down to three companies, you've lost something. You've lost your power to manoeuvre. We were damn short. Our platoons, which were supposed to be thirty-three or thirty-four men, were all down to about sixteen men. We were down to twenty-five at one point in a couple of companies. The 4th Division was even worse off than we were because they had small battalions anyway.

Rowley was left with no alternative but to accept and assimilate raw recruits mid-battle. He deplored the terrible waste and damned those who legislated it:

> It was inexplicable and inexcusable. Anti-aircraft officers in England, who were put through ten days at the Canadian

Army battle school, were literally retreaded and sent to me. I'm not exaggerating when I say that they had no notion of war, let alone at the infantry battalion level. They'd been trained as anti-aircraft gunners. They kept coming in and God — if they lasted twenty-four hours, they were lucky. They just came in, went out on the line, and zap — they were either wounded or killed. They were nice guys, but they weren't much use to me wounded or dead.

We did what I'm sure other battalions did. At B Echelon we set up a battle school where we rotated the men, set them up, and tried to get them used to the war. But when you're fighting a battle like the Scheldt, there was no way you could achieve all that much; there wasn't time.[25]

One of those reinforcements, an SD&G Bren gunner who saw his platoon reduced to just three of the original complement at the end of the Breskens campaign, recalls: "Being so short of men made it difficult to keep up morale. Us raw fellows came in and we didn't know whether we were going to survive to the next day or not."[26]

"They sent us a bunch of reinforcements from the catering corps," scoffed a sergeant from the HLI, "and we got five or six butchers. But they were the wrong kind of butcher than we were looking for. The rate of casualties for the reinforcements was high because those guys almost had to learn everything from the moment they set foot on Breskens."[27]

Officers and men of the Queen's Own Rifles had their own horror stories:

> We were so thin on the ground at the Scheldt that most of the time the company I commanded could do nothing but man the automatic weapons. We didn't have enough men left over to have a rifleman. At one time I had one officer and only twenty-nine other ranks in the company.[28]

> We would bring the men up from B Echelon to spend a night in the line. They had a sort of buddy system there. They'd spend the night, have breakfast there, and if there was any

flak flying, they'd be pulled out for the day, back to B Echelon. That way they figured they were trained soldiers; their chests went out. I found that we really got some damn good men out of those fellows. Most of them wanted it and did the best they could. But they had no training.[29]

They'd send reinforcements up to a company after dark. Those poor guys didn't know where they were. They were scared to death. The old soldiers were making them even more scared by saying, "Wait til you see what happens tomorrow!" and so on.

I had to bellyache back to England that the people being sent from Canada had not had proper training. I got twenty-five driver mechanics who had never been on a tracked vehicle, and yet they were categorized as tracked vehicle people, trained in Canada at Camp Borden. Because of the shortage of tracked vehicles, they had trained them on fifteen-hundred-weight trucks, but they gave them their qualifications just the same as "Driver Mechanics Tracked." These guys had never even been inside one. I took them out and they didn't have the faintest idea of how to change gears in a tracked vehicle.[30]

We were cut off. The only communication link between the front line and the Canadian people had long since been severed on General Stuart's instruction at CMHQ in London. Neither the population at large, nor Parliament — nor even Ralston or King — were aware of the desperate situation the men were facing.

Then, in September, there emerged from beneath a tangle of tubes and needles and plasma bottles an emissary willing and entirely able to take on the Government of Canada singlehanded. Major Conn Smythe, Maple Leaf Gardens founder and hockey promoter, never had a better opportunity for a shot on goal. Severely wounded in France in July, Smythe had spent the next weeks in recovery units in England, quietly assembling the incriminating set of interviews of his fellow patients' experiences in the field. Universally, they recounted shocking stories of undermanned units seeing front-line action, reinforced only with poorly trained replacements.

On the 16th of September, Smythe, still a stretcher case, arrived by ship in Halifax. Two days later, he broke the story to *Globe and Mail* publisher George McCullagh. Torontonians awoke next morning to blazing headlines:

UNTRAINED TROOPS HAZARD
AT FRONT,
SMYTHE COMPLAINS

Major Conn Smythe, M.C., declared in a signed statement last night that "large numbers of unnecessary casualties" have resulted from the fact that "reinforcements received now are green, inexperienced and poorly trained."[31]

Across Canada, other convalescents just back from the front picked up the war cry, and Ottawa was deluged with angry demands by relatives and friends of the volunteer infantrymen, calling for an investigation into the scandal. A startled Ralston announced he would tour the battlefronts and find out the truth for himself. He left for Europe soon afterward.

At the Italian front, the defence minister heard a variety of views, some of them conflicting, from a number of senior commanders. In the course of these interviews, he apparently dismissed Conn Smythe's accusation that troops were badly trained. Possibly persuaded by the reports he had reviewed from the training centres themselves (which would hardly be self-critical), and possibly drawing on World War I experiences, Ralston hypothesized that the real problem lay not in the inferior quality of the training of the enlisted men, as Smythe had maintained, but in the fact that finicky commanders, jealous of maintaining their own authority, were downgrading it.

Before he left Italy, Ralston held a meeting with his senior officers there. "No commanding officer," he maintained, "was ever satisfied with the standard of training that reinforcements received elsewhere."[32]

On the second issue under investigation — the question of whether there was a shortage of manpower — Ralston also received contradictory reports from his senior commanders. But on the day before his scheduled departure, the defence minister ran into an indomitable force in the person of Major General Chris Vokes, who completely convinced him of the acute need for reinforcements. It was a stormy session.

On a Sunday afternoon in the Eternal City, Major General Vokes, relaxing on a rare weekend leave in Rome following the victory of his 1st Canadian Infantry Division at Rimini, received an unsettling telephone call. It appeared that, despite the absence of its commander, the minister of defence had sprung an impromptu weekend visit to Vokes's division. There Ralston had been subjected to some very candid observations from several of Vokes's officers. Now, just before his departure, the defence minister was pressing for an immediate meeting at the Air Ministry Building with Vokes. It was a session that the seasoned Canadian infantry commander would not easily forget:

> I was led into an office where Ralston sat behind a desk. He greeted me in a very surly manner. Then, in a most aggressive way, he said "The discipline in your division stinks!" Taken aback, I said, "Why?" He answered, "I visited all nine of your infantry battalions and each RSM and his NCOs attacked me on the subject of reinforcements."
>
> So I asked, "What did they complain about?"
>
> "They complained that the supply of reinforcements was inadequate; that the rifle companies of their battalions fought in battle at less than fifty percent of establishment strength."
>
> I said, "Colonel Ralston, when I was given command of 1st Division in November of 1943, I had had considerable combat experience as an infantry brigade commander. What the men told you is certainly apparent to me as well, and it is absolutely true. The reinforcement situation in this theatre is desperate. I'm glad my RSMs made their opinions known to you. They know that there are plenty of well-trained soldiers in Canada — conscripts — who cannot be sent overseas unless they volunteer.
>
> "Trained men," I told Ralston, "have a 75 percent chance of survival. Untrained men had none."

Sending untrained men into action was an act of murder, Vokes grimly warned the minister of defense: "Ralston pulled in his horns and said, 'I will look at the situation in northwest Europe, talk to General Simonds, and if the situation there is as it is here I will correct it when I get back to Canada."[33]

General Vokes thought his message was clear enough, and so, he thought, were its consequences. "You can't make an omelette without breaking the eggs" had been the doughty commander's unabashed advice to the Canadian government.

Ralston had given his word: if Simonds corroborated the evidence that the infantry shortages in northwest Europe matched those in Italy, the minister would advise Cabinet to release the trained conscripts for overseas duty. Since this was precisely what transpired, it was therefore quite apparent to Vokes that Simonds would have given similar outspoken and alarmed reports as well.

Then, after four days conferring with General Stuart at CMHQ in London — and a fast visit to see General Crerar at the Canadian military hospital at Taplow — Ralston flew to 1st Canadian Army headquarters in Belgium on the 10th of October. Here he was taken around by General Simonds and Acting Corps Commander Major General Charles Foulkes to divisional and corps headquarters, presumably hearing the same frank revelations.

Ralston's visit had coincided with a critical period in Simonds's command, when everyone from SHAEF down was peering over his shoulder, urging him to get Antwerp opened up. No one could have been more aware than Simonds that these shortages of experienced fighting men were a strong factor in slowing up the Canadian advance at the Scheldt. In other battle theatres, armour could reinforce the infantry role. But the polders were impassable to tanks. Here the most keenly honed infantry skills were demanded — far, far more skills than could be gleaned in a few weeks at a remustering centre.

It was during those brief days of Ralston's fact-finding tour that, just a few kilometres away, the Calgary Highlanders were fighting with desperation to hold Hoogerheide from counterattacks by von der Heydte's seasoned paratroopers. The Royals — some of them boys who had left Toronto just the week before — were struggling through flooded polders, taking heavy casualties as they edged the Germans

Land Mattress crew prepares for shoot.

H/Captain Jock Anderson receives MC from Field Marshal Montgomery.

Major General Knut Eberding, GOC 64th Infantry Division.

Brigadier John Rockingham, Commander 9th Brigade, after being awarded DSO by HM King George VI in Antwerp.

Crossing in Buffaloes, October 1944.

Shelled-out civilians at Sluis seek refuge.

Major General Dan Spry, GOC 3 Canadian Infantry Division.

1st Canadian Scottish Bren gun carriers mired in Breskens mud.

Major Huck Welch, company commander of RHLI.

Sodden polderlands of Breskens Pocket.

Flame throwers in action across Leopold Canal.

Lieutenant Pieter Kloosterman (left) awarded the Bronzen Kruis by HRH Prince Bernhard of the Netherlands.

The shaving of heads — a form of vengeance taken against women who consorted with the enemy.

Denis Whitaker (right) with Major General Foulkes (left) and Brigadier Cabeldu.

Sniper team of Calgary Highlanders on the polders.

Defence Minister Ralston conferring with Lieutenant General Guy Simonds in Belgium.

Dutch civilians arrested in razzias, for forced labour, dig an anti-tank ditch.

back towards Woensdrecht. Ralston's tour would last through the devastation of Friday, the 13th of October, when even the courageous fighting by the Canadian Black Watch could not overcome the fact that 45 percent of its men were in combat without adequate training. While Ralston was making his way around these headquarters, Major General Dan Spry's amphibious assault across the Braakman was committed to wresting mere toeholds of sodden canal bank from an unrelenting enemy, and his battalion commander, Lieutenant Colonel Rowley, was seeing raw recruits join the unit one day and be wiped out the next.

The concerns of these officers and men that Ralston talked to in those tense, pressured days of October, 1944, were focused single-mindedly on the current battle — and on its adverses. And these problems would have been communicated to battalion, division, corps and army chiefs — and to the minister of defence.

Spry could not credit General Simonds with taking any but a supportive position on behalf of his men: "When there are not enough people even to carry the ammunition up for the Bren guns, you know there is a problem," the 3rd Division commander stated. "It was of grave concern to me; I'm sure Guy Simonds knew it too."[34]

When Layton Ralston returned to Brussels, he conferred with Simonds. There were no witnesses to the encounter, no formal minutes of the conversation that transpired. However, certain historians in recent years have chosen to accept an interpretation of the meeting that indicts Guy Simonds for having betrayed his men by assuring Ralston that there was no problem with the standard of training. By a curious convolution of circumstance, although it was Ralston who circulated that ill-conceived and sanctimonious theory that commanders did not want to admit that men were well trained if they had not personally trained them, it was Simonds who took the blame.

The evidence is tenuous. Some thirty years after the fact, and several decades after the deaths of Ralston, King and Simonds, a scribbled note in Ralston's all but indecipherable handwriting was unearthed from the boxes of his personal papers, which had been turned over to the National Archives of Canada by the Ralston family.

This scrap of paper, believed by some historians to be notes Ralston

made of his conversation with Simonds, was then transcribed to read
as follows:

> ### Simonds — Antwerp
> Told of battle. Showed on map.
> 3rd across canal — Told Spry not to send more — Had enough.
> 2nd nearly to road from Peninsula.
> 4th put in on left — had none on foot — did their best job.
>   To do — Go on neck
>   Across from south bank
>   Don't want to flood
>   peninsula.
> Asked about reinforcements.
> Have been down somewhat. Did commanders speak about it?
> Although have numbers very well up — the casualties are in
> rifle companies and larger proportion of shortages conse-
> quently is in these companies.
> Never got to a point where fighting efficiency impaired.
> Stuart had explained to him.
> I said remustering every man possible. Memo seemed to
> show numbers enough till year end.
> Only other source NRMA, which wouldn't be easy.
> Asked about training. Said any CO would say men not
> trained as he would train them.
> They do talk of training sometimes, but when pinned down
> they really haven't any serious complaint.
> Taken as a whole, standard of training of reinforcements very
> satisfactory.[35]

As the defence minister's own war diary attests, one key sentence
of this note had already been voiced, not by Simonds, on the 10th of
October, but by Ralston himself the week before, on the 2nd of October, in Italy: "No commanding officer," Ralston had said on that
occasion, "was ever satisfied with the standard of training that reinforcements received." Of the remaining lines, there seems far too
much ambiguity of who-said-what-to-whom to entertain serious
interpretations or conclusions from this note. Even had the original

secretarial transcription been accurate, and it was not, the overwhelmingly contradictory and subjective appraisal by Simonds's wartime associates would — in my opinion — render the previous interpretation invalid.* The suggestion that Simonds could have declared the training of the troops to be "very satisfactory" is an incredible statement to attribute to a man who had been deluged by reports to the contrary from all his staff. I do not believe he said this to Ralston. Nor do I believe him capable of sloughing off the training issue on such a flimsy excuse as temperamental commanders. It would have been Ralston, a retired World War I colonel, who could have passed off this archaic piece of B Echelon philosophy to men involved in modern warfare.

In branding front-line commanding officers as prima donnas, Ralston demonstrated how seriously out of touch he had allowed himself to become with the realities of war. Sequestered in Ottawa, isolated by Stuart's communication ban, he seemed not to have comprehended that in battle, yardsticks had become very basic. We commanders had long since stopped caring, if in fact we had ever cared, where and by whom an infantryman had been trained. The only pertinent fact was whether or not he had had any training at all.

Clearly, Guy Simonds knew about the infantry shortages, and he must also have known that ill-trained men were being put into front-line duty against professionals like the German paratroops. Simonds was too shrewd a commander not to be aware of the overall situation.

Brigadier Elliot Rodger, chief of staff of the 2nd Canadian Corps at that time, supports this view: "I wasn't at the meeting," Rodger recalls, "but I know that everybody at headquarters was aware of the reinforcement situation and I know that Guy Simonds would not play

---

* For example, if one accepts the transcript as stating: "Asked about reinforcements.

Have been down somewhat. DID COMMANDERS SPEAK ABOUT IT?" it is obviously Ralston speaking.

But quite a different emphasis can be placed on the remarks when, on closer examination and without the additional punctuation added, the words actually read: "Asked about reinforcements.

"Have been down somewhat. DIV COMMANDERS SPOKE ABOUT IT."

These now become Simonds's words.

up to any politician. Reading between the lines, perhaps Ralston was guilty of wishful thinking," he concluded.[36]

Captain Marshal Stearns, who, as Simonds's ADC was constantly at his side, recollects his senior officer's frustrations in trying to deal with the shortage of infantrymen: "Guy had been exasperated for months over the failure of CMHQ to understand that by the time they had filled our requirements for replacements there were new replacements needed because of casualties which had taken place in the meantime. This always seemed to bother CMHQ because they would say, 'You asked for 2,000 men and we sent you them and now you're asking for another 1,000.' General Simonds alerted Ralston to this problem."[37]*

When Ralston returned to Canada, the complexion of the controversy had altered. The Conn Smythe furor had been quietly diverted. ("He told his people not to proceed with any court martial against me because I had been right," Smythe declared, assuming — incorrectly as it turned out — that the situation was being corrected.[39]) But the nation's focus had been neatly shifted from the battle-readiness of the infantrymen to their sheer numbers. About the standard of training, Ralston was silent. Whether he had persuaded himself that the men in front-line action were adequately trained — or was afraid that the world would discover that they were not — he abandoned the investigation. In so doing, he abandoned the thousands of young untried Canadians flung into war with virtually no chance of survival.

The implications of Ralston's damning scrawl, unsigned and unwitnessed, have been allowed to fester, distorting and tarnishing Simonds's great contribution as army commander.

———•———

Back in Ottawa, on the 19th of October, Ralston reported to the War Committee of the Cabinet that the conscripts must be sent to the front. Still reeling from that thrust, King's government received

---

* In a postwar conversation with Brigadier Richard Malone, Simonds adamantly confirmed the fact that he had informed Ottawa by cable of the shortages.[38]

another body blow. General Stuart, hastily ordered to return to Ottawa and explain the situation, coolly admitted he had made compound errors of calculation in estimating casualties. His three-month estimate (from July 1st to September 30th) predicted 10,967 all ranks. Instead, the actual casualty total was 17,941. The reinforcement pool, Stuart reported, would require an additional 15,000 infantrymen.

On Parliament Hill, a choice had to be made by the government in this tug of war: to commit political suicide by admitting its gross mismanagement of Canada's armed forces, or to commit, in one commander's words, "an act of murder" by sending untrained men to war.

Fighting a delaying action with a shrewdness equal to that of the German Army on the polders, King manoeuvred adroitly to avoid political annihilation. For thirteen days, while the 2nd and the 3rd Canadian Infantry Divisions were fighting for every inch of gain on the stubbornly held banks of the Scheldt, the Government of Canada was locked, even within its own ranks, in battle. King was convinced that the issue was a conspiracy by Defence Minister Ralston to dethrone him. He was prepared to back off his obstinate opposition to conscription, but he would not countenance this terminal threat to his reign. Ralston must go. With the lightning reflexes of a survivor, King applied himself to a deft political manipulation that tricked the minister's supporters into submission while, by resurrecting a letter of resignation submitted some months before, it trapped Ralston into resigning. Immediately, the prime minister appointed the popular, anti-conscriptionist General Andrew McNaughton as minister of national defence. And almost as immediately, McNaughton fired General Stuart. Heading up the Historical Section at CMHQ, Colonel Charles P. Stacey found himself in the uncomfortable role of a witness to another's demise: "Stuart was fired. He never came back to CMHQ. McNaughton wouldn't even let him return to London to clear out his personal effects, so it became my job to catalogue all the documents in General Stuart's office. The desks were covered all over with papers, many of them top secret. It was an awful mess."[40]

The man whom Colonel Stacey terms the "Great Survivor" of those CMHQ days, Price Montague, had a less complimentary epithet for Stuart. "General Montague, who outlasted almost everyone else at CMHQ, called Stuart the 'Great Appeaser,'" Colonel Stacey recollects. "Montague said Stuart was a political man who wanted to keep everybody at the War Office and in Ottawa happy."[41]

With the confirmation that the shortage of trained infantrymen was acute, McNaughton had little choice but to appeal to the 70,000 NRMA men, the "Zombies" as they were known, to try to persuade them to volunteer for overseas duty. It was only when these conscripts defiantly refused to comply that King reversed his stand. Cabinet authorized 15,000 infantry-trained NRMA men for service overseas. The grudging legislation was enacted, but far too late to bolster the depleted Canadian ranks when the need was most urgent, and far too late to replace men who should have been pulled out of the line and properly trained in those chill autumn months of 1944.

The first 10,000 NRMAs were finally ordered to sail in January, a full two months after the infantry manpower crisis had peaked. More than three-quarters of these deserted or went absent without leave; fewer than half of that first contingent ever crossed the ocean. By the time the first draft had arrived in Europe in late February or March, most of the intensive fighting was over. Casualties suffered by the Canadian Army in the drive north to Germany were light. As a result, only about 2,500 of the 15,000 conscripts reached operational units. A captured German leaflet revealed that these facts became useful propaganda for the enemy:

ARE CANADIANS COWARDS?

CANADIANS

You are again to assume the offensive. In case you should come into a hopeless situation don't lose courage. Germany treats prisoners of war according to the Hague and Geneva conventions. Your soldier's honour will be respected.

BETTER TO COME ACROSS
THAN GET A CROSS

Never has anybody dared to assert that. Even Canada's enemies rank Canadians among the world's best soldiers.

AND YET

More than 6,500 out of 15,000 newly drafted Canadians have
deserted before the embarkation to Europe, stated Minister
of Defence McNaughton officially. Are these 6,500 boys cow-
ards? No. They simply ran away to return to their families
and to work. They see no point in fighting in Europe, fighting with Bolshevism as allies. They rather see that all over
Canada, in farming as well as in the lumber business, labour
is lacking, men are wanted, production slackens.[42]

So once again, the tug of war was on between self-serving politicians and bureaucratic military leaders. And once again, the fighting
men were to be the losers.

❖ 11 ❖

The Villagers

I N THIS WAR OF THE POLDERS, THE CASUALTIES WERE NOT LIMITED to the fighting troops. Sometimes the Germans elected to build their defence lines in the core of the villages, and the Canadians would be forced to attack, first with artillery, mortar and machine-gun fire, and finally with infantry hand weapons in streets and houses of the towns.

Few places received the crushing punishment of the villages of Woensdrecht and Hoogerheide. For eighteen days, these "restful and peaceable" communities were ravaged mercilessly, their homes burned to the ground or blasted into bits, church towers pulverized, farms laid waste, animals slaughtered, their people killed.

The first grim days of war began with the bombardments on the night of 6 October. In the days to come the towns, and even certain streets and neighbourhoods of a single town, or just one farmhouse strategically located, would change hands two or three times in a day as the two sides fought fiercely. Nine hundred inhabitants in the area were trapped in the bitter fighting until they were evacuated on the 15th, the eve of the final battle.

The struggle to survive began in the cellars. The lucky residents who had sturdy, concrete-reinforced cellars, made room for those with no safe shelter from the relentless shelling.

In Woensdrecht, the seven members of Jac Suijkerbuijk's family experienced fifteen hours of terror while escaping across the exploding battlefields:

In the morning of Sunday, 8 October, we had already seen the Canadians, but later on it was again the Germans who walked up the streets. We had not a good cellar so we fled to a neighbour's. Jac Suijkerbuijk kept a pig on the roof of his workshop. He wanted to give the pig food because he was anxious that the swine would cry out and betray our position. After a long time at last there was a quiet moment and Jac went, in spite of our warnings, to his swine. He returned to our cellar and there was again plenty of shooting. One of the flying bullets hurt Jac in his leg and he was badly wounded. What must we do? We were uncertain whether we could get any help. We lay Jac on his back with his leg upwards and put on a dressing. In the same manner we passed the following night. The boys of the family Suijkerbuijk tried to sleep on the potatoes down in the cellar. The other people had to sit on the chairs. They could hardly sleep.

The next day, the Canadians again had the upper hand in our neighbourhood. Some soldiers set up a look-out post in the upper storey of our house. When one part of the guards kept watch, the others made use of our beds. This day we hadn't the courage to go in the streets, and we exchanged talk with our neighbours. We could not find any help for the wounded man in the cellar.

Then violent shooting from the Germans began again. The roof of the house was heavily damaged and the upper storey completely shot away. In the kitchen lay a dead Canadian that we covered with a tablecloth. So we had another anxious night with German occupation. In the middle of the night we heard a strange noise. The whole house was on fire and we fled to the garden. It was three o'clock in the morning. The streets were crowded with Germans so we ran across the yard to the next road, two of us carrying Jac. Looking back, we saw an enormous fire in the Raadhuisstraat; about twelve houses were on fire: this made an unforgettable impression on us.

The refugees found a wooden wheelbarrow to transport the wounded man. When shelling became intense they had to roll him quickly into a ditch for safety, there being no time to lift him down properly.

Later, everything became quiet and we thought the war was finished. We sat down on the pavement and smoked an English cigarette that we got the day before from the Canadians. Some time later we went further to the polder. The way was inundated by the Germans. We walked on top of the dyke but the wheelbarrow with the wounded man was wheeled through the water. We passed the cafe-house of the family Vreng; nothing was left except a few black, burned walls. Then we drove to the farmyard of Louis Pijnen. There we met the Germans, again drawing up the artillery. We asked where we could stay. The Germans told us that it was too dangerous. They told us that the farmer had run away and showed us some dead soldiers in the farmyard. We had to go further. As we walked, we noticed that there were slit trenches made with concrete in the dykes. The Germans suddenly shot in our direction. We ran back to the nearest slit trench and plunged in. To our great fright we found in the same pit two Germans, and of course they were not very happy to see us. There we were…nine refugee civilians and two German soldiers in the slit trench together in a hole of less than two square metres. The bullets whistled over the dyke and when the shooting stopped, the two Germans began to shoot from our pit, to the polder.

The family was told to move on to the next polder where everyone would be safe. But first they had to cross a ditch by a small bridge consisting of two tree trunks tied together. It was now seven o'clock in the morning. Just then, shooting broke out again from Hoogerheide and Ossendrecht, with shells exploding to the right and left of the family. Struggling to get the wheelbarrow across the makeshift bridge, Frans Suijkerbuijk, Jac's son, was shot in the head. Then Jac's wife was wounded by shell fragments.

The wound bled violently but we had nothing to tie it up with, only a shirt that we tore up for bandages. The shooting continued for a long time, but finally we found again the courage to go on. We made a flag of a stick and a pair of white pants, to show we were civilians. It was an expedition through hell. Every ten metres we had to fling ourselves to the ground, the exploding shells throwing sand over our bodies. At last, at five o'clock in the afternoon, we reached the farm Lakwijk in the next polder where we were safe. The distance from our house to this point in the polder is about five kilometres. We passed this distance in fifteen hours.[1]

———•———

Captain George Blackburn, FOO with the 4th Canadian Field Regiment, RCA, attached to D Company of the Royal Regiment, came to know the Pijnen brothers, and to learn of their devastating experiences. The following is Blackburn's account of the impact of Black Friday on the villagers:

Sjef Pijnen and his brother Louis shared a little farm, surrounded by high dykes, in the flat polder country of South Beveland Peninsula, but the day the Canadians attacked Woensdrecht, a mile or so to the east, Sjef was alone at the farm for Louis was trapped in the village. For several days Sjef listened to the sounds of battle raging around the village. Sjef watched the shells and mortar bombs reducing to rubble his church and, one after another, all the buildings in Woensdrecht, and despaired his brother would live through that cauldron.

Then one foggy afternoon, a long line of Canadians crawled out into the polders from Woensdrecht, and attacked his farm. The Germans dug in on the dykes surrounding it. Shells poured into his fields, his house and his barn. He felt fortunate to escape with his life to a nearby farm.

One particularly stormy night, a steady stream of stretcher-bearing jeeps went up to his farmhouse and came back loaded with wounded. One of his neighbour's boys drove one of the jeeps all night long. He learned from him the name of the regiment which had suffered such appalling casualties, including all their company commanders, trying to take the next dyke — the Canadian Black Watch.

During a lull in the battle one day, he took a horse and cart up to see if he could rescue any of his farm animals that might still be alive. His cows were all dead in the fields. His three big work horses had died tethered in their stalls in his brick barn. Pulverized brick dust from the exploding shells had settled evenly on every part of them. Not one chicken had lived through the inferno.

The only living animals he could find were a few small pigs which had survived in a small brick lean-to at the back of the house, and some of the Canadian soldiers helped him load them in a crate on his cart. Later his little dog "Fanny" showed up, but it had gone mad from the shelling, and the soldiers had to chase it away for their nerves could not stand its insane screeching.[2]

For twenty-four-year-old Sjef Bakx of Hoogerheide and his fifteen-year-old sister Hilda, the violence of the war broke out in all its grimness that same Sunday, 8 October. It was in this town on this date that von der Heydte's paratrooper fire brigade swarmed down on the Calgary Highlanders, but their bullets found their mark on the civilians as well. Sjef Bakx relates:

With our family we stayed outside in the shelter cellar. By want of space we could unfortunately not make an entrance, not even with an eyehook. Through the many German shells that fell in the neighbourhood, we had not the feeling to be safe. In the farmyard was a great straw heap. There we went in. The cut straw would smother the splinters and the bullets. A shell exploded near the straw heap. My sister was hit by a splinter in her head.

The situation was serious. In my wooden shoes and in a sweater, I ran to the vicarage. The hall was full of Canadians.

I tried to make myself understood that my sister was seriously wounded. Again I ran into the Raadhuisstraat and reached the house of the doctor, van de Kar. I knocked on the door and the doctor opened it himself. Immediately I began, "Doctor, come if you please quickly, because my sister Hilda is seriously wounded."

"Listen, friend, it is impossible, because I have to stay at my post, for possibly more wounded," he said. I was completely beside myself. "Doctor, may I bring my sister to your house?" The doctor said it was all right and I left. At the crossroads of Nieuweweg, Raadhuisstraat, Duinstraat and Antwerpseweg it was havoc. In the middle of the crossing lay three dead Canadian soldiers and another badly wounded.

At the municipal hall, I met the village policeman, P. Aarden. I asked him if he had something to transport my wounded sister, a stretcher or something like that. Yes he had. I took the stretcher under my arm, and ran away. A Canadian hospital-soldier who had seen this followed me. At home, he dressed my sister's wound and made an examination. We laid her on the stretcher, and he accompanied us as a second stretcher-bearer.

We got her to the doctor, but he asked me to return the same evening because the situation was very precarious and she might not live till the next morning. The same night, at dusk, I returned with some bread and milk in my bag. In the Raadhuisstraat I was held up by some Canadians who were shooting. They let me by, but further down the road, almost at the address of the doctor, I heard a German voice behind the thick oak tree and I was ordered to come to their side. If not, I would be shot. They took me to a house and there I was interrogated and they kicked me in the face. There was I, quite alone, in the centre of the enemy. It was forbidden to say or do anything, even to dig myself a slit trench. Suddenly there was intense machine-gun fire. A German soldier wanted to withdraw but he was ordered back. The lieutenant colonel hissed between his teeth: *"Krieg ist Krieg"* ("War is War").

At daybreak I got away and finally got back to Doctor

van de Kar. I heard that my sister was dead. Distraught, I returned home. A few days later I was in Ossendrecht and accidentally I met the Canadian hospital-soldier. Shyly I shook his hand, thanking him for his spontaneous helping of the transport of my wounded sister.

The village doctor, van de Kar, who had through the occupation years cared for wounded Allies escaping through the Pilot Line, now found himself ministering to the wounds of his enemy:

On the night of 7 October we were suddenly awakened by heavy knocking on the back door. It was two Canadians, armed to the teeth, apparently scouts. By afternoon, the Canadians had disappeared. Great was our disappointment when in the afternoon we heard again the scraping of German boots on the tiled floors. Leaving the cellar, we saw camouflaged German steel helmets everywhere. Alternately we heard the Germans and the Canadians. Both sides tried to make a stronghold from the house. They were scary and fearful hours.

On Sunday, 8 October, a severely wounded girl was brought into the house. It is a pity, but I could not save her. The battle intensified tremendously that day. The Canadians were fighting for the house with all the means they had. The house was very important as a lookout over the rest of the battlefield. But the Germans were strongly resisting. They did not want to give up their positions. Wounded soldiers were brought into the rooms on the first and second floor. They were moaning from pain and begging for help. In view of my medical obligation I was applying emergency treatments. Several times I went with them to the battlefield to collect wounded persons. It was a complete bloodbath.

Curiously, there were two separate German forces in the area at that time, neither communicating with the other. The Hermann Goering occupation troops were equally despised by the townfolk and by the professional paratroop fighting men. But it was in the ample figure of one Mrs. Soffers-Plompe that the occupiers finally met their nemesis.

In spite of the noise and clamour of the shellfire and mortar bombs, Mrs. Soffers-Plompe, who was at that time pregnant, went from the shelter to her home to get some food. She came upon a large stack of bread piled up on the pavement in front of her house, deposited there for the Germans. Now it happened that Mrs. Soffers-Plompe was carrying home a large, white bedspread that she had just crocheted. She loaded this bedspread-sack full of bread. With the breadsack trailing behind her, this very pregnant woman stole past three firing German batteries to reach the shelter, by then filled with twenty-five hungry persons.

For a week, the people of Woensdrecht and Hoogerheide existed within the vortex of the raging battle. Living conditions became appalling, as one villager relates: "During the first days of the battle we were still able to cook. The meat of shot cows was prepared in a hurry for consumption. Also the milk was cooked. Later on this cooking was forbidden, because the Germans were frightened of smoking chimneys. From then on, the milk was consumed uncooked. With some sugar and Belgian pudding-powder, the milk was given some flavour. For dessert we ate some apples."

Later, the ground became littered with dead animals, but fear of contamination restrained the hungry people from eating the putrid flesh. By then, babies cried for the drops of milk that only desperate, life-threatening forages could find. Many people fled, some north through the German lines to Bergen op Zoom, others to friends or relatives behind the Canadian line at Ossendrecht.

Then, on Sunday, the 15th of October (the day before the RHLI attack), Doctor van de Kar was called out of church during Mass by his wife. The Red Cross had sent an urgent message. By order of the German occupation force, the remainder of the population of Woensdrecht had to be evacuated to Bergen op Zoom immediately. Mrs. Groffen-van Oers, with her husband and two small children, recalled joining the miserable band of refugees:

It was a complete exodus, a real marching out of the population. Human legs were the only means of transport. First the nurses went by, one carrying a white flag, and after a whole row of village people, men, women and children, a few

of them also with white flags. Everybody was carrying bags
and suitcases or just some clothes under their arms. Also there
were some people with pushcarts or wheelbarrows and sometimes a horse and carriage. It was sad to see. Some people
had difficulties to say farewell to their homes and especially
to their animals. One man gave his goat the most precious
place in the house, surrounded by food: he hid the animal in
the master's cupboard-bed, hoping to find the animal still
alive on his return.

I looked back once more at the polders. The bombs were
dropping there like big burning cigars or balls of fire from
the sky. The dykes were burning; there was not much left
of Woensdrecht.

More than eighty refugees were escorted by the Red Cross to
safety. It was a sombre moment for all. Louis Soffers, who had
received a head wound two days earlier, shepherded his family along.
His daughter and two others had also been wounded. But his heart
was heavy for another reason. Earlier in the day — it was Friday the
13th — he had gone home to load the sculpture of the "Holy Heart"
in his barrow. There, on the floor, were four Canadians, guarded by
a Finn with an automatic pistol. "They say nothing, but in their anxious glance I see supplication," Soffers thinks, "but I am powerless."

Leo Timmermans remembers the nightmarish evacuation as a
horror worse than the mortar and shellfire of Woensdrecht: "We suddenly saw a number of English planes coming in our direction. They
dove upon us, firing. The bullets hit the cobblestones of the road as
we pressed against the embankment for protection. The planes went
away. We walked a few hundred metres, but they returned, again in
a nosedive with machine-gun fire close to us. We fled into a house.
When it was quiet we continued on our way. The same shooting
repeated itself later. 'What could be the meaning of these shootings?'
we wondered. Evidently, not far from us were also Germans."

Red Cross officials are to be credited with leading this particular
band of forty-three civilians safely through the misguided strafing, but
not without several critical moments. "The people would flee to the
woods during the attack," the Red Cross commander reported, "but

the woods were sown with landmines. By resolute action, holding the refugees together, the leader guarded them from even more misery."

Finally, the terrified folk completed their journey. Just eight km from raging war, the tranquility of Bergen op Zoom was overwhelming, as Leo Timmermans remembers: "It seemed we were in another world. Here we saw children playing in their Sunday clothes, and for the first time we realized it is Sunday. The people of Bergen op Zoom barely realized the misery and catastrophe only eight km away, and at first looked on us with suspicion as if we were dirty and grubby beggars."

------◆------

Some of the people of Woensdrecht, the older ones, refused to leave. One of these was Cornelis van Beek. Despite the entreaties of his wife and children, Cornelis could not bring himself to abandon the home where he had been born, nor the animals sheltered in his barn. A German pistol finally forced him out.

Inevitably, some people missed the evacuation warning. In the Hooghuis, a former convent on Woensdrecht Hill that was now the farm of the family Lakwijk-Snepvangers, the occupants could not be reached with the evacuation order. The strong brick cellar of this rampart sheltered twenty-six inhabitants, including an eleven-day-old infant and the child's father, who was in hiding from the Gestapo. None of these could forget the Battle of Woensdrecht:

> On Sunday, 15 October, we stayed in our cellar. This day we saw nobody. After that, on Monday, the great battle around Woensdrecht was in full swing. Suddenly we heard a strange clattering. There were no more Germans, but eight Canadians rushed into our home and quietly took possession. We were happy and could hardly realize that we were free. But then, suddenly, hell broke out. There was clamour and violent machine-gun fire all around us.
>
> In a fight of man against man, the Germans tried to reconquer their position. Machine pistols rattled until their magazines were empty. In bayonet fighting doors and cupboards were cracked.

With the head in the hands and the fingers in the ears, we heard this terrible noise from the cellar. How much time this misery took, we can't remember. It seemed this was our last hour on earth.

But finally the noise died away and to our great regret the Canadians [had] lost the battle. One of them was dead in the kitchen, the other seven were prisoners of war. How many the losses were on the German side, we don't know. After this terrible scene, we were ordered to evacuate our cellar while some German officers set up radio transmitters. But like a miracle, they left and we stayed on in our cellar.

How monstrous the Germans behaved after this attack. In the Steenstraat they took two men out of the cellar, Mr. Dons and Mr. Kil, without any form of trial and shot them down behind the hedge of their house. In the same street, at the family Iriks, they threw a hand grenade in the cellar. The result of it was that the seventeen-year-old son, Petrus, was killed and his father seriously wounded.* The fear grew visibly among us. But we waited for our liberators. Shortly after that we were liberated. The "occupiers" had gone for good, but we heard from them still for a long time. First from their mortars, later on via flying bombs.

Gradually, the people of Woensdrecht filtered back to their homes. For most, there was only rubble to be found. Of the fifty families left in the village, thirty people had been killed in the Battle of Woensdrecht and countless others wounded. Louis Soffers met the first Canadians in vehicles, decorated now with flowers. He thought, "Now I know we are free, and the English cigarettes taste excellent (after the first one)." Soffers then returned to his house, but it had been reduced to a rubbish-heap. Cornelis van Beek had had eight cows; only two were left, both wounded, and had to be destroyed. His pigs were all

---

* These citizens had apparently made the mistake of coming out of their cellars and greeting the Canadian liberators when they first arrived, and this was observed by German patrols. When the Canadians were beaten back again, the Germans killed every civilian who had been observed fraternizing with the enemy.

killed, his barn levelled. Amazingly, his farmhouse, which had served as RHLI battalion headquarters throughout the battle, still stood, with only the battle-scars of bullets to attest to the constant firing.

Seventy-two houses had been totally destroyed by the fire; 355 houses were so heavily damaged by mortar and shellfire that they could not be repaired. Two hundred and thirty-five more were damaged to some extent, but these were ransacked first by the Germans, then by the Allies.

This village that depended on farming for its livelihood was ruined. The crops had been destroyed when the Germans opened the sluice gates on the 2nd of September and let the Scheldt flow back onto the polders. What crops they had managed to salvage had been lost. The great food warehouse had burned to the ground.

But it was the slaughter of their livestock that cut to the hearts of these people. Missing or dead, and the account is precise, were 146 horses, 329 cattle, 506 pigs, 448 goats, 3348 chickens, and 3,461 rabbits.

Then a new misfortune befell the people of Woensdrecht: "We were requested by the Canadians to leave again, this time due to danger from typhoid. Dead pigs, sheep, cows and horses were everywhere. The smell was sometimes unbearable.

"Once again we gathered a few personal belongings and went to Bergen op Zoom, this time by truck. In the meantime Bergen op Zoom was also liberated."

Against this catalogue of misery, there was one cheerful event: Mrs. Soffers-Plompe gave birth to a baby girl. For the family Soffers and for the Canadian soldiers it was a joyful occasion: "Many Canadians who were in the neighbourhood came to admire the baby. They didn't come with empty hands. They presented mother and baby with chocolate and many pieces of soap."

12

Race Along the Polders

A T LAST THE POLDER RACE WAS ON. AND EIGHTEEN DAYS AFTER ITS
first advance on Woensdrecht, the 2nd Canadian Infantry Division could finally unleash its drive toward Walcheren. Clearly, it was to be a wretched battle, the cold and wet and constant danger only heightened by the news that Brigadier Keefler had challenged his three brigades to a grim contest. If "Big Sunray,"* as he was known, wanted a race, he would have one. These fifteen thousand men wanted not a moment more of polder warfare than was necessary.

The first objective was the historic Beveland Canal that bisected the peninsula, some fifteen km from the start line. The task was given to the 4th Brigade. Immediately, a major stumbling block appeared. The retreating Germans had blown every bridge, mined every field and road and booby-trapped barns and farmhouses. They had fortified every dyke intersection, burrowing narrow slits through the slopes for machine-gun muzzles. In short, they had pulled out every delaying tactic in the book to stall the Canadian advance.

South Beveland topography was ideally suited to a defensive battle but was hell for attacking troops in the damp, miserable fall of 1944. Since most of the area was below sea level, the land was honeycombed with canals, dykes and polders. In ordinary times, the canals functioned to drain the land and provide water communication

---

* Sunray was the codename for a commander at any level. Thus in an infantry battalion, Sunray was the CO, Big Sunray was the brigade commander, and Big Big Sunray was the division commander, etc.

routes. The dykes were essential to the creation of polders, areas of land reclaimed from the sea for agricultural purposes. These dykes, up to five metres high by ten wide, controlled the water levels in the canals and drainage ditches. Roads ran along the tops of the dykes and were the only routes for land transportation and communication.

The polders formed large fields varying from three hundred metres square to as many as a thousand. Early on in the fighting, the Germans had opened the sluice gates at high tide, inundating the polders at the neck of the isthmus with sea water which lay, in some places, just a few inches deep and in others, several metres. Then, following the RHLI victory at Woensdrecht, the German High Command admitted defeat, authorizing more extensive inundations: "A permanent recapture of the land connection with Walcheren can no longer be expected. O.B. West, therefore, consents to the flooding of the area."[1]

Infantrymen would find it increasingly difficult to traverse the polderland; transport would find it impossible. The only other place for the Canadian tanks and transport to move was along the tops of the dykes. But even when the Germans were driven back and these elevated roads were freed, these passages were found to be ill-suited for carrying large elements of tracked or wheeled traffic. They became, and remained, single lanes of deep mud.

The Germans established strongpoints at the intersections of dykes and covered their approaches with well-sited infantry and antitank weapons, thus setting up killing grounds for any attacking force. With their slit trenches dug into the reverse sides of dykes, they themselves were impregnable, virtually immune to artillery and mortar fire.

To make these strongpoints even more unassailable, the Germans put great effort into laying Teller mines to destroy vehicles, anti-personnel mines to repel intruding infantry, and Schu-mines which were designed to maim an infantryman who happened to step on one. The last mentioned could not be detected by conventional sweep equipment because they were made of wood. On occasion, the Nazis went so far as to lay Teller mines with an additional detonator so that they would explode while being lifted. Another fiendish explosive was the Ratchet mine, a delayed-action Teller mine laid in the road. The first half a dozen vehicles that ran over it would be unharmed, but the seventh or eighth would be blown to bits.* Neutralizing these mines to clear the way for the riflemen was demanding, highly dangerous work, executed by sappers and demolition platoons.

Any diabolical device seemed to be fair game including booby-trapping their own or Allied dead.

The Germans were also ingenious in their use of camouflage. Pill-boxes were painted to look like houses, and concrete casements resembled haystacks. Dutch farmers were forced to paint large numbers on the roofs of their houses and barns. When the Canadians approached one of these numbered locations, the German guns and mortars had easy and quick target identification.

The Canadians learned to be wary of tree stumps, especially large ones located prominently with a panoramic view of the surrounding countryside. Too often, a German soldier was hidden inside this clever piece of staging, either noting our movements for future reference or directing fire upon us.

Adolf Hitler had dictated the chief objective of all the German forces at the Scheldt: the opening of Antwerp Harbour must be denied or at least delayed for as long as possible. Tactics were therefore designed to accomplish this objective. The Germans made skilled use of obstacles. Wherever possible, a main defensive position would be sited behind an antitank obstacle, preferably one containing water. In the Battle of the Scheldt, there was never a lack of such water defences — the Leopold, Albert and Beveland canals among others.

Usually the Germans would position outposts a kilometre or two ahead of a defence line to compel the advancing force to deploy, and thus make the attackers more vulnerable to German harassment. When they had successfully held up the Allied advance, the Germans would then withdraw slowly into their main position on the canal. They fought hard at every fortified post. They counterattacked strenuously to try to catch us off balance. Then, if the pressure became too much, they would skillfully withdraw to take over another previously

---

* An early victim was 6th Infantry Brigade Commander Brigadier Guy Gauvreau, whose jeep struck a mine while he was on a reconnaissance mission, seriously wounding him and breaking the leg of his Intelligence officer, Captain Maurice Gravel of the FMR.

prepared defensive position, possibly only a few thousand metres back.

As the only possible approach was straight up a dyke, this use of tactics presented the Canadian forces with the monumental task of attacking these strongpoints on a one-man front, dyke by wretched dyke, without respite. This was bad enough, but when it had to be done in cold, driving rain, through ankle-deep mud, with little hope of a change of dry clothes or a warm place to sleep, not knowing from one moment to the next if you would be dead or alive, it was a new form of hell.

This was polder warfare.

At first light on the 24th of October, the Royal Regiment led the attack along the narrow neck of land, securing the start line as the Essex Scottish advanced with two armoured columns. Seven field and medium artillery regiments supported the assault. As the Royals moved up, they noted gratefully that even the guns of the 3rd Canadian Infantry Division were firing in support from the south side of the Scheldt.

The first lesson of the polders was the impossibility of moving armoured vehicles up the narrow dykes. "About six hundred yards past the railway the first three [armoured vehicles] were knocked out by a well-placed enemy gun, and the armoured drive came to an abrupt halt," recounts the Essex Scottish History. "The start line was crossed on foot."[2]

And on foot the 4th Brigade stayed, for forty-eight hours of plodding through the salt marshes in the icy, relentless rain, hammering at each fierce crossroad with no cover and no space to manoeuvre for any form of protection from the enemy defensive fire. The child's game of leapfrog had become a necessary wartime tactic as each battalion forged westward, each making hard-earned gains before handing over its position to the battalion coming up from behind. There simply was not room in the narrow entrance to the peninsula for any more troops than one or two companies to lead the pursuit.

Prisoners were bagged by the dozens. Lacking transport to move them back, the Canadians at one point ordered fifteen Germans, as muddy and miserable as themselves, to lie flat on the twelve-metre-high sloping sides of a dyke. A sudden direct hit from their own mortars killed and wounded several of them.

Evacuating Canadian casualties, for much the same reason, was a formidable challenge in polder warfare. Major Cliff Richardson, medical officer to the Essex Scottish during the Scheldt campaign, recalls:

> Casualties first had to be carried by stretcher-bearers onto the dykes. We were all on foot out there, and the medical arrangements weren't very good. There were very few houses where we could set up RAPs.
>
> Once we got them to the RAP, we would send them out by jeep to a forward surgical unit or field dressing station, and from there to a casualty collecting post and back to the clearing station en route to a field hospital. Many of the fellows had been in low-lying land and they were in shock from their wounds and from the wet October weather.
>
> There were quite a few casualties amongst the stretcher-bearers who were getting the wounded on the field. They didn't get much recognition for what they did, but they weren't looking for it, either. A lot of them were conscientious objectors who had volunteered for overseas duty but who didn't believe in fighting or killing anybody. But they weren't afraid, and they made dandy stretcher-bearers. There was one fellow from Kitchener, his name was Gale, and I remember he was really fearless. He'd go anywhere. It gave the riflemen a lot of confidence to know that the stretcher-bearers would come for them if they got into trouble.[3]

One such stretcher-bearer was Corporal Wes Burrows of the RHLI. For a while, Burrows had been having an easy time of it, spending much of his pre–D-Day service investigating Britain's pubs while officially listed as CO's driver. On the side, he played a pretty hot trumpet with his own dance band.

Given the sack for over-zealous "research," Burrows volunteered as stretcher-bearer, transferring his energies into driving a stretcher-jeep onto shell-covered fields to pick up casualties. For more than two hundred wounded Canadians, the sight of Wes Burrows plunging through lethal fire to reach their sides was an incomparable memory.

I got out two hundred, easy, and sometimes I'd help out others as they ran into problems too — like, with another company that couldn't get the casualties out, I'd go and get them. It got a little hairy at times. I lost four jeeps from mortar and shellfire and once a mine blew it up.

You knew the job had to be done. There were chaps there to be picked up and it was just in your mind to get them. You got a little scared maybe when you were on your own going out there, but at the time that you were taking them back you had it in your head to get them out as fast as you could. Those mortars — the faster you'd drive, the closer they'd keep coming; you'd swear they were just trying to catch you. I had the Red Cross flag, but it was drawing fire. I took the flag down.

In Antwerp, Burrows became something of a celebrity with the local populace. While on duty on the docks, he darted out into the middle of a bridge, dodging a hail of enemy machine-gun fire, to rescue a severely wounded Belgian. "He was there and somebody had to get him out. I looked after our own wounded first and then I went back and got him and I brought him back to his home. He was alive. I think his leg got blown up pretty bad. His family owned a bar in Antwerp and they treated me pretty good after that," Burrows remembers.

It was shortly after the RHLI moved out from Antwerp that the Hamilton man got word that he was going home: "They sent home everybody that was over there for five years. We got thirty days' leave. But there weren't too many of us. We lost so many at Dieppe and then we lost a lot going up through France and Belgium. There weren't many left."

Burrows' bravery was rewarded with the MM, the Military Medal. On his way home, after his five years of overseas duty, he had a pretty good feeling: "I thought I had been doing something to help. I had no other training to do anything else." But on the troop ship, rifle drill was called and Burrows, clumsily wrestling with the gun bolt, was hauled up by an English sergeant major: "What do you think you're doing! Hold your head up! What a pitiful sight you are!"

"I guess there were some people who thought I wasn't much of a soldier without a gun," Burrows concluded.[4]

———————•———————

Then it was the turn of the RHLI to leapfrog into the lead, moving through positions that had been won by the Royals. The Rileys noted that in the confusion created by a nighttime offensive, enemy resistance was collapsing. However, the darkness caused problems for the Canadians, too, as they had to peer intently for any tell-tale signs of bricks dislodged in the roads to hide buried mines. Later on, during the second day of the marathon thrust, the riflemen observed gratefully that the peninsula was wide enough to allow them to progress on a two-battalion front. By late afternoon of the 26th, all three battalions of the 4th Brigade had reached their objective on the banks of the thirty-metre-wide Beveland Canal, only to find that all the bridges across the waterway had been blown. In the advance, six hundred Germans had been taken prisoner; a number more had been killed. The exhausted Canadians settled into local villages and farms for a twenty-four-hour rest.

It was now the turn of the 6th Brigade to leapfrog through the 4th, taking over the lead in this miserable race. The brigade's first task was to forge crossings over the broad canal, liberating several canal villages in the process. Some of the towns, abandoned by the enemy in the face of the advance, were taken easily with few casualties and little damage to the centuries-old buildings. Others the Germans stubbornly defended, and these hamlets became the innocent pawns in this tug of war. The gamble, for the Canadians, was to determine whether a village's fortifications were still manned by the enemy. On the night of the 26th–27th, SSR Major Victor Schubert, himself a bit of a gambler,* took a chance that he could lead his company in an amphibious crossing without drawing enemy fire. The gamble nearly backfired, as he recalls:

———————

* Schubert's most audacious gamble was in Normandy when he had been captured by a German patrol. Although wounded, he had bluffed his captor into handing over his weapon and surrendering.

There was a village on the far side. We did a reconnaissance on it — the CO, company commanders and myself — and it didn't look as if it was occupied. So we got a little bold, strolling up and down the bank.

That night we got the boats down and started across the canal. The plan was that if the Germans opened fire on us I was to call down a lot of fire on the village. They opened up all right, so I called for fire, everything we had. I'm afraid it pretty well wiped out that village. But it was necessary; the crossing was successful and we kept on going from there.[5]

The SSRs remember another incident in a lighter vein that occurred during the night of the canal crossing:

One of the very efficient scouts was interrogating prisoners with the initial question *"Haben sie Geld?"* From there on the questions concerned such military objects as watches, cameras and Lugers. By morning the scouts were unknowingly the richest men in the Canadian Army. An unknown officer casually asked one of them if he had picked up any souvenir notes of large denominations, and the innocent scout honestly replied: "Yes, sir," and proceeded to show off his many stuffed pockets. "Oh," said the officer, doing some fast mental arithmetic. "Thousand-guilder notes? I haven't any of those, and these 500-guilder notes are pretty, too, aren't they? My, they will add nicely to my collection, do you mind?" The scout who thought a guilder was of no value, like the German marks, kept on giving the officer all he wanted. Later the scout discovered that a guilder was worth forty cents. He had given a fortune away to an astute gentleman. Later the scout was heard telling a reinforcement, "You got to watch them officers, son, they're sly."[6]

To their right, the Queen's Own Camerons of Canada met fierce fire as they advanced along the top of the dykes towards Yerseke, a picturesque harbour world-famous for its oyster and mussel beds.

It happened that as the Canadians were approaching, the villagers were confronted with a grave crisis. The German commandant of the garrison, facing a critical shortage of manpower to build the defences for the retreating forces, had issued an edict. All male civilians between the ages of sixteen and forty were to report for forced labour. If they failed to comply, the village would be burned to the ground.

Within a few hours, two fishermen from the village had escaped into the marshes, following the shoreline they knew so well until they found the Camerons eight km to the east. There they explained the emergency and told the Canadians that the German garrison was lightly defended. Six hundred men from Yerseke village were saved by the ensuing prompt action of the Camerons.

At the same time the FMR, advancing on the left flank, arrived in the village of Hansweert where the Beveland Canal flows into the West Scheldt. Centuries of international trans-shipping through the town had made its citizens multilingual, so the miserably wet, homesick French-Canadians received a warm welcome in their native tongue.

On a certain day there landed on a nearby beach an officer of such sartorial splendour that at least one Canadian had to look down at his own dishevelment with embarrassment. The encounter is well remembered by Captain T.R. Wilcox of the Royal Regiment of Canada who came upon this Scottish officer on a reconnaissance mission of South Beveland landing sites. The meeting made an unforgettable impression on the tattered, mud-soaked Canadian:

> The brigade major stepped out of his boat; he was really a startling sight. We were absolutely filthy with mud and rain, and he was absolutely spotless, packsack neatly packed as though he had just come off parade. By then we had all lost ours. He had his pistol in a neatly balanced web holster; I had mine in my hip pocket. His maps were carefully packed in his map case; mine was stuck in my breast pocket. His boots gleamed with polish; I was wearing turned-down rubber boots. He must have thought we were the dregs. He asked if I could direct him to battalion headquarters. I did better than that. I escorted him to battalion headquarters. I was taking no chances on losing such a beautiful specimen of a soldier to the German Army. He was really a startling sight; I felt badly that we looked so terrible.[7]

The officer was on the staff of the 157th Brigade, 52nd (Lowland) Division, scouting prospective landing areas for an amphibious invasion in support of the Canadian assault. And at 0330 hours on the 26th of October, the largest flotilla of Buffaloes* and other eccentric landing craft ever assembled for action swam into the black Scheldt waters. Bearing the two brigades of the 52nd (Lowland) Division, led off by the 6th Cameronians and the Royal Scots Fusiliers, the invasion craft embarked under the protection of an intense artillery barrage, landing on the south bank of the peninsula some ten km west of the Beveland Canal. Their objective was to form a pincer movement with the 2nd Canadian Division to cut off the German escape route from South Beveland toward Walcheren.

Fresh to battle, and in fact fresh to the war, this Scottish Division was placed under the command of the 1st Canadian Army for this final stage of the Scheldt battle.

The Scottish unit contained several Canadian officers, men who had volunteered in 1944 to serve with British battalions when severe casualties had depleted them of junior officers.** The Scots were undoubtedly accustomed to idiosyncratic Canadians by then; now they yearned to become as familiar with their turned-down rubber boots as well. For within a few days of their exposure to polder warfare, it was the Scots who envied the Canadians — mud and all: "You were up to your knees in water if you got off the roads at all," one Canadian lieutenant attached to the 7th Cameronians said. "What really bothered us was that the Canadians had been issued knee-high rubber boots, while the British had never been issued any. Finally, I went over and scrounged enough for my platoon — and got in trouble for it!"[8]

It had been, as the division noted, a "fantastic introduction to real war for mountain troops" — for, ironically, having done all its training in mountain warfare, the 52nd was seeing its first action below

---

* A Buffalo could transport thirty men, either "swimming" in water or crawling on land.

** Six hundred and seventy-three Canadians, mainly lieutenants, served as "Can-loan" officers in almost every British division and in every major battle in northwest Europe. Nearly 20 percent of the Canadian volunteers were killed; 75 percent became casualties.

sea level. The invading fleet had crossed the fifteen-km stretch of water with little enemy opposition until it met heavy mortar fire near the beaches. (The deputy brigade commander and his batman were the only survivors of a direct hit on their Buffalo.)

Now baptized, the Lowlanders established their first headquarters in Oudeland, where they soon had an unlikely visitor, Pieter Kloosterman, general leader of the OD (the *Orde Dienst* or Underground Organization in charge of South and North Beveland whose seven hundred members were actively engaged in Resistance for Zeeland Province) and commander of the Group South Beveland. He had come to meet his liberators.

When Kloosterman had heard in his hometown of Nisse that the British had landed some six km away, he led a band of his men through the German lines to meet the unit. With the occupation forces collapsing under the Allied sweep, each day saw more towns and villages of his beloved South Beveland freed at last. Through an interpreter, he offered the services of his band as guides. Now Kloosterman could fight a new kind of war, not furtively from secret cellars but openly, in field headquarters and on battlefields.

But the fifty-one-year-old Resistance fighter received an unlikely welcome from his Allied liberators. A newly appointed IO, replacing the intelligence officer who had been killed earlier during the invasion, had apparently not been briefed on the role of the Dutch Resistance. In the absence of the commander of the 6th Cameronians, Lieutenant Colonel A. Ian Buchanan-Dunlop, Kloosterman was thrown in jail:

> My battalion had very early contact with the Dutch Underground Resistance leader during the assault on Beveland. He had turned up at our first established battalion headquarters in my absence. I do not recall that we had been warned of this likely support and my battalion IO, who had been appointed that morning owing to casualties, incarcerated in a cellar the Dutch Resistance leader as a suspected spy. I cannot now remember his name, nor the extent of his command, but he was certainly the leader for the whole of Beveland, at least. He was a splendid man.[9]

The situation was untangled without rancour. Pieter Kloosterman appointed some of his men to stay on with the battalion as
guides as it advanced steadily toward the causeway connecting South
Beveland to the island of Walcheren.

Climbing aboard the only transportation he had — his bicycle —
Kloosterman entered the village of 's-Heer Abtskerke. He recounts the
hair-raising story of his first combat experience with the Canadians:

> A young lieutenant from a reconnaissance formation had
> taken his platoon to a position under the trees in the village
> centre. The local parson and a "person-in-hiding" brought
> me to this officer. The Dutch gentleman told him who I was
> and the officer asked me to give him all necessary informa-
> tion about the enemy positions etc. in the vicinity of 's-Heer
> Arendskerke. As it was difficult driving through that area with
> its narrow secondary roads the officer asked me to accompany
> him as his guide. I thought it to be my duty to inform him
> that going through the area would be a reckless manoeuvre
> as it represented about forty square km of open, flat terrain,
> so that one single German battery could control the entire
> area. The officer thought I was afraid, but I merely informed
> the officer that I was ready whenever he was and climbed with
> my bicycle on the hindmost armoured car. About 800 metres
> from a level crossing we noticed it was controlled by a Ger-
> man 88mm gun. Our commanding officer thought that this
> antitank gun was deserted, but all of a sudden I saw a flash
> and the almost simultaneous scream of a shell was heard. Our
> party of twelve immediately took cover behind the armoured
> cars. Very soon a second shot was fired, which fell some fif-
> teen metres short. A third knocked out the first armoured car
> and the fifth shot took care of the hindmost armoured car, the
> one with my bicycle. Under heavy enemy rifle and machine-
> gun fire, we were forced to crawl back to our start line, using
> the muddy ditches to stay out of sight. I was wet through.[10]

While the 2nd Division had been making its way westward along
South Beveland, the three squadrons of the 8th Reconnaissance

Regiment (14th Canadian Hussars) under the command of Lieutenant Colonel Mowbray Alway had been employed along the main axis of advance and also as a protective screen on the right. Kloosterman's next encounter with the unit, considerably more productive, was with an officer of a different squadron. The result of that meeting was an unusual diversion that added no slight excitement to the right flank of the battalions.

On the 31st of October, a squadron of the 8th Recce Regiment, commanded by Major C.R.H. (Dick) Porteous, was informed through the Resistance that the Germans were using the island of North Beveland as a transfer point for escapees from Walcheren. North Beveland, Porteous discovered, was an island eleven km long and five in width lying in the East Scheldt, a bare one hundred metres north of the South Beveland shore. The island had not been strongly fortified, although it still held a number of gun emplacements and casemates and was believed to have a garrison of two hundred men as well as German troops awaiting evacuation. The prospect of capturing them, although not on his set list of objectives, was tantalizing to Porteous.

Armed with this information given by the Netherlanders, Major Porteous led his squadron to a ferry station on the coast where they commandeered a barge and a number of fishing boats. By the next night they and their vehicles had navigated the narrow crossing without incident, taking for support a heavy mortar company and a company of machine guns, both from the Toronto Scottish Regiment. They were joined by about twenty-five armed members of the Dutch Resistance. On arrival, the force captured a hospital ship commanded by a German naval officer.

On the morning of the 2nd of November, Lieutenant Colonel Alway and Major Porteous had the squadron wholly assembled on North Beveland Island, ready to take on the German Army, or what was left of it (numbering some 250 men and two officers in the town of Kamperland). An ultimatum was sent to the enemy commander demanding his capitulation. Colonel Alway tells the story:

> The commander said he would fight to the death, but we had the Toronto Scottish lob in a few of their heavy mortar bombs. Then I asked 84 Group for air support. They were

really attacking Walcheren but they got all the twelve to eighteen planes going to Walcheren to fly low so the Jerries would think that they were supporting us. I sent word to the garrison that the Typhoons were coming, and if they didn't get the hell out they were going to get it. The Typhoons did come, barrelling down the highway at about fifty feet and the Germans all folded because they were frightened to death of them. The commander changed his mind and came out in a hurry.

In this action the 8th Recce captured 367 enemy with no casualties. The task still remained of cleaning up the eastern end of North Beveland where it was rumoured that an escape would take place that night. Alway recalls the frustration of that long wait:

The thing that broke my heart was that they were still evacuating Germans at the end of the island. Each night, a German destroyer would come in and take them off. We had our own 6-pounders; we had eight of them. I took those down and we dug them right into the dyke, camouflaged them, and then I issued instructions. If this vessel had come in that night I had two guns that were going to fire at the bridge with HE. There were going to be about four guns just firing at the water line with armour-piercing shells, plus a couple more where we estimated the rudder would be. If she had come, we would have sunk her sure as hell. We would have surprised her; we were at the right spot; we were camouflaged and we were just praying she'd come. But she didn't.[11]

So concluded the last known attempt by a reconnaissance regiment of the Canadian Army to sink a German naval destroyer. It would have been one hell of an accomplishment.

The arms of the pincer were closing in as Scottish and Canadian troops moved quickly westward toward their rendezvous at the

Walcheren Causeway. The enemy was retreating, in some cases just an hour or two ahead of them. After a stiff fight, the Cameronians liberated Ellewoutsdijk on the south coast of the peninsula but met little opposition thereafter. In rapid succession, the towns and villages of central Beveland — Goes, Nisse, Nieuwdorp and Heinkenszand — fell to the Canadian troops, now warming to the finish line. Major Tim Beatty sent some Royals to intercept a column of Germans "clunking down the road with all their equipment in horse-drawn wagons. So we just got into the ditch on both sides of the road, fired in the air and they all surrendered. It happened twice that way. The first time, we sent the horses and wagons along with the prisoners back to battalion HQ. But the CO got on the blower to say he didn't want any more horses or wagons. 'Next time, send the prisoners but get rid of those horses,' he said."[12]

A highlight for RHLI scout platoon commander Lieutenant John Williamson was the night he was sent out to arrest one German and came back with fifty-five:

> Three German soldiers came into the RHLI HQ saying that there was a German captain out there who wanted to surrender, but he would only surrender to an officer. The CO kept one German behind as hostage and sent my patrol off with the remaining two Germans to get the captain. It was kind of nerve-wracking. We had to walk down the centre of this road that was all lit up by burning barns around us. Eventually, the Germans came to a barn and called, "*Hauptman, Hauptman!*" and this German officer came out. He was wearing riding breeches and had his pistol at his side. But at first he wouldn't give it up. He looked at me and said, "He's not a captain, he's only a lieutenant." But Joe Gates, one of my scouts who spoke German said, "Our colonel says that if we are not back in an hour he is going to put in a battalion attack on this place — and you'll have no chance to surrender to a lieutenant or anyone else."
>
> Finally the captain agreed, but said he had to go back inside for his bicycle and his men. "How many men have you got?" we asked. "Oh, about twenty," he answered. So they

started coming out of the barn and I started counting: twenty...thirty...forty...there were fifty-five of them.[13]

But there was one final fortification on South Beveland which the enemy was prepared to defend to the last. On the 30th of October, the Germans halted in their retreat and dug in their men at the eastern end of the only land-link from Beveland to Walcheren: the fifteen-hundred-metre Walcheren Causeway. The strongpoint was known to be heavily fortified with machine guns and antitank artillery pieces in concrete-reinforced fire positions.

The Royal Regiment of Canada arrived on the scene first, winning the race for the 4th Brigade but also earning the unenviable task of destroying this major enemy obstacle. An Orders Group was called and the commanding officer, Lieutenant Colonel R.M. Lendrum, issued the order that the battalion was to make a frontal assault on the fortification the next day.

One of the company commanders, Captain Jack Stothers, did not agree with the plan. He plainly stated his dissatisfaction. Major Ralph Young, 2/I-C of the battalion, recalls the bitter meeting:

> It was the only time I ever saw the CO's order questioned and changed. Stothers objected and asked to be allowed to advance and assault along the outside of the dyke on the rather muddy shoreline. His appreciation of the situation proved correct and with little opposition he got in behind the German positions, including their gun emplacements, and the whole lot was in the bag with some 200 prisoners.
>
> It was a bold stroke on Stothers's part. He had only just rejoined the battalion, did not know the CO, and yet had the guts to question his method. He of course was right. He was recommended for a DSO-immediate award. He was awarded an MC as were two of his platoon commanders, Berry and Gillespie.[14]

Lieutenant Morris Berry's platoon was pinned down by enemy fire from a concrete pillbox. In order to get his men moving again, Lieutenant Berry crawled forward alone and silenced the opposition

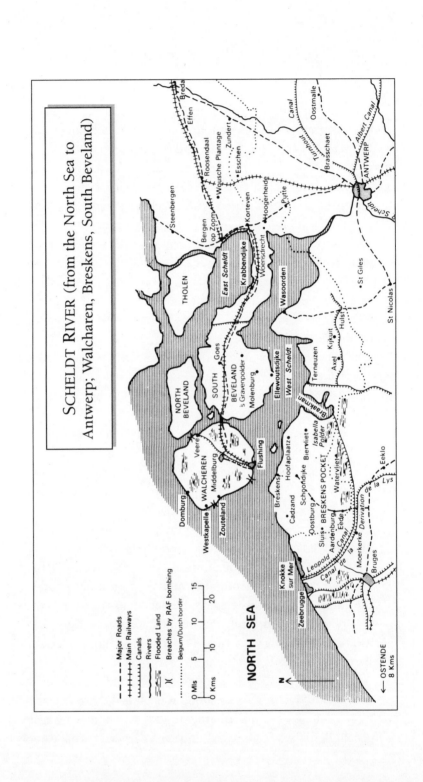

SCHELDT RIVER (from the North Sea to
Antwerp; Walcharen, Breskens, South Beveland)

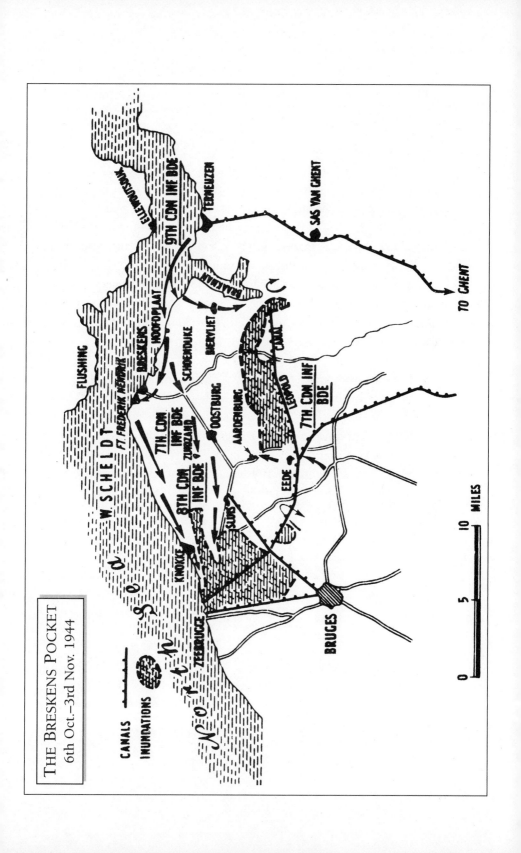

THE BRESKENS POCKET
6th Oct.–3rd Nov. 1944

CANALS
INUNDATIONS

0   5   10   MILES

W. SCHELDT

FLUSHING

FT. FREDERIK HENDRIK

N o r t h   S e a

ZEEBRUGGE

KNOKKE

7TH CDN. INF BDE

8TH CDN INF BDE

SLUIS

ZUIDZAND

OOSTBURG

AARDENBURG

BRESKENS

HOOFDPLAAT

SCHOONDIJKE

BIERVLIET

EEDE

LEOPOLD CANAL

7TH. CDN. INF BDE

ELLEWOUTSDIJK

9TH CDN INF BDE

TERNEUZEN

BAARLMAN

SAS VAN GHENT

TO GHENT

BRUGES

with grenades. Major Tim Beatty recounts this action admiringly: "The two flanking companies got in very close. Moe Berry actually put a grenade right through one of the loopholes in a pillbox. He took the pin out first and then put it in by hand, a pretty gutsy thing to do. That knocked the whole damn strongpoint out."[15]

The Royals, as it turned out, had won more than a race. They had won a reprieve from what was to be one of the bloodiest battles of the Scheldt, the crossing of Walcheren Causeway. That assignment went to the loser of the race across South Beveland, the 5th Infantry Brigade.

So, after six weeks of almost continuous fighting, the 4th and 6th Brigades were retired from the Battle of the Scheldt, their tasks completed. On 1 November, a long line of weary, muddy infantrymen plodded slowly back down the road that would take them away from the Scheldt:

> The men were indescribably dirty. They were bearded, cold as it is only possible to be cold in Holland in November, and wet from having lived in water-filled holes in the ground for twenty-four hours a day. Their eyes were red-rimmed from lack of sleep, and they were exhausted from their swift advance on foot under terrible conditions. Yet all ranks realized with a certain grim satisfaction that a hard job had been well and truly done.[16]

13

The Water Rats

WHILE THE SECOND CANADIAN INFANTRY DIVISION WAS SLOGGING dyke by deadly dyke along the north side of the Scheldt, the 3rd Division was struggling for supremacy at Scheldt Fortress South, a small pocket of land encircled by water courses that came to be known to Canadian troops as "Breskens Pocket."

By the end of September, under pressure from the Poles and the 4th Armoured Division, the Germans had been forced to withdraw to a firm defensive line along the Leopold Canal which ran from Heyst in the west to the Braakman Inlet in the east, an area thirty-five km long by fifteen wide. Once more the enemy had shrewdly elected to rely for their defence on this barrier of water; Breskens Pocket was virtually an island, a fortress island of Hitler's design.

From their vantage points at the raised crossroads of the dykes that partitioned the "island," the Germans could pick out the smallest movement; scouts trained to patrol with stealth were no exception. Reconnaissance was virtually impossible. In daylight, the Canadians had no choice but to sit it out on the sodden polderland, huddling their already soaked bodies in steaming, stinking mud. Such immobility was their only defence. Because of their flooded surroundings, the 7th, 8th and 9th Brigades of the 3rd Canadian Infantry Division took on the sobriquet of "The Water Rats."

To further confound the Allies, the Germans, as they had done elsewhere, flooded large tracts of Breskens Pocket, rendering the polders impassable to tracked vehicles and even to foot soldiers. An RCASC officer noted that the cobblestones would actually sink under the weight of the wheels of heavy supply trucks, and then bob up again, giving the impression that the trucks were "riding on soup."[1] Then came a new enemy, the October rains, relentlessly pounding the land and those upon it. Even the areas not inundated became quagmires of mud. It was a wretched land.

General Simonds's plan, rejecting as unfeasible the use of armour in the assault, called upon the 3rd Division to clean out the Pocket as soon as the Channel ports had been secured. The fact that SHAEF put such little emphasis on the importance of opening Antwerp Harbour diverted the Canadians from what should have been their main task of clearing the Scheldt. Instead, the foot soldiers were delayed through all of September, when the fine weather would have allowed greater mobility on land; in addition, the absence of fog and rain would have made greater air support possible.

Thirty-two-year-old Major General Dan Spry, the aggressive, young 3rd Division commander, was finally free to launch his assault on Breskens Pocket early in October. Spry was informed by Acting Corps Commander General Foulkes that Canadian Army Intelligence reported the defenders numbered only about 1,750 infantry. It was expected that there would be a total of some 4,000 troops, including support services, and these were reported to be of low morale and fighting ability. A matter of a few days' work, Spry was told.[2] In fact, the assault on Breskens Pocket was to require twenty-nine nightmarish days of slogging in one of the filthiest and bloodiest battles the Canadians faced in World War II.

The 1st Canadian Scottish War Diary noted with surprise that the enemy showed a considerable amount of fight. "They are good," exclaimed the diarist. Indeed, the 64th Infantry Division defending Scheldt Fortress South was of the best. The Canadian Intelligence estimate of an enemy strength of 4,000 men in the Pocket requiring "three or four days" to mop up was far from accurate: the 64th Infantry Division comprised three Grenadier Regiments, with a total well in excess of 10,000 men.[3]

Of all the divisions of the German 15th Army that escaped through Walcheren, the 64th was the most strongly armed and manned — and commanded. General Knut Eberding and the men of the 64th would prove to be a foe of formidable proportion.

Eberding's nephew, now a Canadian citizen, describes the experiences of the two world wars that made this man a seasoned commander: "My uncle joined the army at the age of seventeen. While he was still eighteen he fought in World War I in Russia and Flanders in a Jaeger [Ranger] Battalion. After the war he fought in the so-called Freekorps against separatists and communists, returning to the infantry in 1926 as a career soldier. He was the coach of the German Gold Medal handball team in the Berlin Olympics in 1936 (they were all soldiers of one battalion). In 1943 he became a major general." [4]

The 64th Division, too, was a veteran unit of first-class fighting men, professional soldiers who had been committed to the German military even as youngsters in the Hitler Youth Movement before the war.

"You'd throw a grenade at them and they'd throw it right back at you," a 9th Brigade senior officer remembers. "Especially those Feldwebels, field sergeants, they were really hot. But they all knew their business. They were tough kids. Bad boys." [5]

Although it was newly formed, having been thrown together hastily during the latter part of June and July, 1944, the 64th comprised experienced fighting men on leave from the Russian, Italian and Norwegian fronts. This "Leave Division" was dispatched to the Normandy front in August, but missed the main action and joined the remainder of the 15th Army in its flight across France and Belgium to be evacuated, through Breskens, in early September.

Here, the 64th was stopped on Hitler's order, and assigned the vital task of defending Scheldt Fortress South. With their comrades distracted by evacuation procedure, the men of the 64th had little trouble scrounging a considerable extra quantity and variety of guns and ammunition.

At the onset of the Breskens Pocket battle, the division, which included miscellaneous army, navy and air force elements, comprised three hundred officers and 10,700 men. Its strength included 489 machine guns, numerous mortars, and more than 300 guns from 20mm to 150mm, as well as twenty-three of the dreaded 88s.*

---

* The 88 was a very high-powered and versatile weapon. It could be used as an anti-personnel gun, as an antitank gun or as an anti-aircraft weapon. Its high velocity gave little warning of an approaching shell. The Allied forces had nothing comparable.

The Germans had also strongly fortified both banks of the Scheldt against enemy attack from the North Sea. In the Pocket, from the port of Breskens all the way west to Knocke on the Belgian border, they had six coastal batteries each with four long-range naval guns, heavily fortified in concrete. Just five km across the estuary, on the southern coast of the island of Walcheren, the batteries of heavy naval guns at Flushing were a powerful dual threat both to attacking amphibious forces and to land forces advancing across the Pocket.

It was to the German defenders of the fortresses that orders were issued by Adolf Hitler that would change them from merely competent soldiers to men obsessed with their mission. From the onset of the battle, General von Zangen, 15th Army commander, had made his troops' task clear to them: "Each additional day that you deny the port of Antwerp to the enemy...will be vital."[6]

Now, just prior to the invasion by the 3rd Canadian Division, they received a new order: defenders of the fortress were to fight to the last man and to the last round of ammunition. Those who surrendered or were captured would be considered traitors, subject to the death sentence, as would their families back in Germany. The Canadians soon were to witness the potency of that command.

Early in October, the 1st Canadian Scottish noted in their War Diary that: "Artillery prisoners of war taken this morning stated that their officers held them to their gun positions at the point of a pistol, and that reprisals would be inflicted on their families by the Gestapo if they surrendered."

Forward troops from the Canadians reported a new forcefulness in the German rifleman, a savagery that saw the use of fists and clubs, knives and bayonets in hand-to-hand fighting. This was hardly the ragged, demoralized foe reported to be running from Normandy.

The do-or-die order was attributed to Eberding. But in a letter dated December, 1968, the German general emphatically denied authorship of the threats, calling them "heroic ornaments":

The mentioned order of October 7, '44, was not my decision, but a passing on of an order from higher up which instructed us to give "obstinate defense," as this tactical form of fighting

was called in the German Army. Without doubt this order
came directly from Hitler, who always personally gave this
order whenever it regarded a strategic important position.
Heroic ornaments like "to the last man" were then the rule,
as I had experienced a few times in Russia. During October,
1944, on my representations, this order "obstinate defense"
was changed to "holding defense," a fight to win time.

It was necessary then that instead of obstinately defending we prevent so long as possible the use of the port of
Antwerp for the Allied force, because the decision for the
offensive in the Ardennes for the middle of December, which
was now known to me, depended on the non-function of the
port of Antwerp for the Allies.[7]

The German strategy revealed by Eberding explains the single-
minded tenacity of the enemy in attempting to thwart the Allied plans
to open Antwerp Harbour. Eberding was aware that the German High
Command was even then planning a major counterattack through
the Ardennes in December. The thrust had little chance of success if
the Allied supply lines were established at Antwerp, close to the front.
Antwerp was roughly 160 km from the designated German attack
point at Bastogne. The supply route to the port must not fall into
Canadian hands. Not yet.

Tactically, the German defensive plan was efficient and thorough,
and for one month, workable. A captured enemy battalion commander outlined the plan:

We really anticipated that the water would be our greatest
defence. You would therefore be forced to advance on the
surfaced roads at the top of the dykes, a very difficult thing
to do. We felt that you would try to cross the Leopold Canal.
We had you cold as far as the canal was concerned as we had
it heavily defended.

Every potential attack point was defended and we had
our artillery sighted to bring fire to bear on every position
there. If your forward troops tried to establish a bridgehead,
no matter where it was, we didn't have to range in our guns.

That had all been done long before. We could drop shells on you wherever you were.[8]

Eberding deliberately turned his back on the north coast of the Pocket, feeling that no approach by the Allies from this direction was feasible. The heavy gun batteries along the coast prohibited any invasion from the sea. From the east, moreover, he felt equally free from threat. The mud flats along the shores of the Scheldt and the Braakman Inlet would surely discourage a landing from this direction.

So Eberding lined his three regiments in depth along the Leopold Canal, and waited, confident that his position was impregnable. Against such a plan and in such fighting conditions, the Canadian infantry found its skills and resourcefulness sorely challenged.

On the 6th of October, the Canadians made a second attempt to pry the Germans from their stubborn hold on the Leopold Canal. The first canal assault in September by the Algonquin Regiment of the 4th Canadian Armoured Division had proved costly as well as futile. Entrenched in the reverse side of the broad, raised, canal bank at Moerkerke, almost impervious to artillery fire, the Germans used their advantage of complete protection to bring the full power of their defensive strength directly upon the attacker. Forty-two percent of the intrepid Algonquins — some 153 men — were casualties in that action.

Now, three weeks later, the 7th Infantry Brigade of the 3rd Division would try its luck — and this time the odds of winning were more in its favour. There would be three battalions throwing their weight into the attack: the 1st Canadian Scottish Regiment, the Regina Rifles and the Royal Winnipeg Rifles. And they had studied the problems the Algonquins, with only a third of that strength, had faced.

The important priority in this crossing was to devise some means of keeping the enemy's head down during the critical first few moments of the attack across the canal. After considerable research by the Chemical Warfare Section, the solution presented was to use a battery of flame-throwing projectors mounted on Bren gun carriers; these carriers were called Wasps.

The pilot experiment, "Operation Hotshot," was organized by Captain Norman Mould, technical officer (chemical warfare), 1st

Canadian Army, and rehearsed in a heavy downpour just two after-noons before the attack over the Leopold. He describes its successful pilot trial: "We found that our earlier ideas of 'raining' the fire [on the target] were not effective. But we had enough force to ricochet off the front of the dyke and 'bounce' the flame up and over the bank into the slit trench behind."[9]

For Norm Mould, the night before the attack was a long and hazardous one. Setting off on foot, well aware that he was exposed to enemy surveillance — by sight or even by sound — Mould made a personal survey of the routes and positions for each of the eleven Wasps. He designated these routes by laying white tape, and himself led each of the carriers to its position, always under direct mortar and machine-gun fire. His citation for the Military Cross describes the action:

> He stayed with the carrier and himself directed the fire of the flamethrower equipment to ensure that they functioned properly and that all possible support was available to the assaulting infantry. The action of the flame throwers was so successful that the enemy immediately defending the dyke were all eliminated and the crossing of the two leading companies of 1 Canadian Scottish Regiment was achieved with no casualties. This crossing was essential to the success of the plan for the destruction of the Breskens Pocket. The success of the assault by 1 Canadian Scottish Regiment, as compared to the partial success of the battalion on the left, is attributable in large part to the skill, bravery, coolness and disregard for personal safety of Captain Mould.[10]

Two hours before the attack, the massed artillery of 327 guns deployed along the divisional front opened up, adding the essential firepower factor without which few infantry attacks could be successful. Although the actual fighting was to be done by these infantrymen, much of their work depended on support from the various other arms and services. Of all these, the artillery was the most indispensable and saved many lives in the Scheldt battle.

The most important source of firepower in each infantry division was its field artillery-three regiments each of twenty-four guns capable of firing a twenty-five-pound shell 13,500 yards with extreme accuracy, at a rate of up to five rounds per gun per minute. These guns were capable of concentrating all their fire upon a single spot in a matter of seconds. The Royal Canadian Artillery also had an Antitank Regiment and a Light AntiAircraft Regiment attached to each division. The 2nd Corps and 1st Canadian Army could provide additional support with their RCA Medium Regiments. These each had sixteen guns which fired 100-pound shells.

To add further depth to the firepower, there were the medium machine guns and 4.2-inch mortars, twelve of each in a battalion; the air force made available under special arrangements their heavy, medium, and fighter bombers, and rocket-firing Typhoons.

For this attack, the artillery programme, laid on by Brigadier (Artillery) Bruce Matthews, 2nd Canadian Corps, and Brigadier P.A.S. Todd, senior gunnery officer at 3rd Division HQ, consisted of a sixty-minute series of concentrations fired by all guns on known enemy positions, beginning two hours before H-Hour. This would be followed by a half hour of counter-battery fire — Allied guns firing at enemy gun positions — to "soften" some thirty hostile batteries. Then, in the fifteen minutes immediately preceding the infantry assault, the corps guns would fire heavy concentrations along the canal bank, after which batteries would be employed in corps and divisional tasks, both pre-arranged and on call, on various known or suspected strongpoints. This weight of fire constituted more than five times the regular artillery strength of a division.

The 7th Brigade launched its bid to establish a bridgehead over the Leopold Canal at the village of Strooiburg, seven km east of the Algonquins' battle site. The two battalions spearheading the assault, the Canadian Scottish on the east and the Reginas simultaneously attacking two km farther west, were to link up on the far side. The Royal Winnipeg Rifles was held back in reserve.

The assault craft were waiting, and the riflemen in position to go over immediately the flame throwers had completed their task. This time, no groundwork of errors would be allowed to mar the success of the operation.

At 0530, in the pale half light of the cold October morning, leaning into a bitter wind, the grimly determined men of the 7th Brigade moved stealthily along the dirt verges of the cobblestone roads near the canal's edge.

Suddenly, the world seemed ablaze. Black rods of pressurized fuel were shot thirty-five metres across the canal. As the hot liquid bounced over the dyke, it burst into flame, falling directly on the entrenched enemy. It was a flame so vicious that there was no way the frantic victims could extinguish it. Many who were not burned alive were terror-stricken, shocked into immobility by the horror of the moment. Even the Canadian observers described the moment as "terrifying."

The flame throwers had only twenty seconds' firing time before their fuel was exhausted. The respite, as brief as it was effective, depended upon split-second timing. The instant that the Wasps shot their molten death into the midst of the enemy, the assaulting companies leaped into their boats and were quickly paddled across the canal.

The Canadian Scottish crossed successfully without coming under fire. The Regina Rifle's left-hand company — the RMRs — also got across before the enemy recovered. This was a fine effort by a company with little battle experience. As First Canadian Army Headquarters Defence Company, the RMRs (Royal Montreal Regiment) had been in training since the early war years for their role. After five months' intensive training in England it had recently exchanged duties with B Company of the Reginas to gain further experience in action.

Experience they gained that grim morning on the Leopold — but at what a price. The company, commanded by Major Robert Schwob, plunged across swiftly under that protection of flame. But the remaining Regina company on their right ran into difficulties, giving the enemy an opportunity to open up heavy machine-gun fire on all the attackers.

Now both companies were pinned down by incessant counter-attacking. "The entire front was a flat, coverless field of fire for dozens of machine guns," the Reginas reported. Major M.R. Douglas, commanding D Company in reserve, was stopped from crossing by a canal-side pillbox that "was eventually silenced with very heavy losses on our part."

The man who did this silencing, Major Douglas, was awarded a well-deserved Knight of the Crown of Belgium and La Croix de Guerre for his aggressive action: "I got all the Piats I could put my hands on. We laid those on the pillbox and I told my men to shoot at the Germans through the pillbox slits."[11]

The deadly mortaring and shelling took a fearful toll on the Montrealers. Of the original 118 RMR men, ten were killed, forty wounded, and twenty-one were reported missing. Their numbers became so few that they officially ceased to be a company and were reclassified mid-battle as "remnants." But that didn't stop the determined RMRs.

"There were enough of us still on our feet to prevent the enemy from pushing us into the canal," Major Schwob reported.[12]

Too soon, it seemed, the enemy recovered. Those who had escaped the flames were directing mortars, machine guns, and grenades at the attackers. Undeterred by the heavy fire, the Canadian engineers and pioneers started constructing a kapok bridge to enable the follow-up companies to cross. They were startled to see its first passengers — four German soldiers running across toward them, arms outstretched in surrender.

Just fifty minutes had passed.

Throughout the long morning, the troops fought desperately to keep their narrow hold on enemy territory. Platoons deployed in houses and barns were infiltrated time and again by Germans taking up positions just metres away in adjoining buildings. A sharp exchange of fire would ensue. A farmhouse would become ominously quiet. There would be no one left on either side to fight.

The operation required almost superhuman resources. The canvas boats for canal crossings were manned by troops from the North Shore (New Brunswick) Regiment, on loan from the 8th Brigade. These men, always in full view of the enemy, were continually under concentrated German fire. But they persevered in keeping fresh supplies and ammunition moving across the broad thirty-five-metre canal to the far bank, ferrying back casualties and hauling up bridging material to the engineers. Their efforts were monumental.

Just getting the bridging material to the site had demanded exceptional courage, and won a Military Cross for Lt Edwin Eperson of No. 34 Corps Troops Composite Company in the Royal Canadian Army Service Corps (RCASC). Eperson was in charge of a transport platoon moving bridging equipment to the launching site when two of his vehicles were hit by shellfire. One was destroyed, the other set alight, drawing continuous enemy fire on the illuminated target.

Eperson not only led his men through shellfire to extinguish the blaze but also evacuated the remaining vehicles after off-loading the essential bridging equipment to the engineers at the time and place where it was needed.

By the end of the day, with all their companies committed, the Reginas had a mere toehold on enemy territory — a narrow strip that was 350 metres in length. In places, they had penetrated fifty metres inland; elsewhere, troops had their feet in the canal water, their hands grasping clumps of grass on the banks.

The Reginas, Scottish, and Winnipegers literally clung to their bridgehead by their fingernails; in several locations they held no more than their side of the steep slope of the dyke with the Germans dug in on the opposite side, just the width of a narrow road away.

"For the next five days we got the hell kicked out of us," Douglas remembers. "We couldn't move, couldn't get anywhere. It was all polders out in front of us, all water. There was only one way we could get at the Germans and that was along the dyke, but the Jerries had it completely covered. I lost all my officers and ended up with twenty-seven men and myself."[13]

Canadian war correspondent Ross Munro, who witnessed the action, reported: "By all the rules of war, the bridgehead should have been lost; the battalions should have been wiped out or forced to withdraw...it was only by sheer guts that the western units hung on to their positions."[14]

But it was the nights that were the worst. Hand grenades were lobbed over the bank into the trenches on both sides; some of our men threw as many as twenty-five in a night. Fortunately, the balance was in our favour as the Canadian No. 36 grenade was considerably more powerful and effective than the German "potato masher" grenade.

The enemy was remembering his vow; he would never give in. In the early hours of the 7th of October, he launched still another savage counterattack. Overrunning a platoon of the Scottish that was guarding the left flank of C Company, 150 Germans rushed in to crush first a section of the platoon and then its headquarters. In an hour-long blazing battle, the remaining men of the platoon fought on against impossible odds until just one man, its commander Sergeant A. Gri, was left. The Scottish history *Ready for the Fray* recounts the terrible outcome of this skirmish:

> Ammunition exhausted, his uniform scorched by the flames of the house burning down around him, Gri was overwhelmed and taken prisoner. Then, turning on the C Company headquarters building, the Germans initiated the same punishing treatment. The fight put up by this platoon had helped Captain Schjeldrup and his company headquarters to battle longer with the enemy. The action here was every bit as fierce, with the enemy throwing grenades through the windows and pouring machine-gun fire through the doors...Once again, the enemy managed to set the buildings on fire with his tracer bullets, and with the building in flames there was nothing for the survivors to do but to surrender.[15]

It was later found that sixty Germans had been killed or wounded by this handful of stalwart Scottish.

In the grey half light of dawn, men of the Scottish witnessed a spine-chilling sight. Silhouetted against the horizon, a column of their own officers and men, including the commander of C Company, Captain V.R. Schjeldrup, was marched off towards the German lines, the captors mixing in with the main body of prisoners to protect themselves from retaliatory fire.

Captain Schjeldrup recounts how the Canadian prisoners were interrogated by German Intelligence: "The enemy tried every trick to find out the location of the other brigades from the prisoners, but with no luck. A brand new reinforcement to the unit captured at this time still wore his 'Rocky Mountain Rangers' shoulder patch, which made the enemy's intelligence officers scratch their heads."[16]

Some of the captives devised their own escape, including the indomitable Sergeant Gri, who had hidden a knife in his clothing when the Germans captured him. Of the 110 men of C Company who had followed the flame across the canal two days before, only one-third remained. But the Canadian Scottish had succeeded in preventing the enemy from breaking through to the canal and had given the Winnipeg Rifles time to press forward and close the wedge between the Scottish and Regina Regiments. Then it was the Winnipegers to the rescue. Fighting furiously to close the gap made by the infiltrating enemy, they finally broke through to German HQ, liberating those Canadians imprisoned there.

Still the battle anguished on, neither side yielding an inch. For Major Andrew Bieber, a company commander with the Royal Winnipeg Rifles, it was "one of the worst parts of the war — just a terrible, terrible show. The ground was so flat, and with no cover; maintaining supplies for just that small perimeter was impossible. We lost a lot of good people — wounded and killed. I get an uneasy feeling even thinking about it."[17]

The Germans were desperate, fighting with every resource, laying on an intense bombardment — the heaviest laid on the Canadians by the enemy since D-Day — to try to drive the invaders off. Enemy gunfire and mortar-fire saturated the narrow dyke area continuously. Even the big German coastal guns of Flushing on Walcheren Island and at Cadzand on the North Sea coast of Breskens Pocket were used, pounding relentlessly on the Water Rats. But the Canadians were laying on their heavy artillery too, and the ever-useful rocket-firing "Typhies," flown by the RAF, were seldom still.

Casualties on both sides were heavy. The medical officer of the Regina Rifles reported on the 12th of October that there had been between 250 and 300 casualties go through the Regimental Aid Post since the assault began on the 6th. Official figures for the three battalions listed 533 casualties in seven days' fighting.

Evacuating the wounded required immense acts of individual courage. Casualties had to be carried the length of the treeless, sodden ground on the enemy side, then ferried across the canal, always with no cover from German shellfire or the single, skilled German sniper. At one point, a German sergeant asked for — and got — a twenty-minute truce so each side could pick up its dead and wounded.

Lieutenant Colonel Seigfried Enfirth, commander of the German 1039 Grenadier Regiment, described the fighting as "extremely violent," deploring that his regiment had lost more than half its strength, amongst them the commanding officers of two companies.

Despite Hitler's orders, he approved the brief truce: "I was well aware of the Fuhrer's order according to which it was forbidden to make any such arrangements with the enemy. But I followed the voice of my conscience and agreed with the suspension of arms and gave the order for a temporary cease-fire within my sector. Friend and foe together carried their wounded and dead from the battlefield. Afterwards both sides took up their former positions again — which were approximately eighty metres apart — and resumed the fierce fighting."[18]

For the riflemen, it was a living nightmare. Forced like animals to crawl through flooded trenches to reach the front lines, they stumbled continually on the bodies of Germans and Canadians killed by commando knife or bayonet in the savage hand-to-hand fighting that erupted when enemy troops stole through the lines at night and infiltrated the trenches.

The already bad conditions had now become appalling, as a private soldier recounts in the Toronto Scottish War Diary on the 9th of October: "Living conditions at the front are not cosy. Water and soil make mud. Mud sticks to everything. Boots weigh pounds more. Rifles and Brens operate sluggishly. Ammunition becomes wet. Slit trenches allow one to get below the ground level but also contain several inches of thick water. Matches and cigarettes are wet and unusable. So the soldier shakes his head, cleans his rifle, swears a good deal and dreams of what he'll do when he gets leave (if)."

To many of the survivors of the 7th Canadian Infantry Brigade, including one sergeant with the Regina Rifles, it was the ground that left a lasting memory. "It seemed we had to have someone cleaning our Bren guns and rifles all the time. And you couldn't dig in very well. The trenches would just fill up with water. Sometimes the only way to get protection was to wedge your body horizontally into the dyke. But much of the time we were more or less out in the open. Just sitting ducks."[19]

And always, there was the water. Fighting on land flooded by the Germans and soaked by the raw October rains, the riflemen were continually wet and cold. To Dan Spry, this was the unbeatable foe: "The troops were always soaked and really exhausted. If we'd had fresh, warm dry men to put in there we could have done the job faster. As it was, we finally had to pull some out, send them through the mobile baths, give them clean, dry uniforms and socks, serve them a decent meal and a few tots of rum and then we'd leapfrog them back into the fight and pull some other poor Water Rats out."[20]

At a time when grimness took on a whole new meaning, the smallest particle of humour could be life-saving. Spry recalls the incident that sent a wave of chuckles through the trenches. Feeding the troops was just one of the major difficulties in moving supplies forward. Only at night could Compo-rations,* heated up in vats of hot water, be ferried over by crews from the quartermaster's store. To troops isolated in sodden trenches, a tin of hot food tossed from a passing rowboat was a welcome break.

"In the course of heating up the tins," Spry smiles, "the labels would sometimes get burned off. One night, a soldier broke silence with a roar of protest. 'Goddamn it, this is the third night in a row I've been given tinned jam!'"[21]

Slowly the pressure eased on the Canadians. The 9th Brigade's brilliant flank assault on the German rear lines and the 8th Brigade's successful follow-up had taken off some of the heat. By the middle of the month, the 7th Brigade was able to extend its bridgehead considerably, and a few days later was relieved by the 157th Brigade from the British 52nd (Lowland) Division.

More of the Breskens slogging match awaited the Water Rats of the 7th, but not until they'd been given a few days to rest and dry out, and a few tots of Dan Spry's rum to block out their nightmare experiences on the Leopold.

---

* Compo-rations, which were usually packaged in units of fourteen meals, consisted of a variety of tinned goods that were supposed to provide all the daily dietary needs. Each pack would contain several kinds of meats — sausage, stew, spam, bully beef, etc. — vegetables, fruit, cheese, butter and jam, as well as cigarettes, candy and toilet paper.

❖ 14 ❖

In the Back Door

Y OU'VE GOT TO BE A SPECIAL KIND OF CAT TO BE A GOOD INFANTRYMAN.
What people don't seem to understand is that different people have
an affinity for a certain environment. My environment is the ground
and I feel good on the ground. I feel at home in that environment and I
reckon I can fight in it.

I had no urge, at any time in my life, to join the air force and bore
holes in the sky at 40,000 feet with some German up my backside. I had
no urge to do that, nor did I have any urge to go to sea and be a sub-
mariner and meet my Maker wrapped up in a submarine at sixteen fath-
oms. When you take it down a little further, would you rather be in the
armoured corps or would you rather be in the infantry? Personally, I
wouldn't want to die in a tin box.

To be a good infantryman, you've got to know and want to know
about your weapons, and how to look after them. This is one thing you
can't be lazy about. You can be dirty, slovenly, and unshaven, but you've
got to know how to fight with your weapons and you've got to have
them with you. If you feel better with a knife on your side — I'm not
talking about the colour, I'm talking about something that gives you a
feeling of security — then it's important to wear that knife, all the time
you're out there.

You have to have an instinct for survival, the capacity to make a tactical appreciation in a millisecond. I can go out, look around, and almost
without thinking about it say to myself: "There's only one place for me to
be. If I'm going to get from here to that house, I've got to go that
way…now!…maybe on my belly for the first ten yards." You've got to be

able to make that instantaneous kind of appreciation of a situation, almost unconsciously, in order to make right decisions.

It takes a very special set of skills, being an infantryman. A lot of fellows don't start out with them — they have to be developed along the way. But there's one thing sure: you can't be out there very long and survive unless you learn the tricks.[1]

Lieutenant Colonel Roger Rowley

It was apparent at 1st Canadian Army headquarters that the German line on the Leopold Canal was not going to yield without a terrific struggle. After forty-eight hours, the 7th Brigade's frontal attack was still stalemated.

But Guy Simonds was ready with the second phase of his battle plan to wrest Breskens Pocket from German control. Two days after the 7th assaulted the Leopold, the 9th Brigade of 3rd Division was ordered, in the words of its commander, Brigadier John Rockingham, "in by the back door."

Simonds's skill for reading the enemy's mind came once more to the fore. The Germans, he pondered, had assembled most of their infantry strength along the "island's" south defence line on the Leopold. They would be depending on their powerful coastal guns on the "outer crust" of Breskens and on Walcheren to ward off any invader from the North Sea.[2]

That left just one approach, one so impossible that the Germans might never expect it — the mud flats of the Braakman Inlet on the West Scheldt, behind enemy lines.

Intelligence reports assured him that this stretch of beach east of the port of Breskens showed a thinning out of defence fortifications with only a few prepared defensive positions; concrete fortifications were all spaced west of the port towards the sea. The Germans probably assumed that the mud flats would effectively discourage any attempted landing. But the Germans were not reckoning on the propensity of 3rd Division's Water Rats for managing mud.

Still to be ironed out were the dual problems of exactly where to plan the landing and how to transport troops to the site. Major

General Dan Spry's subsequent 3rd Division report noted that, in late September, Intelligence had examined possible landing sites, studying the precise nature of the shore from aerial photographs and "from details supplied by a Dutch engineer."[3]

That Dutchman was Peter de Winde, member of the tough-fighting Knok Ploeg, commander of interior forces for West Flanders, savage Resistance fighter, son of the indomitable Sara, and brother of Hannie who smuggled weapons under her skirts. The account of how this tough young lad braved the frigid waters of the Scheldt for eight hours to bring information to the Canadians has not been told before in the English language. In the official Dutch history, the chapter describing the following adventure is entitled: "DE MESSIE VAN P.H. DE WINDE."*

On 11 September, the whole of the port of Breskens had to be evacuated because heavy RAF bombardment had nearly destroyed the town. Nineteen-year-old Peter de Winde went with his family to Schoondijke where his mother and sister continued offering refuge to the Underground. At this time, Prince Bernhardt, chief of the Underground, appealed to all the diverse Resistance groups to unify under one command. De Winde was appointed commander of interior forces for West Flanders.

He had come out of hiding following *Dolle Dinsdag*. The new German force that had returned to reimpose military rule over the country after that traumatic day would not recognize the slim, open-faced youth as a member of the Resistance. His papers, and he had several sets, stood up to the closest scrutiny. On occasion, he would be a member of the Todt Organization; his greenish-brown jacket of this paramilitary German labour force was a safe passport to permit the youth access to explore the district. On other occasions, he might roam the agricultural hamlets of Breskens Pocket freely in the guise of a cattle dealer.

On 27 September, Peter and a friend made a reconnaissance, by

---

* "The Mission of P.H. de Winde": de Winde's account, although incredible to imagine, has been authenticated by Professor-Doctor L. de Jong, in his official history of the Netherlands in World War II, and by his successor, Dr. A.H. Paape, Director of Documentation, RIOD, Amsterdam; by Dr. C.M. Schulten, Chief of the Army, Historical Section, Sectie Militaire Geschiedenis, HQ Royal

bicycle and on foot, of the south bank of the Scheldt to the west of
the Braakman Inlet. They confirmed their suspicions that the region
was heavily defended by the Germans in the coastal fortresses of
Breskens and Fort Frederik Hendrik. He was concerned to note that
they had also begun to build up a line of defence along the western
shores of the Braakman as well. But de Winde observed that there was
a gap: the enemy was not strong in the area between these positions,
near the snail beds of Hoofdplaat. He thought that an attack at that
point, behind enemy positions, might be successful in surprising the
German defenders.

That night, his reconnaissance completed, de Winde stole along
the marshy mud flats of the Scheldt. He had with him three possessions of Flight Lieutenant Raymond Gordon Sim, a Canadian who
had been shot down over West Flanders two weeks before and was
in hiding in his mother's cellars: Sim's RCAF battle-dress jacket and
identification card, and an RCAF rubber dinghy.

De Winde had determined that there was only one way to get his
vital information to the Canadians. Even with his forged papers, he
would never be permitted through the German front lines along the
Leopold, nor would he survive an attempt to steal across. He was
trapped in this water-encircled "pocket" of West Flanders. The only
way out, he reckoned, was by sea. If he were captured, it would go
easier on him if he were identified as an escaping Canadian flyer
rather than a Dutch Underground fighter.

Climbing into the boat, the courageous young man pushed off.
Almost immediately, he was in trouble. Stakes hammered into the sea
floor as part of the German shore defences gashed the rubber dinghy
irreparably.

Now he had no option but to plunge into the freezing waters and
swim the Scheldt. For eight hours, de Winde struggled against the
storm-blown waves. Fighting a heavy tidal current, against a gale
force of 7, the lad swam a distance of some six and a half km across

---

Netherlands Army, 's-Gravenhage; also, by Dr. Von Druten, Director of the
Archief van de Binnenlands Strydkrachten, Kerkrade, where original corrob-
orative reports were filed by Chief of Documentation Colonel S.I.X., heading
a postwar tribunal that examined and evaluated each account of each Underground member.

the Braakman Inlet to reach Canadian lines. It was impossible to keep on course; the distance he covered nearly doubled as he was buffeted by the powerful currents. Once he paused to rest, feet barely touching the slimy bottom. The silence of the black night was broken by the sound of a dog barking, then voices, German voices, nearby.

Finally, he reached the opposite shore near Terneuzen and found help at the home of a dyke worker who opened his door to the frozen lad. There, exhausted and with arms severely weakened, he rested for two hours before walking on to Terneuzen where the Canadians picked him up by jeep for the last leg of his escape to 4 Canadian Division HQ at Eekloo. By noon of the next day, de Winde had given a full report to intelligence officers at the headquarters. A few days later he was transferred to the Intelligence Section of 3rd Canadian Infantry Division HQ when it took command of the area in early October. He worked with the Canadians as an interpreter until his homeland was liberated.

Besides detailing enemy fortifications, de Winde estimated the strength of the German 64th Infantry Division as numbering twelve to thirteen thousand, a far more accurate estimate than the Canadians had been given previously. This intelligence, brought across the lines so dramatically, assisted the division in determining the ultimate landing sites for its invasion — one of which was Peter de Winde's take-off point for his bitter swim.[4]

Transporting a fighting force of two thousand men, their vehicles, weapons and supplies across a stretch of open water, and landing them on a bed of oozing mud required the development of a vehicle that could swim in water, slither effectively in ooze and land its human cargo safely ashore. It was called the Buffalo, and it was about to make its debut in one of the most ingenious amphibious invasions of the war.

Just as incongruous as the creature he invented was the story of its originator, a retired British general who became a corporal in the Home Guard and then a general again, just in time to invent this cunning vehicle.

Major General Sir Percy Hobart's love affair with the tank went back more than two decades. After World War I, Hobart became Britain's foremost exponent of tank warfare. Many of his new theories for the use of armour were not appreciated by the somewhat stuffy British High Command. Immediately before World War II he was shunted off to Egypt where he formed and trained the famed 7th Armoured Division that later fought victoriously in the 8th Army in North Africa.

However, the maverick tankman continued to rankle the staid members of the War Office, who finally forced Hobart into early retirement in 1940. He promptly joined the Home Guard where, armed with broomstick and pitchfork, he continued to defend his country, now as a corporal.

It was Winston Churchill who rescued him from obscurity a year later, elevating his rank by eleven grades and giving him command first of the 11th Armoured Division and, soon after, of the newly formed 79th Armoured Division.

With this latter command Hobart was given a free hand to develop weapons which would enable the infantry to attack successfully the heavily fortified or otherwise inaccessible enemy positions anticipated in the Northwest Europe campaign.

Presumably, the lessons of Dieppe had been heeded. The formation of the 79th occurred shortly after the disastrous Canadian raid in 1942, when appalling casualties were sustained by troops helpless against the concrete fortifications on the Dieppe beaches.

Hobart went about this new challenge with zest, and his flair for new ideas resulted in his division's eventually being 21,000 strong with over 1,600 tracked vehicles designed to accomplish a variety of unusual feats by innovative means. These vehicles, often of extremely peculiar appearance, earned them the name of "The Funnies."

The initial creation was the Flail. This was a Churchill or Sherman tank modified to carry up front a rotating drum with chains attached. The chains would beat the ground to explode mines as the tank moved forward, thus clearing a passage through a known or suspected minefield for vehicles and foot soldiers.

Then in rapid succession came a number of strange and inventive ideas. The Crocodile was a flame-throwing tank that spread panic and fear in its wake. The versatile AVRE could perform as a cannon, firing a highly penetrating and destructive charge that could demolish concrete emplacements. Alternatively, the AVRE could carry a small bridge to span narrow gaps, or it could drop bundles of fascine into the smaller antitank ditches, making them passable for armour.

Then there was the miraculous DD or amphibious tank, and, finally, the Buffalo or LVT (Landing Vehicle Tracked), a weird-looking creature that could transport a platoon of thirty infantrymen or a fully equipped carrier or jeep plus personnel across water. It had a limited capability on land as well.

Marvellous as these were, Hobart must still have harboured some personal insecurity after the somewhat cavalier treatment he had received throughout his career. His plaintive request is recorded in the 2nd Canadian Corps War Diary on 18 September: "Gen Hobart, 79 Armd Div, visited HQ to discuss further the plans for capture of [Breskens and] Walcheren and to ask that his 'gadgets' not repeat not be forgotten when the move to the Ghent area takes place."

Canadian journalist Ralph Allen wrote this appreciation: "How many lives this Hobart-inspired or Hobart-encouraged menagerie saved before the war was over there is no way of guessing. But they were many more than the lives lost at Dieppe, and according to the impersonal cost accounting of war and in the jargon of the military college blackboards, the final verdict may be that Dieppe was a tactical failure but a strategic success."[5]

Without Percy Hobart's "Funnies" in the Battle of the Scheldt, the mines, the concrete fortifications, the flooded terrain, the ditches — all the defences that the Germans had peppered across Zeeland — might very well have succeeded finally in slowing down or halting the Canadian drive. And without the Buffaloes, in its desperate assault on Breskens Pocket, 3rd Canadian Infantry Division could have become yet another Dieppe tragedy.

Rockingham's "back door" assault was like the man — audacious, intrepid and mercurial. Its success depended upon a lightning attack, with a beachhead secured before the enemy could pull his defences together. Literally under the muzzles of enemy guns the whole time, the Canadians had first to descend in Buffaloes down a thirty-km-long canal from Ghent to Terneuzen before emerging into the West

Scheldt. Subsequently they had to cross the Braakman Inlet. All movement had to be effected at night. Secrecy and surprise were key elements to the success of this amphibious invasion.

The three battalions of the 9th Brigade — the North Novas (North Nova Scotia Highlanders) and the HLI (Highland Light Infantry of Canada) which were to lead the attack, and the SD&G (Stormont, Dundas and Glengarry Highlanders), the reserve battalion — were given the briefest of introductions to the Buffaloes.

Then, in late afternoon of the 7th of October, this curious armada of ninety-seven Buffaloes set forth from Ghent, wallowing and belching as they struggled over dykes and through murky canal waters toward the Scheldt.

For Rockingham it was a long night. Security seemed almost impossible to maintain. Efforts were made to seal off the area, but without success. The Buffaloes could only manage a speed of eight km per hour. Cheering Dutch civilians following the flotilla by bicycle were highly amused that they could proceed faster than their liberators.

"It was just like you were setting off for a picnic," North Nova Scotia Highlander Major Morris Clennett recalls. "Only you sort of wondered if every German in town knew you were coming."[6]

The troops were sure that some collaborator would report their intent, or that their positions would be revealed to the enemy either by the flares that had to be dropped to lead the way or by the incredible noise of the Buffalo motors. Their aeroplane engines created a sound so like the roar of aircraft that as far away as Flushing the anti-aircraft guns began to fire sporadically — "Which suited us just fine," Rockingham said gleefully.

Then one of the locks broke down and sappers had to erect steep wooden ramps to get the Buffaloes over the six-metre-high dyke and into the Scheldt, a slow and difficult task for the vehicles. The coming of daylight forced a twenty-four-hour postponement of the invasion, but this, too, threatened the security of the operation until the entire flotilla was camouflaged and buttoned down out of sight and sound of the enemy observation posts just a few kilometres across the water. To a man, 9th Brigade spent an uncomfortable Sunday night in a ditch.

In the early hours of Monday, the 9th of October, the Buffaloes took to the water and the assault group formed up on the canal bank in two sections. The first, the North Nova Scotia Highlanders, was guided by British Naval Lieutenant Commander Robert Franks, attached to the Canadian Army, who had volunteered to lead the flotilla to the landing beaches. He later gave this account:

> At 0030 hours we were lying off the sea ramp in our little motor boat showing two dim red lights astern. Well on time, the first LVT [Buffalo] waddled down the ramp and splashed into the water. We moved slowly out to the canal entrance as more and more took to the water and formed up astern. It was a nearly ideal night — calm and quiet with a half moon behind light cloud but a bit of haze which restricted visibility to one mile at the most.
>
> We went slowly and as far as could be seen all our Buffaloes were formed up and following. I then set course due west across the entrance of the Braakman Plaat. Just as we cleared the land our artillery barrage started up, "plastering" the far beaches and other targets. The noise effectively blanketed our sounds and was generally most heartening.
>
> Our touchdown was planned to be on either side of a groin, which proved to be a good landmark. We were able to identify it and then lay off, flicking our lamps to guide the Buffaloes in. They deployed and thundered in past us, looking and sounding most impressive. The landing was successful and I could see through my binoculars the infantry disembark on dry land and form up and move off.
>
> The artillery barrage had by now of course ceased and there was silence except for the roar of the engines and an occasional rifle shot. There was no problem disembarking the infantry but there was some trouble experienced by the craft-carrying vehicles which had to negotiate the dyke to discharge their load.
>
> The amphibians then made their way back across the Braakman independently to pick up the SD&G and Brigade Headquarters. These went over in one long convoy at 0900 hours. The voyage was skillfully screened from the far

shore by our smoke laid down from the DUKW and storm boats working with smoke floats in the river…It ensured a safe crossing for the LVTs as the enemy was only able to shell "blind."[7]

The first wave of Canadians had the combined protection of surprise, darkness and the barrage to bring them safely across the inlet during their ninety-minute run under the menace of German guns.

The second wave, a convoy comprising Rockingham's brigade headquarters and his reserve battalion, the Stormont, Dundas and Glengarry, as well as essential supplies, had none of these. The force embarked at 0900 hours, in a morning turned cloudy and raining, swimming directly towards an alerted enemy.

But once more, 1 Canadian Army's Chemical Warfare Section came to the rescue with an important contribution to the Breskens Pocket attack. They had made flames for the 7th Brigade; now they would produce smoke to screen the 9th Brigade's flotilla from enemy eyes.

They called the smoke generator, with great affection, "Smokey Joe." And they gave it a lot of the credit for getting the troops across unharmed, as Rockingham recalls: "We had a motor launch running just slightly behind us that carried smoke canisters. I can remember watching it — poor old 'Smokey Joe' — it got shot at all the time. I could see enemy artillery shells flying all around it."[8]

So seemingly simple an operation was in actuality a technically complex task that was handled by the chemical warfare men. Over 250 tons of smoke-generating equipment were required, including 4,140 generators, 2,150 floats and 656 barrels of fog oil. "It was our first big operation," Major J. Temple Hugill, G.2. (General Staff Officer 2), Chemical Warfare, recalls:

Lieutenant Colonel Reg Sawyer was my boss. For seven days there at the Scheldt we didn't do anything but make smoke, but we sure did a lot of that. It was *Ad Hoc* with a capital A H. My God, we really learned as we went along. My HQ was in one of those lovely big German fortifications about a mile off the Terneuzen Canal. We brought up a bunch of engineers to maintain the storm boats. I remember they were run

by those Evinrude engines that gave us continual trouble. To
keep eight boats in operation, sixteen engines were required
with two fitters working full time tuning them up. After the
first couple of days we anchored rafts out in the estuary itself
and then we got four DUKWs to ferry the smoke floats out
to the rafts.

For seven days, until a land route was driven through to connect
the brigade with a supply line, Tempy Hugill and Smokey Joe kept the
amphibious gateway open, allowing the ferrying of essential supplies
to the fighting force while serving also as a popular target for the
enemy. Tempy Hugill sums it up like this: "Flame came into its own
with the Canadian Army fighting on the dykes; then a few days later,
smoke did too. Our operation at Terneuzen worked pretty well con-
sidering it was our first major go. It must have been successful because
everybody screamed and hollered for smoke from thereon in."[9]

The skilled navigation of Commander Franks deposited the
North Novas safe, dry and still undetected on Green Beach, just three
km from the fishing village of Hoofdplaat.

The HLI was not so lucky. Several of their craft experienced difficulty negotiating the sand bars and mud flats of their landing beach
and came in thirty minutes late. HLI Sergeant Roy Francis, who had
already lost one brother in Normandy and was to see another brother
killed the next day by German mortar, recalls the landing clearly:
"The mud seemed bottomless; you almost had to swim in it. You had
to carry your rifle and try to keep moving or you'd start to sink.
There was a sort of fitful moon, and from one hundred yards out the
beach looked like hard sand. But when the Buffalo went aground and
we all piled out, it wasn't sand. It was just ooze. It was a pretty
ghastly experience."[10]

By mid-morning, the three battalions of 9 Brigade had firmly
planted their boots on enemy soil, with no intention of backing off.
The Germans, although momentarily caught off balance, were fanat-
ically determined to sweep the Canadians out of the Pocket. As Spry
had anticipated, General Knut Eberding lost valuable time recovering from the surprise amphibious attack on his rear position. He was
to become increasingly disconcerted at the ferocity and courage of

these lead troops from 9th Brigade. Most of all, Knut Eberding was to discover that he had a formidable opponent in its commander, John Rockingham.

More than in flame, or smoke or strange fighting monsters, Rockingham believed the strength of his brigade was in its men and in their leaders. A man of great physical and mental toughness, lightning quick in action, spirited in temper, staunch in loyalty, "Rocky" roused the enthusiasm and gained the affection of the ordinary soldier possibly more than any other Canadian brigade commander. The War Diary of the 9th Brigade admired his style: "Brigade commander visited the units several times during the day; in fact, during an attack he is more easily found conducting the battle from his scout car, well forward, usually under fire, than he is at Tac HQ."

Rockingham was intrepid, given to flamboyant actions, to thumbing his nose at the rulebook. Hanging around the front line was a frequently repeated infraction of procedure at brigadier level, a fact that impressed him not at all:

> Maybe I differed from a lot of other guys, but I didn't believe you could get the feel of the battle, the smell of the battlefield unless you were up at the front line where the troops were, where you could see how their morale was, whether they were happy or unhappy, why they were unhappy, why they were happy. So I believed that the front line was where a brigade commander belonged, at least part of the time.
>
> I used to take the little armoured car I rode around in, it had a big 52 radio set and I could talk for thirty miles back, so I could relay messages directly from the front to my headquarters and my battalions.[11]

To the men, and to one junior officer at least, their brigadier seemed omnipresent, sometimes dangerously so. "Sure, you can't read the battle from twenty-five miles back up the road, from a cellar someplace," one lieutenant agreed, "and Rocky would never commit troops to ground he hadn't looked over. But he sometimes carried things to the other extreme.

"He would come up to our forward positions (he seemed so

huge sticking out of that little scout car of his), and he'd pop off a few shots, stir things up. After he left, we'd get the hell pounded out of us with counterfire. But the men loved it. They thought he was God."[12]

But it wasn't always like that. Highland Light Infantry Padre Captain Jock Anderson, who had landed with the battalion at D-Day, is one of Rocky's greatest boosters. However, he recalls a time when the men detested Rockingham. Anderson described the pressure-cooker situation that Rocky walked into when he was sent by Simonds to replace a commander who had objected to an order to commit his men to what he felt was a no-win battle:

> They fired our brigadier and the COs of the Novas and Glens, and, as well, our CO had been badly wounded. Everyone on the ground in Normandy on the 8th and 9th of July knew we couldn't possibly regroup to make a night attack. So when Rockingham was appointed brigade commander, we felt this was a slap in the face to us. The men were resentful. Then, one Sunday evening as I was finishing a service, he stepped up and asked if he could say a few words. He told those men in no uncertain terms that orders were orders — he would obey any order he was given and he demanded the same from the men.
>
> The fellows were really mad, but after a while they respected him. He was always seen when the battle was toughest, and everybody thought the world of him then.[13]

The showmanship was part of the dashing Rockingham facade, the morale booster. But the philosophy of command, the issue of preservation of life of those troops that he loved, was a lot more serious. War was business with Rockingham:

> There is no peacetime job that can compare with the demands of wartime command. If you're really conscientious and really think about what you're doing, you're exposing the lives of thousands of men in everything you do. And they've got to follow you; they have no choice. So you'd better be right. In

business, if you take a wrong decision, you lose a lot of money or get fired. But that's pretty easy compared to losing a lot of lives.[14]

A Canadian private in 9 Infantry Brigade put it this way:

My best friend, Bob, he was a super guy. I'm sure he was just as scared as the rest of us but he never showed any signs of fear in Normandy.

But when we made that landing at Breskens, we were facing one another going across in the Buffalo. He had a ring that was given to him by a girl friend back in Canada, came from Long Branch. She was a Catholic, though I don't think Bob was. But anyway, he was sitting there rubbing this ring and it had a little cross on it and it was the first time Bob ever showed any real fear.

So I said to him, "What's wrong, Bob?" and he said, "I don't like this." One guy shows signs of going down, that's when you buck up yourself; a sort of natural reaction. I looked over to the next Buffalo and there was Brigadier Rockingham and I said, "Hell, Bob, this is not going to be that bad, the brigadier's here." But it was; it got rougher as it went. The next day Bob was killed in the barn. I guess he had a premonition that maybe he was going to get it. They say that sometimes happens.[15]

But the troops were only as good as the officers that commanded them, and most of all, Rocky esteemed his three COs. "I played my commanding officers like musical instruments in an orchestra," he would say. "There were certain jobs that fit each of them: Don Forbes, CO of the North Nova Scotia Highlanders, was the real staid, slow and steady Nova Scotia type — always got things done. Roger Rowley, SD&G commander, was just exactly the opposite — flashy and flamboyant — always in a hurry and a bit careless about what he left behind him. Phil Strickland, HLI, was a cross between the two of them — terribly clever, full of courage and ability. I admired him most in the world, I think."[16]

One of Rocky's so-called musical instruments, Lieutenant Colonel
Roger Rowley, commander of the Glens, echoed these sentiments:

> Rocky was absolutely superb, a first-class commander.
> Nobody had the big, black whip out like he did, but he kept
> us going. He was also, and I say this with respect, the best
> corporal in the Canadian Army: he knew more about tactics
> at the eyeball level than anybody I've ever seen.
>
> He told me once his analogy about playing us like an
> orchestra and he was right. Don Forbes was a super soldier
> and a very good tactician, a very meticulous, methodical
> kind of guy, used to smoke a big curved pipe. Phil Strickland
> also had his sort of personality and I guess I had mine.
>
> When Rocky wanted something cleaned up in a hurry
> or somebody to go somewhere, he always got me kicking out
> in front. Then he'd have to send Don Forbes in behind to
> clean it up, to pick up the pieces I'd left behind. Rocky was
> very good at that. He understood people. He understood his
> subordinates and what they were capable of. He put his
> money on that and he had a pretty good band. He played
> good music.[17]

During the initial assault by the two lead battalions, Rockingham
and Rowley waited anxiously on the near side of the Braakman.
Through the long pre-dawn hours, they sorted out the sporadic and
confused reports from the assault battalions. Rowley recounts the
ensuing events:

> At 0900 hours Rocky finally said, "You and I will go over
> now, Rog, anyway. We'll take your battalion over and you'll
> break out."
>
> The HLI had reported that they were on their objective,
> so when we got across the Braakman, Rocky and I decided
> to go and see them.
>
> We went through the enemy barrage and arrived in
> two carriers at what was supposed to be the HLI battalion
> headquarters. All of a sudden it got very quiet. There wasn't

anybody there but Germans; it was a very dicey little operation getting back to the farmhouse behind the beach where brigade tactical HQ was set up.[18]

A furious Rockingham got onto his 52 set and hollered for his brigade major, Phil Strickland, to get the hell across the Braakman and take over command of the HLI from its present commander. Strickland arrived on the beach and was told that the battalion had been cut off. "They're somewhere over there," Rockingham waved airily, "but the Germans are in between." The incumbent CO borrowed some North Nova carriers to make the plunge across 1,500 metres of German-held territory to reach his new command.[19]

Of the three battalions, the Highland Light Infantry was experiencing the most difficulty. One of their companies was prevented for some time from landing by heavy German machine-gun fire, and then was surrounded on three sides. Finally, with the help of flame throwers, they linked up with the battalion the next morning.

"For a while at the beginning we were in potential isolation," reported the new CO, Lieutenant Colonel Strickland. "We had no one on our flanks. The enemy could have encircled us and cut off part or all of the unit and infiltrated to the landing beach."[20]

The HLI, despite every effort, was unable for the moment to reach their objective, which was the small village of Biervliet just 1,500 metres inland. They were, instead, pinned down for several days by enemy counterattacks and bombardment. The beach had become a "hot spot." The Germans had turned the great guns of Walcheren on them.

There was a complete absence of protective cover for the troops, except in the lee of the dykes or in occasional buildings. The only vehicles with the landing troops were jeeps and carriers. But with all the roads on top of the dykes, these could be used only at night, and then at considerable risk.

"Mortar fire was coming down continuously, at the rate of three bombs every minute," reported Corporal E.C. Brownhill, of a mortar section of the Cameron Highlanders of Ottawa who landed in support of the HLI on this first assault wave: "I would get up, take some steps, and then drop down again. But I got so tired of doing that that

I just said to heck with it. I always tried to hang on to some kind of spiritual experience, and something told me to just get up and walk to that beach…you're going to be all right. And I did. Later on that first morning we had one guy come so close to three shells — three times they buried him in mud. But the mortars were exploding deep in the ground and most of their blast went straight up in the air. He refused to go back; he was absolutely bomb-happy." [21]

At 2100 hours the evening of the invasion, Captain Alf Turvey, RCASC, and his eighteen-man unit responsible for setting up a supply depot for the assaulting troops, were deposited on the beach by the Buffaloes. But by the time the service corps men made the crossing, the Germans had directed accurate fire on the landing beaches, knocking out all landing guidelights. Turvey, with 300 tons of vital ammunition and petrol on deck, was dumped on an unselected beach. He was awarded the Military Cross for his subsequent actions: "The Buffaloes let us down at the wrong spot. The important thing was to set up an ammunition dump, but we landed under continuous shelling and we had no idea where we were. We had two jeeps; mine was blown up. I finally found brigade HQ in a cellar. Rocky just looked up and said, 'What do you want?'"

Turvey reconnoitred alternative areas for supply depots throughout the night and organized the off-loading of the ammunition while still under heavy fire. He maintained the supply line for the forward troops for the next twelve days, bunking in with his men in the main floor of a farmhouse. "There were twenty civilians in the cellar," he recalls. "A few of them asked permission to return to their home in the next farmhouse about four hundred yards away. I said, sure they could go. I didn't know there were some Germans still in there. They opened up on one of the civilians when he was halfway there; we had to go over and actually clear the Germans out." [22]

Captain Jock Anderson, HLI padre, landed with the battalion as well. "He was always there," Major Ray Hodgins remembers. "He acted as counsellor, stretcher-bearer, doctor, the whole bit. Nothing was too much for Jock Anderson. He got two Military Crosses, and he was very deserving of them.

"And he also had, always, a crock of real farm butter in the back of his jeep that he'd share out with any of us. That was his loot." [23]

When the HLI landed on the mud flats of Breskens, Anderson, with his corporal and a handful of stretcher-bearers, rolled off the Buffalo in his ambulance jeep. The troops soon found out this was like no other battle they had ever been in. Padre Anderson agreed: "As soon as you landed on that first wave, there you were right in the middle of it. The Germans were on the next dyke, a couple of hundred yards away at most. It was almost like standing at one edge of a square. There would be one lot of them on this side, one on that and one ahead of you. You could almost feel it, it was so close."[24]

Heaving over the first dyke, they spotted a red-brick farmhouse just ahead, and very soon, working with the battalion doctor, they had begun setting up the Regimental Aid Post.

By 2200 hours, twenty-five casualties had been brought in. The wounded were evacuated by incoming Buffaloes. The death of CSM Johnny MacDonald was keenly felt. Twenty-nine years old, from Galt, Ontario, MacDonald had been with the battalion since mobilization; his brother had been killed in Normandy.

Anderson observed that the men were experiencing many more severe casualties than usual from small arms fire. "In other battles, it was mostly the mortar fire that caused the casualties, but only about 20 percent were fatal. At the Scheldt, many more casualties were from small arms fire, and these resulted in as much as 50 percent fatalities."[25]

On the afternoon of the 10th of October, standing on a dyke trying to locate the position of a particularly lethal machine gun, Forward Observing Officer Captain J.L. Murdoch of 19 Army Field was killed by the very fire he was attempting to pinpoint. This was reported to Anderson:

> I was told that Captain Murdoch's body was out there between two dykes. We couldn't go for the body right away because there were snipers around. But that night I went out for it. I said to the fellows, "I'm going out there in a jeep to try and find an officer that was killed. So don't shoot."
>
> So Mitch and I went out there and were going around and around until we finally found him. I always had a hook and a long rope. I would crawl in and put this on the

soldier's belt and then pull, because the Jerries were booby-trapping the dead. We'd been told if a body had lain out in the open for any length of time never to move it unless you moved it that way. We took his revolver off him and put him onto the stretcher and got him onto the jeep.

Just at that moment, three Germans walked up. Anderson had learned not to wear his Red Cross armband; it drew enemy fire. He was surprised to see that one of the Germans was carrying a Red Cross first-aid kit although he wasn't a first-aid man:

> They looked at me and I looked at them and I knew they were going to surrender. So I said, "All right, get in the jeep." They got in the jeep with us — Captain Murdoch, Mitch and me — and we drove down the road. There was a POW cage right on the beach so I turned them in.
>
> Later, I ran into the Provost who knew me quite well and he said, "Did you search them?" I said, "You know me better than to ask a question like that."
>
> But I had taken the German's first-aid box from him because I thought the civilians might need it as some of them were getting hit. That night I opened it up and there was a layer of bandages and underneath it was nothing but Belgian francs — all sorts of denominations. Later on, when we got a couple of days off, we went down to Brussels and we had a whale of a time doing our Christmas shopping with that.[26]

Three days after the landing, the HLI attacked Biervliet in a slogging house-by-house action bitterly contested by the enemy. Just before midnight, the Germans succeeded in infiltrating behind an HLI Company position until hand-to-hand fighting drove them off. "Private Beaudreau," reported the HLI War Diary with satisfaction, "broke his rifle and also an enemy weapon over the head of one of the attacking force."

It was evident that the Germans were obeying the edict to fight to the death. They had to win, or be shot down by their own guns. That this was no idle threat, the Canadians soon found out to their horror. HLI Major Tom Prest relates the incident: "By the second day, we had got quite a number of German prisoners and wounded. We put them in two large open farm carts and had the more able-bodied prisoners push them down the road to the evacuation point. They were on high ground, clearly visible, on a bright day, with the Red Cross flag displayed very prominently on the wagon.

"Next thing we knew, the Germans were shooting at the wagon full of their own men. They shot them all to pieces with a battery of 20mm German anti-aircraft guns."[27]

Captain Anderson, who came by at that point, saw the piles of dead and wounded German prisoners lying in carts by the road and tried to give help: "One of the Jerries tried to get up, so I jammed on the brakes, and Mitch and I ran over and got him on the jeep. While we were doing this, a Jerry was shooting at us from the field. Then I went over and felt the others. There were two that were still alive and we got them down. The Jerries were killing their own people. It's a horrible feeling to be trying to help a Jerry when his buddies are shooting at you."[28]

The biggest problem about the Scheldt was the fact that there was no let-up in the fighting. Other battles were wound up after a day or two. But at the Scheldt, from the time you went in until the time it was over, you were never away from it. The next days blurred into a seemingly endless series of skirmishes as the Highlanders forced a wedge westward. "I was soaking wet the whole time," recalls Tom Prest. "I don't think I ever had my shoes off during the whole Breskens battle."[29]

———◦———

The North Nova Scotia Highlanders had landed at the same time on dry beach to the right of the HLI, as Commander Franks had noted, but it didn't take the Germans long to come to life and start plastering the beach with every conceivable type of artillery shell and mortar bomb. Eberding had rushed reinforcements over from Walcheren Island and the Canadian artillery and infantry were kept busy driving off fresh counterattacks.

The battalion fought tenaciously; the enemy would not willingly yield an inch. In the first twenty-four hours the Novas' gain was a fragile three hundred metres. During the next week, they advanced some seven to eight km. And the polder war continued to provide surprises even for veteran riflemen, as the German troops, vastly underrated in intelligence reports to General Spry, fought with skill. The War Diary of the North Nova Scotia Highlanders reflects this: "This dyke to dyke fighting is very different to what we have been doing. It appears that the enemy here are a much better type than what we have been running into lately."

There was another difference. The battle for Breskens Pocket had been reduced to desperate slogging matches between platoons. The dyke roads ran in squares or blocks, and the Germans would be dug into the crossroad where two dykes intersected. One platoon, two at the most, with some carriers or flame throwers, would be sent in to clean them out.

Major Morris Clennett, commander of D Company with the North Nova Scotia Highlanders, recalls the appalling human cost of this "platoon war": "It was basically an NCO's and platoon commander's battle most of the time, at least as my company faced it. What happened was you were constantly moving across these polders. The only way to go was up the dykes, so this became a one-man front. That meant that somebody had to lead, and that job was always given to an NCO or a platoon commander. The result of it was I lost every lieutenant I took in, and I lost every NCO."[30]

"Finally the battalion started to run out of lieutenants," echoed the 2/I-C of the North Novas, Major F.A. Sparks: "In the end we only had one left. This guy had to be shuffled from company to company; he was killed by a blast of machine-gun fire on the 15th. Almost every company commander that went into that Breskens battle became a casualty — not wounded, killed."

A full keg of rum told its mute story of the heavy casualties. Sparks had all the rum ration sent over to the fighting troops, about six or seven hundred ounces a day: "A number of the men never took their rations and A and B Echelons didn't get much, so we ended up with gallons of rum. But by then we just didn't have enough officers or men to drink it up."[31]

The morning of October 15th was an ordinary day in the Breskens battle: wet and cold, a day with more dykes to conquer. Lieutenant

R.H. Tingley, cool, efficient D Company veteran, moved his platoon up against a German dyke position. He had been bothered with a bad leg but would not go to the medical officer as he knew he was needed very much in the line. Lieutenant Tingley was killed that morning attacking a little cross-dyke, leading his platoon in the attack.

That same morning, Lieutenant G.A. Godfrey was shot during a skirmish with German troops after leading his platoon in an all-night patrol. An outstanding officer, Lieutenant Godfrey had been requested to lead another platoon into battle the previous day. Returning to base after a long tough day, he learned that his original platoon was going out again on patrol and insisted on leading them. It was on this patrol that Godfrey was wounded.

Later that day, C Company of the North Novas was forced back twice from its objective by enemy machine-gun fire. The battalion history recounts the story of yet another lieutenant's action:

> A third attack was teed up, with more artillery support, and was finally successful chiefly because of the good work of the "Wasps" and Lieutenant G.A. Gibson. The enemy was dug in beneath piles of hay which Dutch farmers had placed on the dykes to dry.
>
> A squirt of flame at each pile caused a row of fire which quickly produced prisoners. Gibson's platoon then moved in quickly. This officer had fought with every company as he was superb in leading attacks. He rushed a post, secured a prisoner and marched him in front as he moved from one enemy slit to another, making the Germans emerge with hands up. All the slits were cleared in this manner and the first objective had been secured when another German climbed from a dyke hole to surrender.
>
> Lieutenant Gibson went out to make sure of him and was killed by a blast of machine-gun fire from a post 1000 yards away. His loss was a heavy one for the battalion.[32]

To add to their difficulties, the RAF in error strafed the mortar platoon, and, in spite of frantic signalling, injured two men and destroyed a carrier.

"Not far from the dyke where we landed there was a busted down farm with a little apple orchard," Major Sparks recounts sadly. "We had about seven or eight casualties at that point. Someone said, 'What will we do with these casualties?' I said, 'Let's bury them just at the back of the orchard.' When we came back at the end of the Breskens Pocket fight the whole orchard was filled.* It was just a mean, rotten damn month."[33]

But day after day, dyke after dyke, casualty after casualty, they pushed on. Lieutenant Burton Fitch, who commanded a twelve-man platoon with B Company, recalls the mindshattering fatigue of those days: "For seven days, just before the attack on Fort Frederik Hendrik, we were running on a total of about seven hours' sleep. You got to the point where you would hear an 88 shell being fired, making a lot of noise as it streaked across toward you, hear it land, hear it explode, and then you would duck. That's how tired we were."[34]

While the HLI and the North Nova Scotia Highlanders were struggling to establish and then enlarge a firm base to the rear of the enemy, the Stormont, Dundas and Glengarry was given the by-now familiar chore, in the words of Lieutenant Colonel Rowley, of "kicking out in front."

The SD&G's role in Operation Switchback, as it was officially known, was to act as breakout battalion. Its orders were to break out from the right flank of the bridgehead as soon as it was established by the North Nova Scotia Highlanders and cut west along the coastal seawall to the small port of Hoofdplaat. Because of the size limitations of the Buffalo, the force was of the absolute minimum assault scale.

A good portion of 3 Division's artillery had been deployed in support of 7th Brigade on the Leopold. In support of the 9th's amphibious assault was one regiment from the 4 Canadian Division and the 10th British Medium Regiment, which was used to fire DF(SOS) at

---

* Thirty-five Canadians, almost all of them from the HLI, were buried temporarily in that plot during the period of the Breskens Pocket battle. Their graves along the sea-dyke were cared for by Suzanna de Bruyne (now Mrs. de Koeyer), who lived in Schoondijke. The bodies were later reburied in the Canadian War Cemetery in Adegem, Belgium.

Breskens.* These guns were positioned on the shores of the Braakman, across the inlet, their fire directed by the FOO attached to the Glens. The artillery history, *The Gunners of Canada,* describes the action: "Four times next morning and twice more in the afternoon the SD&G came under increasingly violent counterattacks, and each time these were driven off with the help of the 4th Division's guns. Busy Canadian FOOs calling down neutralizing fire on the German positions on the dykes suffered a number of casualties. Captain E.E. Campbell of the 15th Field was twice wounded by shellfire while observing for the SD&Gs at Hoofdplaat." Campbell's assistant, Lance Bombadier Benjamin Clark coolly continued directing fire, earning a DCM for his heroic efforts.[35]

After a stiff fight, the battalion reached its objective the next afternoon. Once in Hoofdplaat, Rowley soon found out that not only was he travelling light, he was also travelling alone. The North Novas, who were to have moved up on the SD&G's left, had been unable to get on their objective. The Glengarries were isolated, their right flank on the Scheldt, their left flank completely exposed.

To add to the seriousness of their position, the Glengarries discovered they had advanced beyond the reach of their own field artillery. They now had to rely only on support from the medium guns, as well as the machine guns and mortar fire of the Camerons of Ottawa to repel a fiercely counterattacking enemy. Because of heavy rain, little or no air support could be given. Colonel Rowley recalls the complete isolation in which he suddenly found himself:

> For three days we were surrounded by Germans. It was a very messy operation. Not only were we on our own, we had very little artillery support. In fact, we had run out of our own field artillery because we had advanced so far. We had crossed three thousand metres of water at the Braakman; then we went another six thousand on land. This put us out of range of the field guns.

---

* A DF(SOS): literally SOS (Save Our Souls) Defensive Fire — a prearranged artillery target to bring the greatest fire in the least time on the prime line of approach of an expected enemy attack.

We were being severely shelled from the big placement guns at Flushing across the way. They were in concrete fortifications with closing doors. We tried to get the Typhoons to low-level attack, which they did, but it didn't make much difference. It was very difficult to knock these gun positions out.

In those grim days, from the 9th to the 11th of October, fifteen Glengarries were killed, and forty-six wounded.

"Finally, the Novas came along to protect our left flank and we moved on," Rowley said. "I thought it was endless. You'd get to Hoofdplaat and somebody would say, 'Take out Driewegen.' And then somebody would say, 'Take out Hoogeweg'…'take out Roodenhoek.'"

Then, on 21 October, someone at a very high level said to Colonel Rowley, "Take out Breskens."

Rowley recalls the difficulties that beset him, one after another:

Breskens was a fortified city, completely surrounded by an antitank ditch, mine fields, wire and every other conceivable defence. The plan was that we would have the support of a squadron of "Funnies" from 79 Armoured Division. We were to have the AVRES to knock out strongpoints, Flails to break their way through the mine fields and wire, plus the flame-throwing Crocodiles. We were also supposed to have heavy bombardment from the RAF bombers before we went in.

Then a tragedy occurred:

The squadron of the 79th was in a circle refueling at IJzendijke. There were ammunition trucks coming into this laager. A Ratchet mine was buried in the road and about the fourteenth vehicle hit it and blew it up; it blew the whole squadron to kingdom come. There was nobody left alive who was not either blind, or deaf, or both. The rest of them were dead. There were eighty-four casualties; ten armoured vehicles were knocked out.

These vehicles were intended to get us through the defences and across the antitank ditch into Breskens. That was the first piece of bad news. It came through that afternoon and we were supposed to attack at dawn the next morning. The next bad news we got was that the heavy bombers couldn't take off from England; the weather was bad. So that meant I had no support.

Rocky went to Dan Spry, who told the corps commander that the operation had to be cancelled. But before long, a message came back from Mr. Churchill himself that not only was it on, but it would go on time.

On the sort of personal side, I was having my brother over to dinner. The outlook had been so grim, I didn't think I'd ever see him again. Then the news came through that the operation was cancelled. So we had a hell of a good time for about a half an hour or an hour. Then the bad news came that we were to go anyway.

Rowley found he had to change the whole plan in a hurry:

What we did was to go in on a one-man front. We went along the seawall and used kapok bridging equipment which got us over the antitank ditch into Breskens. Of course the Germans never believed that anybody would be so foolish as to put in an attack from there, so we got in with very few casualties. We were in on top of them before they knew what had happened and took 150 prisoners.

Then the shelling started at point-blank range from Flushing. They must have known we were in there. They were firing over open sites. What we found out later was that the Germans were trying to hit the docks that had been prepared for demolition. If they'd ever hit them, they would have blown the whole place out of the water, but they never did.[36]

Rowley's citation attests to his courage and that of his men:

CITATION — BAR TO DSO — IMMEDIATE

Lieutenant Colonel Roger Rowley led his battalion in the face of heavy enemy opposition with such brilliance, courage and speed as to capture the garrison of Breskens and prevent a further escape or reinforcement of the entire German garrison north of the Leopold Canal.

On 22 October, the SD&G were to attack with a squadron of armoured vehicles of Royal Engineers against the strongly fortified port of Breskens, which was surrounded by a twenty-foot antitank ditch full of water twelve feet deep. Shortly before the operation was due to commence an accidental explosion destroyed the majority of the squadron and a new plan had to be made.

In spite of the shortage of time, Lieutenant Colonel Rowley planned and ordered the new attack with such brilliance and led it with such determination that the garrison was quickly overcome and Breskens was captured.

The capture of this port cut off the last remaining line of retreat, support or reinforcement for the German garrison and contributed largely to the ultimate defeat of the German garrison.

B.L. MONTGOMERY

On the 21st, the North Nova Scotia Highlanders were in reserve position for the SD&G's successful assault on the port of Breskens. The next day, D Company of the North Novas was ordered to act as a patrol in force and occupy the ancient Dutch fort of Fort Frederik Hendrik, just northwest of the town of Breskens. One of Hitler's fortresses, it was strongly defended. But the North Novas had a secret weapon in the person of Lieutenant Colonel D.F. Forbes.

Behind the staid, pipe-smoking facade, Don Forbes had become a legend within his own battalion for his frequent reconnaissance patrols to the front line. It was a well-kept secret; even Rockingham, who was noted as a front-line adventurer, would have disapproved of such risky ploys by one of his battalion commanders.

"Don was absolutely fearless," recalls HLI Commanding Officer Phil Strickland. "If he had an attack to put in and there was some doubtful point, Don would go up personally, perhaps with a Bren gunner behind him, and have a look. If his FOO wasn't getting accurate artillery concentration, Don would get up there and call it down himself.

"I did it once or twice myself, just because Don shamed me into it. But we never reported it to Rocky."[37]

But it seemed that no amount of reconnaissance or planning could crack the concrete fortress. Each of the two attacks over two days against the moated fortification was repulsed by severe fire from German machine guns and mortars. Two officers, again both lieutenants, were killed.

A third attack, more massive in scale with supporting arms and air bombardment, was scheduled to go in at dawn of the 25th. However, during the previous night, three Germans drifted into the Glengarry headquarters in Breskens to announce that there were only fifty men left in the fort, and they wanted to surrender. Thus fell Hitler's mighty fortress.

So, on the high note of success on all fronts, the morale of all three battalions of 9 Canadian Infantry Brigade was jubilant. Fighting first in perilous isolation and then in finely coordinated interactions, each battalion had met its objectives, wresting the eastern half of the Pocket from the enemy. On the 21st of October the SD&G took Breskens; the next day, the HLI attacked Schoondijke and, two days later, the North Nova Scotia Highlanders had Fort Frederik Hendrik — three important German strongpoints.

Sixteen days after being deposited by the Buffaloes onto the mud flats of the Braakman, after fighting without a minute's respite from the dual enemies of ceaseless mud and German fire, the Water Rats of the 9th Brigade were placed in reserve and sent back to IJzendijke for a four-day rest.

And Major Tom Prest of the HLI finally got to take his shoes off.

———•———

The original Switchback plan called for the 8th Canadian Infantry Brigade, made up of the North Shore (New Brunswick) Regiment, The Queen's Own Rifles and the Régiment de la Chaudière to break out through a bridgehead established by the 7th Canadian Infantry Brigade across the Leopold Canal.

In line with this, on the 6th of October, two companies of the North Shore (New Brunswick) Regiment were attached to 7th Brigade to carry and maintain the service of the boats during and for several hours after the actual assault on the Leopold. Owing to the inability of 7th Brigade to expand the bridgehead, the original plan was cancelled by General Spry and replaced by an assault crossing of the Braakman by the 8th Canadian Infantry Brigade utilizing the 9th Brigade landing area to reinforce success. The 8th Brigade was then to press south with the twin objectives of opening a land route from the area south of the Leopold Canal into Breskens Pocket and of relieving the pressure on the 7th Brigade.

The North Shores embarked and crossed the Braakman at 0600 hours on 11 October in Buffaloes, and by the evening of the 12th all three battalions were across and established in the area just north and east of Biervliet.

Private Jack Martin of the Queen's Own Rifles remembers the frightening trip: "Crossing on those Buffaloes was probably the most terrifying part. You were down so deep below the water surface, like you were in a submarine. Thank God they only travel ten or twelve inches above the surface so there is very little target to shoot at."[38]

On the 13th of October, the North Shores captured the ground to the east of Biervliet with the help of strong support from the artillery. Then the Queen's Own relieved the Highland Light Infantry in Biervliet.

On the 15th of October, the Queen's Own made contact with the Argyll and Sutherland Highlanders of the 4th Canadian Armoured Division, thus opening a land route to the Pocket. This alleviated a pressing problem for transport and supplies.

After that a period of prolonged mud slogging developed. The dykes, the mud, the water, the lack of manoeuvrability, the lack of reinforcements, the strength of the German defences and his resolution not to give in all contributed to the fact that the ten-day period from the 15th to the 24th of October saw the advance going at a snail's pace.

An infantry officer spoke for all the men when he wrote:

Do you know what it's like? Of course you don't. You have never slept in a hole in the ground which you have dug while someone tried to kill you. It is an open grave — and yet graves don't fill up with water. They don't harbour wasps or mosquitoes, and you don't feel the cold, clammy wet that goes into your marrow. At night the infantryman gets some boards, or tin, or an old door, and puts it over one end of his slit trench; then he shovels on top of it as much dirt as he can scrape up nearby. He sleeps with his head under this, not to keep out the rain, but to protect his head and chest from airbursts. In the daytime he chain-smokes, curses, or prays — all of this lying on his belly with his hands under his chest to lessen the pain from the blast. If it is at night, smoking is taboo. If there are two in a trench they sit at each end with their heads between their knees and make inane remarks such as, "Guess that one landed in 12 Platoon."[39]

Casualties soared. "The whole Scheldt battle was company attacks, day after day," said Major Corbett of the North Shores, "sometimes two or three attacks in twenty-four hours. The weather was wet and we were soaked all the time. Along the dykes was the only place a soldier could dig in. Down on the flats, water would drain in at once. We gradually worked our way along but every day saw some casualties."[40]

Captain Ben Dunkleman, mortar officer with the Queen's Own, developed a healthy respect for the enemy: "Those Germans of 64 Division, they were the cream. They were regulars. Most of them had a number of years of experience. War was their business. They were brave, well trained and disciplined. Damn good soldiers."[41]

Fighting was at this point the same for all three battalions of 8th Brigade. It was slow, tedious and dangerous work. With no cover, and enemy strongpoints on all the dyke crossings, the men had to inch their way forward either along the raised, exposed dykes, or below, in the water-filled ditches. It was this sort of lethal, one-man front, highly weighted on the side of the defence rather than the attacker, that can erode into and blunt "the cutting edge of a division," as General Brian Horrocks once put it: "In a section of ten men, as a rough guide, two lead, seven follow and one would do almost anything not to be there at all. The two leaders take most of the risks and are usually the first to become casualties."[42]

On the Scheldt, rank did not spare a man from bullets. On the 17th of October, Lieutenant Colonel T.A. Lewis, acting 8th Brigade commander, went missing. Lewis had gone forward to the Chaudière start line the night before an attack. The following morning, his body was found, along with his wounded driver. The driver reported that he had taken a wrong turn, driving straight into an enemy strongpoint. The Germans had apparently ambushed them, dressed the driver's wounds, and left. Four gunners of the 13th Field Regiment had made the same tragic error on the previous day. (One was discovered dead, three subsequently were found to have been taken prisoner.)

Lieutenant Harry Hamley of the North Shore Regiment made his mark on the German troops, with an unorthodox attack that inspired German awe. Hamley ordered his men to fix bayonets, borrowed a rifle for himself and led his platoon in a wild charge that so startled and frightened a German gun crew that they did not fire a shot but threw up their hands and surrendered. The North Shores captured a German major who talked of what he called the "Canadian SS troops": "We can handle the Yanks and the Limeys within reason," he said, "but you Canadians come at us at night with flame throwers, mortars, machine guns, everything — yelling like hell. And you simply terrify our troops."[43]

By the 17th of October, IJzendijke had been taken and by the 22nd, Schoondijke. But the Germans were still shelling all units constantly. Two platoons of the Régiment de la Chaudière were under a particularly heavy concentration of fire. One of the men, somewhat shaken by the bombardment, stuck his head out of his slit trench and demanded whether it was our fire or the Germans'. An officer replied, *"N'aie pas peur, c'est la nôtre."*[44]

Next, on the 24th of October, the Queen's Own was ordered to capture the strongly held town of Oostburg. The attack was launched from the south and by dint of an intrepid bayonet charge led by Lieutenant J.E. Boos, A Company, a foothold at the entrance to the town was established. Boos received the MC for this valiant effort. By the 26 October, the Germans had had enough and surrendered. Some two hundred prisoners were taken.

However, there were other pockets of enemy who would never give up, as the Chaudières discovered on the 24th when one whole company was cut off and captured:

> B Company attacks about noon and captures twenty-two
> prisoners. A half hour later, B Company reports "We are

counterattacked — more later." D Company from an observation post can see that a battle is raging. As it was impossible to communicate via radio, a battle group was sent to make contact with our troops and to learn what had happened. The group could not reach B; the enemy had surrounded them and consolidated their position. Lieutenant R. Nadeau was killed during this counterattack as well as twenty soldiers. During the night, fifteen men escaped and got back to our lines. They told what had happened. The Germans had let the company advance without much opposition, simulating a retreat. While our troops were advancing, the enemy covered the flanks, then finally closed the circle and concentrated the fire of their automatic weapons on our troops who found themselves completely surrounded. It was a slaughter. The survivors were taken prisoner.[45]

During the afternoon of 29th October, Lieutenant Colonel James Roberts was placed in command of 8th Brigade. He arrived just in time to have a bridge named after him:

By the end of that day, 30 October, the Chaudières had advanced right up to the canal and had even crossed the water obstacle to form a small bridgehead directly in front of Sluis. The matter of a bridge built to replace the blown one was solved by the Chaudières with French Canadian ingenuity, by simply driving a Bren Gun Carrier into the narrow canal and piling earth, fill, wooden planks and steel beams on top of the almost submerged carrier. It worked perfectly, and next morning the Queen's Own Rifles passed over it. Régiment de la Chaudière, typically courteous and thoughtful, named the small but usefully improvised bridge "Roberts Bridge"; the men even took a photograph and gave it to me later to retain among my souvenirs.[46]

After passing through the Chaudières, the Queen's Own Rifles took Sluis and pressed on to their final objective, Westkapelle. Major Charles O. Dalton was in command. A large concentration of artillery was ready to support any advance. The approach was a narrow, straight road which stretched for a kilometre with water lapping at both verges. There was no cover. Dalton's brother, Elliot, commanding B Company, was in line to lead a frontal attack.

But then the scouts reported that they thought Westkapelle held a lot of civilian evacuees. Using the guns would undoubtedly kill and injure the innocent Dutch. Charlie Dalton faced a terrible decision: his brother's life versus the lives of many civilians:

> We could only use one company because of the narrowness of the road. That morning it had to be B Company, commanded by my brother Elliot. The question was, would I send him down this mile-long road where he and his troops would be mowed down if the Germans started firing on them, or would we flatten the place first with artillery? After spending the night thinking about it, I eventually decided we'd go in dry and hope for the best. Much to the astonishment of all there were no casualties, no shots fired and the Germans just gave up.[47]

During the Battle of the Scheldt, the support arm utilized to the largest extent was the artillery. The Canadian Infantry Division's standard complement of three regiments (twenty-four guns each) was bolstered at times by additional field, medium, heavy, antiaircraft and antitank regiments.

All the tasks of these weapons were coordinated by Brigadier Bruce Matthews, senior gunnery officer at 2nd Canadian Corps. Their assistance to the infantry was invaluable. Infantry and artillery worked together to achieve the ultimate in cooperation and coordination. Awkward, difficult and even perilous situations were restored time after time by the accuracy and deadly effectiveness of the Canadian artillery. Most attacks would not have been successful without artillery support.

This teamwork gave split-second results. Brigadier John Rockingham recalled that on many occasions he would say to his artillery representative, Lieutenant Colonel Hal Griffin, "Hal, quick! Get a concentration of fire down here!" And in a few seconds Griffin would come rushing up, "It's in the air, it's in the air."[48]

The commander of the 13th Field Regiment, Lieutenant Colonel Frank Lace, worked out a system which provided comprehensive support to the infantry:

> We engaged in a practice that was utilized in other places, but not, in my experience, to any great extent. We would make a series of potential targets on known or suspected enemy positions. Then I would spend the night passing that information down to the batteries, numbering each concentration and coding each group.
>
> I could then make up a fire plan on a moment's notice. If the infantry wanted to attack so-and-so, I would look at the concentrations we had, maybe add one or two to them and the code name of some little group of concentrations, for example, "MABEL." I would then give the order, "MABEL INTENSE for ten minutes," give them a zero hour, and away they'd go. So it was a flexible fire plan which normally takes quite a long time to prepare, but it already was pre-prepared. We made them up as we went along and this speeded the whole process up.[49]

On one occasion, the most brilliant, and certainly the most unique aspect of the Canadian artillery throughout the Breskens battle, occurred when it was able to shell the enemy from behind, in front and on his flank at the same instant. "That's probably one of the few times in history when the infantry was advancing towards its own artillery fire," observed Brigadier Stan Todd, Commander of Royal Artillery, 3rd Division Headquarters.[50]

In fact, the guns of the 13th Field Regiment were firing north from their position along the Leopold Canal as the Canadians were advancing south against the enemy. That one regiment fired 82,700 rounds, equivalent to one thousand tons of high explosive, in the final four weeks of the Scheldt battle.

The 14th Field was also shelling the German line, but they were firing from across the Braakman, from the flank of the Canadian troops and with "impressive accuracy," according to Major Prest of the HLI. "They brought down fire within at least one hundred yards of our positions, sometimes less," he recalled.[51]

At the same time, the 15th and 19th Field Regiments provided artillery support in the orthodox manner from behind the advancing Canadians.

Much of the success achieved must be attributed to the Forward Observation Officers. These FOOs were artillery captains or lieutenants who were attached to the forward infantry battalions, usually two to each one.

Their job was to move with the infantry, keeping in constant communication with their own regiments and gun positions, and signalling for fire if, as, and when infantry needed it. To do this, they had to be in the forefront of the battle, in a position to see where their shells were landing, and to then make necessary corrections if required.

Frank Lace had this to say about FOOs:

Of all the gunners that fought, they were the heroes of the artillery. So many of them were older, like Jack Hooper. He was a FOO from D-Day right through to the end of November. I don't suppose he was ever out of action; the guns never were. This is not to say that we didn't need the rest. The infantry might be off-duty, but we'd be supporting somebody else. As far as I know, the guns were never out of action from D-Day until we got to Nijmegen in late November when the war settled down. They were supporting somebody all the time. While the guns are in action, somebody has to be directing them. So those FOOs were out there.

They walked forward with the company or platoon commanders in the attacks; they were with them on the defence, usually exposed. When the company received relief, the FOO would be switched over to another company commander and still go on sweating it out. Some of them would begin counting — the ones that had missed them and the ones that didn't miss. When the casualty figures get so high, you begin to say the odds are getting pretty small.

I think of Jack Hooper particularly; he's a typical example. He was getting very, very uptight. I had to get him some reprieve. There wasn't enough attention paid to relieving those guys. I don't say they were all good, but the FOOs became a very important part of our infantry.[52]

A number of other branches of the Canadian Army had important roles to play in infantry support. A vast number of men had been trained to precise skills in very specific fields: there was the Royal Canadian Army Service Corps, where Lieutenant Eperson distinguished himself, providing transportation for all supplies. The Royal Canadian Engineers was an arm of the Canadian Army that seemed invariably to be employed in high-risk areas. On the Leopold, they worked — often under heavy enemy fire — to build the bridges. When enemy shelling destroyed their work, they would build it again. And again. As well, the engineers prepared demolitions, cleared mines and took on many other technically demanding and critically important jobs.

The Royal Canadian Army Medical Corps was the life-saver of the services, managing the care of the wounded man from the flooded field where he fell to the forward dressing station and then back to the security of the Canadian medical theatre. The Royal Canadian Signal Corps was responsible for all communications, the Royal Canadian Ordnance Corps for supplies, the Royal Canadian Electric and Mechanical Engineers for the maintenance and repair of vehicles.

The Division's Reconnaissance Regiment provided the Division's eyes and ears, a fast-moving, mobile unit of which the prime responsibility was to gather information about the enemy. Not a part of a Division, but available on call, were the units of the Royal Canadian Army Tank Brigade, whose tanks served either to eliminate enemy tanks or strongpoints, or to cooperate with the foot soldier in the basic tactical principle of fire and movement by shooting the infantry onto their objectives.

Each of these services had a unique contribution to make, but for each man it was his own branch of the service that was the best. A corporal in a mortar platoon of the 3rd Canadian Infantry Division put it this way:

I think everybody did their own thing. The guys in the tank corps used to talk to us guys in the mortar platoon: "Gees,

I'm glad I'm not out there with you guys. You have no protection." And we'd answer, "You're too big a bloody target." And you know when a tank gets hit, most times it's game over. Those poor guys don't even get out; they're on fire.

The guys in the infantry thought the guys in the carrier platoon and the antitank carriers had it easier than those guys that walked, but we were the first vehicles up the road. That could be really rough because of the mines and stuff.

I'm not belittling the infantry at all — my God, my heart goes out to those guys. They had to do patrols and that hand-to-hand stuff, something I was glad I never had to do. Patrols were pretty tough going, pretty scary; it would take a lot of guts.

And the guy in the air force, he comes back to white sheets and pubs every night, and he's saying the same thing, "Gees, I look down and see you guys down there and I'm glad I'm not with you."

So each guy picked his own environment, where he was familiar with his surroundings and could put up with what the hell he had to put up with.[53]

———— • ————

On the 20th of October, after a few days' rest and refit, the three battalions of 7 Brigade took up the fight, with the task of clearing the north coast of the Pocket from west of Fort Frederik Hendrik. All units fought against enemy-delaying tactics as they slowly edged their way westward towards Cadzand, where German batteries still pounded at the attackers. It was a miserable ten days for the brigade, still enduring the raw wet and cold of late October weather, and the continual threats of numerous enemy mines and constant shelling.

The Regina Rifles described one attack where a company pushed into what looked like a neat little Dutch village: "Just as [we] assaulted the place the men suddenly felt quite sick — the 'village' turned out to be pillboxes, all daintily camouflaged as stores, houses and sheds. Fortunately, what could have turned out to be slaughter was an almost painless show. Once in the 'village' the garrison streamed out to surrender. [We] had taken 250 prisoners by nightfall."[54]

To Major M.R. Douglas, the final surrender at Cadzand offered a tense moment:

> The Cadzand battery was still firing. A man came out to me under the white flag, a doctor, asking for a cease-fire until they could pick up their wounded. I wouldn't let them do it. We had pretty good pressure on them and we figured they just wanted a little time. So we didn't want to take the pressure off.
>
> The man came back out again. Our troops picked him up, put a blindfold on him, and brought him to my HQ where I questioned him through an interpreter. Then I went back with him and took the surrender. We brought out about 300 Jerries from there, the whole battery.[55]

By the 2nd of November, the pressure from chiefs of staff to get Antwerp open had become intense. But the peculiar nature of the fighting still demanded slow methodical plugging. Progress was being made, though, and the Reginas were impressed with a firsthand view of the enemy defence positions: "The fortifications along the coastline were modern and well equipped with underground chambers, casements and small arms positions. Everything was made of concrete, from the coastal gun positions to the outlying slit trenches."[56]

In the early morning of the 2nd of November, a white flag was raised over the remaining strongpoints and the show was over for the 7th Brigade.

Meanwhile, the 9th Brigade saw action again on the 31st of October when the SD&G and HLI crossed a north-south canal and established a bridgehead at Retranchement, an ancient village near the Dutch/Belgian border, whose fortifications dated back to the Napoleonic era. The North Nova Scotia Highlanders passed through with orders to deploy across the Belgian border towards Knokke. Advancing during the night and surprising the Germans along the way, the Novas took many prisoners including a German colonel and his staff. However, a still bigger prize awaited them not far away: their final objective, the elegant seaside resort of Knokke. Poised at its boundaries, the battalions were planning a full-scale attack with heavy artillery and air bombardment to capture this last German outpost.

What occurred can only be described as the miracle of Knokke. On the night of October 31, 1944, one Camille Vervarcke, a member of the Belgian Underground, came out of his attic hideout for a brief walk, and made a discovery that was to save his hometown of Knokke in Belgium and many of its citizens from certain destruction.

Throughout the war years, Vervarcke's job had been to utilize his skill as an artist in drawing maps of defences; these sketches were then sent by the underground route to the war office in London. He spoke fluent English, so Vervarcke was also required to take note of all news bulletins from the BBC and to make reports on their contents to the local head of the Resistance. Then, in 1943, the young Resistance worker was arrested and sent to a forced labour camp.

In the fall of 1944, he had escaped from the Gestapo, making his way cautiously back to his home in the town of Knokke, where for the next year he was forced to go into hiding. It was, however, his custom to take a nocturnal stroll, and it was on one of these secret outings that Vervarcke made his discovery.

Just around the corner from where Vervarcke had been in hiding from the Gestapo, two hundred Canadian troops had been held prisoner in the cellar of a large garage. Some of these men were members of the Régiment de la Chaudière. However, standing in front of the garage on Kustlaan Bunnen that night, brandishing German guns, were several of the Canadian prisoners, now clearly in control of their captors.

Young Vervarcke immediately went to the house of his commander on Elizabethlaan to report this news. He discovered from other agents that the Canadian troops, who were poised for attack on the outskirts of the city, had sent advance patrols towards the city, and that the Germans were in full retreat. Vervarcke was instructed to report these findings directly to the Canadian authorities. Immediately, he set out into the night on his bicycle, crossing the German lines. Finally, he came upon the HQ of the SD&G. In Vervarcke's words: "The officer asked me to guide his men in a Bren gun carrier through the minefields. 'You will ride in the first one!' they told me. I was happy because I expected to ride triumphantly with the first troops into Knokke. However, we were stopped further along the road and I had to repeat my story several times more. Finally, they asked for a password. I had not been given one, but I remembered that my commander signed his papers 'ALEXANDER 7001,' which proved to be the correct password."[57]

Officers of the SD&G still remember the last-minute order cancelling the artillery barrage that would have flattened Knokke. For this heroic service Vervarcke was awarded the Croix de Guerre with Bar, equivalent to the Military Cross.

The last German stragglers at Knokke surrendered to the North Novas on the 2nd of November and after neutralizing three or four enclaves on the coast near Heyst, which afforded little opposition, the Battle of Breskens Pocket was over.

On the 1st of November, a German officer appeared with his hands in the air before a company commander of the North Novas; he stated that his divisional commander wanted to arrange terms for surrender. Lieutenant Colonel Don Forbes gave them until 1600 hours to give themselves up, and exactly at the appointed time Major General Eberding, commander of the 64th Infantry Division, and his staff of one hundred, came out of the fortified pillbox and were marched off to the POW cage. There had been, the German recalled, no alternative but to surrender: "My staff and I were in Knokke in bunkers; no further troops were available between us and the enemy. We were between buildings from which armed civilians shot at us from out of the windows and from roofs and we had casualties by them. Then, as a few Canadian tanks appeared, I ordered the end of resistance."

But even in his defeat, Eberding clung to the cockiness of the victor. He had achieved his goal, he claimed with arrogance; the Allied forces had been held back: "The 64th Division prolonged this struggle, longer than in other fortresses. On the other side there were tactical errors made by the attackers, which I have pointed out, but which don't show up in any of the books on the Allied side."[58]

An eyewitness to the arrest of the German commander described the elaborate cases of "loot and luggage" that filled one entire jeep. The Intelligence Summary of the 3rd Canadian Infantry Division confirms the remarkable details of the procession: "When General Eberding of 64 Div decided surrender was inevitable, he determined to relax and enjoy it — in his own way. He told his servant Frank to pack his bags for a long captivity, and not to forget his chess set and books. So Frank piled in the staff officer's trousers, the polished high boots, the suit of civvies, the fur-lined gloves, the extra stock of generals' insignia, hats various, the underwear, and above all, the general's chess library — some fifteen printed works and manuscript notebooks."[59]

Sitting in front of a large camouflaged canvas tent that was Tactical Headquarters of 3 Canadian Infantry Division, Major General Knut Eberding, commander of the 64th Infantry Division, downed three fingers of neat whisky. Before him stood Major General Dan Spry. These two men had known during the four-week clash of command skills that this meeting was inevitable. The imponderable had been merely which one would be sitting and which standing in the confrontation.

> Now, General Spry began the interrogation: We sat [Eberding] down on a deck chair and I had my specialist people like the gunner and the engineer, the medical and the signals, with me. We gave him neat whisky and got him talking.
>
> Eberding was a smart well-turned-out professional soldier, well educated and well trained. He spoke some English and it went very well. In fact our signals people dug up an underground cable, a civilian cable that ran back to his HQ and we got him to talk to them while we were interviewing him.
>
> We then persuaded him to get up and mark on our map his medical locations on the pretext that I didn't want to bomb or shell our own captured/wounded in his medical installations, and he got up and marked them on the map for me. Of course, once you see the medical layout you can pretty well figure out what his troop layout is. And we then ordered no bombing, no shelling, no mortaring in those areas for the sake of our own wounded/captured. A few days after that we overran the whole thing and it was all finished.[60]

On the 4th of November, Dan Spry's Water Rats thankfully turned their backs on the Scheldt, earning a few days' respite from war. "They said that it would only be a few days' work...that there were only six thousand Germans in the Pocket. But it took a month. And we took over twelve thousand prisoners," related Spry.[61] The men of the 3rd Division had lost 314 dead and 2,077 wounded, with 231 reported missing in action. The German High Command did not release their casualty figures for the Scheldt operation; indeed, the figures have never been released.

More telling were the statistics that each man who fought remembers still. In a single company of the North Novas, as a grim example, every sergeant and corporal became a casualty, as did most of the lance-corporals. With the single exception of Major Clennett, every officer of the company who made the original assault at the Scheldt, and three others who joined after the fighting began, had been killed or wounded. Certainly, in this war by platoon, every NCO and every lieutenant in the company became a battle statistic — a personal statistic, much of the time, as in brothers seeing brothers, or friends seeing friends lying wounded or dead in the despised polderland.

The Causeway

IN THE MEDIEVAL BELGIAN TOWN OF BRUGES, THE CONFERENCE ROOM of the Grand Hotel seemed shrouded in perpetual smoke as team after team of experts worked throughout the month of October developing final plans to attack the fortress island of Walcheren.

By the last day of the month, the troops had achieved three of the four hard-won tasks assigned to the 1st Canadian Army: the 3rd Canadian Infantry Division, with preliminary help from the 4th Canadian Armoured Division and the 1st Polish Division, had all but cleaned up Breskens Pocket, securing the south bank of the Scheldt. That operation had taken seven weeks in total. The two armoured divisions had then joined up with the 1st British Corps and the 104th U.S. Division to drive the Germans back from the area in the eastern periphery of the Scheldt, providing essential right flank protection for the Canadian Army.

While their flank was being secured, the 2nd Canadian Division had moved up from Antwerp, where they had pushed the enemy out of the port and collapsed his defences on the Albert and Turnhout canals. The strategically sensitive area of Woensdrecht at the neck of the Beveland Peninsula had been consolidated. This action had absorbed the attention of the three brigades of 2nd Division for the subsequent eighteen days in a series of battles, each more bloody than the one before.

Finally, the 2nd Division turned full circle to the west, clearing out the forty-km-long Beveland Peninsula in less than a week against softening enemy resistance. On the 26th of October they linked up with the British 52nd (Lowland) Division, which had made an amphibious landing on the underside of the peninsula.

Of the German defences, only Walcheren, with its menacing gun batteries, remained. But that was enough to guarantee enemy control of the shipping lanes of the Scheldt. The pressure was on. From the 16th of October, both Eisenhower and Montgomery had belatedly decreed that the clearing of the Scheldt and the opening of Antwerp Harbour were to take priority over all other Allied operations. The task that Ramsay and Simonds had urged be given immediate priority early in September was finally receiving long overdue attention. And the word from both London and Washington was, "Hurry up — open Antwerp!" This urgency filtered down through the 21st Army Group, the 1st Canadian Army, the 2nd Canadian Corps, the 2nd, the 3rd and the 4th Canadian Divisions to all brigades and battalions. And at a number of levels, more than one resentful commander remembers being hauled back from the front to receive an important communication, which always began: "This is big, big, BIG Sunray ...why in hell aren't you moving faster?" The causeway battle typified that state of high urgency; the pressure accelerated as the prize grew closer.

General Simonds had realized from the start that Walcheren would be the last, and possibly the toughest, nut to crack. His plan was three-fold: first, the breaching of the island's dykes to destroy by flooding all enemy communications, cutting off his supplies and forcing him to concentrate his forces; second, the intensive "softening up" of the major gun batteries by bombers; and finally, when all other German positions in Zeeland had been wiped out, the invasion.

The island was to be invaded, more or less concurrently, from three sides. British commando and infantry troops would make two of the assaults: one, at dawn on the 1st of November, on the city of Flushing at the mouth of the Scheldt; the second, four hours later, at the Westkapelle strongpoint on the west coast of the island.

The third invasion, leading off early in the afternoon of the 31st, was to be from the east across the Sloe Channel, a narrow waterway that separated Walcheren from the mainland of South Beveland. The task of establishing a bridgehead on the enemy side of the channel would begin as a Canadian operation, its final action in the Scheldt campaign, with the British 52nd (Lowland) Division passing through it almost immediately to strike out into the heart of the island.

The 5th Canadian Infantry Brigade was given that job. Immediately, they ran into problems. "On the quarter-inch-to-a-mile map back at 5th Brigade HQ, the channel showed up as a half-mile strip of blue," remembers Brigade Major George Hees. "So we figured that was enough water for boats to get across and we ordered up the assault boats. When the Germans pulled back and we had our first good look at the channel, this so-called blue water came up only twice a day; the rest of the time it was soft mud. That cancelled any idea we had about getting an amphibious crossing. There was only one way over and that was on this damned causeway."[1]

The epithet was well deserved. The Walcheren Causeway, the only land-link between South Beveland and the island, was an ordinary raised embankment standing some seven metres above the high-water line. It was dead straight, about twelve hundred metres long and forty metres wide. The familiar rows of poplars, so typical to Dutch landscapes, bordered an elevated rail line, a two-lane highway and the inevitable cycle path that served the Zeelanders in normal times.

But as the planners of the 5th Brigade well knew, these were not normal times, and the causeway *was* damned. The Germans, their backs to the sea, were far from beaten. They had prepared a monstrous reception for their Canadian enemies. On the Walcheren end of the causeway, a wide water-filled ditch and a broad dyke ran along the banks of the Sloe Channel. Here the Germans had built concrete strongholds armed stoutly with mortars, 88s, heavy machine guns and "Vierlings" (four-barrelled 20mm ack-ack guns) and, behind these, a tank was dug in and an antitank gun sighted to fire straight down the centre of the road. Mortars capable of withering fire covered the length of the causeway.

The German engineers had not been idle. The railway track had been torn up; the road, path and embankments were thick with mines, planted even under the cobblestones. Deep craters pockmarked the crossing. Just west of the halfway point one huge, water-filled crater rendered the causeway impassable to any vehicle, including tanks. Only the splintered stubs of burnt-out trees showed against the horizon.

The German guns were sighted squarely down this narrow strip of raised roadway that they knew the Canadians would be forced to cross. There was, they believed, no alternative. In 1940, as pursuers this time of a French Armoured Division, the Germans themselves had attempted to cross the Sloe and had seen 150 of their comrades drown.

For the Allies, timing was everything. Two highly dangerous amphibious assaults were being launched on 1 November on the exposed western and southern sea coasts of Walcheren: army commandos spearheading an infantry attack at Flushing and the naval and Royal Marine invasion at Westkapelle. To give these risky assaults an edge, the Canadian attack on 31 October at the causeway was designed to convince the enemy that the main Allied thrust was coming by land from the east, thus diverting some of his firmly entrenched forces from the vulnerable western sea coast.

It fell upon the Black Watch, bone-weary and still recoiling from Black Friday, to make the first attack — and on its brigadier, W.J. Megill, to formulate the battle plan. At 1000 hours on Tuesday, the 31st of October, a Brigade "Huddle Red" ("O" Group) was called. Almost immediately, the Black Watch was given orders to commence an attack, a daylight assault to "feel out the enemy defences."[2]

On a raw Hallowe'en morning, in the first thrust across the Walcheren Causeway, C Company of the Black Watch approached the causeway, leaning into the lashing rain while the enemy came to life. A, B and D companies followed. The still desperately under-strength battalion was down to fifty or sixty men in each company, half its usual complement, including the LOBs (Left Out of Battle).

Enemy artillery and mortar fire pounded the Canadians. German snipers, positioned in the marshes bordering the causeway, shot with deadly accuracy. At 1345 hours additional artillery was called for as C Company was being held up by snipers, light machine guns, mortaring and shelling. Under its cover, one platoon of C Company, under Lieutenant J.P. Jodoin, pushed forward to within seventy-five metres of the enemy bank, but under increasingly heavy mortar fire. The Black Watch War Diary chronicles the grim conclusion: "At 1430 hours, the tanks in support were prepared to move...down the causeway, but were informed that the road was impassable. C Company had to wade through a crater, through water up to their armpits. The enemy had his guns sighted to give cross-fire on the causeway, with one tank dug in, and an antitank gun firing down the centre of the road...The enemy was firing at least one very heavy gun, the shells of which raised plumes of water two hundred feet high when they fell short. He was also ricocheting armour-piercing shells down the causeway, which was hard on the morale of the men...The jeeps evacuating the wounded were having a difficult time as the roads were coming under heavy mortar fire."

Meanwhile, B and D companies were preparing to inch forward into the holocaust. Major William Ewing was commanding A Company, whose forward elements were hard on the heels of the lead company with orders to pass through it when they reached a certain point on the causeway. But they could make no progress against the obstinate German defence. To Ewing, it was an exercise in futility: "We never got that far. We were going nowhere at all. The company ahead of us was bogged down. What I was really critical of, later on, was our artillery — it was probably five or six hundred yards off target. I don't know what the hell they were trying to do."[3]*

By then, it was pitch dark. Regimental Sergeant Major Alan Turnbull remembers trying to get some protection from the relentless hammering the men in C Company were taking: "We were trying to dig in on those bricks, and it was hell trying to dig out even a six-inch slit trench while they had their tanks and their 88s lined up at us just like a bowling alley. We just couldn't dig in. Halfway across, Major Ewing gave me command of the company while he went back to talk to the colonel about the useless position we were all in. Finally, he got back to us and we withdrew towards our side."[5]

By 1930 hours, C Company had been ordered to withdraw to a line two hundred metres from the near end of the causeway. The remaining companies were also withdrawn, with the exception of a

---

* Colonel Ritchie, CO of the Black Watch, had also observed that the Field Artillery Regiment in support was firing short, and that consequently his men were not getting the proper support. After the battle, he launched an investigation into the guns and discovered that "the whole field regiment in support of us was calibrated to one faulty gun. Our men never got the right fire support out on the causeway."[4]

party left behind to carry out C Company's casualties.* Lieutenant Jodoin and the four men of the lead section of C Company — two of them now wounded — had by then advanced to a position just twenty-five metres from the end of the causeway. In spite of the darkness, the evacuation of the casualties farthest out was found to be impossible; at the slightest sound or movement, the enemy fired down the roadway. A heavy artillery barrage had been scheduled to start at 2340 hours, and the casualties were then forced to go to ground, unable to withdraw before the Canadian barrage started. They huddled in a German slit trench on the causeway and watched the exploding shells.

And in the month's final hour, men of the Black Watch, who were crouching silently behind the near bank of the channel, saw the pyrotechnics of war explode around their wounded and trapped comrades. It was four-dimensional hell: "The red fire of Bofors laced the dark sky, mortar shells could be seen bursting on the far bank, and the sound of heavy artillery was everywhere."[6] The attack had been, to Lieutenant Colonel Ritchie, "monstrous":

> When we got the order to bounce the causeway, one thing that hit me right off the bat with that order was that the brigade failed to realize that when you move a battalion under observation of the enemy, then you have to string them out a bit. An engineer got in touch with me after we'd taken Goes. They had bridging equipment. It was an alternative order to bouncing the causeway, to try to go along a broader front.
>
> The higher command seemed to depend more on the so-called intelligence provided by the overprints on the maps. In the experience of the Black Watch, this was often found to be faulty. You would have thought that even the aerial photographs would have indicated [another way]. But I was told to bounce it, and we did bounce it. And it was our Black Watch Platoon — C Company, 13th Platoon — that went across.[7]

---

* The battalion casualties in the eighteen days since Black Friday now numbered eighty-five.

While the men of the Black Watch were thus engaged through the long hours of the 31st in their struggle through this "killing ground,"[8] Brigadier Megill held a succession of Orders Groups as plan after plan to make a crossing was considered, adopted and then discarded. On the morning of the 31st, it was decided that Major Ross Ellis, acting CO of the Calgary Highlanders, would launch an amphibious crossing of the channel on either side of the causeway. By afternoon, Brigade had learned that there would not be sufficient water to "swim" across, although there was too much mud for tracked vehicles. Brigade was now aware, as well, that the Black Watch probe had turned into a bloody battle. The enemy, it seemed, would not easily relinquish this gateway to Walcheren. Finally, at 1830 hours on the 31st, the Calgaries were ordered to mount before midnight the second stage of the causeway attack with a frontal assault. The battalion was instructed, with considerable optimism, to move out to the right when it reached the German end of the causeway, at which point it would be followed by the Régiment de Maisonneuve, fanning out to the left.

Brigadier Megill's battle plan was predicated on a fairly quick and easy in-and-out. The British were to take over the bridgehead; the 5th Brigade had been stuck with the job of merely establishing it. As far as Megill was concerned, "We had been promised to get out of the line and we wanted out. We were trying to do it with a minimum of casualties. We were quite frankly not really interested in fighting at that point at all."[9]

But there were men of the three committed Canadian battalions whose units would fight courageously for fifty-three consecutive hours for a position on that single, slender land-bridge. They did not see their assignment as anything other than an all-out effort. Some of these considered the operation to have been so hastily patched together that alternative crossings were not fully investigated: "The Limeys, on the other hand, when they assaulted Walcheren, they did it with class — not as a sort of spur-of-the-moment thing," one officer commented acidly.[10]

Perhaps the strongest justification for the after-taste of bitterness was that in fact there *was* an alternative, and when the Canadians had all been withdrawn a Limey battalion *did* assault it — with class.

The Calgaries, still to be initiated into this inferno, had to wonder what kind of task had been given them as they waited their turn. To attack directly into those guns, at least the elements of surprise and manoeuverability ought to have been there. But they were not. The attack would be recorded as "the most brazen" of all frontal assaults in history.[11]

Major Ross Ellis had become acting commanding officer of the Calgary Highlanders during the Hoogerheide-Woensdrecht conflict.* Interviewed shortly before his death in 1983, Ellis, too, found the accuracy of the intelligence questionable. And his recollections of the management of the battle had persisted throughout his life as "disturbing":

> The intelligence was about as bad as anything we ever got. The intelligence report said that we couldn't use an amphibious attack across the canal because it was impossible to cross, that the only way we could do it was to cross on that causeway. It was ultimately found out that we could have gone across in a number of places without the slightest difficulty, spread our troops out and been much more successful than we were. These are some of the things that are a bit disturbing.
>
> We were directed to go across at the causeway, then afterwards drive into the main city, which was Middelburg and take it. We were told that the enemy were some 350 "White Bread" cases, ulcer cases, in other words, just a kind of semi-hospital unit of Germans holding that as a base with no ability to fight or anything. They kicked the hell out of us.[12]

The Calgary Highlander history tells its own grim story:

> Promptly at midnight, 1 November, under the cover of mortars from the Queen's Own Cameron Highlanders of Canada and the Black Watch, B Company's gallant men began to edge along the narrow ribbon of land. Discarding every conceivable

---

* His command and his colonelcy were confirmed shortly after the causeway episode.

element of surprise, medium and light artillery, bofors, anti-aircraft guns and heavy mortars concentrated on the German positions.

As the heroic band edged along the causeway under a hail of enemy artillery and small arms fire, the watchers on the bank waited with bated breath. They had crossed half the distance to the island when the enemy fire became so intense that further forward movement was impossible. Even the [eastern] entrance to the causeway was under heavy enemy fire.[13]

Major Francis Clarke, in command of the lead company, lost many of his men, including most of 12 Platoon in the attack. Clarke requested permission to withdraw the remnants of his men. He was then called back by Ross Ellis on the order of the brigadier to discuss further plans: "I advised that we start a creeping barrage well out on the causeway and covering well down the flood bank on each side of the island. This barrage was to be followed very closely by whatever company was selected. Bruce McKenzie (D Company) was selected to move behind the barrage and once again B Company was detailed to move through them southward along the flood bank toward a group of farm buildings behind the bank and about 500 or 600 yards down."[14]

At dawn, McKenzie launched a second attempt to break through the thick enemy fire screen. In the face of heavy shelling, the men inched their way along until they could see the strong German roadblock at the far end. The history relates: "Despite the hottest of cross fire from both sides and directly ahead, this gallant band of Calgary Highlanders rushed the roadblock and seized it, taking fifteen prisoners. Meanwhile, artillery attempted to nullify the opposition from beyond the barrier, all at extremely close range. Heavy casualties did not deter D Company from making good its objective and by 9:33 A.M. it was able to report that a small bridgehead was secure. A platoon was even working along the dyke south of the causeway."[15]

Now the remaining companies followed the magnificent advance of their forerunners. Crossing the causeway in the steady drizzle of rain, under the incessant pounding of mortars, they proceeded to reinforce them. A and C companies dug in on the causeway itself. Clarke pushed across to join McKenzie.

In spite of murderous fire the Canadians stuck tenaciously to their foothold. A bulldozer started filling the huge craters but was driven away by a volley of 88mm shells. The Germans launched a ferocious counterattack.

Led by 10 Platoon with Lieutenant John Moffat in command, Clarke's company advanced under fire in the only way possible, single file, between the bank and the water. They dug in along the near side of the floodbank — vertically — as Captain Clarke recalls:

> For manoeuvring, we just had the space between the top of the dyke and the water at the back of it. When the tide came in, it wasn't very much. The enemy were using 8.1-cm mortars on us at less than fifty-yard range. They were dug in on the land side of the floodbank and we were on the water side.
>
> We could see our command HQ across the water but our communications were completely lost in the mud and sand. We had an 18-set and 38-set but those damn radios didn't work. I sent two runners out because I wanted to get some mortar down on a group of buildings that I had to get to. The runners didn't get through.
>
> We lost the full front end of Johnny Moffat's platoon.* We were strung out in a long, thin line and couldn't do anything; we couldn't move one way or another. Each time we tried to go over the dyke, we took a hell of a beating. About this time Jerry launched a counterattack at the end of the causeway at our point of contact with D Company. It was here that Sergeant Lalonge earned his DCM in fighting almost a one-man counter-battle with hand grenades.
>
> D Company was being forced back; that would leave us exposed at both ends — our rear was now in danger. I had to try to maintain contact with them and eventually we

---

* Ross Ellis: "That was the only place I saw Germans using flame throwers on our troops. We lost Johnny Moffat when his group got involved with the German flame throwers." [16]

moved back behind the crater in the middle of the causeway and held on. It was here that Major George Hees contacted us in search of A Company, which he was to command.[17]

Meanwhile, Brigadier Megill had sent his brigade major, George Hees, forward for a situation report. Then, at 1545 hours, Acting CO Major Ross Ellis and Hees crossed the causeway and contacted all companies. They returned at 1610 hours. It was learned that heavy losses to the Calgaries threatened the operation. Captain Wynn Lasher was wounded (for the third time). A Company had now lost all its officers and was faced with withdrawal.

At this point, Hees volunteered to lead the company. Captain W. Newman, the artillery FOO, offered to go in as his second-in-command. Major Ellis recalled the incident: "When we learned that A Company had lost two company commanders and a couple of platoon commanders, Hees said, 'Well, I'll go up and take over.' He called back and got permission from the brigadier. I remember Hees was wearing a staff cap which he always wore, the ordinary officer's cap. So we got him a tin hat and had one of the scouts take him out and show him how to run a Sten gun. Then I took him up onto the causeway. Later, he got shot in the arm. What he did was very commendable; it took a lot of guts for a guy who had never been in action to go into a hell-hole like that one."[18]

Finally, D and B companies, the "heroes of the assault," were ordered back into battalion reserve. The remaining two companies took up defensive positions to hold the bridgehead. The gallantry of the action was summed up by the battalion history: "No Calgary Highlander who served in that battle will ever forget the ferocity of the fighting for almost forty hours. The great courage of those forward companies inspired supporting arms to equal feats of bravery."[19]

But the pride of achievement was overshadowed by a strong sense of the futility of the action. In Ross Ellis's own words: "You put a bunch of guys in a cannon, push them up to the mouth...our main accomplishment was that we got as many as we could get out alive. The actual battle didn't develop much of anything. It was a bad deal."[20]

In two days, two Canadian battalions had been flung down the causeway chute into the muzzles of the German guns, with no

significant success. The third and final one, Le Régiment de Maisonneuve, was now ordered to follow suit. At 2100 hours, 1 November,
an "O" Group was held, designating the order of advance: D Company first, then B, C, and A companies following. H-Hour was 0400,
the 2nd of November. The battalion was to establish a bridgehead on
Walcheren, passing through the Calgaries who were still wearily holding on at the now infamous rendezvous point of the crater halfway
along the embankment. This next attempt was optimistically forecast
to take a single hour to complete; the 1st Battalion of the Glasgow
Highlanders, 52nd (Lowland) Division, was instructed to relieve the
Canadians at 0500 hours. The Maisonneuves sardonically expressed
their disbelief in the operation: "The commander of the 5th Brigade
obstinately remained convinced that Walcheren could be taken in a
night attack with artillery support. He decided therefore to hold
another assault, this time using his last battalion."[21]

The single hour turned into ten. The bald facts tell little of the
terrible ordeal that befell the Maisonneuves on the far side of the
bridge. It is known that of the four companies, only one, D Company,
managed to advance beyond the crater. And just one of its platoons,
plus the remnants of two more, succeeded in actually crossing the
fiery causeway.

Those ten hours have never been fully documented. But fragments of the action were witnessed and even recorded by four separate groups: two of these were Canadians and Belgians who fought
the battle, a third was a member of the Dutch Underground, and the
fourth comprised commanders from both Canadian and British
units involved.

The three officers of the Régiment de Maisonneuve who somehow led the courageous handful of French Canadians across the carnage of the causeway — Lieutenants Guy de Merlis and Charles
Forbes and Major Dan Tremblay — clearly remember every moment
of those hours.

Segments of the story have lain in a drawer of a Belgian home,
unheralded, in an ordinary child's autograph book hand-titled *Memoires d'un Combattant,* and in the diaries of two Belgian businessmen
who fought as volunteers at the side of the Maisonneuves through
all the Scheldt campaign and beyond. The two Belgians, Jacques

Cantinieaux and Roger Mathen, had offered their services to the Maisonneuves when the battalion first arrived at the Albert Canal in September. Overcoming the Canadians' initial reluctance to take them on, the Resistance fighters had persisted until finally they were accepted. They had, however, to meet conditions; they had to sign away all claim to wages, and they had to agree that neither they nor their families could expect support or assistance however serious the outcome of the action. Lieutenant Guy de Merlis, commander of 16 Platoon, D Company, Régiment de Maisonneuve, summed up this unorthodox employment: "They got food, clothing, a bit of glory — that was all."[22] "They fought marvellously," his fellow officer, Lieutenant Charles Forbes, agreed.[23]

The prelude and aftermath of the battle were recently revealed by a Dutchman, the third witness to the episode. Along with three other men of the Underground, a respected patriot had been in hiding from the Gestapo for ten days in the home of the Resistance family Almekinders in the village of 's-Heer Arendskerke, just east of the causeway. 18 Platoon, Régiment de Maisonneuve, established headquarters in this house.

The Zeelander recalls 18 Platoon commander, Lieutenant Forbes, who with his batman with the quaint nickname of "the Snake," spent two days in the house before the battle. Throughout the long hours of waiting, he remembers the officer's friendliness as he chatted in fluent French and English about his home in Montreal. And he remembers being shown more than once the thumb-worn news clipping from the *Montreal Star* of a beautiful debutante who was Forbes's fiancée. In the early hours of Tuesday, the 2nd of November, the Dutchman stood on the rain-swept cobbled walk in front of the house as his liberators left to join the other members of D Company on their causeway assault — and he stood watch until the battered survivors of 18 Platoon limped back that same afternoon: "Their eyes were red-rimmed, their hands were shaking, they were soaked and covered in mud — they said they had been through hell. They could not talk. We put our arms about them and wept."[24]

And in that final hour of the month, the fourth group that would witness a segment of the causeway drama — Scottish and Canadian commanding officers — stood in silent clusters in the 5th Brigade

HQ. Men of the 157th Brigade of the 52nd (Lowland) Division, observing the action of the past days from Canadian headquarters, had been shocked to hear the order that had committed a second Canadian battalion and then a third one to repeat the futile efforts of the first. Soon, they learned, the Scottish would be required to follow as the fourth battalion flung into the chaos of the causeway. It was an order that has been tersely condemned by one high-ranking British officer as "an elementary infringement of a principle of war, i.e., a reinforcement of failure." [25]

But to Brigadier Megill there was a different set of priorities and pressures. The brigade had been in constant action since Normandy. He felt that it was important that it be given a brief respite from active duty. And while there was some pressure from senior ranks to force the causeway crossing,

> it wasn't all that heavy. I don't remember [Guy Simonds] taking any strong part in it; I don't even remember Charles Foulkes taking any strong part in it. The main thing that was said was that if [we] didn't get over there, we weren't going to get out for our rest period.
>
> Originally, I told the Black Watch to just get out there with some patrols and see how far they could go — just feel it out. And, of course, they were untrained. I should have known better, they were not up to it. So they went blindly right out and they just blundered into a lot of fire about halfway down the causeway and came right back. Well, it was perfectly clear to me that they were the wrong people, so I just pulled them back and then I put the Calgaries in there and when they got in there, they were spread all along the causeway, more or less, but very thin. The only reason for putting the Maisies in at the end was that the Calgaries were there and it made a cleaner job if I put a fresh company right in at the end. [26]

H-Hour, 0400 hours, 2 November

For Major Hees, the past twelve hours in the desolation of the shell-pocked causeway had been a startling introduction to the front line.

Crouched in his crater fortress with the Calgaries he still commanded, Hees experienced for the first time the seemingly endless enemy bombardment throughout the long night. Then the Canadian barrage came down. For forty-five minutes, six artillery regiments thundered in unison, their positions marked by the fire in the sky behind the heads of the Calgary Highlanders.

> [Roger Mathen:] Imagine a black night, the rain pouring down, a muddy road with holes of one and two metres deep. If you fall into a hole you are muddy, dead beat and without your gun or ammunition. The road is ten metres wide, without trees to take cover. Imagine a dyke leading to nowhere, enemy soldiers on both sides with heavy machine guns and light cannons. Then let start a barrage of 296 shells over the Germans, then observe a counterattack with 88mm and 105mm mortars coming from the other side. Now, send to the other side of the dyke some hundred men, platoon after platoon, the men ahead following the edge of the water, with their faces to the unknown.[27]

The Glasgow Highlander commander stayed beside the commander of the Régiment de Maisonneuve throughout the battle, the two men clinging anxiously to the snatches of communication that came through from the forward companies to the Tac headquarters farmhouse. There was little to say. The total darkness was relieved only by the searing gunfire and the awesome sight of the banks of the causeway seemingly all ablaze.

The Maisonneuve moved up under the protection of the creeping barrage, D Company in the lead. But at 0426 hours, when the barrage lifted, withering German fire assailed the Canadians, explosion after explosion from shells "falling down like rain," as Lieutenant Robert Saey, who was wounded in the action, remembers: "It seemed as if all the guns on the island, they had only one place to shoot and that was on the causeway. We started out with eight officers. In twenty minutes we had three."[28]

These three remaining officers from D Company were the 2/1-C of D Company, Major Dan Tremblay, and the young commanders of

16 and 18 platoons, Lieutenant Guy de Merlis and Lieutenant Charles Forbes. ("We were just twenty-two years old, Charlie and I," de Merlis recalls, "and we'd been together since July. If there was a raid or a patrol, we'd be on it — just daredevil kids. It was either stupidity or innocence.")[29] They commanded a mere thirty Canadian soldiers, supported by a handful of Belgian patriots. They had only the light weapons they could carry. They faced two hundred crack German troops with two tanks. But still they pressed on.

Lieutenant Charles Forbes commanded 18 Platoon, the point platoon of the advance. Even in these difficult circumstances, the reinforcement problem plagued the company. "I handed a Bren gun to one man as we approached the causeway," Forbes recounts. "He was forty-two years of age, a Service Corps type who announced that he had never fired a Bren gun in his life. So I said, 'Well, you're a big man. If you can't fire it, carry it!'"

Forbes had been briefed on the location of the large crater midway across the causeway where the Calgary Highlanders were dug in, waiting to be relieved, and he had ordered his men to shoot at anything that moved on the enemy side of it. No one had mentioned that there was a second, smaller crater before he reached the main one. "It was all in confusion," he describes bitterly. "Madness! My men opened up when we passed the crater — what we thought was the only crater — but we quickly found out we were firing on some of the withdrawing Calgaries. I feel very badly, even now, about this.

"Further on, Major Hees came running up, pushing up, yelling 'Go'…'Go'…We moved on. Finally, we pooled what was left of numbers 17 and 18 platoons — we then had only twenty-two men including seven Belgians. Lieutenant de Merlis, commanding 16 Platoon, had fifteen men."[30]

[Roger Mathen:] 18 Platoon, with Lieutenant Forbes, Bidoche and Reeves started first. Then 16 Platoon, de Merlis's, followed with Jacques Cantinieaux, Jules [cousin of Roger], Snake and myself. Before us, there was shelling and shooting. I fell down in a mortar hole. I got up slowly; I was wet and I started to shiver. Just when I got up, a great salvo made me jump to the ground again. Next to me, Bidoche fell down, a bullet through his head. Jules, standing in the water up to his hips, helped a Canadian. I asked Jacques what time it was. I called like a deaf person. Even one metre away, Jacques didn't hear me. I progressed slowly, clinging to the ground under the enemy machine-gun fire. Again, I dived into the hole; there were two dead soldiers already in that hole. I waited about two minutes and then ran ten metres. I saw two Germans; they passed by without seeing me. I fired one shot but it was useless. The mortars and heavy machine guns were overpowering everything. I heard men cry like madmen; this is impossible, wake me up please! Others are so calm — they die without making any sound, with a smile on their faces. That night the artillery swallowed men. It drove some who were attacking between two walls of fire and there they died.[31]

H-Hour plus 30

The lead platoon under Forbes was nearing the end of the land-bridge. Thirty minutes had passed. "We captured a German antitank gun that was firing down the causeway at us," Forbes remembers. "I was wounded in the left wrist. Then I was across, looking for the mainland, but the ground was submerged and difficult to identify. I actually passed my objective by six or seven hundred metres. I had lost contact with de Merlis."[32]

> [Jacques Cantinieaux:] 17 Platoon advanced between the German machine-gun nests. Roger was hit. We advanced past the enemy end of the causeway, beyond the crossroads and even beyond the objective. We dug trenches around the house on the left of the road. Only D Company had crossed, protected by the artillery barrage. A, B and C companies could not make it. German machine guns swept the cause-way from all directions.[33]

> [Roger Mathen:] At a certain moment, when I tried to free myself from a muddy pool, I saw Lieutenant Forbes next to me. I took him by the arm. A warm liquid flowed over my hand. Snake told me that the lieutenant was wounded.

17 Platoon, crushed by the fire, didn't exist any longer as a fighting unit.

A man drowned in the water. How many were we? I called Jules, Jacques and de Merlis. I fixed my eyes straight on the dyke. I saw shadows but they didn't answer my call. A shell exploded next to me, I fell into a hole. A great pain tortured my side. Before I fainted, I felt my leg and side were like lead.[34]

H-Hour plus 60

[Jacques Cantinieaux:] At five o'clock the British were ordered to take our place. We didn't see them. Lieutenant Forbes sent his runner, the Belgian Dumais, with two Canadians to try to contact our relief. He didn't know the way; the road was out. We were surrounded. It took them an hour and a half to reach headquarters of D Company.[35]

At this moment, a confrontation of some heat was apparently flaming up at Canadian HQ.* Brigadier Megill instructed his British counterpart, Brigadier J.D. Russell of 157 Brigade, that he wanted all the Maisonneuve relieved. The Scottish commander, who was desperately investigating — under orders from his divisional commander — alternative means of crossing the Sloe, was evidently not willing to commit his men to a major assault of such futility. He retorted that he would send in only as many of his men as there were Canadians on the causeway, "after deducting casualties."[37]

The CO of the Maisonneuve, Lieutenant Colonel J. Bibeau, estimated that there were not more than forty of his troops alive on the causeway, and the 1st Glasgow Highlanders then agreed to relieve the Régiment de Maisonneuve with one platoon. The Glasgow Highlanders crawled through the mud on the slopes of the causeway

---

* Brigadier Megill recently said that his recollection of the night of the 1st–2nd of November differs somewhat. He had, Megill said, been unable to contact Brigadier Russell to initiate the relief when it would have been less hazardous. "The first night, when we were trying to tidy the place up [during the Black Watch and Calgary attacks], he was there at Tac HQ. When things didn't go well, I told him: 'Look, it's no use. There is nothing you can do. You are not going to be

embankment toward Walcharen, running into small groups of
Maisonneuve. And, as per plan, the Scots gradually took over the
Canadian positions on the causeway.

0700 Hours

Just before dawn, Major Hees coolly reappeared at 5th Brigade Tac
HQ with the information that he had just been across the causeway
and could guide the British to their positions. The Maisonneuve, he
reported, were on their first objectives: "The Germans were being
very quiet at that moment; there was no resistance. I knew the British
were moving through and I thought it was important to bring them
up to take over and do a recce before first light."

It was just when Hees reached the far end of the causeway again
that he was wounded: "I forgot that dawn was beginning to break and
I would be silhouetted. Suddenly, a sniper fired. I was hit in the
elbow; it felt like a heavy, ball-headed hammer."[38]

The sniper's shot heralded a return to the vicious onslaught of
enemy fire. The Glasgows, following their forward platoon, were
caught in the concentration of fire. Progress became almost impossible. The battalion was being "led into hell." The Division history
records the incredible odds these Scots faced: "To move a foot in daylight was nearly impossible; to advance a yard in the darkness was an
adventurous success."[39]

But advance they did, untried troops proving themselves on one
of the war's most challenging battlefields. By now, all of the Maisonneuve had been relieved except for the few stubborn defenders hanging onto their sorely won positions on Walcheren Island.

At dawn, Lieutenant Forbes saw a startling sight: "A whole column of Germans was withdrawing along the road towards Middelburg. They were very casual — some were even carrying boxes of

---

able to take over tonight at all. How about going to bed and forgetting about it?'

"But he insisted on staying up all night — I had a snooze myself — and then
the next night when we had it more or less clean after this fracas of bringing
[in] the Maisies, I felt now was the time he could take it over. But he had left
strict orders with his brigade major that they were to do nothing without his
personal OK. Then he wasn't available. So that meant that the actual takeover
didn't take place until morning."[36]

ammunition in their arms. They seemed completely unaware that we were between them and the main German position. They were coming right at us. We realized that they would have to go through our position. We opened fire as they came closer; it was an awful moment. Then a German tank came up, but too far away for us to engage them."[40]

From across the dyke, defending the far side of the railway underpass, de Merlis, too, was watching that German tank move in on him. Then he heard the welcome roar of 84 Group Typhoons diving in for the kill. Several times that morning, the Typhies swooped down to help the beleaguered Canadians and their rescuers.

[Jacques Cantinieaux:] Daybreak — grey and dirty. Three 20mm machine guns take our position apart. Fortier is killed.* The CSM has been shot in the foot. Several men were wounded more or less seriously. The worst was that we could not possibly evacuate them.

0830 Hours

While rockets harassed the German positions and gunners fired devastating air bursts above them, the Glasgow Highlanders forced their way onto the narrow strip of Walcheren with its handful of Canadian captors. For six hours more, Scot and Canadian clung together to their small foothold on the fortress. Conditions worsened; retreat was impossible. The survivors of the Maisonneuve's D Company numbered no more than twenty. One soldier from de Merlis's Platoon, J-C Carrière, advanced in a ditch full of water and with a Piat destroyed a 20mm gun. The act earned him the Military Medal.

[Jacques Cantinieaux:] I left with Dumais, the lieutenant and Ouellet. We crawled in fifty centimetres of water. We arrived beside the bridge. We met three POWs taken by 18 Platoon and put them ahead as we walked five metres behind them. Nobody fired at us. Then we contacted the British. We got as far as the railway bridge at the crossroads. Suddenly, the

---

* Guy de Merlis reports that Private Fortier, severely wounded in the action, actually died in England seven days later.

20mm machine gun opened fire. We had only time to dive into the little canal alongside the road, Lieutenant de Merlis, the British and me. We stayed for one and a half hours in the water. Our teeth chattered terribly. The bullets passed ten centimetres over our heads. On top of that our artillery opened fire but it fell too short. We received shell bursts.

1030 hours

The lieutenant and I left, crawling in the water to try to rejoin our HQ. We crossed the road on the run. The house was our objective. The 20mm gun blasted the walls. We literally dove into the cellar. Two men are wounded.

I left with one man and the Piat to try to knock out the 20mm machine gun. The water was up to my thigh. We advanced 150 metres into the German lines but the 20mm was mounted on a moving truck. We located an ordinary machine gun; I returned to ask permission to fire three grenades. I took twenty-five minutes to get to the end of the ditch under fire of the German machine gun. I dove literally into the water; I was almost exhausted. When I raised my head above the water I heard the machine gun crackle, bullets hit the rim, but too high to hurt me. I crawled back under the wire, arrived at our position, ran across the road and threw myself into the house.

I explained the situation to Lieutenant de Merlis. It was necessary that I go back with the Piat. Bullets crashed against the door around me as I re-entered the battle scene.[41]

Back at Brigade Tac HQ, the atmosphere was growing extremely tense as the battle dragged on. The events of the next moments are reported in the Scottish history: "Commander 5 Canadian Brigade stated that if his troops were not relieved at once he would have to bring back tired troops on his own to extricate them. At this stage, commander 5 Infantry Brigade appeared to be of the impression that his troops were offering organized resistance to the enemy. According to reports from the CO of 1st Glasgow Highlanders they were completely disorganized and only a few remained."[42]

Finally, at 1445 hours, the Maisonneuves and a single platoon of rescuers withdrew under cover of a smokescreen laid on under the direction of Lieutenant D.G. Innes of the 5th Field Regiment, RCA. Innes, a FOO who had supported the Maisonneuves even after being wounded, was awarded the Military Cross for this effort. Corporal Lappin and two other ranks remained behind in the cellar of the house to take care of a wounded man of D Company, and three companies of Glasgow Highlanders clung grimly to the bridgehead.

But withdrawing, even with artillery support, was hazardous. "It was all open field," de Merlis recalls, "without much cover, and with deep water in every ditch. We had to work our way across this — it was every man for himself."[43]

[Jacques Cantinieaux:] For ten minutes our artillery concentrated on the German positions to enable us to move without too much risk. At the first shellburst, a dash — a desperate escape across the road — a jump into the icy water that paralyzed the limbs and blurred the sight. Some stumbled in the barbed wire. Death whistled its little song in our ears. We reached the railroad, then climbed the side of the dyke to safety. After several minutes we walked. It didn't matter if we were fired on; we followed the road in a dream. It was unreal. Life floated and danced in front of our eyes. Time after time, we stumbled in a shell-hole like a blind man.[44]

John Colligan, a British gunner with the 79th Field Regiment, Royal Artillery, supporting 52nd Division, came on the Maisonneuve position later that day:

We reached the farmhouse where they had been. On the floor were letters, a lot seemed to be French. There was a dyke beside the house and the Germans were dug in underneath the dyke. I helped move some of the Canadian dead; there were about half a dozen who had been killed when the Germans and Canadians were throwing hand grenades at each other from foxholes about five yards from the dyke.

We picked up two lads who were in the same foxhole. One had been wounded, and the other had apparently crawled in to help him. And that's how we found them: one had his arm around the other, patching up the fellow's wound. Both were dead.[45]

Back at the red-brick house at 's-Heer Arendskerke, Lieutenant Forbes and his men were greeted by the waiting Zeelanders. Forbes could not bring himself to talk about the past hours. "I was badly shaken. I lay on a bed in the house and all I could hear was bullets."

But his mind would not rest, and he could only think: "Christ almighty! You send one...then another...then a third battalion into the same battle. Reinforcing failure — what a typical example!"

And today, he thinks still, "The whole thing left a very sour taste in my mouth. It was bad, and especially bad on morale which was already very low."[46]

Soon, the remnants of D Company, Régiment de Maisonneuve, joining their battalion comrades, wearily picked up their kits and turned away. It was no longer their battle. In three days of fighting, one hundred and thirty-five of their brigade comrades had fallen, dead or wounded. The survivors could not help reflecting that they had paid an incalculable penalty for losing that race along the South Beveland Peninsula.

Now, the 2nd Canadian Infantry Division was withdrawn from the Battle of the Scheldt. The deathblow would be delivered by British troops; the Canadians could enjoy a week's hard-earned respite from war. From the time the division had set foot on the South Beveland Peninsula, until the debacle at Walcheren Causeway, a period of a little over a week, close to one thousand men had been killed, wounded, or taken prisoner.

In the entire South Beveland campaign, 5,200 German prisoners had been taken, half of these during the last week. But the statistic becomes even grimmer for the Canadian infantrymen. The skirmishes at Merxem and Oorderen, the long battering-down of German defences at the Albert Canal, the ferocious struggle to capture Hoogerheide and Woensdrecht, the seemingly endless mud-slogging through mine-filled polders had all taken their grievous toll: 3,650 men of the 2nd Canadian Division alone had been killed, wounded or taken prisoner in the action.

While the shambles at the causeway was continuing, the Germans were also being threatened by two Allied invasions from the sea approaches to Walcheren, both launched on 1 November. But, despite the threats, these Germans would not let go, not on this last hold on Zeeland. At best, the Allies could claim only narrow bridgeheads on the strongly defended fortress. Each Allied commander of this triple assault was aware that he must not permit the pressure to ease up on the trapped enemy.

At this point, although 1st Canadian Army still maintained overall control of the operation, the command of all land forces on Walcheren shifted from Canadian responsibility to that of the British Lowland Division.

Major General Sir Edmond Hakewill Smith, commander of the 52nd (Lowland), had been dead opposed from the beginning to the 5th Brigade's frontal assault on the causeway. He had backed up his brigade commander of the 157th, Brigadier Russell, in the latter's confrontation with Brigadier Megill.

Now, made resolute by his increased power, Hakewill Smith challenged the authority of General Foulkes, GOC 2nd Canadian Corps and hence his senior officer on the Canadian side, to command more of his men into the inferno. In the early morning hours of November 1st, Foulkes appeared at 52nd Division HQ, inciting a head-on clash with the Scot. The pair had a fiery meeting.

Foulkes ordered Hakewill Smith to send his division across the causeway. The Scot argued forcefully that while he had to accept the order of a superior, a protest stressing the likelihood of very severe casualties would, he threatened, be lodged at 21st Army Group headquarters. Further, Hakewill Smith demanded that Foulkes issue the order in writing. A blank piece of paper was passed angrily across the table. Foulkes furiously backed off. Hakewill Smith recalls even now the difficult encounter:

It was not easy to refuse the direct order of my senior commander. However, I said I did not consider that an attack down the 1,500 metres of straight causeway covered by German guns and machine guns dug into the banks of the dykes was a viable military operation, and that we would try to find another route. The Canadian Corps commander said there was no other route and that we had to go in at dawn the next morning. I again protested that it was not a viable military operation, that we would have very heavy casualties and achieve nothing. My Corps commander was insistent, and after further argument he departed, saying that if we did not put in this attack there would be a new commander of the 52 (L) Division immediately.[47]

Hakewill Smith had, however, won a reprieve of sorts. Foulkes grudgingly gave him forty-eight hours to come up with an alternative plan...or look for a new job.

Meanwhile, on the 31st of October, Pieter Kloosterman and his wife Christina enjoyed a rare moment of peace in their home in Nisse. From their parlour window they could see a British corporal on a motorcycle round the tranquil village green and approach their house. The message delivered in such haste instructed Lieutenant Kloosterman to report to Captain G. Brook at 157 Brigade headquarters.

The farmhouse of the Widow Blok near Nieuwdorp served as headquarters for the 157th. Immediately on arrival, Kloosterman was quizzed about alternative routes over the Sloe Channel. He gave this report: "I had already understood that the frontal attack across the causeway was of no use and that the Allies had better cross the Sloe sea-branch. The ford in the Sloe Channel where they could cross was long ago indicated to me by two workmen with the provincial waterworks. Neither German nor Dutch authorities knew about that fordable lane across the Sloe Channel. By their assault via this route, the Allies [could] outflank the German positions near the Bijleveld Polder, so that they could 'roll up' the entire line of defence."

Lieutenant Kloosterman had with him a map on which all dispositions, strongholds and blockhouses had been indicated. He now handed this over to the officer: "I had stolen the map from a German officer in the house of the widow Sturm at Kapelle where I had a meeting with three local Resistance leaders. In an adjoining room was the office of a billeted German staff officer. After a good breakfast, the German gentleman left the room to follow the call of nature and left the map on the table. On the way out after the meeting, I passed the open door of the German's room and noticed the map. I pinched this and fled on my bicycle."[48]

The Scot told Kloosterman that he was "very pleased" with the suggestions, that he thought they were worth trying, and that he would take them up with his senior officer. At the same time he gently turned down an anxious offer by Kloosterman that he be allowed to help as a guide in leading troops across.

Incomplete records at this juncture do not indicate whether it was this information that led the Scottish troops to find the fordable land through the Sloe, or if, as their Divisional Commander Hakewill Smith claims, independent investigation by the 52nd Division the following day found, by chance, the identical route.

But inspiring a concept is one thing; executing it is another. Two venturesome young British sappers from 202 Field Company Royal Engineers would now pull off a daring venture that would spare the battalion the grim assignment of making yet another frontal assault over the fatal path that was Walcheren Causeway.

On the night of November 1st, at the moment when the commanding officer of the Glasgow Highlanders was being pressured to put a token force on the causeway to rescue the isolated Maisonneuves, these British sappers were cautiously inching their way through the mud flats of the Sloe.

The Sloe sea-branch was a stream of water bordered by muddy marshes and fields of sea-flora. When the tide was in, that "ribbon of blue" that Major Hees had noted on his map was in fact a three-hundred-metre strip of sea, with water enough to be traversed by assault boat. But on the far side, the sea water gave way to a stretch of saltmarsh of some thousand metres in width, interlaced with muddy creeks — a network impossible for vehicles or boats to cross or men to swim. These were the optimal conditions. When the tide went out, much of the blue turned to grey — a glutinous, slimy ooze that could suck a man up to his knees or waist. Such were the conditions the two Scotsmen faced when they began their crossing. The 52nd (Lowland) Division history relates: "They were just two lonely, apprehensive but skilled and watchful young men, who set out thus in the dark to prospect foreign soil held by a resourceful and pitiless enemy. Ambushes, the crack of the sniper's rifle, the roar underfoot of the deadly Schu-mine — these might at any second terminate the adventure."[49]

The sappers somehow made the crossing, confirming that there was a fordable lane, though one so narrow two men could barely pass. They crawled up the firm ground of Walcheren until they heard the voices of enemy troops.

The next night, as soon as darkness fell, the men retraced their passage across the channel, this time marking the route with white tape for the riflemen. At the same time, engineers were frantically clearing the thickly sown mines from the steep take-off bank on the near side of the Sloe.

Now it was the task of the 6th Battalion, the Cameronians, to follow the rapidly muddying ribbon of white that would lead them through the black night into the enemy camp. Remembering their comrades of 52nd (Lowland) Division, isolated in the hell-hole of the narrow causeway bridgehead barely two km north, the Cameronians were determined to force a way across and link up with the Glasgows. The initial wave of infantry crossed with considerable success, rowing over the open water in small assault boats and then tackling the miserable stretch of mud the only way it could be tackled — on foot. With surprise on their side, they rushed the enemy position and immediately took more than sixty prisoners.

But problems arose several hours later as a sudden storm bringing gale-force winds lashed at the flimsy boats, causing several drownings. A guide dog actually saved his handler from drowning when he was being swept away by the tidal currents.

Enemy gunfire continually peppered the crossing. The narrow take-off point became a confusion of personnel. Men waiting to cross, some wrestling with ungainly cases of supply for the front line, slithered and slid their way down the mud chute, colliding with incoming wounded and bewildered German prisoners. The sappers struggled to maintain the narrow passage through the minefields. The battalion commander, Lieutenant Colonel Ian Buchanan-Dunlop, describes the next events:

> Movement over the mud marsh was very hazardous, both in darkness and when daylight came, and the enemy artillery got busy. It was not until I asked for and got a large quantity of kapok bridging that we were able to get ammunition forward and casualties back over the salt-marsh flats.
>
> The assault achieved surprise, and gained a foothold on the bund, but attempts to push through a follow-up encountered very strong resistance, particularly on the left where we got a bloody nose. The follow-up company on that flank sustained heavy casualties and the company commander [Major Charles Sixsmith] was killed trying to bring in his wounded. The other company on that flank* really saved the whole operation. Although pushed back, it managed to hang on to its original bridgehead position and withstand counterattack and much shot and shell until a two-company attack could be put in...to win the battle.[50]

The next afternoon, the Highland Light Infantry (157 Infantry Brigade) passed through the position the Cameronians had so sorely won. It was their Private McGregor who, rushing a machine-gun post with his Bren gun and killing six Germans, eliminated the last obstacle before reaching the Glasgow Highlanders still holding a bridgehead on the causeway. After four bloody days, the Germans were finally pushed back. Many surrendered, feeling the bite of the trap that was encircling them. But others would never surrender, and they machine-gunned down some of their comrades who tried.

---

* Its company commander, Major Stanley Storm, was awarded a Military Cross for this action.

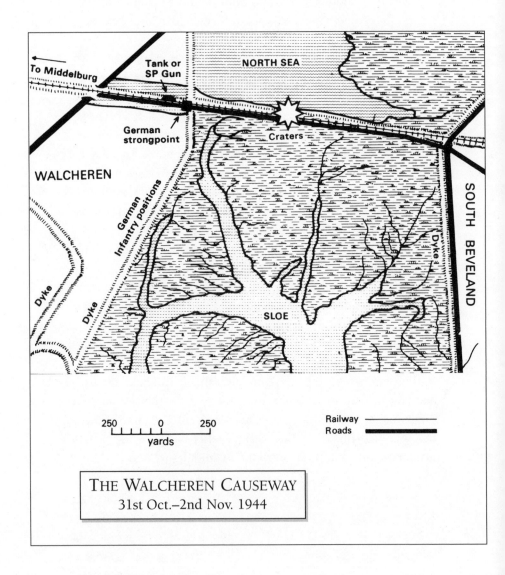

To Middelburg

Tank or
SP Gun

NORTH SEA

German
strongpoint

Craters

WALCHEREN

German infantry positions

SOUTH BEVELAND

Dyke

Dyke

Dyke

SLOE

250   0   250
yards

Railway
Roads

THE WALCHEREN CAUSEWAY
31st Oct.–2nd Nov. 1944

✦ 16 ✦

Red Hot — Best of Luck

WHILE THE CANADIANS WERE BATTLING FOR A FOOTHOLD ON THE causeway link to the fortress island on the 1st of November, two waterborne assaults, using British formations under Canadian command, were also being launched on Walcheren. At Flushing, just across the mouth of the Scheldt from Breskens, No. 4 Army Commando would spearhead one invasion, with infantry close behind. The knock-out blow would be delivered less than four hours later at Westkapelle, some fourteen km northwest. A fresh wave of troops — marine commandos this time — would make the assault with the support of Force T, a specially formed naval group whose task it was to escort the commandos safely through the North Sea and onto the new beaches. These were the beaches that Simonds had created, one on each side of the gap in the Westkapelle Dyke, when the RAF bombers made their raids in early October.

The logistics of the operation were of overwhelming complexity, second only to the Normandy landing itself. Planning continued for thirty days, producing enough verbiage to fill five volumes of books, each with 1,005 pages. The several thousand men involved in the assault had to be located from many battle theatres, assembled, and then trained, all in a short period of time. All their special crafts, vehicles and weapons had to be assembled as well. The invasion date had to be decided upon. To select a time that would offer optimal chance of success — and survival — tide and weather charts, all-important with the winter storms threatening, had to be considered.

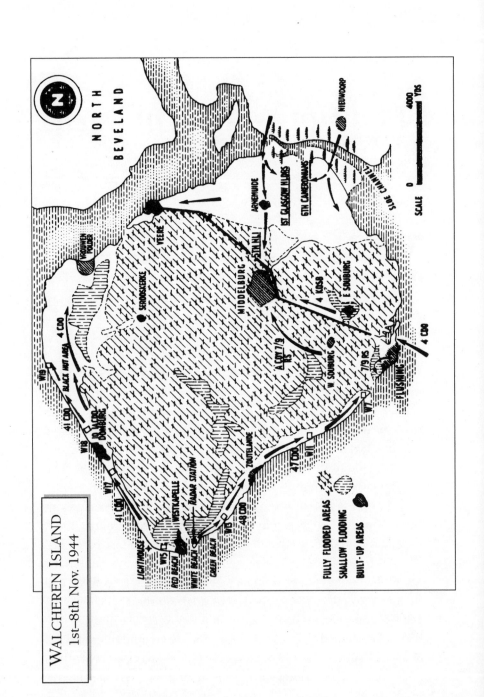

WALCHEREN ISLAND
1st–8th Nov. 1944

The Force T naval and military commanders, Captain A.F. Pugsley, RN (who in turn reported to Admiral Ramsay), and Brigadier B.W. Leicester of the 4th Special Service Brigade (who would hand over command after the landings to Major General Hakewill Smith, GOC 52 (Lowland) Division), urged General Simonds to commit the assault at the earliest possible date. Simonds countered that the operation would not go until "it was definitely established that defences were softened."[1] With that proviso agreed to, the Canadian notified Admiral Ramsay that the invasion was set for the 1st of November, weather permitting, to which the British admiral wired back: *"Red hot. Best of luck."*[2]

Ramsay knew full well the terrible risks of the operation. The weather, now into worsening winter conditions, could not be expected to produce more than one day in every six when the heavy swells would permit small craft to land.

The single advantage on the Allies' side was the fact of the island's flooding. Encouraging reports had been coming in to the Canadians throughout the month of October about the destruction of many of the enemy's strongpoints by the bombing of Walcheren's dykes and consequent flooding. With its dunes and dykes rimming the perimeter of the island, and its flat polders forming an inland cavity, Walcheren soon became inundated. Twice each day, the tides had poured furiously in through the ragged breaches in the dykes, icy brown sea water plunging over farmlands and homes, encroaching farther and farther upon the heart of the island.

The Germans were aware that when they controlled the flooding by opening the sluice gates, as in the "tame" flooding they had perpetrated in South Beveland and Breskens Pocket, they maintained control of their own roads and communications. But when the Allies caused so-called wild flooding by damaging the dykes, the Germans could not maintain that control. Simonds's bombing tactics, therefore, severed the Germans' communication with their outposts. Transportation of supplies was reduced to a minimum; troop mobility was almost nonexistent. They were isolated. Desperately, the Germans ordered all men of Walcheren to report to labour parties to construct emergency dykes around key towns and villages. They staged *razzias*, threatening the death sentence in case of disobedience, and in at least one instance, a Zeelander was executed. But subsequent Allied bombing erased these rebuilding efforts.[3]

For the civilian population of Walcheren, conditions caused by the inundations were very bad. Three-quarters of their homeland was rendered uninhabitable, destroyed by salt water. But the courageous people stolidly hung on to the shreds of their former lives, uncomplaining as they watched their "Garden Island" sink into a mire.

Only at the last moment, when the waters were at the threshold of their villages, would the populace leave, cheerfully hailing each other from borrowed dories or on footpaths knee-deep in bitter sea water. It was reported that one woman — it being a Saturday — proceeded to scrub the pavement at her front door while her neighbours were preparing to evacuate. Some villagers waited in attics, hoping for a reprieve. Others used improvised rafts to float to safety their most important household goods, and even their cattle. Amazingly, in this haphazard exodus, no more than about a dozen people drowned.

But there were few places to which they could escape. Hardly any locations had been spared from the devastation, and these were soon inundated by a different kind of flotsam — the starving homeless refugee. The centre of the inland capital city of Middelburg, protected by its ancient ramparts, harboured 40,000 people, doubling the city's population, straining its resources as it made room for the homeless. A section of the city of Flushing, and most of the eastern side of the island at the causeway, also remained above water, the last refuge to the evacuees. German guards forbade any passage of civilians across the causeway to the relative safety of South Beveland.

The fortress island had been made virtually impregnable. Hitler's inventive engineers had devised a complex and intensive system of defences that capitalized on the topography of the island. Forced labour executed the plan. The western shores of the diamond-shaped island, protruding into the North Sea, formed the island's strongest defences. Each section of coastline was some fourteen km in length, rimmed by huge sand dunes, some as high as ten metres and as thick as one hundred metres at the base. The slopes were steep, particularly on the ocean side, making them ideal defences against any attack from the North Sea. They would be unscaleable by wheeled vehicles, nearly impossible even for tracked armour to ascend, and could be climbed only by determined infantry.

Dangerous shoals and sandbanks punctuated the approaches to these two coastlines. It was along here the enemy's heaviest fortifications lay. The dunes, natural defences against the sea, and the dykes constructed over many years by the Dutch to keep out the frequently raging North Sea, now had been reconstructed into walls of concrete incorporating a sufficient number of heavy arms to repel any seaborne incursion. All of the more than twenty-five gun positions were enclosed in four-metre-thick casemates reinforced with concrete and steel.

These had escaped inundation by the onrushing sea and so it was these batteries that were earmarked as top priority targets for the RAF. 84 Group gave target numbers to these batteries ranging from W3 to W19. In total, the defences comprised some sixty guns of heavy calibre. But the batteries to prove most lethal were W15 and W13, on either side of the four-hundred-metre-wide gap in the dyke made by the RAF at Westkapelle, the island's most westerly town. Ironically, W15's armament, which consisted of four high-velocity 3.7-inch anti-aircraft guns, had been captured in the rout of the British in 1940. W13, with four 150mm guns, sat safe and dry on the other side of the Westkapelle breach. These guns had a very high rate of accurate fire. To give further depth to the defences, there were numerous 88mm and 50mm dual-purpose weapons, all of which were cleverly sighted with mutual support in mind.

The beaches were heavily mined, and multi-strands of barbed-wire and every kind of booby trap and explosive honeycombed the entire western coast. More than twenty thousand mines had been laid on the coastal floor. On the shores, thousands of mines and obstacles defied the safe entry of any amphibious vehicle. Inland fields were strewn with many more thousands of mines.

In determining the most vulnerable area of the dykes for bombing, Simonds's engineers, "Spot" West foremost, had automatically dictated the invasion sites. This would by now be evident to the Germans as well. Intelligence reports indicated that there were some ten thousand Germans defending Fortress Walcheren. It was a curious formation. Sixty-year-old Lieutenant General Wilhelm Daser's 70th

Infantry Division had been charged by Hitler's direct order to hold the island. He had been told that the fate of Berlin rested on his success in keeping the Allies' shipping out of Antwerp. His was a very special oath — there could be no surrender.

Most of the men of the 70th were seasoned veterans, but of an unusual sort. In German military circles they were known as the "White Bread" or Stomach (*Magen*) Division, all of them men recovering from stomach wounds, or digestive problems such as stomach ulcers who could not tolerate the heavy, dark German flour. With typically Teutonic efficiency, the German High Command grouped together these thousands of men into special units to cater to their dietary needs such as fresh milk, eggs and white bread. In August, 1944, these troops had been posted to guard duties in the abundant lands of Zeeland, forcing the conquered Dutch farmers to contribute to the recovery of their captors.

But as one British infantry officer later remarked bitterly, "I don't care if the guy behind that gun is a syphilitic prick who's a hundred years old — he's still sitting behind eight feet of concrete and he's still got enough fingers to press triggers and shoot bullets."[4]

In addition to the 70th Infantry Division, there were troops from the 64th Infantry Division who had escaped Canadian pursuit in Breskens Pocket, and naval personnel of the 202nd Marine Artillery Battalion manning the heavy coastal batteries and other special artillery. The troops assigned to carry out the defence of the city of Flushing were those of 1019 Regiment commanded by Colonel G. Reinhardt, an officer absolutely loyal to Hitler's decree. In the thick of the ensuing battle, he found time to issue a warrant, later captured by the Allies, ordering the arrest of an antitank platoon commander who had withdrawn his men without orders, "in spite of repeated official warnings that this must on no account be done."[5]

Flushing, situated at the entrance to the Scheldt at the southern tip of the island, provided its own special problems for the invaders, the result of a very carefully planned system of defence fortification. A sheer seawall of some eight to ten metres in height guarded the southwest water approaches to the city. Strongpoints and pillboxes entrenched in the embankment above the wall made any Allied landward approach almost an impossibility. Seaward, the mines, wires and ten-foot-long poles buried on the floor of the sea would discourage an approach from that direction. Some of the more important buildings along the Esplanade, such as the barracks and the Britannia Hotel, had been fortified and flanked with heavy concrete pillboxes. No corner of the city had been overlooked by the zealous engineers — even some of the city manholes in the streets had been capped with protective steel cupolas.

But of all the enemy defences on Walcheren, it was the heavy gun batteries along the whole west coast that Simonds had feared most, and that he had most energetically urged Bomber Command to destroy. These were the gun positions that had harassed troops of the 3rd Canadian Division throughout October while Eisenhower vacillated on the bombing issue. These were the gun positions that Air Chief Marshal Tedder had refused to bomb, calling them "a part-worn battery" that the Canadian Army, "drugged with bombs," wanted destroyed.[6] It was these guns that were to become responsible for the excessive Allied casualties in the coming days.

Few operations during the Battle of the Scheldt had involved such a broad cross-section of offensive troops, or had required such precise planning as the Force T assault on Westkapelle. Pugsley would have the terrible responsibility of shepherding the commandos into the very muzzles of the guns.

The end result of over a month of planning was a flotilla of 182 craft lying off the west coast of Walcheren under sullen clouds in the early hours of the 1st of November. Each had an important function. To silence the deadly batteries, Pugsley had added three heavy warships to his team: HMS *Warspite*, HMS *Erebus* and HMS *Roberts*. This was an inspired idea, but the execution of it was somewhat less than inspired. Had more ships been available, and earlier, their continuous bombardment could have compensated for the lack of interest and action of Bomber Command. Repeated poundings from the ships' fifteen-inch guns could have had sufficient force to smash through the thick casemates that protected the German batteries. As it was, the ships arrived only in time to cover the assault; a three-day reloading trip after their ammunition was expended made further use of them impossible.

Nor, unfortunately, were these ships all in top condition. The rear turrets of the battleship *Warspite* were unserviceable, leaving her with only four fifteen-inch guns. The remaining ships had two guns each, but turret failure was to silence one of them for the first critical hour and a half of battle.

A more serious drawback, and one that would backfire badly in the coming battle, was the fact that the accuracy of the fire was largely dependent on directional aid from air spotters. The Spitfires assigned to this duty had the highly important task of observing the fall of shot and of signalling corrections to the ships. Without them, the guns were much less accurate and less effective.

Forming a formidable part of Force T for the Westkapelle assault was SSEF (Support Squadron Eastern Flank), so named because it had provided eastern flank protection for the vast armada of craft lying off the Normandy beaches for nearly three months. The squadron had just been released from that operation and was on leave in Dorset when it was recalled to active duty for the Walcheren strike.

The responsibility of the Support Squadron was to protect the troop-carrying landing craft during their sweep onto the Westkapelle beaches by directly attacking the enemy batteries, thus inviting fire on themselves that would otherwise be brought to bear on the assaulting troops. Twenty-five ships were available for the job. The total SSEF assault team at Westkapelle was six hundred Royal Navy personnel and five hundred Royal Marines, the latter handling the guns.

Commander K.A. "Monkey" Sellar, better known in prewar days as an international rugby star, had no illusions about the dangers of the mission for the SSEF. He was facing defences that had been described as "the most formidable of their kind in the world."[7] He determined that "close action was justified and losses acceptable"[8] if they met their objective of diverting German fire. in fact, had the enemy midway switched their targets from the SSEF to the landing craft, he was prepared to order his men to approach the shore at even closer range to force the Germans to fire upon them.

Such was the dedication of the short-lived SSEF: born to defend the Normandy beaches and disbanded in tatters after its heroic sacrifice in the chaos of the Walcheren assault.

The shock troops that would make the initial landings were from the 4th Special Service Brigade, commanded by Brigadier B.W.

Leicester. No. 4 Army Commando, a force of 550 men, embarked for Flushing from Breskens in twenty LCAs (Landing Craft Assault) — small landing craft built with ramped bows to allow easy evacuation when landing on the beaches. One Dutch section of eleven men and two troops of French commandos were attached to the British unit. The task of the strike force was to gain a foothold in the city, after which time the infantry would take over. In this case, 155 Brigade, 52nd (Lowland) Division, the final uninitiated unit of the "mountaineers," would soon be blooded to polder warfare.

Commandos for the Westkapelle attack comprised Nos. 41, 47 and 48 Marine Commandos and No. 10 Inter-Allied (IA) composed of Dutch, Belgian, and Norwegian troops whose countries were all occupied by German forces. Theirs was a special vendetta.

Accompanying the first assault wave of commandos to Westkapelle were three Canadian medical units, charged with providing medical and surgical care and also with evacuating the wounded troops. These were the 8th and 9th Canadian Field Surgical Units, Royal Canadian Army Medical Corps (RCAMC). A section of No. 17 Canadian Light Field Ambulance was to land with each of the two commando units that went in on either side of the Westkapelle gap. Casualties were then to be collected and taken to a beach dressing station which would be set up in the sand dunes by No. 10 Field Dressing Station. As none of the personnel involved had had experience in amphibious operations, they were placed under command of the 4 Special Service Brigade for training exercises.

These medical units had one of the toughest assignments of the Northwest Europe campaign. They faced the prospect of handling the accumulated casualties of two weeks' fighting, during which time they might be cut off from all sources of supply. Instruments and medicines for every conceivable type of injury had to be consolidated into the limited space of a Buffalo. Tents that would withstand the high winds on the dunes, reliable power supply, fuel for the sterilizers, safe drinking water — these were just a few of the challenges that had to be met. When all equipment had been assembled, the medics were placed behind barbed wire at Ostend along with the rest of the assault group, maintaining maximum security as they waited for D-Day in cold and barren surroundings, without heat or light.

The assault troops and support personnel were to be transported in LCTs (Landing Craft Tank) — ramped beach landing craft built to carry about one hundred men as well as the Buffaloes in which these men would disembark.

The control centre for the operation was at Major General Foulkes's 2nd Canadian Corps headquarters near Breskens. But the traffic jams were at Ostend, the assembly point for the various craft and vehicles, where personnel was pouring in as D-Day grew closer.

There were so many chiefs, each with a different set of pressures and problems and objectives, but at the top of the complex command structure, feeling the enormous external pressure to activate the plan, and bearing the ultimate responsibility for its success, was General Guy Simonds. Brigadier Bruce Matthews, in charge of all artillery support for the operation, observed the unceasing leverage exercised on the acting army commander: "At the 1st Canadian Army HQ the pressure to get that damn thing done was really incredible. Hour by hour we'd get calls, 'Where are you going…what are you doing…what's happened in the last hour?' It wasn't just a strategic decision at Army Group; it was also a political decision right in the War Office in Washington."[9]

Shortly before dawn on the 1st of November, a force of 550 men of No. 4 Commando Group landed at Flushing on an unassuming refuse dump, now charted as Uncle Beach, just west of the harbour. Dodging anti-landing stakes, the troops scrambled up a mole to secure their first objectives.

The planned last-minute bombardment of the casemated batteries at Flushing had been vetoed by the Deputy Supreme Commander, Air Chief Marshal Tedder, who was concerned about damage to the town and its inhabitants. In any event, bad weather would have prohibited a bombing raid on D-Day. Artillery support was coordinated by Brigadier Bruce Matthews of the 2nd Canadian Corps, who laid on a massive barrage, using every available Canadian and British gun, 314 of them, to support the troops.

The 4th King's Own Scottish Borderers (KOSB) of 155 Brigade,

52nd (Lowland) Division, followed the commando shock troops onto the landing beach; all of the assault companies had landed in comparative ease by 0800 hours of that morning. It wasn't long before the surprise element gave way to determined German defence. And it was a dirty, bloody fight. Street fighting was the only possible form of combat, hour upon hour of crawling over rooftops, edging down narrow alleys and back gardens, even "mouse-holing," blasting holes through walls of houses in densely built-up areas to get from one house to the next.

Yet, in a curious way, the battle took on a macabre sort of carnival atmosphere. The more courageous civilians ventured out in small groups to see their street liberated, and kindly commandos took a moment to warn them of impending danger. The Germans put up a frantic defence, but by evening, the centre of the old inner town was securely in British hands. At 2200 hours the commander of 155 Brigade, Brigadier J.F.S. McLaren, landed at Flushing.

Major pockets of enemy resistance still had to be mopped up, often with the support of the FOO and a summons of help to the Canadian artillery commander across the Scheldt on the south bank. In the case of the more stubborn German strongholds, cab ranks of Typhoons obligingly did the job.* In all, the Royal Air Force Typhoons and Spitfires flew 150 missions during the day.

Street fighting continued through the night and into the next day. Suicide squads of now desperate snipers took to the shipyard cranes and gantries where they could fire down on the troops. This caused problems until the 52nd Division put their mountain training to good, if unusual, use. The Scots had ferried some of their mountain artillery over with them to Walcheren. These were 3.7-inch guns, relatively light, designed for mobility in rough, mountainous country. Some men wrestled the dismantled parts — still heavy enough to cause considerable strain — up the narrow stairs of a Dutch home and reassembled them in an upper bedroom where they could easily silence dangerous enemy snipers perched in the cranes. Bombardier John Walker of 52 Division recalls his unexpected descent: "We were

---

* "Cab rank" is air force terminology indicating planes attacking in line, one after the other — like taxicabs at a railway station.

called on to set up a 3.7 in a house to knock out a sniper position. Our crew kept firing, very accurately, but the impact of the recoil and the weight of the gun gradually started to collapse the floor of our house. Finally, just as we destroyed the objective, the floor caved in, saving us the trouble of hauling the gun back downstairs again."[10]

In prewar days, the imposing Britannia Hotel dominating the western approaches of the city's esplanade was a popular tourist mecca. Now it was a German stronghold, and on November the 3rd, three companies of the Royal Scots Fusiliers of the 155th Brigade were assigned the task of clearing it out. It was to prove a challenge far more demanding than was originally anticipated, when it was estimated that not more than fifty Germans occupied the building.

Protruding grotesquely from the encroaching flood waters, the luxury resort had been transformed into a strongly fortified garrison — the headquarters, as it transpired, of the German commandant of Flushing or, as the War Diary of the 155th Brigade dubbed him, the King of Zeeland. An elaborate system of trenches and bunkers encircled the building, guarding all approaches. Pillboxes lined the steep embankment that protected the south side of the building overlooking the Scheldt. The hotel was moated by the escaping sea water, which in places was waist and shoulder deep and ran strongly with the tide.

H-Hour was set for 0315 hours. The best approach which provided cover to within three hundred metres was from the north. Forming a human chain to prevent being swept away by the current, the troops carried their weapons and equipment above their heads as they struggled by moonlight through icy waters, almost defenceless against the alert enemy mortar and machine-gun fire. As daylight broke, the extent of the German defences soon became evident and each pillbox encountered demanded a quickly improvised attack plan. However, under covering fire, the Scots stormed and knocked out a pillbox while two platoons forced their way into the ground floor of the hotel.

Through the long morning, incredible acts of heroism were performed by the Scots. The single way to silence the enemy fire was to take the strongpoint head on. A machine gun and a 20mm gun were firing from the flat roof of the hotel until a handful of men charged the building, gaining access at the cost of the lives of two company commanders. It was impossible now to call for support fire from the artillery as Scot and German were locked in hand-to-hand combat. Communication back to brigade headquarters became hopeless. The battalion commander, Lieutenant Colonel Melville, was severely wounded when he came up to assess the situation. His signaller was killed. The sole remaining company commander took charge and led a successful attack on the last of the pillboxes by scaling the embankment. By now, the building was on fire and three junior officers, rushing a door to the extensive cellars of the hotel, accidentally uncovered a thick concrete shelter packed with hundreds of trapped and badly frightened Germans.

It was a rich haul. Six hundred prisoners were taken, including the Garrison Commandant Oberst Reinhardt, CO of the 1019 Grenadier Regiment. Fifty Germans had been killed. In this, their first major battle of the war, the Royal Scots had casualties of twenty dead and more than twice that number wounded. But they also had the satisfaction of knowing that their extensive mountain training had indeed had some valuable application, even in below-sea-level · polder warfare.

There is a Canadian postscript to this gallant Scottish victory. Back on Breskens, the First Canadian Rocket Battery of Field Artillery, Eric Harris's and Mike Wardell's Land Service Mattress team, was jockeying with all the other artillery regiments for space on the boggy Breskens terrain. Because of mines and impassable ground, there were almost more guns than there was space to set them up. The team's first launching pad proved to be in an area thick with mines. A launching site was finally found behind the sea dyke near Fort Frederik Hendrik, a fortunate move as on the afternoon of the shoot the area previously selected received ten direct hits from enemy coastal guns. The Walcheren invasion was the immediate raison d'etre of the rockets, their maiden efforts designed to knock out the Flushing batteries. Eric Harris remembers the pair's excitement:

> We made a predicted shoot in the darkness just before first light. Then, as the light came, we continued fire by observation. I controlled it from the top of an abandoned and wrecked lighthouse, close to which we had chosen our battery position.

Mike Wardell arranged to go over with the attacking troops in their amphibious craft, so that he could see and assess the results of our fire. The attack was successful and many of the enemy troops were captured. Among them was the commander of the enemy garrison, and Mike was able to interview him. He was still jittery about the rockets, and couldn't figure just what they were. They had had, he said, a devastating effect, not only by knocking out the battery upon which he was depending, but also on the morale of his garrison.

It was great news for Mike Wardell and me! Some eight months after our first Larkhill [British School of Artillery] talk, we had seen Mike's conception make good in battle. And the battery was now proven, and it was available for further fights ahead.[11]

———— • ————

The German postscript is considerably less jubilant. A commander of one of the commando groups reported the demoralized state of Colonel Reinhardt on his arrest:

At about 1000 hours, along with a line of dishevelled and badly shaken German officers, standing miserably on the parade ground outside the arsenal barracks, Colonel Reinhardt was brought into a shelter for interrogation. But he was far too much upset by his recent experiences to be coherent about anything. He was obviously very much the worse for the bombardments he had endured and was also greatly distressed because he had surrendered his command. During the interview he both wept and urinated freely. His adjutant, who was subjected to a much more exhaustive examination, proved equally uninformative, but by no means uninteresting. He gave the impression of being a somnambulist, so utterly dazed was he after the bombardment and the trials with the floods that had been brought in their train. Throughout his interrogation he was shaking violently and uncontrollably and when he did speak he poured out hysterical curses at the destruction wrought by water everywhere on the island. All the officers testified to the havoc the water had played with all forms of communication, and to the appalling effect it had on morale. To anyone who spoke with these officers, there could be no question but that the flooding policy had been a decisive success.[12]

———•—•———

The battle for Flushing, which had begun on the 1st of November with the commando assault, concluded two days later, almost at the same moment that the Cameronians were forging a passage through the mud flats of the Sloe Channel on the other side of the island.

The last of the three attacks on Walcheren scheduled for 1 November was the naval and marine commando attack of Force T on Westkapelle, the North Sea village midway up the western coast of the Walcheren diamond.

As the armada of 182 craft made its final seaborne approach on the gap between the sheltering dunes of Westkapelle, its commanders were heartened to hear the sharp retort of the German battery at the north of the island exchanging fire with the Canadian artillery in Breskens. Apparently, the enemy had not yet discovered the presence of the invaders.

Captain A.F. Pugsley anxiously studied the message that had just been handed him. Simonds and Ramsay had ordered the Force T commanders to proceed with the assault, but because of the terrible risks involved they had given Pugsley and Brigadier Leicester the final veto at the moment of attack. Now, a message from Major General Churchill Mann, Chief of the General Staff at 1st Canadian Army headquarters, had just come, so urgent that it was sent in clear to save vital moments: "Extremely unlikely any air support, air spotting or air smoke possible owing to airfield conditions and forecast."[13]

Dense fog was already closing in on England. It was very unlikely that planes would be able to take off. The final "softening up" of the dreaded gun batteries would not take place. Of equal seriousness was the fact that because of the weather the air observation planes of the three ships could not cross the channel to be on hand to direct naval fire on the casemates. Pugsley was being told, in effect, that he was on his own, isolated from outside support.

Pugsley had two mandates: he should only proceed if the weather on the target area seemed positive, and then only if the enemy appeared "not more than very weak."[14] These proved to be incompatible instructions.

The weather *was* positive for landing, but it was negative in England, where ground fog prevented the heavy bombers and spotters from taking off.

In regard to enemy strength, Pugsley knew that Simonds had called for a reconnaissance of the enemy defences after the projected air poundings, in order to assess whether Walcheren could be assaulted successfully and with minimum casualties. Reports were disappointing. Codenamed "Tarbrush," small units of men from the navy and the marines, faces blackened to escape detection, had made several sorties to the Westkapelle shores, each time finding an alert enemy with guns and searchlights ready. Clearly, the low priority given the project by Bomber Command was having its effect. There was no evidence of any perceptible softening of the defences. Moreover, although all but one of the batteries was at that moment quiet, there was nothing to indicate that they were damaged or would remain so.

On the other hand, although the sea was quiet and the weather conditions for the landing good at the moment, there was every chance that they would worsen in the next days, probably postponing the assault until the next forecast favourable tide in mid-November. By then, the troops of 52nd (Lowland) Division, now landing at Flushing, would have been beleaguered on the island for many days, in serious jeopardy from German counterattack.

The factor which probably influenced his decision most was the enormous pressure from the War Office to open the port of Antwerp.

Pugsley cast his vote; the code name "Nelson" flashed over the wires. In the tense headquarters of 1st Canadian Army, Simonds and Ramsay exchanged grim glances. Their long weeks of planning now depended on the skill of the men executing the operation — and on a sizeable amount of luck. Lieutenant Colonel Bill Anderson records the next moments: "In the Walcheren operation, the second [Westkapelle] part of it, Guy finally decided, despite the weather and lack of air-cover, to let the commandos loose with the navy. We didn't have any bomber support. I was around for every single agonizing conference about the weather, of when it was likely to lift. I was certainly conscious of what was meant by the loneliness of high command when that man, and that man only, with the naval man beside him said, 'We're going.'"[15]

The Westkapelle assault was on.

At 0820 hours, the *Warspite, Erebus* and *Roberts,* still some twenty km offshore, opened fire on the German batteries. Forty minutes later, under the umbrella of these heavies, Sellar moved his Support Squadron unwaveringly through the unswept minefields towards Westkapelle, its lighthouse forming a target as prominent as "a match sticking out of an apple."[16] But twenty-five Allied craft steaming steadily towards the German position in broad daylight could hardly be called inconspicuous. The enemy soon sighted their guns on this new threat, and within moments the Support Squadron craft came under fire. Using their own 4.7s, 17-pounders, and other weapons designed to destroy the enemy emplacements, the marines returned the fire, inviting further retaliation as they closed in.

Sellar had expected casualties, but what he saw through his binoculars was, quite simply, a slaughter. It was far worse than he could have anticipated when he so resolutely took on Europe's toughest fortress.

A new disaster overtook the men. There were five rocket-firing ships in the Support Squadron. The other support craft and Typhoons were to hold their fire until the rocket broadsides had been discharged. But suddenly, Sellar's crews were horrified to see the rockets plastering their own ships. One of the ships had been hit by a shell from W13, causing the boat to lurch and involuntarily fire off half its load of rockets into the midst of the Support Squadron's own craft. Then two other rocket ships began inadvertently firing on their own men. Faulty radar ranging had caused them to fire more than three thousand metres short.

But still the SSEF craft coursed in, those that still could, provoking the infamous German batteries into uneven battle, finally at point-blank range. And fresh disasters overtook the men. A single craft, steaming steadily towards land, would receive hit after direct hit, almost beyond count, and even when completely crippled would go on firing. The captain of one LCG (Landing Craft Gun), wounded and lying on the shattered deck, guided his ship by passing orders that were relayed through a hole in the deck of the ship to the wheelhouse. A motor mechanic had himself lowered down the side of his ship where he perched in a gaping shell-hole, playing a hose on a fire raging at the fuel tanks by his feet.

Two boats were under orders to deliberately beach, one on either side of the four-hundred-metre-wide gap. LCG 101 remained on the north beach for nine minutes, exchanging fire with a pillbox less than fifty metres away. Her commanding officer, Lieutenant G.A. Flamank, RNVR, attempting to free the anchor, was shot dead. Riddled with holes, the LCG limped back to sea and sank. LCG 102, commanded by Lieutenant D.T.V. Flory, scored a number of hits on her target on the southern beach before being set on fire. The three LCS (Landing Craft Support) supporting her elected to close in, deliberately beaching at point-blank range. They too were blistered with enemy fire and burned out. This action allowed safe passage to the commandos landing on the beach. But of Lieutenant Flory and his crew of forty-one there were no survivors, and only one from the craft that supported her.[17]

In less than two hours, the Support Squadron was virtually wiped out. Only five of the original twenty-five attacking craft were not disabled; nine had been sunk. One hundred and seventy-two men had been killed, and two hundred and eighty-six wounded, many of them seriously. But in those two hours, the Support Squadron had achieved its objective. By deliberately drawing all the enemy fire upon themselves, these "gallant young amateur sailors," in Pugsley's words,[18] had given safe conduct to the commando landing. From his flagship *Kingsmill*, Pugsley ordered the hovering Typhoons to buy a brief respite for the commandos by plastering the area with their rockets, the first of 150 sorties that morning.

The assault force came in LCTs and LSIs (Landing Craft Infantry) in the wake of their Support Squadron escort. They were scheduled to land on beaches formed on each side of the gap. Three troops of 41 Commando with two troops of 10 Inter-Allied Commando landed on the north side, with the immediate assignment of capturing the nearby town of Westkapelle and destroying all batteries in the area, and in particular, W15. 48 Commando landed on the beach on the south side. Its mission was to capture W13.

The Germans had made a serious mistake when, taken in by Sellar's ruse, they directed all their fire on the Support Squadron. They eventually realized their error but by the time they did so, it was too late. The landing craft had gained the security of the beaches where the enemy emplacement guns could not be depressed enough to bring direct fire upon them. Now, however, heavy indirect gunfire peppered the beaches, causing a number of casualties.

But the operation was threatened once again with disaster when the powerful guns from the Force T ships proved themselves virtually useless without their "eye in the sky," the fast, spotting aircraft scheduled to direct their fire. These were grounded by fog on England's south coast, as Pugsley had been alerted. Substitute OPs (Observation Posts) from the continent were brought in to replace them, but they had never worked with the British Navy. Unrehearsed in communications and in naval techniques for directing fire, these planes were of little use in the assault. This was clearly a fumble by T Force, whose enlistment of the substitute air spotters was an impromptu, slipshod arrangement, as this report reveals: "Air OPs from the continent had been arranged as a secondary means of observing, and eventually was procured, but these arrangements had been made a few days before the assault and there had been no opportunity of exercising them with T Force. Some difficulties of procedure and the unsuitability of the Air OP wireless sets for this type of work made the spotting ineffective."[19]

The battleships, lacking that vital air spotting, could not find their targets. After firing three hundred rounds at W17, the *Warspite* was not able to register a single hit. The artillery bombardment over in Breskens was seeking to disable those dread batteries. But only 10 percent of the guns — the 155mm heavy and super heavies — could reach the target area to the north of Westkapelle gap. For the rest, Bomber Command had been expected to provide this support — until policy reversals and bad weather had legislated against it.

41 Commando touched down at 1012 hours, and at 1056 hours they reported that the village of Westkapelle with W15 was almost

completely in their hands. Minutes later, a troop attacked and captured the lethal battery W15, taking 120 prisoners.

Things were tougher on the south side of the gap where 48 Commando, under the command of Lieutenant Colonel J.L. Moulton, suffered heavy casualties. The German infantry and artillery troops defending W13 put up a tough fight. It was nightfall of D-Day before this battery that had caused the most severe casualties to the Support Squadron earlier in the day fell. Ironically, it was later discovered that at the precise moment when W13 could have finished off the last few SSEF craft, the four guns of the battery ran out of ammunition, and none could be brought up because of the flooding. Guy Simonds's decision to breach the dykes was further vindicated.

Meanwhile, 47 Commando, which had been scheduled to follow an hour behind the two leaders, was in difficulty. The intensity of enemy fire and some confusion in their orders as to which side of the gap to land on caused 47 Commando to become scattered and disorganized. Some of the troops, mistakenly landing on the north shoulders of the gap, had to cross four hundred metres to the south beach, fighting riptide currents that swept them away from shore. Many men were lost and valuable equipment sunk.

Hobart's "Funnies," expected to play an important role, encountered difficulties as well. Over one hundred Buffaloes and eighty Weasels were brought to the beaches in landing craft, and many were immediately put to use. The 79th Armoured also provided special detachments of armoured vehicles, and few of these escaped crippling damage from the combined threats of a fast-moving tidal current and the enemy guns.

An invasion rehearsal that would normally have been held for an assault of this dimension might have avoided this sort of confusion, but the rehearsal had been deliberately shelved by the T Force commanders in order to advance the date of the invasion.

The assault troops in this hazardous mission were mainly British, although still under the command of the 1st Canadian Army. But Canadians filled another important role in the invasion of Walcheren: they were responsible for the medical services. One of the first to land was Major John Hillsman of 8 Canadian Field Surgical Unit, RCAMC. Coming in, in the wake of the first assault wave, Hillsman watched,

Simonds and Montgomery confer on the plan for the Walcheren amphibious attack.

General Wilhelm Daser, Commander,
Walcheren defences.

Queen Wilhelmina of the Netherlands views damage at Flushing.

*Montgomery with
the mayor of Antwerp
salutes the opening of
Antwerp Harbour.*

horrified, as the Support Squadron advanced to its annihilation: "Pinpoints of light sparkled from the south batteries. The Germans were opening up at last. The whole line of support craft broke into flame and smoke. Ships blew up and were swallowed in one gulp. Others drifted aimlessly around, out of control."

Then an LCT immediately in front of him — a hospital craft especially fitted for stretchers — hit a sea mine. To the bespectacled, sandy-haired surgeon, it was a devastating sight: "There was a tremendous explosion and the entire ship was hurled into the air. It settled rapidly. Men jumped into the sea. Some were picked up by the following craft. Others floated face down in their life belts."

German fire was beginning to find the range of the assault craft now, and the commanding officer of Hillsman's LCT yelled through his megaphone that they were going to try to land ahead of schedule to get away from the fire from the shore batteries: "We grounded with a grating jar, and the sergeant in charge of the Buffalo yelled above the din, 'Hold on! We're going off!' The Buffalo lurched down the ramp and into the gap. Fragments were shrieking overhead. Sand and water were blown by the continual explosions all over our equipment. A Buffalo to our right hit a mine. It burst into flames and men poured over its sides. The wireless operator threw back his turret and started to climb out. His clothes were blazing. He got half out and fell back into the flames."[20]

Although most of the vehicles around him had been hit, somehow Hillsman's got through the gap and onto the minefield behind the dunes on the north side of the breach. It took five attempts before the second section of the surgical unit could get through the intense shelling on the south side to swim ashore.

The sappers were also having problems finding the correct landing beach and getting their heavy equipment off-loaded; because of mines and cratering, most of the essential equipment was lost, including all but one of the armoured bulldozers required to clear the beach of obstacles. Consequently, the beaches became jammed with craft, some stuck in the sand or mud, some holed, some simply torn to bits by mines. As soft sand was compacted by traffic, buried mines became a menace; finally, the beach area had to be swept for mines every two hours.

The assault troops found themselves seriously short of vehicles, guns, ammunition and armour. Some of the sappers, lacking equipment for their own work, fought as infantry troops. The 1st Lothians and Border Yoemanry of the 79th Armoured Division originally had two Sherman tanks, six Flails, eight AVREs and four bulldozers, but in the end only the two tanks and two AVREs beached successfully.

Regardless, 48 Commando continued to drive south through the dunes to Zouteland, which fell into their hands late the next morning; 150 German prisoners were taken. The next important objective was W11, the last battery whose shells were still pounding the landing beaches. 47 Commando made the attack the afternoon of the 2nd of November but was beaten back by savage resistance. With darkness falling and all three troop commanders wounded, the commando troops became dispersed and disorganized. Their confidence had been badly shaken by the events of the day and by the poorly executed landing attempts the previous day. Despite the urgency of the task, their commander did not believe he could mount another attack that night. The next morning, however, the attack was reorganized successfully and the deadly battery finally silenced.

During the next four days, the enemy fought determinedly for the last foothold on the fortress. That special Walcheren oath of Hitler's devise was infecting the defenders with stern determination. They had sworn: "I am pledged to hold this fortified sector to the last, even to sacrifice my own life. Even if the enemy should already have broken through on my right and left, I am not empowered to give up this sector or to negotiate with the enemy." [21] Even the act of suicide was expressly forbidden. Offenders would be buried, in total silence, in civilian plots.

Despite its depleted ranks, 47 Commando continued its thrust southward, eliminating several other *stutzpunkts* until, finally, they made contact with the Flushing assault troops to ensure complete domination of the southern half of the island.

In the meantime, 10th Inter-Allied Commandos had been holding firm in Domburg, northeast of Westkapelle. Reinforced by 41 Commando, they now began a sweep up the island's northern coast towards W18 with its four 105mm guns, and finally, the last and northernmost of the heavy batteries, W19. During this period, the work of the two surviving tanks and two AVREs of the 1st Lothians was invaluable as they supplied the only fire support available to the ground troops.

The going was very treacherous as the Germans had mined, wired and booby-trapped all the approaches to the batteries. And, just as the 2nd and 3rd Canadian Infantry Divisions had been forced to fight a German delaying action dyke by dyke, the commandos now had to fight dune by dune to drive the Germans back. Using each elevation defensively, the enemy would put up savage resistance to the British, even driving them back with the intensity of their defiance, and then stealthily withdraw back through the dunes during the night to the next strongpoint.

On the 6th of November, after a three-day struggle, the commandos captured W18, taking three hundred prisoners. W19, the final objective, was known to be heavily fortified. But first, "Black Hut," a strongpoint in the woods that defended W19, offered fierce resistance. "Typhies" and the tanks dealt with this obstacle. It was then learned that the much-feared W19 had been evacuated, its crew having just retreated south through the woods.

As the commandos inexorably pushed the enemy into the sea, the Canadian medics were struggling under appalling conditions to care for the seemingly endless stream of wounded. On the first day of the invasion, 150 casualties were collected and treated. It was decided that it was preferable to evacuate the wounded to Ostend rather than risk operating on the still heavily shelled and mined beaches. At midnight, one LCT pulling out with a load of casualties struck a mine and burned, killing many of the wounded. After that, they were taken out in Buffaloes.

It was while the medical staff were having their lunch on the second day that a salvo of shells hit three nearby Buffaloes that were being unloaded of some seven tons of ammunition by German prisoners. For the next forty-five minutes, exploding small arms ammunition and mortars from the vehicles raked the crowded beach, killing twenty men, including the quartermaster of the Field Dressing Station and five other ranks as well as ten German POWs. Canadian, British and German wounded were no longer enemies as they shared the common denominator of pain and fear.

All of the medical officers were trapped in the dugout where they had been eating their lunch, with only Captain Lew Ptak of the Transfusion Unit and Major Hillsman free to help the wounded. Hillsman described the next minutes: "We had to crawl two hundred yards on our bellies with the exploding ammunition shooting at us from one side and the Germans from the other…One of the medics went inside an exploding Buffalo to reach a wounded commando. He was blown half in two by a mortar bomb. For the next half hour we lay on our faces in the sand, dressing wounds, stopping hemorrhages and splinting fractures. Constant explosions were blowing sand over us as we worked."[22]

That night, the long expected North Sea gale descended with force, lashing at the defenceless men with sleet and cutting winds. Evacuation was now out of the question; the assault force troops with their wounded comrades were isolated from all outside support, alone on an island and surrounded by their enemy.

Hillsman crawled around the heaving tents examining the wounded. Five men urgently needed surgery. Major Hillsman operated that evening under appalling conditions. "With great difficulty we pitched the 160-pounder tent. This gave us an Operating Room some nine feet long and six feet wide. We could just get the table, three men and some hand basins in without moving around too much. It was impossible to use open fires for sterilizing so we put the instruments and some rubber sheeting in chemical solution in basins on the floor…Captain Merkeley was almost bent double giving the anaesthetic and I had to crawl under the operating table when I wanted to change sides."[23]

When the generator packed it up, the final operations were completed by the light of an acetylene lamp. The next day, November 3rd, the weather had worsened and the slim hope of evacuation disappeared in the face of driving snow and rain. There was no alternative to setting up the main surgical tent. It took forty men to put it up, erecting it on the only available flat ground — on top of the dyke, fully vulnerable to wind and enemy. They thought gratefully of their pre-invasion drill when they had raised tents with specially made six-foot-long pegs until they could manage the task almost in their sleep. One man worked tirelessly, pounding in tent pegs as tall as himself.

As fast as he pounded them in, the wind would loosen them. Petrol and ammunition dumps surrounded the tent; the dead lay wrapped in blankets on one side of the entrance. German prisoners huddled in huge crater pits nearby. Men were given goggles so they could go out in the blowing sand to find more wounded.

In two days, fifty-two operations were performed by Hillsman and his small medical team. On the afternoon of the 4th, a brief lull permitted the evacuation ship to pull into the beach. As the casualties were being loaded by the German POWs, Hillsman remembers the yell that went up: "A sea mine had been sighted just off the stern of the ship, and, loaded with wounded as she was, the captain was afraid to stay or to back out. I'll never forget the sailor who jumped into the water and, clinging to the mine, removed the detonator." [24]

As the last stretchers set off down the beach to the ship, the gale blew up again with such force that the captain had to pull out to sea. Twelve wounded men faced a dismal return to their bleak hospital quarters on the dunes.

For twelve days the Canadian medics endured the desolate, frigid wastelands of Walcheren, working around the clock in what is considered to be the most dangerous medical action in the Northwest Europe campaign. "There was really no comparison," one senior officer recalls. "Ordinarily, with the exception of units such as the RMOs [Regimental Medical Officers] and stretcher-bearers, the medical setups were far enough back from the action to be relatively safe. But on Walcheren, the medical section actually landed ahead of a lot of the combat troops. There, on the island, we were all sitting ducks." [25]

The medics had had to fight to get on the island; now, with the battle finally concluded, they had to fight to get off it, too. Waterlogged, tired, discouraged, they slogged their way through mud and rain to reach Flushing, where they found themselves stranded. Private Roy Connors, of 8th Field Surgical Unit, RCAMC, remembers a friendly sea captain offering them a straight swap: "When they took us to Flushing we stayed in a woodwork factory. We even slept on the factory benches. Then a big load of food came in, a lot of canned stuff, and they told us the only way we were going to get back to the mainland was if we unloaded the food for the people. We had to go and unload it all before they'd take us back." [26]

Back in their old quarters in Ostend, Hillsman was handed a routine order from Corps: "I was told that all lost equipment must be listed and indented for by nine o'clock that night. I didn't have the heart to rout the boys out of their beds. I guessed at the items and multiplied by three. One gets used to the vagaries of the army after a while." [27]

———————

The Germans had set up their defences behind the vast canal system of Zeeland in September, falling back on one water barrier after another to stall the Allies' advance. Now, two months later, they retreated behind the single last body of water left to them in all of Zeeland: the flooded waters lapping around the venerable, moated town of Middelburg in the centre core of Walcheren, now bloated with refugees.

It was the good fortune of its Dutch inhabitants that Middelburg lay on a slight elevation, the ancient quarter high and dry while flood waters completely encircled the rest. And they shared their good luck willingly with other Zeelanders forced from their homes by the floods from the bursting dykes. In just a few weeks, their population had doubled. Forty thousand people now crowded into the town and conditions had become appalling. The water mains had all been destroyed; the only drinking water anyone on the island had was rainwater from cisterns. Poor sanitation facilities brought new threats of disease, and with it the realization that medical supplies were at a premium.

There was another refugee from the floods and the bombardments who was not welcome — the German soldier. The headquarters of 70th Infantry Division and its elusive commander, the balding, middle-aged Lieutenant General Daser, had now been established behind the city's moated walls, confident that its garrison could repel any Allied attack. All the land approaches were submerged except the narrow, raised embankments of the Middelburg Canal, and these were sown thick with mines and punctuated with pillboxes. For the rest, twice a day the tides swept the flood waters into the outskirts of the town, entirely submerging whole streets of homes in up to twelve metres of water, sparing only the centre core. And the Germans had one other advantage: they held forty thousand Dutch civilians as hostages against attack.

It was in these circumstances that a civilian doctor from the town, a Zeelander, escaped by night to the waterlogged suburbs of Middelburg where he stole a canoe and crossed the German lines. He paddled almost five km down the canal that linked Middelburg with Flushing, skirting the mine-sown banks, until he finally reached the headquarters of Brigadier J.F.S. McLaren, infantry commander of 155 Infantry Brigade of the 52nd (Lowland) Division.

The doctor described the desperate plight of the people of Middelburg, and begged the British to rescue them. The Germans, he reported, were determined, but they might back down with a show of strength from the Allies. Get your tanks in and I'm sure they will surrender, he implored.

The British were under orders not to bombard these civilian outposts. So, once again, Hobart's "Funnies" were called in to play a useful and imaginative role. While tanks could not cross submerged land, Buffaloes could — and Buffaloes looked enough like tanks that they might outbluff the enemy. That was the gamble of the handful of men of the 7th/9th Royal Scots who set out at noon on the 5th of November to capture the last German troops holding out on Walcheren. It was a curious flotilla. The 120 men, with the only eight Buffaloes that could be requisitioned, swam their way across the navigational nightmare of inundated land, thickly sown with mines and obstacles.

The strategy was a complete success. The small band reached Middelburg by mid-afternoon, entering the town behind the main enemy camp before he was even aware of their approach. The British officer in charge of the company, Major R.H.B. Johnston, immediately sent an order to General Daser demanding the surrender of the garrison. The German replied that he refused to surrender to an officer junior to himself. Borrowing some pips, Major Johnston promptly promoted himself to the "local and temporary" rank of colonel.[28] His honour satisfied, General Daser formally surrendered to the British and two thousand of his men obediently paraded into the main square in front of the town hall and laid down their weapons.

An anxious nine hours followed with two hundred British guarding two thousand prisoners still milling about the square in confusion.

To compound the potentially dangerous situation, hundreds of civilians and a force of Dutch Underground crowded in to share the excitement of liberation — and liberal swigs of Dutch gin — with their neighbours. Relief finally came from the east where the HLI of 52nd Division had broken through the causeway. Almost simultaneously, more help arrived from the west with the 4th KOSB coming in from Flushing.

Later in the same day, the 7th Cameronians under the command of Lieutenant Colonel C.F. Nason, captured Veere with its garrison of over six hundred Germans, again with little opposition. Small pockets of resistance continued to occupy the Scottish liberators for several days, but the battle for Walcheren, and for the Scheldt, was to all intents concluded.

The enemy had fought well and bravely; his losses had been staggering. In all, 41,043 Germans had been taken prisoner. No one will ever know how many more there were who were killed or wounded, or who had escaped Lieutenant Colonel Alway's net on North Beveland, or had slipped away with von der Heydte's paratroopers in Woensdrecht. The 1st Canadian Army, in the same period of the 1st of October to the 8th of November, had 12,873 casualties, killed, wounded and missing. Half that number were Canadians.[29]

The cost in human life during the eight-day struggle to drive the Germans off the island had been high. Allied casualties neared 7,700 including one in every four Support crafts' crew, and two out of every five commando troop officers.[30] In refusing to bomb the Walcheren gun casements in support of the Canadian assault, in labelling infantrymen as "drugged" on bombs, Air Marshal "Bomber" Harris was said to have boasted that he could "capture Walcheren with his batman after all the bombs that had been dropped on it." Admiral Pugsley added later, "I wish that he had been with us that day!"[31]

There were many men of the Support Squadron and the commandos who would have echoed that wish. Air Marshal Harris and Lord Tedder must bear some responsibility for the fact that W13 and W15 destroyed ten support craft. W13 was the direct cause of 250 to 300 of the casualties suffered by the assault force. W15 claimed 150 to 200 killed and wounded.[32]

For the 52nd (Lowland) Division, no battle could have been

tougher than their first one, nor fought with greater valour. For the commandos, the Walcheren assault was "the finest thing they did in the entire war."[33] For the Support Squadron, it was their finest and last. In that brief two-hour span, by deliberately sacrificing themselves to direct enemy fire, they ensured the safe landing and successful campaign on Walcheren.

Epilogue

FOR EIGHTEEN MONTHS, DUTCH AND ALLIED ENGINEERS WORKED furiously to restore the destroyed lands of Walcheren. It was an enormous task: nearly 80 percent of the island's 47,000 acres had been inundated.

In 1945, a great deal of work was achieved, and that fall the race against winter saw the first gains against the elements. By 1947 new trees were planted, and with them came the birds, and soon the crops, more abundantly than ever before.

And slowly, stiffly, the people of Zeeland picked themselves up from the chaos of the war years and entered on the long, painful process of making a new beginning. The years following the Battle of the Scheldt have been coloured by the lasting gratitude they have for their Allied liberators.

But many military commanders and historians remember the battle for Antwerp as one of the war's most costly blunders. It cost us Arnhem, it might easily have cost us the Ardennes — and it certainly cost us many thousands of lives needlessly wasted as the war dragged on into the winter of '45.

The Allies' neglect in intercepting the escaping German 15th Army offered a valuable opportunity to the enemy to regroup their forces for the defence of the approaches to Arnhem. Our failure to establish a bridgehead over the Rhine before the onset of the winter storms and floods had a direct bearing on extending the war by many months.

The continuing reluctance to give military priority to the Canadians for the Scheldt campaign only helped the German strategy. And although the campaign was a brilliant victory by the 1st Canadian Army, the lengthy struggle still deprived the Allies of the use of the front-line port for nearly two months. This dangerously stalled the build-up of essential war supplies, which continued to be dependent on truck convoys from the Normandy coast. On the 1st of November, while British Army and Marine commandos were engaged in their desperate bid to capture Walcheren, the first minesweepers of the Royal Navy braved enemy fire at the mouth of the Scheldt to begin clearing the river of mines. On the 26th, 150 of these craft had completed the tough and dangerous assignment: 267 mines had been swept and detonated from the eighty-five km channel to Antwerp. Within a few days, the first ten thousand tons of vital supplies were off-loaded from Allied ships at Antwerp Harbour.

Just two weeks later, the great German counteroffensive in the Ardennes began. The enemy raced for the American and British supply dumps, capturing vast stores. Had Antwerp Harbour not been open to bring up fresh supplies for the dwindling Allied reserves, the Germans might well have been successful in breaking through the line and isolating the British and Canadian armies in the northern part of Belgium and Southern Holland. Cut off from supplies, that vital arm of the Allied offensive would have been paralyzed.

By the narrow margin of two weeks, Antwerp's opening forestalled this threat. It was that close. A single mistake in executing the battle plan to free the Scheldt, one error in strategy or an isolated slip in judgement could have jeopardized the entire Northwest European campaign.

Eisenhower's major blunder — failing to open Antwerp Harbour quickly enough — was the manifestation of the victory euphoria that infected so many. It was this euphoria that caused him to lose his direction in the campaign and his control over its commanders. Removing himself from direct communication with his land commanders, abandoning his influence with SHAEF's air marshals, plainly ignoring the advice of his top naval man, and even neglecting Ultra's strong warnings, Eisenhower, for the moment, allowed the conduct of war to slip from his grasp. An unparalleled opportunity to end the conflict was tragically lost.

Personal ambitions were unleashed. The will to win the war was still up front, but what's-in-it-for-me? was becoming the silent motivator. Dozens of minor conflicts between the principals of those times emerged — rivalries that Eisenhower's skilled diplomacy had until now kept submerged. Mistrust was rampant. Jealousies sprang up everywhere — Americans quarrelled with British, British with Canadians, the French with everyone. Had the Belgian Government-in-Exile trusted their king, or the Royalist Resistance group that supported him, the Albert Canal bridges would almost certainly have been captured intact, as "Harry" had pleaded that they be. Had Montgomery or Dempsey ordered Horrocks to advance over the bridges immediately, the German escape channel would have been cut off.

Instead, a night's work took two months. Had essential supplies been diverted earlier to the 1st Canadian Army, along with urgent orders to secure the Scheldt approaches, a major battle could have become a minor skirmish. And had Simonds's request for bomber support been heeded, the German defences of Breskens and Walcheren would have been diluted, clearing the way for a fast victory…and sparing, in the process, so many lives of Canadian infantry, British Commandos and Support Squadron personnel.

Even among the various arms of the Allied forces, the war effort was briefly stalled by mistrust: the lofty attitude of Bomber Command towards the infantry, and the lack of communication between air force and army were but two examples of this prevalent mood.

And who was listening when lone commanders stood up against the unnecessary wastage of their men? It was expedient for Mackenzie King and his governmental appointees to play their dangerous game, paying little heed to the untrained Canadian volunteers who were being sacrificed on the polders.

The simple conclusion would seem to be that even in time of war, the enemy is not always on the other side of the hill.

———————◆—◆———————

On the 28th of November, Allied naval and military chiefs from Belgium, Great Britain and the United States gathered with the Burgemeester of Antwerp and dignitaries of the municipality for a reception to formally open the port of Antwerp to Allied shipping. The band played the Belgian national anthem and the British one, too.

Admiral Ramsay, who was killed in an air crash two months later, attended the ceremony, as did British minesweeping personnel who had performed the dangerous task of clearing the Scheldt of hundreds of mines in record time.

Not present, not having been invited, were members of the Secret Army. Somehow, Reniers' name, and Colson's too, had not warranted inclusion in the celebration.

With a single exception, there was no Canadian representation there either. General Crerar, by then recovered and back in command of the 1st Canadian Army, was not invited. Nor were General Simonds, nor anyone from Canadian Military headquarters. But, proudly steaming up the Scheldt as the first supply ship to enter Antwerp Harbour, was the Canadian-built *Fort Cataraqui*, manned by a crew of the British Royal Navy. 12,873 casualties of the odd-job Canadian Army would have to be content with that.

Afterword

I N 1995, A DUTCH MOTHER HELD UP HER BABY TO A PASSING LORRY-load of veterans. She gently put one of her child's tiny fingers in the hand of a Canadian veteran. "I want to be able to tell my child that she held the hand of a man who brought us freedom," she said shyly.

This was the moment for us when *Tug of War*, the book, became tug of heart, an ongoing emotional experience, an unexpected off-shoot of the book that has dramatically changed our lives.

Before *Tug of War* was published in 1984, we were going full tilt in a number of directions. Denis (Denny, to friends, comrades, and readers) had a challenging financial job with Burns Fry Ltd. (now Nesbitt Burns). He was also chairman of the Canadian Equestrian Team, having led that team to a fistful of Olympic and World Championship medals over two decades. He was a co-founder and board member of the Olympic Trust of Canada and had been named *Chef de Mission* to the boycotted 1980 Olympic Games in Moscow.

I was also wearing several hats: a sports writer running my own successful public relations firm, marrying up corporations to amateur sports bodies, as well as freelancing for a variety of newspapers and magazines on sports, travel, and business. Oh, and I was raising four young daughters.

Then Denny went lame.

It wasn't sudden and traumatic, although it seemed so. One day he was fit and healthy; overnight, canes and crutches littered our front hall. His failed and infected hip transplant was to have a deep impact on our lives.

"What shall we do?" we cried in unison over a plate of spaghetti that was steaming mightily with oregano and basil. A hearty sprinkle of parmesan. Red wine. Our favourite "O Group" think-tank time.

"Let's move to Europe and write a book about the war!" It made sense. In the interim period since the war — some 35 years — very few books had focused on the achievements of Canadians fighting in Northwest Europe. Literally *no* book had been written at that time about any Canadian WWII battle by an officer who had commanded it. No Canadian general had ever written a book. Worse, though we had some outstanding general officers, there wasn't a single publication about any of them. The British and American historians and veterans wrote their hearts out during that period, acclaiming their leaders and describing their military actions. But Canadians? Not a word! The veterans weren't talking: they had hung up their uniforms — and reminiscences — when they came home.

But we didn't just want to write about war. We wanted to capture the feel of the battles, and the feelings and motivations of the men who fought them — the human elements of war. We interviewed hundreds of men: British, Canadian, American, Belgian, Dutch, and German. We also sought the views of European civilians who had endured so many terrible years of the Occupation. We came to know well many of the Belgian and Dutch Resistance fighters whose courage and sacrifice made the job for the liberators easier. We now count several of them as close friends.

Tug of War was thus conceived, and three years later, on April 29, 1984, was born (written, by the way, on an ancient Apple computer with a 64K memory!). That day is nostalgic for us: we welcomed our first grandchild, boy Graham, at 4 a.m. Too excited to sleep, we drove to our Oakville home, tied a large blue bow around an old oak tree, and wrote the final pages of the book.

As novices, we were surprised and delighted that this first effort at writing won the John W. Dafoe Award as the Best Book on International Affairs for 1984. At the presentation dinner at the Manitoba Club in Winnipeg, the city where I was born, I had another surprise. The *Winnipeg Free Press* photographer posed us under a portrait of one of the club's founders. When my mother later saw the print, she was startled. Gazing down approvingly from the wall above us was my grandfather — a man who had died thirty years before I was born, a man who had made a significant contribution to the development and history of western Canada — Major William Sherwood Bell.

That first book turned into four books, and one year became twenty, and we were still not done. Happily, we have thus far avoided the agonies of our books being shredded. They still sell, in three or four countries and as many languages.

We have returned to Belgium and Holland a number of times since *Tug of War* was published. We picked up the threads of a wartime camaraderie forty years later when we interviewed Harry — now sea captain Colonel Eugene Colson — about his role as head of the wartime Resistance in Antwerp's docks. The relationship between Denis and Harry began uniquely, and endures to this day.

On September 16, 1944, the Royal Hamilton Light Infantry (RHLI) moved into Antwerp. Its commanding officer, Lt-Col Denis Whitaker, set up Regimental Headquarters in Antwerp's harbour. Colson, a burly dockworker operating under the code name of "Harry," strode into Denis's HQ. He introduced himself as a member of the Belgian Secret Army, commanding a unit of six-hundred dockworkers whom he had hand-picked and secretly trained as a resistance battalion. These men had risked their lives daily, often enduring imprisonment and torture by the Gestapo during the four years of German occupation to protect the docks.

He explained the importance of the Antwerp docks to the Allied cause. By September 1944, the Americans, British, and Canadians had overextended their supply lines. They were fast running out of fuel and ammunition. Without access to Antwerp's vast docks — the only ones in free Western Europe that were still intact — the Allied forces would not have had the logistical power to finish the war. Harry had tried vainly to convince the British of this when they liberated the city ten days before, but they were ordered out before securing the docks. In the interim period, waiting for the Canadians, this amazing Belgian patriot and his men had been holding the port against vicious German attacks. Their only weapons were a few antiquated machine guns, and a much more potent one: their intimate knowledge of every inch of the 20 square kilometres of dock area. The enemy — determined to destroy those vital docks — fought with tanks and 88mm guns.

During the "Streetcar War" that ensued between Second Canadian Infantry Division and the Germans, Harry and his men gave invaluable assistance to all the Canadians fighting to secure the docks and canals around Antwerp.

Colson's passion has never wavered for his *wapen broeders* (brothers in arms), the men of the Resistance who fought under his leadership. Every year these patriots meet formally at the Monument to the Resistance they erected in 1989. They observe the "Last Post" for the twenty-one young men brutally shot down in one dark moment by German attackers, and for the scores more who gave their lives in the following weeks of battle. When the Canadians finally secured the port in early October, many of the Resistance volunteered to remain with the Canadians, fighting alongside them as they pushed north to the Belgian–Dutch border and even further into southern Holland to clear the banks of the Scheldt. In this way, Harry and Denis became *wapen broeders*, too.

We have also had enduring relationships with the Dutch. In Chapter 9 of this book we relate in some detail the story of the harrowing battle for five days between the RHLI and General von der Heydte's crack German paratroopers. Denis's battalion headquarters were in the white-stuccoed van Beek farmhouse in the village of Woensdrecht. It is one of the few WWII landmarks utterly unchanged by the decades – bullet-holes and all!

In 1944 the family had been ordered to evacuate, but Cornelis, the owner, refused to leave the homestead where he had been born. Besides, what would he do with his eight cows and a barnyard full of pigs? The Germans seized his farm and ordered him out at gunpoint. While fighting for their very lives in the next days, the men of the RHLI took the time to feed and water the cattle (the pigs, alas, were killed by mortar shells).

When we turned up four decades later, Cornelis's son and daughter-in-law were working the farm. We're going to walk the battlefield, we said. Back in half an hour. When we returned, half the village was waiting for us. We had a grand *sckoll* and schnapps reunion. Grandson Cornelis ("Corny" they called him), then a schoolboy, interpreted. Cards flew back and forth over the ensuing years.

In 1995, traveling with a bus full of veterans, we parked briefly in Woensdrecht. We were too many, we thought, to invade yet again the van Beek farmhouse. A loud rapping on the bus window revealed a broadly grinning *Mevrouw* van Beek gesturing at me through the bus and beckoning urgently.

She had something very exciting to show us; we must come to the farm right away! There was a great bustle, and who should toddle shyly towards us but twin baby girls. These were the 1944 farmer Cornelis's great granddaughters — and we became honorary grandparents!

We were similarly honoured in our own country by the grand-children of Chris Kruter, the president of an Ontario branch of the Dutch-Canadian Legion, with whom we became friends. Although the Dutch-Americans have a national organization, the Canadian association is the only foreign branch of the Dutch Legion. All its members are *wapen broeders,* who served under the Dutch flag before emigrating to Canada.

An unexpected byproduct of these ventures into military history has occupied quite a lot of our time. The bond that we forged with Harry and the Antwerpens in the early '80s elicited an invitation to join them in Antwerp's celebration of the 45th year of Liberation, and later, their 50th — six of them in recent years. Bring some veterans, they generously requested. In the end they hosted dozens of Canadians and their spouses for a week on the town.

Antwerp, we discovered, was *some* town. When we weren't sampling Beluga caviar on silver spoons, sipping the finest wines, nibbling their world-famous chocolates, or relaxing over the incomparable Antwerp café specialty, *moules frites*, we were cruising the Scheldt or swapping war stories with the many British and Belgian veteran invitees.

We struck up a strong friendship with Major General "Pip" Roberts — that splendid British commander whose 11th Armoured Division liberated the city of Antwerp a few days before the Canadians freed its port. Burgemeester Bob Cools, one of the main catalysts behind these reunions, had great fun teasing Pip and Denis about who was the *real* liberator — this historical event having a subtle but important impact on the outcome of the war.

There was a memorable parade when Denny rode in a vintage World War II vehicle, a four-star American general's jeep, which had been reverently preserved all these years by a European group called "Keep 'em Rolling." The irrepressible Cools leaped forward from the reviewing stand as the jeep pulled up and bodily lifted Denny down with a big bear hug.

An unforgettable moment came one night when we sat in bleachers in Antwerp's incomparable flood-lit main square, Grote Markt, to witness an incredible tattoo of massed bands from every liberating country. The climax occurred when Dame Vera Lynn reduced us all to tears singing "We'll Meet Again." Winston Churchill, the grandson, was bouncing up and down in excitement in the adjacent seat. The Antwerpens erupted.

On a more solemn note, at the Canadian Military Cemeteries of Bergen op Zoom and Adegem we honoured the 1,816 Canadians killed in the Scheldt campaign.

On another day we were taken in rather lavish style in the Burgemeester's private barge down the Albert Canal to the tiny village of Wyneghem, which had been liberated by the Calgary Highlanders. The local mayor and councillors met us formally in the town hall. Speeches and gifts were exchanged, all of us wreathed in smiles without understanding a word of what the other was saying.

Through an interpreter, one woman explained that she had been a child during that bloody battle. Since the Liberation, for all those fifty years, she had taken it upon herself to tend the grave of the one Canadian soldier buried there. Every week she laid fresh flowers by the tombstone.

But now she was concerned. Was there no relative in Canada who might want to know that the Canadian was buried there, and that his grave is well tended? she wondered. These thoughts had weighed heavily on her as she grew older, so much so that a few years before, on her behalf, a member of the Wyneghem town council wrote to the Personnel Records Division, National Archives, seeking the address of the next of kin.

The reply was dismal and curt: "We are forbidden to release this information to a third party." Luckily, we were able to intervene and find one sister, now in her nineties and living in Calgary. She was the only survivor of the soldier's four brothers and four sisters. Her joy at finally learning of her brother's burial place was very moving.

We were less successful in helping a Belgian woman who wept as she described her search for a father she had never known. He had served with a French-Canadian unit and had had a brief affair with her mother, a local girl, who braved the derision of the villagers and stoically bore the child. But to this day she has stubbornly refused to tell her daughter the name of the father. Somehow, the daughter discovered the name of her father's unit and came to Canada in hope of finding him. She received no cooperation in Canada and finally returned home empty-handed.

The Belgian–Canadian bond is strengthened each year in many ways. In Antwerp, every Remembrance Day, Colson and his *wapen broeders* each pick the name of one fallen Canadian and honour his resting place at Antwerp's municipal cemetery, Schoonselhof, with flowers and, one suspects, a few tears.

Thousands of Belgians and Dutch and a surprising number of British and Canadians join in the annual Canadian Liberation March in November from Hoofdplaat in Holland to Knokke on the Belgian coast. This follows, for thirty-two kilometres, the route of the liberating Canadian Army, stopping at Adegem cemetery where 848 young Canadian soldiers are buried. Far from depressing, the march is a shared international outing with families frolicking and bands playing along the route. The march is organized each year by a personable young Belgian, Danny Lannoy.*

For many hundreds of years the seaside resort of Knokke, with its elegant and historic architecture, has attracted visitors from all over Europe. The intervention of a young Belgian resistance fighter, Camille Vervarcke, during the war spared the city from being flattened by a planned Allied artillery barrage, as we describe in Chapter 14. We kept up friendly correspondence and occasional meetings with Camille and with Dutch underground fighter Peter de Winde (also in Chapter 14) until, sadly, black-edged letters arrived from both widows.

A compelling side trip from Knokke is a visit to Adegem cemetery and to Gilbert Van Landschoot's nearby Canadian Museum. Professor Terry Copp, military historian at Wilfrid Laurier University,

---

* Preregistration is required. Write to Danny Lannoy, Canadian Liberation March, Graaf Jansdijk 300, 8300 Knokke-Heist, Belgium.

has written an excellent book, *A Canadian Guide to the Battlefields of Northwest Europe*, which walks the visitor through all the important battlefields and monuments, and informs the reader about the best restaurants and hotels near the World War I and II battlegrounds.*

For the 50th anniversary of Antwerp's liberation, Denis was able to convince the Governor General of Canada, Romeo LeBlanc, to decorate Eugene Colson with the Meritorious Service Medal. It was a well-deserved but seldom-awarded honour for a non-Canadian.

On October 25, 1998, Denis was honoured in a similar way by the Belgian government. By order of King Albert he was invested as a Commander of Belgium's Order of the Crown, a medal equivalent to our Order of Canada. We were told he was one of the few Canadians ever to have received this honour. (Since the publication of *Tug of War*, Denis has also been named as a Member of the Order of Canada, an Officer of the French Legion of Honour, and a Doctor of Military Science (honoris causa) by the Royal Military College. He was also inducted into Hamilton's Gallery of Distinction and Canada's Sports Hall of Fame.)

In Kalmthout, a new memorial was unveiled in 1998 by Ambassador Claude Laverdure, with Brigadier General (Ret'd) Denis Whitaker representing Canada, and Lieutenant-Colonel Eugene "Harry" Colson and Kalmthout Mayor D. Freygers representing the Belgian people.

The monument is startlingly realistic. Two life-sized bronze statues represent a Canadian commanding officer encountering a Belgian Resistance fighter. They could well be Denny and Harry meeting in 1944 on the Antwerp docks. Columnist Peter Worthington wrote fittingly, "It's nice that each of these warriors has been recognized by the other's country."

Canada's ambassador to Belgium said to us: "Canadian diplomacy was relatively young in the early '40s. The first *real* ambassadors we sent to Europe have been our soldiers. Now, fifty years later, you have come back, fulfilling the good name of Canada."

---

* Terry Copp, *A Canadian Guide to the Battlefields of Northwest Europe*. The Laurier Centre for Strategic and Disarmament Studies, 1995. Contact Wilfrid Laurier University, Waterloo ON N2L 3C5.

It is easy to be good ambassadors in Europe. The people there understand and appreciate Canada's contributions to World War II. They insist that their children be keenly aware of them too.

In the years since *Tug of War* was launched, many veterans have written books — good books — about their war experiences. But here's the conundrum: unhappily, most Canadians of postwar vintage still don't know very much about our role in World War II. How could they? It is only scantily — and sometimes erroneously — taught in our schools. It has also become something of an academic trend for a few revisionist historians to write articles and documentaries denigrating Canada's role in World War II. The power of TV is frightening. With its mass audiences, it can in one hour destroy the efforts of all of us who have been trying to make Canadians proud of their history.

Our politicians and bureaucrats pay lip service to veterans and their contributions to this country but, unhappily, many seem to view these occasions primarily as photo-ops. When Antwerp celebrated its 50th anniversary of Liberation in 1994, with thirty Canadian veterans as special guests of the city, Prime Minister Jean Chrétien snubbed the event and instead attended ceremonies twenty miles away in Brussels — a city where no Canadians ever fought. In 1995, he again rearranged history to fit his schedule. He staged his own remembrance ceremony two days early in Holland so that he could join Bill Clinton in Moscow on May 8. We all know how many Canadians sacrificed their lives in Russia — none.

June 6, 1994, the anniversary of D-Day, anguished the many of us who were muscled away from the main beaches to make room for the politicians. Tight security made passes difficult to come by.

One of our group, then a young corporal in the Queen's Own Rifles, had been shot in the stomach shortly after the landing on that fateful day in 1944. He had lain on that beach in the chaos of battle the entire day before he was evacuated. Now he could not get a pass to attend the ceremonies on the beach.

"I own a corner of Juno Beach, after the awful day I lay there," he told us. "And I brought my wife and daughter to see, after fifty years, an important moment in my life. And now the Canadian bureaucrats won't allow me back."

At Dieppe's 50th anniversary the Canadian minister of veterans affairs was scheduled to attend services at each of the Canadian memorials commemorating some of the nearly one thousand Canadians killed and two thousand taken prisoner on that dark day in August 1942. The veterans — none younger than 70, most much older — were assembled, waiting. They were appropriately dressed in wool blazers and berets for the occasion, but not for the blistering August sun. They had no shelter and no place to sit. They waited ...and waited. After two hours, each unit finally went ahead with its own services. The minister, who had lingered for after-luncheon coffee and liqueurs, was seen hours later marching forlornly with his bugler along the nearly abandoned esplanade.

Jack Granatstein has asserted that "no nation treats its military past as shabbily as Canada,"* and he might be right.

The veterans are doing what they can to correct this deficit in Canada's history. They have established the Battle of Normandy Foundation. This volunteer organization sends twelve qualified Canadian university history students every year on a battlefield tour of France, Belgium, Holland, and Italy under the skilled direction of a military historian. Contributions by individuals and corporations fund the enterprise, but the candidates pay half the cost themselves and commit to disseminating the story of Canada's efforts in the two world wars to students back home. Denis and I joined them in 1998 and found their enthusiasm contagious. If our future lies in the hands of these fine young people, we have no fears for the future.**

On a personal note, I have been walking the battlefields of Northwest Europe for twenty years through the eyes of the hundreds of men from six countries whom we have interviewed for our books. It took giant steps for a former sports writer, still a girl-child in braces in the war years, to keep up. Yet in a sense, war and sports are not that far apart. We all admire the Olympic athlete who strains almost beyond the limits of ability for team or country. Our citizen soldiers were Olympians on every battlefield.

---

* *National Post*, 19 April 1999.

** Contributions would be welcomed and tax receipts provided. Send to Lt-Gen Charles Dalziel, Battle of Normandy Foundation, c/o Canadian War Museum, 330 Sussex Drive, Ottawa ON K1A 0M8.

What a rare privilege to walk back into history with my husband and these distinguished patriots. What an honour to gain their confidence, to learn of their challenges, their fears, their loneliness, and their pride of achievement. What a startling thought for this Canadian to absorb, that freedom is not an accident. The veterans bought it for us, and the price was high, but worth it. They shared one all-encompassing passion: they loved Canada — and they despised the Nazi regime that threatened our freedom. That made it worthwhile for them to give up an important chunk of their lives when they could have been finishing school, carving a career, marrying, rearing sons and daughters. For some, it was even worthwhile to die.

Now, increasingly, their efforts and sacrifices are regarded as a bore, or as politically incorrect war-mongering. In his fine book *Who Killed Canadian History?* Jack Granatstein quotes a letter from a man whose father had been killed fighting in Normandy. "When he read several recent texts in Canadian history, he discovered that 'the Second World War has disappeared. The years between 1939 and 1945 are still there, but the war is gone. My father and thousands of other Canadians have been airbrushed out of history.'"

Granatstein asks some hard questions about the indifference of government and educators in promoting and stimulating the study of the history of Canada in the schools. Our history, he says, is "a great story…exciting." Our war efforts are part of that greatness.

Granatstein has inspired another dynamic initiative. In April 1998 BCE chairman Red Wilson read Granatstein's book and was appalled at the poor quality or absence of Canadian history taught in our schools. Wilson believes that learning and understanding our history are an essential preparation for responsible citizenship.

If history is dead, what can we do to bring it back to life? That was the challenge. "If the government's not going to do it, it's up to the private sector," Wilson said, and dug into his own pocket for the first half-million dollars to launch "Historica," a Foundation for the History of Canada.

"Somebody had to step off the curb. Charles Bronfman came forward with a challenge grant of up to $25 million. Then we had a series of meetings in every city across Canada and lined up commitments of support from some of Canada's most powerful corporations." One columnist called them the "village elders." With men like Peter Lougheed, John Cleghorn, and Tom Axworthy aboard, and corporations such as Bell Canada, the Royal Bank of Canada, TD Bank, the Bank of Nova Scotia, George Weston Ltd., McCain Food Ltd., Imasco Ltd., and CanWest Global, the foundation is now looking at raising a potential $50 million.

This new Canadian foundation is using a 21st-century medium — the Internet — to reach and teach Canadian schoolchildren about their history: *all* their history, not just the regionalized, sanitized, politically correct fragments taught today. "The Internet has no boundaries," Wilson said. "It will be impossible to stop."

Histori.ca, the proposed "web site of web sites," will make the Internet an accessible, reliable, and valuable resource centre for students and teachers, creating and disseminating the rich fabric of Canada's developing years.

Veterans of the two wars believed that Canada's history was worth dying for. And today Denny and I and a growing number of Canadians of all ages believe it is still worth fighting for.

Below, two of our colleagues comment on Canada's role in World War II and our efforts to keep history alive.

IT IS FLANDERS' DUTY TO REMEMBER THE CANADIANS!
Bob Cools, Mayor of Antwerp

It is said that memories tend to fade after fifty years; facts then enter history. However, history is written by different authors, who tell such different stories. For all these years as deputy mayor, mayor, and as a member of parliament, I have always tried to prevent memories from fading away. I found that the best way to do that is to bring together, as often as possible, the actors of the glorious deeds that helped liberate Antwerp and the port area. These gatherings are not meant to glorify war; on the contrary, they teach us, especially the young, lessons for the future.

Flanders and its historic cities have been invaded many, many times in history. It was innumerable times a battlefield for neighbouring countries, and became an everlasting resting place for more than 400,000 youngsters of the British Commonwealth. Among them, the Canadians occupy a very important place in our hearts. Twice in half a century they came, as volunteers from a distant country. They generously sacrificed their young lives in West Flanders in WWI and on the River Scheldt and the Dutch-Flemish border in WWII.

For that reason in particular I insisted on giving these soldiers the opportunity to revisit the site of their deeds. Brigadier Denis Whitaker, together with Captain Eugene Colson, both blessed by longevity, became the soul of these meetings. We brought them together with other Allied commanders such as our good friend "Pip" Roberts (who passed away about two years ago), Brigadier Harvey, Major Dunlop, Major Thornburn, and of course the many chaps of the resistance groups.

It was exciting for us to find among the Canadian liberators "boys" of Flemish origin, such as our good friend Fransoo. So it was an exceptional experience in 1996 for our Antwerp delegation to "walk" all through Canada and meet them in Winnipeg at the Belgian Club in the armoury, and of course to meet Denis and Shelagh Whitaker in Hamilton and Toronto.

We were all so happy that Gene Colson and the friends of the "Memorial of Gratitude" succeeded in raising the money for the monument at Kalmthout, which will be the everlasting memento of the contribution of the Canadians to the liberation of our region and the seal of eternal friendship between the Canadian volunteers and the resistance groups. Such a monument is necessary to explain its meaning to younger generations. We are happy that the local school is patron of the Canadian monument in Kalmthout.

We are also pleased by this second edition of *Tug of War*. Books like this one are a major contribution to our struggle in trying to end war. We must indeed not forget that a few months ago there was once again a war in Europe. Once more we welcomed refugees, and for some of us it was as if we were back in 1940.

We sincerely hope that *Tug of War* will not be read only in Canada and the U.S. but also on the European continent.

PORT OF ANTWERP AND THE RIVER SCHELDT
REMEMBRANCE
Col Eugene Colson, Underground Army, leader of the
Resistance Fighters Group for Antwerp and the River Scheldt

How can one ever forget the birth of our friendship for the Canadian brother-in-arms?

They had a tremendous experience in warfare, from 1942 in Dieppe through the landing at the Juno and Gold beaches; the gigantic battle resulting in the annihilation of the enemy trapped within the Falaise–Argentan pocket; the crossing of the Seine River; the clearing or neutralizing of all the coastal ports up to Ostend and the Breskens Pocket.

We were self-trained underground soldiers prepared to safeguard our harbour and eager to pursue the enemy until he fled out of the country and off our soil.

We were at first sustained by the British 11th Armoured Division. But a drastic change within the policy of the Supreme Command made us meet, from then on, the unforgettable Canadians of the 1st Army and especially the 2nd Infantry Division. The change of attitude towards us was heart-warming and an endless dedication for those new friends was soon born.

We stayed at their side until the battles for the port of Antwerp and the river Scheldt were won. Such friendship will last until the last one of us enters the evergreen fields to roam amongst old soldiers still wearing their boots.

The former mayor of Antwerp, Bob Cools, was the pivot of many reunions of the still-living brothers-in-arms. Such reunions were held each fifth anniversary of our liberation. It was on the forty-fifth that Bob Cools reunited all the still available leaders and their ladies: General Roberts on the British side, General Whitaker on the Canadian side, and also two leaders of the underground army. We inaugurated then a monument of remembrance to pay an everlasting tribute to all who gave their lives, or were absent, achieving this victory. The monument lies a few feet off the embankment of the Scheldt where the first vessel of the first convoy moored with her full load of the much-needed logistics to beat our loathed enemy. This vessel was Canadian-built and named *Fort Cataraqui*.

Our fraternal connection with Canada goes on still very strongly. The last visit was a coast-to-coast voyage from west to east, on which the Belgian group had great pleasure in meeting many old friends, especially in Winnipeg, Hamilton, and Toronto, where we were received by the Lieutenant Governor at the Ontario Legislature, where General Whitaker, Bob Cools, and I were cited for our everlasting fraternal brotherhood.

Nevertheless, our advancing age (fate grant us a generous duration of time) may call us over to the other side of the fence.*

---

* Sadly, Col Colson died on January 22, 2000, shortly after writing this letter of friendship.

RESEARCHING OUR MILITARY ROOTS

Am trying to find information on Canadian regimental WW2 D21336. Charles Ray, my grandfather. Would just like to see his name on something saying he was in the service. Please direct me or can you help. Thanks, Dave.

This e-mail from the U.S. hit our web page not too long ago. A similar one came recently from Australia. Searching the military past of deceased relatives is becoming an increasingly important pastime as boomers age. In a typical scenario, Dave and his ilk either didn't get around to asking Dad or Grandpa — or Mom — what they did in the war, or these veterans were reluctant to dredge up old and unhappy memories.

Similarly, while researching *Tug of War*, we lived for several months in Bruges. We saw a steady stream of young people passing through on their way to the war monuments, seeking answers to questions they never thought to ask, until it was too late.

If you are looking for information about a veteran, Tom MacGregor, assistant editor of *Legion Magazine*, suggests you write and request an insertion in "Lost Trails."* It's a one-time-only public service of this popular and well-written Canadian magazine for veterans. *Legion* is published five times a year and has an average circulation of 400,000. "Lost Trails" is a poignant page, with plaintive and sometimes strange pleas for contact: buddies searching for buddies; widows seeking bomber crewmates with whom their husbands flew (or crashed); the Dutch seeking wartime connections.

Recent examples include: "Stalag 11-B – Salt Mines, Germany, October 1944–May 1945. Fellow POWs sought by comrade"; "Willy the Cook – Cdn soldier, Raalte, Holland. Sought by 5-year-old who befriended him"; "17th Dyrch ...who helped liberate Kampen, Overijssel, by rowboat";

---

* *Legion Magazine*, 407–359 Kent St., Ottawa, ON, Canada K2P 0R6

"Smith, RFMN Arthur S. Regina Rifles. Killed in action Juno Beach, June 6, 1944. Those who knew him sought by cousin."

In placing such an ad, give as much information as possible: details of a relative's regiment, date and/or place of enlistment, which war he was in, plus his full name and birth date, serial number (if known), next of kin at the time of enlistment, date of death etc. *Legion* doesn't require all of that information — but the more information they have, the better the chances of success. One area that *Legion* won't touch is the increasingly frequent requests of illegitimate children seeking their fathers.

Alternatively, you can write to the National Archives of Canada, Personal Records Centre,* giving the same information, and requesting data on the relative. Personal Records is very careful to preserve the privacy of the veteran. If he has been deceased for twenty years or more, it's easier. You need to send proof of death and proof of relationship (a death certificate or even an obituary notice citing grandfather's and grandson's names would be sufficient) plus the same data listed above for *Legion*. Obviously, as most veterans from the First World War have been deceased for more than the stipulated twenty years, records about them are easier to obtain.

Problems do arise — and data is much more limited — if Grandpa died less than twenty years ago, or if definite kinship cannot be proven. Then the Canadian Access Information Act and the Privacy Act has put up real roadblocks. A third person cannot have information unless his or her request is reviewed and approved by an Access to Information officer.

---

* National Archives of Canada, 395 Wellington St., Ottawa, ON, Canada K1A 0N3

Notes

THROUGHOUT THIS BOOK, THE AUTHORS HAVE LEANED ON THE WORKS of a number of distinguished Canadian and international historians. *The Victory Campaign* by Colonel Charles P. Stacey details a comprehensive account of Canadian action at the Battle of the Scheldt. As Canada's official military historian in those wartime years and for several decades thereafter, Colonel Stacey was assigned to CMHQ in London during the war to collect, painstakingly catalogue and, finally, recount the actions of Canada's overseas forces. Australian historian Chester Wilmot, a BBC war correspondent, published *The Struggle for Europe* in 1952, just two years before he died in a plane crash. Wilmot based his conclusions on firsthand observation of immediate postwar interrogations and trials of Nazis and German military commanders. His book is aptly sub-titled *How We Won the War but Lost the Peace*.

Captain Liddell Hart and Major Milton Shulman also contributed books of great value to the researcher, based as they were on personal interviews of German commanders fresh to defeat and Allied commanders who had not yet inflated their roles in the victory. Several Canadian veterans have written fascinating accounts of their battalions' roles in the Northwest Europe campaign; in all, we found close to fifty books, many privately published, most now out of date, that depict war as it was.

Finally, contemporary Canadian historians, such as Terry Copp of the Laurier Centre for Military Strategic and Disarmament Studies, have kept the wartime research data from growing stale and out of context with current new information.

1 — *Dolle Dinsdag*

1. Alexander McKee, *The Race for the Rhine Bridges* (London: Souvenir Press Ltd., 1971), 100.

2. Sir Brian Horrocks, with Eversley Belfield and Maj-Gen H. Essame, *Corps Commander* (Toronto: Griffin House, 1977), 70.

3. Chester Wilmot, *The Struggle for Europe* (London: Collins, 1952), 537.

4. Horrocks, *Corps Commander*, 69.

5. Omar N. Bradley and Clay Blair, *A General's Life: An Autobiography by General of the Army Omar N. Bradley* (New York: Simon & Schuster, 1983), 319.

6. Hugh Darby and Marcus Cunliffe, *A Short Story of 21 Army Group* (Aldershot: Gale & Polden Ltd., 1949), 63.

7. Sir Arthur Bryant, *Triumph in the West* (London: Collins, 1959), 284.

8. Wilmot, *The Struggle for Europe*, 523.

9. Ibid., 281.

10. John Eisenhower, *The Bitter Woods* (Toronto: Longmans Canada Ltd., 1969), 75.

11. Stephen E. Ambrose, *The Supreme Commander* (Garden City, N.J.: Doubleday, 1970), 498.

12. John Harvey, ed., *The War Diaries of Oliver Harvey, 1941–1945* (London: Collins, 1979), 355.

13. Bryant, *Triumph in the West*, 334.

14. Ladislas Farago, *Patton: Ordeal and Triumph* (New York: Dell Books, 1970), 647.

15. Bernard Law Montgomery, *The Memoirs of Field Marshal Montgomery* (London: Collins, 1958), 271.

16. Maj L.F. Ellis, CVO, CBE, DSO, MC, *History of the Second World War, Vol. II: Victory in the West* (London: Her Majesty's Stationery Office, 1962), 10.

17. Walter Warlymont, *Inside Hitler's Headquarters, 1939-1945* (Bristol: Western Printing Services, 1963), 243.

18. Mollie Panter-Downes, *London War Notes* (New York: Farrar, Strauss & Giroux, 1971), 340.

2 — *The Secret Army*

1. Translated abstract of the text delivered to a conference by Lt-Col E.J. Colson, alias "Harry," March, 1965; *Rapport Concernant la Preparation du Plan de Defense du Port d'Anvers et de son Execution*, filed and signed by E. Colson ("Harry"), Lt-Col (December 21, 1944): W12 V, Centre de Recherches et d'Etudes historiques de la Seconde Guerre Mondiale, Brussels, Belgium; Personal interview with Lt-Col E.J. Colson.

2. Ibid.

3. Ibid.

4. Interview with Hauptfeldwebel Berghauser by Marc Van de Velde, Boom, Belgium.

5. Alastair Hetherington, "Robert Vekeman's Secret War" in *The Manchester Guardian*, 1 September, 1969.

6. Darby and Cunliffe, *A Short Story of Twenty-One Army Group*, 64.

7. Lieut-Comdr P.K. Kemp, *History of the 4th Battalion KSLI* (Shrewsbury: Wilding & Son Ltd., 1955), 114.

8. Horrocks, *Corps Commander*, 80.

9. For sources, refer to this chapter, note 1.

10. Letter from Lieut G. Stubb, 7 November, 1969: CWO II, Centre de Recherches, Brussels.

11. For sources, refer to this chapter, note 1.

12. Letter from Maj-Gen G.P.B. Roberts, 17 September, 1969, CWO II, W12 V: Centre de Recherches, Brussels.

13. Sir Brian Horrocks, *A Full Life* (London: Collins, 1962), 205.

14. Wilmot, *The Struggle for Europe*, 486.

15. Kemp, *History of the 4th Battalion KSLI*, 119.

16. Horrocks, *A Full Life,* 204; Horrocks, *Corps Commander,* 80.

17. Horrocks, *Corps Commander*, 82.

Comments

The facts as presented here were gleaned in part from first-person interviews with Colonel Colson, Lieutenant Vekemans, Frans De Moor and Edouard Pilaet. Immediately following his exploit of guiding the British 3rd Royal Tank Regiment across the bridge at Boom, Vekemans was appointed liaison officer for the Secret Army, working first with the British battalions and ultimately with the Canadians. Colson and a number of his men fought in support first of the Royal Hamilton Light

Infantry and then of the Essex Scottish; Pilaet was in command of a number of Belgians who served for some weeks with the FMR (Les Fusiliers Mont-Royal) under Major (now General) Jimmy Dextraze in the liberation battle of South Beveland and northern Belgium; De Moor supported the 1st Canadian Army in Breda. Many of these actions are detailed in a report filed on May 17, 1945, by Lieutenant Colonel Gonze and catalogued at the Centre de Recherches et d'Etudes historiques de la Seconde Guerre Mondiale in Brussels. Attached was a letter of appreciation written by Captain H.S.C. Archbold, GSO 111, 2 Cdn Inf Div, thanking the Belgians for the "very great assistance...given us during our military operations."

In Antwerp, the Secret Army is still proudly remembered, and many of the Resistance fighters have been honoured with the most prestigious decorations by their own and other Allied countries.

Reniers remained in the Belgian Army, attaining the rank of a full general before he died. Lieutenant Colonel Eugene Colson, "Harry," is now retired from sea-captaincy, but actively holds an executive position at the port he once saved.

His medals are numerous. He has been awarded the highest honour given to a Belgian, the Grand Officer de l'Ordre de Leopold. In addition, he received Belgium's Croix de Guerre 1940 avec Palme.

In a full-page feature article, "Robert Vekemans's Secret War," in the *Manchester Guardian* on 1 September, 1969, Alastair Hetherington, then its publisher, wrote a detailed account of Vekemans's actions at the River Rupel, segments of which are quoted here. The source was unassailable; Hetherington was intelligence officer with the 11th Armoured Division during its headlong advance into Antwerp.

At a ceremony held by the mayor of Antwerp to honour Lieutenant Vekemans on the 9th of September, 1956, Major John Dunlop described Vekemans's action as "an act of solitary courage, performed in isolation. Many men are capable of acts of courage performed amid the ranks of their comrades, executing familiar tasks for which they have been trained. The courage needed to persist with a solitary operation is more rarely seen."

In December, 1944, in the Grand Place of Brussels, Robert Vekemans received the rare honour of being awarded the British Military Cross, pinned on his chest by Field Marshal Montgomery. From his own country he received the Croix de Guerre. Bob Vekemans's work as an engineer took him to America for some postwar years before his final retirement to a home of his own design on the Brittany coast of France where he now lives quietly with his wife and seventeen-year-old son Steven.

Professeur Docteur Jean-Léon Charles, himself a student hiding from German arrest in those dark days, is now professor of military history at the Ecole Royale Militaire in Brussels. He offered invaluable guidance in our research of the Secret Army actions.

The Centre de Recherches et d'Etudes historiques de la Seconde Guerre Mondiale in Brussels provided many substantive documents, including reports made to their commanding officers by the men cited here just a few weeks after the liberation battle. In addition, the Centre has on record letters signed by General Roberts, Lieutenant Stubb, and Brigadier Churcher (Brigade Commander, 159 Infantry Brigade) who experienced the events here described.

Other important resource material at the Centre included "The Belgian Underground Movement 1940–1944," written in 1951 by George Kilpatrick Tanham as a thesis for the Department of History at Stanford University; the *Livre d'Or de la Resistance* with its tragic casualty statistics for the occupation and liberation (in Antwerp alone 1,020 men and women were killed); Civil Affairs Information Guide Concerning the Belgian Underground as of 5 October 1944 (War Dept No. 31-194), confirming the careful pre-liberation planning of l'Armée Secrète.

3 — *The Great Escape*

1. Anthology of recollections of townspeople following the liberation: *Woensdrecht en Hoogerheide in de Bange Dagen van Haar Bevrijding* (Woensdrecht and Hoogerheide — From Anxious Days until Their Liberation). Published by the Town Council of Woensdrecht: Translation by Peter Ooms and Leo Timmermans.
2. Ibid.
3. Ibid.
4. Ibid.
5. Personal interview with Peter Eekman and Hans Tuynman; Winston G. Ramsey, ed. *After the Battle, Walcheren, Number 36* (London: Battle of Britain Prints, 1982).
6. Correspondence with Fl Sgt (now the Reverend) D.R. Jennings; Personal interview with G.A. Claeys, Oostburg, West Flanders.
7. Ibid.
8. Ibid.
9. Ibid.
10. Personal interview with Nellie van Nispen.
11. Woensdrecht Anthology.

12. Personal interview with Sara and Peter de Winde.

13. Milton Shulman, *Defeat in the West* (London: Secker & Warburg Ltd., 1947), 175.

14. Personal interview with Sara and Peter de Winde.

Comments

In the course of the war, 23,300 Netherlanders lost their lives as a result of belonging to the Dutch Resistance. (See CAB 101/301, Public Record Office, England.) It was a privilege to meet some of the survivors, whose exploits are cited in the coming chapters. Several of these deeds border on the incredible, and have been the subjects of exhaustive investigative research by a number of the Netherlands' own military historians during the past forty years. The accounts have in every case been authenticated.

We are grateful for the invaluable assistance shown us by the following noted historians: Dr. Leo de Jong, military author and Official Military Historian to the Netherlands, and his successor, Dr. A.H. Paape, Director of Documentation, RIOD, Amsterdam; Dr. C.M. Schulten, Chief of the Army, Historical Section, Sectie Militaire Geshiedenis, HQ Royal Netherlands Army (and his most helpful assistant Mrs. Lea Strik), 's-Gravenhage; and Dr. Von Druten, Director of the Archief van de Binnenlands Strydkrachten (the Archives of the Underground) in Kerkrade. At the latter archives we also found original reports by Chief of Documentation, Colonel S.I.X., heading a postwar tribunal that examined and evaluated each account of each Underground member.

Although much of the background material on conditions in Zeeland and West Flanders was obtained from the above, as well as from Dutch citizens reliving their experiences, often painfully, during the occupation, useful information was found in *A Liberation Album* by David Kaufman and Michiel Horn, and in Walter B. Masse's *The Netherlands at War, 1940–1945*.

We have quoted liberally from the book *Woensdrecht en Hoogerheide in de Bang Dagen van Haar Bevrijding*, a collection of anecdotes written by the survivors of that most bloody battle for Woensdrecht, who remember all too vividly the liberation of their municipality by men from the 2nd Canadian Infantry Division. The book was compiled by the SOF (Foundation Public Festivities), Hoogergeide-Woensdrecht, published by the Burgemeester of Woensdrecht, Mr. J.M. de Leeuw, and its Town Council in commemoration of the 30th anniversary of the Liberation, 5 May 1975, and translated in its entirety especially for inclusion in *Tug of War* through the kindness of Leo Timmermans and Peter Ooms. In addition, *The Battle of Woensdrecht*, the recollections of a civil servant of

Woensdrecht in October–November 1944, was translated for us by the present town clerk of Woensdrecht. We also had the opportunity to interview a number of citizens who lived in Woensdrecht in those days, including Leo Muysken, codenamed "Charles," who escaped from the Germans to volunteer as interpreter with the Royal Hamilton Light Infantry; Maria Verboven, who was simultaneously hiding "Charles" in her attic and a German deserter in her cellar, all the while billeting German troops in the main bedrooms; Louis and Sjef Pijnen, Leo Timmermans, Peter Jacob, L.W. Lijmback and Mr. von Klamm of the Hoogerheide Town Council; Cornelis van Beek, in whose farmhouse I established my battalion headquarters for several days during the Woensdrecht battle, his sons Jan and Frans and grandson Cornelis, "Corny," who now farm the land. It was only during a recent visit to the van Beek farm that I learned of an incident that has been part of the local history for all these years: the night that my battalion made its assault on the German paratroopers defending Woensdrecht, some of my men took the time to feed and water the van Beek cattle in the barn!

The unfailing courtesy and support offered us throughout our tour of Zeeland reflects the gratitude and friendliness still keenly demonstrated by the citizens of these towns toward their Canadian liberators.

Pieter Kloosterman still lives in Nisse in the neat cottage on the village green. He is ninety-one years old. In January, 1983, he and his wife received the authors in their home. Christina Kloosterman had taken great pains to dress in formal Zeeland attire; her long black dress with colourful shawl, and her traditional starched white linen head-covering adorned with disks of pure gold almost dwarfed this diminutive lady. We were not aware that she had terminal cancer. Christina died two weeks after the interview, with the same dignity with which she had conducted her life. As leader of the Resistance movement in Zeeland, Lieutenant Kloosterman saved countless Dutch and Allied lives. For his valour, his government awarded him the Bronze Cross and the Resistance Remembrance Cross.

In the attractive West Flanders town of Oostburg, we met Pieter de Feyter, Gerard Claeys, Pieter Simpelaar and the helpful Town Clerk, Mr. W. J. Robyn.

Peter Eekman stayed on in Flushing, turning a boyhood experience into an adult vocation. With his friend Hans Tuynman he founded the "Documentation Group Walcheren: 1939–1945," with the objective of preserving the history of Walcheren in World War II. Their collection of archival material, exhibited only every two or three years because of lack of funds, includes thousands of pamphlets dropped by both protagonists during the conflict, photographs taken by civilians during the actual liberation battle, a variety of arms, and even a one-man sub마-rine that was discovered, still with its pilot, some ten years ago.

And Sara de Winde, ageless and ever gracious, lives on in Breskens, still on Dorpstraat, where with great dignity, not sharing even a single word of the others' language, she served us coffee not long ago. The Resistance Remembrance Cross has been awarded to Mrs. de Winde, her daughter Hannie, daughter-in-law Margaret and son Peter. The latter also has been honoured with the Bronze Lion, one of the highest military awards of the Netherlands. Hannie has died, but Peter is in Amsterdam, a successful businessman despite the disability in his arms incurred when he swam seven hours through the frigid Scheldt to give a warning that would save many Canadian lives. As it has for most other Resistance members, the agony of those years has left its mark.

4 ～ *The Adversaries*

1. Farago, *Patton: Ordeal and Triumph*, 578.
2. Maj-Gen E.K.G. Sixsmith, *Eisenhower as a Military Commander* (London: Batsford, B.T. Ltd., 1973); *British Generalship in the Twentieth Century* (London: Arms & Armour Press, 1970); Personal interview with Maj-Gen E.K.G. Sixsmith.
3. Wilmot, *The Struggle for Europe*, 536.
4. Farago, *Patton: Ordeal and Triumph*, 595.
5. Russell Weighley, *Eisenhower's Lieutenants* (London: Sidgwick & Jackson Ltd., 1981), 266.
6. Horrocks, *Corps Commander*, 81.
7. Ellis, *History of the Second World War, Vol. II. Victory in the West*, 16.
8. J.L. Moulton, *Battle for Antwerp* (London: Sam Allan Ltd., 1978), 64.
9. Rear Admiral W.S. Chalmers, *Full Cycle: The Biography of Admiral Sir Bertram Home Ramsay* (London: Hodder & Stoughton, 1959), 514.
10. Personal correspondence with F.W. Winterbotham; F.W. Winterbotham, *The Ultra Secret* (New York: Harper & Row, 1974), 124.
11. Personal interview with Maj-Gen E.K.G. Sixsmith; Correspondence of Gen G. Simonds to Maj-Gen Sixsmith, 1971/2; E.K.G. Sixsmith, *Eisenhower as a Military Commander; British Generalship in the Twentieth Century*.
12. Ibid.

13. Ibid.
14. Colonel C.P. Stacey, *The Victory Campaign: Vol. III* (Ottawa: Queen's Printer, 1960), 304.
15. Ibid., 304.
16. Maj Roy Farran, *The History of the Calgary Highlanders* (Calgary: Bryant Press Ltd., 1949), 173.
17. Personal interview with Lt-Col W.A.B. Anderson.
18. Personal interview with Lt-Col Walter Reynolds.
19. Personal interview with Maj-Gen H.A. Sparling.
20. Anon.
21. Maj K.J. Macksey, on General Guy Simonds, from *The Canadian at War,* ed. Douglas How (Montreal: The Reader's Digest Association, 1969), 487.
22. Personal interview with Brig J. M. Rockingham.
23. Personal interview with Lt-Gen Frank Fleury.
24. Richard Malone, *Missing from the Record* (Toronto: Wm. Collins Sons & Co. Ltd., 1946), 65.
25. Personal interview with Maj-Gen C. Vokes.
26. Personal interview with Lt-Col W.A.B. Anderson.
27. Lt-Gen G. Simonds, Private Papers, on loan from Col Charles Simonds.
28. Personal interview with Brig J.M. Rockingham.
29. Personal interview with Brig-Gen W.K. Lye.
30. Personal interview with Maj Elliot Dalton.
31. Anon.
32. Personal interview with Maj Elliot Dalton.
33. Personal interview with Lt-Col W.A.B. Anderson.
34. Malone, *Missing from the Record*, 65.
35. Personal interview with Maj-Gen E.K.G. Sixsmith: Correspondence of Gen G. Simonds to Maj-Gen Sixsmith, 1971/2.
36. Ibid.
37. Letter written home by a German soldier, First U.S. Army G-2 Report, September 1944.
38. Personal interview with Maj-Gen E.K.G. Sixsmith; Correspondence of Gen G. Simonds to Maj-Gen Sixsmith, 1971/2.
39. Shulman, *Defeat in the West*, 174.
40. Personal interview with Brig-Gen (then Lt-Col) F. von der Heydte, September, 1983.

41. Canadian Participation in Operations in NW Europe, CAB 44-301, Public Record Office, London (PRO).

42. Personal interview with Lt-Col v. d. Heydte.

43. Interrogation Lt-Gen Schwalbe, Canadian Participation in Operations in NW Europe, Part IV — 23rd August to 30th September, No. 183 Historical Section CMHQ.

44. United Kingdom Records, SHAEF Intelligence, 9 September 1944.

45. Personal interview with Lt-Col v. d. Heydte.

46. Steven Ambrose, *Supreme Commander*, 510.

47. Enemy Document captured 28 October 1944 by Toronto Scottish (MG).

Comments

We are greatly indebted to Colonel Charles Simonds, son of the late Lieutenant General Guy Simonds, for releasing his father's private wartime papers for our research. It was a matter of great curiosity to the British, Dutch, Belgians and Germans whom we met in the course of seeking research material that no Canadian has to date written a book about General Simonds. Even the most obscure European general, had he commanded his nation's army, would warrant at least one or two books dedicated to his achievements. But for Canada's most outstanding general of World War II...not even ONE?

We are grateful, too, to Major General E.K.G. Sixsmith of Somerset, England, for opening his home to us, sharing his views, offering his counsel on this chapter, and providing us with copies of original correspondence between himself and General Simonds written in 1971–72, shortly before General Simonds's death. Of the overall assigning of responsibility, Simonds confided in General Sixsmith that neither Crerar nor Montgomery appeared to fully grasp the strategic importance of that critical point in the war: "To be quite honest," Simonds wrote, "Crerar had no grip of the situation, and Monty was distracted by the arguments over further strategy."

General Sixsmith, the author of *Eisenhower as a Military Commander* and *British Generalship in the Twentieth Century*, presents a convincing argument in apportioning the blame in the affaire d'Antwerp: "There is no doubt that Eisenhower and Montgomery failed; it was their one great strategic mistake of the war. Horrocks is blameless." Sixsmith added: "The failure of the people at the top to understand and make it clear that the capture of Antwerp involved the whole of the Scheldt and not just the port itself, in view of what the Navy told them, was inexcusable."

On the Island of Sark, we sought out historian Eversley Belfield, co-author of *Corps Commander* with Sir Brian Horrocks and Major General H. Essame. On this charming Channel Island outpost, we spent some hours reviewing this chapter with Mr. Belfield, and examining his thesis that the Canadian Army was at the time of the Scheldt "treated as a kind of odd-job organization, thus given a very low claim to supplies."

The fact of Ultra, finally released for publication in 1972, gives the present-day author a great advantage over those who "wrote blind" in the decades before the Official Secrets Act lifted the ban. We were fortunate to receive assistance from an ex-Enigma cryptographer from Ireland, John Smith-Wright, who very kindly edited our draft on Ultra, and offered helpful suggestions. In addition, we had fruitful correspondence with Mr. F.W. Winterbotham, author of *The Ultra Secret*, and Mr. Ralph Bennett, who wrote *Ultra in the West.*

While the enormous advantages of having a pipeline into the enemy camp have been made obvious to us in the past decade, the procedure has somewhat defrocked those commanders who were negligent in their handling of this fragile tool. It borders on the incredible that Horrocks was not alerted to the Ultra decrypts concerning the escape of the 15th Army. However, it is the images of his senior officers, Dempsey, Montgomery and even Eisenhower, that are tarnished for their failure to advise him of this vital intelligence. While postwar protestations by Allied commanders of ignorance of enemy plans were once given credence, we must now reexamine their innocence.

After a search of over a year, we located and interviewed Brigadier General von der Heydte at his Bavarian home in September, 1983. He was a fit seventy-six: "I missed you by just ten minutes!" was his greeting to a former antagonist recalling our near confrontation on Woensdrecht Hill when our battalions were engaged for five days in desperate, sometimes hand-to-hand combat. It was the first of three confrontations we two were to have in the Northwest Europe campaign.

Von der Heydte's last military action occurred only two months later during the German counteroffensive in the Ardennes, where he was captured by the Americans and sent to POW camp in England. After his release, he resumed his career as professor of International Law at the universities of Munich and Wurzburg. He has two doctorates in the field and twenty texts bear his name. He retired from the German Army in 1967, highly decorated in forty-two years of service.

Far more simply, Private Alexander Schmidt was unearthed through the simple expediency of initiating small talk in a German pub one evening. "You're writing about the Scheldt?" he asked in amazement. "I fought the Canadians at the Scheldt!"

5 — *Groundwork of Errors*

1. Extracts from War Diary of GOC in C., 1 Cdn Army, September 1944, CAB/1064, Public Record Office, London.
2. Ibid.
3. Reported in a letter from Maj-Gen Knut Eberding to the executive committee of *Legion Magazine,* Ottawa, 12 December, 1968.
4. Personal interview with Maj-Gen E.K.G. Sixsmith; Correspondence from Gen Guy Simonds to Maj-Gen E.K.G. Sixsmith, 1971–72.
5. Public Record Office: AEF/First Cdn Army, Docket 1, Vol 1; Summary No 66, 3 September 1944, Appx D.
6. Personal interview with Capt William Whiteside.
7. Stacey, *The Victory Campaign,* 361; Army Ops Log HQ, 1 Cdn Army, 13 September 1944.
8. Ibid., 361.
9. Maj George Cassidy, *Warpath* (Toronto: Ryerson Press, 1948), 138.
10. Ibid., 140.
11. Ibid., 143.
12. Ibid., 145.
13. WO 205/1021: 245 Inf Div, Special Interrogation Report, Maj-Gen Sanders, Public Record Office, London.
14. Cassidy, *Warpath*, 146.
15. Ibid., 148.
16. Ibid., 150.
17. Personal interview with Pte E.A. Gale.
18. Personal interview with Pte Ray Perry.
19. Personal interview with Pte E.A. Gale.
20. Cassidy, *Warpath*, 160.
21. Personal interview with Maj James L. Dandy.
22. Operations of the Polish Armoured Division supplied by John Grodzinski.

6 — *Sinking of an Island*

1. Personal interview with Lt-Col W.A.B. Anderson.
2. Lt-Gen G.G. Simonds, Private Papers, on loan from Col Charles Simonds: Public Archives of Canada, RG24 Vol. 10799, File 29,

July to December 1944: "General Simonds's Appreciation of the Situation Concerning the Scheldt, 21 September, 1944," issued at Main HQ, 2 Cdn Corps at 1600 hours.

3. Ibid.

4. Personal interview with Lt-Col W.A.B. Anderson.

5. Lt-Gen G.G. Simonds, Private Papers, Public Archives of Canada.

6. Personal interview with Lt-Col W.A. B. Anderson.

7. Lt-Gen G.G. Simonds, Private Papers, Public Archives of Canada.

8. Personal interview with Lt-Col W.A.B. Anderson.

9. Lewis H. Brereton, *The Brereton Diaries: The War in the Air in the Pacific, Middle East and Europe, 3 October 1941–8 May, 1945* (New York: William Morrow, 1946), 340.

10. Ambrose, *The Supreme Commander*, 525.

11. Public Record Office, CAB 44/301 Cdn Military Ops.

12. Lt-Gen G.G. Simonds, Private Papers, Public Archives of Canada.

13. Personal interview with Brig Edward Beament.

14. Ibid.

15. Personal interview with Lt-Col W.A.B. Anderson.

16. Personal interview with Brig Edward Beament.

17. Personal interview with Maj Wm. Lye.

18. Public Record Office: CAB 44/301 Cdn Military Ops.

19. Col C.P. Stacey, *The Victory Campaign*, 376.

20. Personal interview with Capt Marshal Stearns.

21. BBC Written Archives Centre: Voice of SHAEF No. 37 for release at 1305 hours, October 2, 1944.

22. "Documentation Group: Walcheren 1939–1945": Peter Eekman and Hans Tuynman.

23. Personal interview with FO Thomas Clayton, RAF.

24. "Documentation Group: Walcheren 1939–1945": Peter Eekman and Hans Tuynman, Correspondence between Eekman and Sidney Aldridge.

25. Personal interview with Capt Marshal Stearns.

26. Personal interview with Lt-Col W.A.B. Anderson.

27. "Documentation Group: Walcheren 1939–1945": Peter Eekman and Hans Tuynman.

28. Walter B. Masse, *The Netherlands at War* (London: Abelard Schuman, 1977), 193.

29. Public Record Office: CAB 44/301 Cdn Military Ops.

30. "Documentation Group: Walcheren 1939–1945": Peter Eekman and Hans Tuynman.

31. Col C.P. Stacey, *The Victory Campaign*, 398.

32. Maj-Gen H. Essame, *Battle for Germany* (New York: Scribners, 1969), 47.

33. Personal interview with Fl Lt Bill Walker.

34. Col C.P. Stacey, *The Victory Campaign*, 411.

35. Montgomery, *The Memoirs of Field Marshal Montgomery*, 283.

36. Ellis, *History of the Second World War, Vol. II: Victory in the West*, 91.

37. Personal interview with Lt-Col W.A.B. Anderson.

38. Lt-Col W. Eric Harris, *Mike Wardell and the Canadian Rocket Battery*, D. Hist. Kardex 147.97(2), 1956; Col G.W.L. Nicholson, *The Gunners of Canada, Vol. II* (Toronto: McClelland & Stewart Ltd., 1967), 376.

39. Lt-Col Eric Harris, *Mike Wardell and the Canadian Rocket Battery*.

Comments

Lieutenant General (then Lieutenant Colonel) Anderson's comments were extracted from personal interviews in 1982 and 1983, and from excerpts of a speech he delivered at a seminar at 11th Anscol, Washington, D.C., on the 14th of August, 1945. General Anderson culminated his army career with the position of Vice Chief of the General Staff at Canadian Army Headquarters. At the time of the Scheldt battle he was General Staff Officer, Operations, 1st Canadian Army.

Others who contributed to our research on General Simonds's work during those critical weeks of planning the Scheldt campaign include Brigadier Edward Beament, Anderson's senior officer, now a practising lawyer in Ottawa; Captain Marshal Stearns, Simonds's personal assistant, a stockbroker in Toronto; and Major (now Brigadier General) Bill Lye, G2 Engineering.

Concerning the bombing of Walcheren, Marshal Stearns had this postcript: "Although everyone thought the island would be ruined for agricultural purposes, I believe that three years after the bombing, with the infusion of salt water, Walcheren had never been more fertile. I understand the crops were magnificent."

The issue of the bombing was a serious matter for the Dutch, and is revived periodically by certain nationalists. In recent years, prolific and highly esteemed Dutch military historian and writer, Dr. L. de Jong, raised the question in a television interview as well as in volume 10A of his ambitious chronicle of World War II, *Het Koninkrijk der Nederlander in de Tweede Werel Doorlag,* that the Dutch Government-in-Exile had never been warned of the intended bombing. Nor, Dr. de Jong maintains, were the War Cabinet in London or the Dutch representatives at SHAEF consulted about the planned raid.

After the war, in 1949, the Dutch prime minister, Prof-Dr. Gerbrandy, told a Commission of Enquiry that not only had he been so informed, but that "Dutch experts prepared the bombardment of Walcheren." And in 1955, Gerbrandy again emphasized that "requested approval was given."

A year later, however, he mysteriously backed off somewhat, saying that the consultation had been so hasty that he had not had the opportunity to consult the other ministers.

"Our approval was asked," the former prime minister now stated, "but only twenty-four hours before. It was too late to say no." De Jong recounts with some relish the dramatic highlights of the evening confrontation when he claims to have wrung the confession from the minister: "One supposes that he [Gerbrandy] was fantasizing the story of requested approval in order to hide the fact that the Allied military had been walking over the Dutch government," de Jong wrote acidly in 1980.

The details of Land Mattress were gleaned from a paper written as a tribute to his English friend Wardell by Colonel Eric Harris.

"I am wondering," queried Colonel Harris in his fulsome postwar account entitled *Mike Wardell and the Canadian Rocket Battery,* "whether the Maritimers know what a bonnie fighter they have now enlisted."

In fact, Michael Wardell never let go his close ties with Canada. He died not long ago in Fredericton, N.B., where he had lived out his life, working for many years, first as publisher of the *Daily Gleaner* in Fredericton while also heading up the University of New Brunswick Press, and latterly as founder and publisher of *The Atlantic Advocate,* designed to promote the interests of the Maritime provinces, Mike Wardell's most rewarding challenge.

7 — *Streetcar War*

1. Bryant, *Triumph in the West,* 285.
2. Seminar by Lt-Col W.A.B. Anderson, 11th ANSCOL, Washington, D.C., 14 August, 1945.
3. Wilmot, *The Struggle for Europe,* 626.
4. Horrocks, *Corps Commander,* 128.
5. Cpl Arthur Kelly, *There's a Goddamn Bullet for Everyone* (Paris, Ontario: Arts and Publishing Co. Ltd., 1979), 282.

6. Personal interview with Sgt Peter Bolus.

7. Farran, *The History of the Calgary Highlanders,* 172.

8. Maj D. J. Goodspeed, *Battle Royal* (Published by the Royal Regt. of Canada), 488.

9. David Kaufman and Michiel Horn, *A Liberation Album,* 39.

10. Anon.

11. Personal interview with Capt Maurice Gervais.

12. John Ellis, *Sharp End of War: Fighting Man in World War II* (Newton Abbot, Devon: David & Charles Ltd., 1980), 327.

13. Personal interview with Pte Douglas Vidler.

14. Personal interview with Capt Lyle Doering.

15. Goodspeed, *Battle Royal,* 489.

16. Personal interview with Capt Osborne Avery.

17. Translated abstract of the text delivered to a conference by Lt-Col E.J. Colson, (alias "Harry") March, 1965; Personal interview with Lt-Col E. J. Colson.

18. Brereton Greenhous, *Semper Paratus* (Hamilton: The RHLI Historical Association, 1977), 274.

19. Personal interview with Sgt Peter Bolus.

20. Personal interview with Lt-Col E. J. Colson.

21. Greenhous, *Semper Paratus,* 274.

22. Personal interview with Lt John Williamson.

23. Personal interview with Lt J.A.B. (Joe) Nixon.

24. *Toronto Telegram,* 27 September 1944.

25. Ellis, *Sharp End of War,* 56.

26. Greenhous, *Semper Paratus,* 275.

27. Goodspeed, *Battle Royal,* 489.

28. Lt-Col G.B. Buchanan, *The March of the Prairie Men* (South Saskatchewan Regt.), 39.

29. Pamphlet distributed by Germans to FMR: 49 Inf Div Int Summary.

30. Buchanan, *The March of the Prairie Men,* 41.

31. Ibid., 41.

32. Pamphlet distributed by Burgemeester of Brasschaet to its citizens, 3 October 1944.

Comments

Current, reliable intelligence about the immediate enemy was the most essential element to a battalion commander's assessment for taking his next objective. While Ultra provided the intelligence at the top, little or none of it could — or did — filter down to battalion level. In the military lingo of the day, we would be informed, with a "broad brush" of the "big picture." It may have given us a glimpse of the strategy of the moment, but it was of little help in determining the tactics.

We learned to rely on the skill and courage of the men on patrol, the two scout commanders mentioned representing the many who volunteered for this unrelenting, dangerous job. Lieutenant John Williamson, although wounded three times in the Northwest Europe campaign, probably logged more time in action than any other lieutenant in the RHLI. Lieutenant Joe Nixon took on the job commanding the Black Watch Scout Platoon, in the knowledge that six men had been casualties in that job in the previous month.

8 — Black Friday

1. (*Woensdrecht en Hoogerheide in de Bange Dagen van Haar Bevrijding*). Personal interview with Leo Timmermans and Peter Jacobs. *The Battle of Woensdrecht*, by C. van Elzakker, translated by the Town Clerk of the Borough of Woensdrecht. *A Liberation Album* by David Kaufman and Michiel Horn (Toronto: McGraw-Hill Ryerson Ltd., 1980).

2. Battle Report MS/B-798. Imperial War Museum. Translated by Captain Sjoerd Westra (Ret), Army of the Netherlands.

3. Personal interview with Lt-Col Friedrich von der Heydte.

4. *The Campaign in North-West Europe, Information from German Sources. Part III: German Defence Operations in the Sphere of First Canadian Army* (23 August–8 November 1944), No. 77, Historical Section (G.S.) Army Headquarters, Public Archives of Canada

5. Personal interview with Pte Al Butler.

6. Goodspeed, *Battle Royal*, 501.

7. Personal interview with Major David "Tim" Beatty.

8. Personal correspondence with Maj Mark Tennant.

9. Personal interview with Maj F. Clarke.

10. Battle Report MS/B-798. Imperial War Museum. Translated by Captain Westra.

11. Personal interview with Lt-Col. B. Ritchie.

12. Ibid.

13. Ibid.

14. Ibid.

15. PRO, Lt W.J. Shea, 10, The Black Watch, 15 October, 1944 AEF/5 Cdn Inf Bde/C/D/Docket 4 Folio 2 — The Action at Woensdrecht — 8–14 October 1944; War Diary, 13 October.

16. Personal interview with Maj William Ewing.

17. Personal interview with Lt-Col Bruce Ritchie.

18. AEF/5 Cdn Inf Bde/C/D/Docket 4 Folio 2 — The Action at Woensdrecht — 8–14 October 1944; War Diary, The Black Watch.

Comments

"On Friday, October 13, 1944, Private Donald Whitman Cook of the Black Watch finished his duty in a third wave of fighting that resulted in 145 casualties. I had always wanted to visit the battleground where my father died and last fall, after thirty-nine years, I stood before his grave in the Netherlands."

This passage was published in *Legion Magazine,* in May, 1984. The author, Gregory Cook, recounted his search to resurrect "at least a moment of his [father's] past."

This was, by coincidence, the man we had encountered so briefly in 1983 at the Canadian Military Cemetery in Adegem, the nameless man who had left so deep an impression that we dedicated this book to him. Gregory Cook has recorded his impressions and experiences of his search through the battlefields for truth in his third book of poetry, *Love in Flight,* soon to be released.

9 — The Guns of Woensdrecht

1. Maj D.W. Grant, *The History of the Toronto Scottish Regiment* (MG), 107.

2. Personal interview with Capt W.D. Stevenson.

3. John Ellis, *Sharp End of War*, 46.

4. Personal interview with Lt-Col von der Heydte.

5. Ibid.

6. Ibid.

7. Ibid.

8. Ibid.

9. Personal interview with Sgt Peter Bolus.

10. Ellis, *Sharp End of War*, 98.
11. Personal interview with Cpl Arthur Kelly.
12. Personal interview with Sgt Peter Bolus.
13. Personal interview with Maj J.M. Pigott.
14. Personal interview with Sgt Harold Hall.
15. Personal interview with Sgt Peter Bolus.
16. Personal interview with Capt Lyn Heigelheimer.
17. Personal interview with Cpl James Bulmer.
18. Personal interview with Maj J.M. Pigott.
19. Ibid.
20. Public Archives of Canada.
21. Personal interview with Cpl J. Bulmer.
22. War Diary, RHLI, 16 October 1944.
23. Personal interview with Lt-Col von der Heydte.
24. Ibid.
25. Personal interview with Lieut A.R.G. Wight.
26. Personal interview with Lieut John Williamson.
27. Personal interview with Sgt Peter Bolus.
28. Personal interview with Cpl Arthur Kelly; Kelly, *There's a Goddamn Bullet for Everyone*.
29. Personal interview with Lieut A.R.G. Wight.
30. Personal interview with Capt Guy Levesque.
31. *Centans d'histoire d'un Régiment Canadien-Français, 1869–1969:* History of the Fusiliers de Mont-Royal (FMR), 239.
32. Personal interview with Capt Robert Beauvin.
33. Observations by Maj Kenneth A. Smith in R.W. Queen-Hughes, *Whatever Men Dare: Regimental History of the Queen's Own Cameron Highlanders of Canada, 1935–1960*, 138.
34. Queen-Hughes, *Whatever Men Dare*, 139.
35. Personal interview with Sgt Major R. Adams, 1985.
36. Queen-Hughes, *Whatever Men Dare*, 142.
37. Regimental History, *Fusiliers de Mont-Royal*, 241.
38. Stacey, *The Victory Campaign*, 390.
39. Gen Simonds's Private Papers, Public Archives of Canada.
40. Personal interview with Lt-Col von der Heydte.
41. Polish Armoured Division Report.
42. Personal interview with Pte Alexander Schmidt.

43. Algonquin War Diary, 1 October 1944 to 31 October 1944.

44. Personal interview with Capt W.G. Whiteside.

45. Personal interview with Maj James Swayze.

46. Personal interview with Capt W.G. Whiteside.

47. War Diary: Argyll & Sutherland Highlanders of Canada.

Comments

The experience of the RHLI company commander — a man who had served in a command position for so many months with no relief from the constant pressure — is remembered by many of the officers and men of the RHLI with the compassion it deserves. "If he is alive, I would like to put an arm about him and tell him, it's all right, we understand," one veteran recently said.

Postwar studies such as the official American report "Combat Exhaustion" (*The Face of Battle* by John Keegan) have demonstrated that after over three months of continuous action, men had probably been pressured to the point where they had reached their upper limits of effectiveness. They could only become steadily less valuable in ensuing weeks. John Ellis states in *Sharp Edge of War* that between 10 and 15 percent of all battle casualties were battle fatigue–related: "For every five soldiers wounded, another was killed and another became a psychiatric casualty."

Sheer fatigue, seen in its extreme manifestation at the front, can itself exert enormous pressures on mind and body. At a certain point, the resulting symptoms of stress can debilitate a soldier just as effectively as a bullet.

Compounding the stress of unceasing combat, of the miserable conditions that tugged at a man's morale, of the dizzying fatigue, and the growing sense of the inevitability of death as each new day sees one more comrade fall — there is the terror-inducing barrage. Then shell shock becomes a very real and specific condition. An American study cited by Ellis notes that "out of one sample of 115 consecutive patients, 105 were suffering from a form of acute anxiety largely resulting from exposure to a nearby explosion."

H/Captain Jock Anderson, padre of the Highland Light Infantry of Canada, believes that everyone at the front experiences fear — at least some of the time — and "everyone has his breaking point. I found I had mine." The padre recalls that moment of emotional disintegration very clearly: "It was right after the battle at Buron when we had so many killed and wounded. I was out all the next day trying to pick up the dead and finally I had to go back to echelon to get more blankets. I remember walking into a tent full of senior officers having an 'O' Group, and then

I thought, 'what am I doing here?' and I started to cry. The colonel took me out and said, 'Take the padre down to Field Ambulance. He's had too much.' So they put me on a stretcher and then they put a tag on me: 'battle exhaustion.'

"Later, I hid the ticket, got out on the road and found my way back to Caen. That evening they came and put me under field arrest and took me back down to field ambulance. I had complete control this time. I begged them: 'I'm all right. If you send me out, you're going to ruin me. I'll never forgive myself for leaving the fellows. Let me stay.' So they sent me to the MO for twenty-four hours' good sleep and I was right as rain.

"But the thing is, if I hadn't broken, I wouldn't have been able to understand other men later on when I found them crying or hanging back in slit trenches."

10 — *Johnny…Which One Was That?*

1. W.A.B. Douglas and B. Greenhous, *Out of the Shadows: Canada in the Second World War* (Toronto: Oxford University Press, 1977), 134.

2. Col C.P. Stacey, *Arms, Men and Governments: The War Policies of Canada, 1939–1945* (Ottawa: Queen's Printer, 1974), 426.

3. Ibid., 426.

4. Ibid., 427.

5. Ibid., 436.

6. Ibid., 438.

7. Ibid., 440.

8. Anon.

9. Personal interview with Maj Joseph M. Pigott.

10. Personal interview with Lt-Col Roger Rowley.

11. Personal interview with CSM Robert Hibberd.

12. Personal interview with Sgt Peter Bolus.

13. Personal interview with Cpl Edward Newman.

14. Personal interview with Lieut John Williamson.

15. Personal interview with Maj J.M. Pigott.

16. Personal interview with Pte Al Butler.

17. Personal interview with Capt T.R. Wilcox.

18. Personal interview with Maj Tom Stewart.

19. Anon.

20. War Diary: The Black Watch (Royal Highland Regt) of Canada.

21. Personal interview with Lt-Col Bruce Ritchie.

22. *Maclean's Magazine,* 15 August, 1944.

23. Personal interview with Lt-Col Frank Lace.

24. Personal interview with Lieut Robert Saey.

25. Personal interview with Lt-Col Roger Rowley.

26. Personal interview with Pte Bob Favlaro.

27. Personal interview with Sgt Roy Francis.

28. Personal interview with Maj Elliot Dalton.

29. Personal interview with Lt-Col Steven Lett.

30. Personal interview with Maj Charles Dalton.

31. *Globe & Mail,* 12 September 1944; Conn Smythe with Scott Young, *Conn Smythe: If You Can't Beat 'Em in the Alley* (Toronto: McClelland & Stewart Ltd., 1981), 167.

32. Public Archives of Canada; M.G. 27, III B II, Vol. 62.

33. Personal interview with Maj-Gen Christopher Vokes.

34. Personal interview with Maj-Gen Dan Spry.

35. Public Archives of Canada; M.G. 27, III B II, Vol. 62.

36. Personal interview with Brig Elliot Rodger.

37. Personal interview with Capt Marshal Stearns.

38. Personal interview with Brig Richard Malone.

39. Scott Young and Conn Smythe, *Conn Smythe: If You Can't Beat 'Em in the Alley,* 169.

40. Personal interview with Col C.P. Stacey, Official Military Historian for Canada.

41. Personal interview with Col C.P. Stacey.

42. PRO, German propaganda leaflet.

11 — *The Villagers*

1. We are indebted to the people of Woensdrecht and Hoogerheide for the use of material from a book written in the spirit of commemoration, and translated from the Dutch language expressly for *Tug of War.* The book, which was published by the Town Council of Woensdrecht, titled *Woensdrecht en Hoogerheide in de Bange Dagen van Haar Bevrijding,* contains a number of firsthand accounts of the effects of the Battle of Woensdrecht on the villagers (translation by Leo Timmermans and Peter Ooms).

In addition, we used material derived from a translation of a diary of events written on the 20th of October, 1945, by a civil servant, C. van Elzakker.

Despite the fact that it was largely Canadian shellfire that flattened their towns, the villagers are nonetheless grateful for their liberation and are keenly hospitable, even now, to their liberators. The Canadian casualties from these battles have been buried in the Canadian cemetery at Bergen op Zoom, tended carefully by grateful civilians. One Canadian is remembered with extraordinary loyalty by his namesake, as Captain Blackburn relates:

> Among the first Canadian casualties in Holland was Gunner J.W. Wells. He died in shellfire in a water-logged field outside Ossendrecht near the Van Dyks' farmhouse. When, the next fall, a baby boy was born to Cornelia Van Dyk-Joppe, Cory christened him Josephus Wilhelmus. Later she learned that the "J" stood for "Johnny" and her boy became known to all as "Johnny." Today Johnny is older than his namesake, whose grave he and his family care for in the Canadian cemetery at Bergen op Zoom near their home.

2. An excerpt from *Reader's Digest,* June, 1971, by George Blackburn.

12 — *Race Along the Polders*

1. W.D. O.B. West, 16 October 1944 Cdn Army Intelligence Reports; *The Campaign in North-West Europe, Part III: German Defence Operations in the Sphere of 1st Cdn Army (23 August–8 November 1944)*, No. 69, Public Archives of Canada.

2. *1 Battalion, The Essex Scottish Regiment History (Allied with the Essex Regt), 1939–1945* (The Wellington Press, 1946), 53.

3. Personal interview with Maj Cliff Richardson.

4. Personal interview with Cpl Wes Burrows.

5. Personal interview with Maj Victor Schubert.

6. Lt-Col G.B. Buchanan, *The March of the Prairie Men*, 43.

7. Personal interview with Capt T.R. Wilcox; D.J. Goodspeed, *Battle Royal: History of the Royal Regiment of Canada*, 510.

8. Personal interview with Lt George McRae.

9. Personal correspondence with Lt-Col Ian Buchanan-Dunlop; War Diary, 52nd (Lowland) Division.

10. Report No. 1626, filed by Lt P. Kloosterman, 15 August, 1946, with the Netherlands Interior Forces, 21/08/46. Department of His Royal Highness Prince Bernhard; Ministry of National Defence, Den Haag; Citation for Bronze Cross published in *Netherlands Gazette,* June, 1951; Personal interview with Pieter Kloosterman, Nisse, Zeeland. (Translation: Burkunk)

11. Personal interview with Lt-Col Alway; War Diary, 8 Reconnaissance Regt; Maj T.M. Hunter, "The Capture of North Beveland," *Canadian Army Journal,* April 1957.

12. Personal interview with Maj David "Tim" Beatty.

13. Personal interview with Lt John Williamson.

14. Personal correspondence concerning the South Beveland operation with Maj Ralph C. Young, 2I/C of The Royal Regt of Canada.

15. Personal interview with Maj David "Tim" Beatty.

16. Goodspeed, *Battle Royal,* 509.

Comments

Polder fighting was a form of warfare unique in the history of modern combat — unique in that the Canadians, by then the foremost authority, were requested early in 1945 to prepare a major report on the tactics of fighting in the polders for distribution to Allied forces.

Unique, too, was the assault on the German Navy by the 8th Reconnaissance Regiment. Lieutenant Colonel Alway was so delighted at his squadron's capture of the enemy naval vessel that he decided, in jest, to ask a reward: "We put a salvage claim into the admiralty. I put it in tongue-in-cheek, but I got a very official letter from them, two pages long, explaining why they couldn't do it."

13 — *The Water Rats*

1. Arnold Warren, *Wait for the Waggon: The Story of the Royal Canadian Army Service Corps* (Toronto: McClelland & Stewart, 1961), 315.

2. Personal interview with Maj-Gen Dan Spry.

3. Information received by Historical Section (G.S.) from General Eberding on 6 July, 1954. The report states that "It is expected that several of these statistics have been downgraded by General Eberding for propaganda purposes."

4. Personal letter from nephew of Maj-Gen Knut Eberding (Christoph S.), Vancouver, B.C.

5. Personal interview with Lt-Col Roger Rowley, CO, SD&G.

6. Cdn Intelligence Report No. 46, PRO: CAB 44/301, von Zangen report.

7. Letter from Maj-Gen Knut Eberding to the executive committee of *Legion Magazine,* Ottawa, 1968.

8. Lt-Col Siegfried Enfirth, Cmdr 1039 Grenadier Regt, PRO AL2795, from a text titled "Encircled."

9. Personal correspondence with Capt Norman Mould, Chemical Warfare, 1st Canadian Army.

10. Public Archives of Canada, Citation for the Military Cross: Capt Norman Mould.

11. Personal interview with Maj M.R. Douglas: History, 1st Bn, The Regina Rifle Regt.

12. Personal correspondence with Col (then Maj) Robert Schwob, 27 March 1988.

13. Personal interview with Maj M.R. Douglas.

14. Royal Winnipeg Rifles Pamphlet, 75th Anniversary, 1883–1958 (quoting Ross Munroe, *Gauntlet to Overload*).

15. R.H. Roy, *Ready for the Fray: History of the Canadian Scottish Regiment* (Evergreen Press Ltd., 1958), 332; Public Archives of Canada: Citation Sergeant Gri, DCM.

16. Roy, *Ready for the Fray,* personal narrative from Capt V.R. Schjeldrup, 332.

17. Personal interview with Maj Andrew Bieber, Royal Winnipeg Rifles and outstanding Winnipeg Blue Bomber player.

18. Lt-Col Siegfried Enfirth, "Encircled," PRO AL2795.

19. Personal interview with Sgt J. Campbell, Regina Rifles.

20. Personal interview with Maj-Gen Dan Spry.

21. Ibid.

14 — *In the Back Door*

1. Personal interview with Lt-Col Roger Rowley.

2. Lt-Gen G. Simonds, 21 September 1944, Appreciation, 2 Cdn Corps.

3. Battle Narrative, Historical Office, 3 Cdn Inf Div, AEF 45/3 Cdn ID/C/S, PRO.

4. Dr. L. de Jong, *Het Koninkrijk der Nederlander in de Tweede Werel Doorlag, Vol. 10A* ('s-Gravenhage/Staat Suitgeuerij, 1980); Personal interview with Peter de Winde.

5. Ralph Allen, *Ordeal by Fire* (Toronto: Doubleday Canada Ltd., 1961), 406-7.

6. Personal interview with Maj Morris G. Clennett.

7. Lt-Cmdr R.D. Franks, R.N., "Narrative of Amphibious Operation"; Battle Narrative HQ 3 Cdn Div, PRO.

8. Personal interview with Brig J.M. Rockingham.

9. Personal interview with Maj J.T. Hugill; Maj J.T. Hugill, "Report on the Smoke Screening for Op Switchback, 31 November 1944"; Lt-Col W.R. Sawyer, "Report on Smoke Screens Carried on by First Canadian Army (In the Field, 15 July, 1945)"; Printed in the Field by 1 Cdn Mobile Printing Section, RCASC.

10. Personal interview with Sgt Roy Francis.

11. Personal interview with J.M. Rockingham.

12. Anon.

13. Personal interview with H/Capt Jock Anderson.

14. Personal interview with Brig J.M. Rockingham.

15. Personal interview with Pte Douglas Vidler.

16. Personal interview with Brig J.M. Rockingham.

17. Personal interview with Lt-Col Roger Rowley.

18. Ibid.

19. Personal interview with Lt-Col Phillip Strickland.

20. Ibid.

21. Personal interview with Corp E.C. Brownhill.

22. Personal interview with Capt A.J.S. Tuvey; Arnold Warren, *Wait for the Waggon*, 316.

23. Personal interview with Maj Ray Hodgins.

24. Personal interview with H/Capt Anderson.

25. Ibid.

26. Ibid.

27. Personal interview with Maj Tom Prest.

28. Personal interview with H/Capt Anderson.

29. Personal interview with Maj Prest.

30. Personal interview with Maj Morris G. Clennett.

31. Will R. Bird, *No Retreating Footsteps: The Story of the North Nova Scotia Highlanders* (Kentville, N.S.: Kentville Publishing Co. Ltd., 1954), 259.

32. Ibid.

33. Personal interview with Maj Sparks.

34. Personal interview with Lt Burton Fitch.

35. Col. G.W.L. Nicholson, *The Gunners of Canada, Vol. II,* 365.

36. Personal interview with Lt-Col Roger Rowley.

37. Personal interview with Lt-Col Phillip Strickland.

38. Personal interview with Pte Jack Martin.

39. John Ellis, *Sharp End of War,* 47; Broadcast by Canadian Infantry Officer Capt Athol Stewart, 23 November, 1944.

40. Will R. Bird, *North Shore (New Brunswick) Regiment* (Brunswick Press, 1963), 451.

41. Personal interview with Capt Ben Dunkleman.

42. Sir Brian Horrocks, *Corps Commander,* 34.

43. Bird, *North Shore (New Brunswick) Regiment,* 446.

44. Maj Armand Ross and Maj Michael Gauvin, *Le Geste du Regiment de la Chaudière* (1968), 71.

45. Ibid., 77.

46. Brig James Roberts, *Indian Summer,* 99.

47. Personal interview with Maj C.O. Dalton.

48. Personal interview with Brig J.M. Rockingham.

49. Personal interview with Lt-Col Frank Lace.

50. Personal interview with Brig P.A.S. Todd; Brig P.A.S. Todd, "Artillery in Operation Switchback," 2 December 1944.

51. Personal interview with Maj Tom Prest.

52. Personal interview with Lt-Col Frank Lace.

53. Personal interview with Cpl E.C. Brownhill.

54. The Regina Rifle Regiment, *1st Battalion, 1939–1946,* 54.

55. Personal interview with Maj M.R. Douglas.

56. The Regina Rifle Regiment, *1st Battalion, 1939–1946,* 54.

57. Personal interview with Camille Vervarcke, Knokke, Belgium.

58. Personal letter from Maj-Gen Knut Eberding to his nephew (Christoph S.), Vancouver, B.C.

59. Intelligence Summary No. 52, HQ 3 Cdn Inf Div, Appx B, Public Archives of Canada.

60. Personal interview with Maj-Gen Dan Spry.

61. Ibid.

15 — *The Causeway*

1. Personal interview with Maj George Hees.

2. War Diary: 5 Cdn Inf Bde HQ, 's-Heer Arendskerke, Tuesday, 31 October 1944.

3. Personal interview with Maj William Ewing.

4. Personal interview with Lt-Col Bruce Ritchie.

5. Personal interview with RSM Allan Turnbull.

6. War Diary: The Black Watch (RHC), 31 October 1944.

7. Personal interview with Lt-Col Bruce Ritchie.

8. H.A. van Lith, *Liberation of Walcheren: Middelburg* (G.W. den Boer, 1970).

9. Personal interview with Brig W. J. Megill.

10. Anon.

11. Maj Roy Farran, *The History of the Calgary Highlanders,* 188.

12. Personal interview with Maj Ross Ellis.

13. Maj Roy Farran, *The History of the Calgary Highlanders,* 188.

14. Ibid., 190.

15. Ibid., 188.

16. Personal interview with Maj Ross Ellis.

17. Personal interview with Maj F. H. Clarke.

18. Personal interview with Maj Ross Ellis.

19. Major Roy Farran, *The History of the Calgary Highlanders,* 189.

20. Personal interview with Maj Ross Ellis.

21. Jacques Gouin, ed., "et quelques anciens du Régiment de Maisonneuve"; *Bon Coeur et Bon Bras, Regimental History of the Régiment de Maisonneuve 1880–1980* (Montreal: Régiment de Maisonneuve, 1980), 137. Translation from the French language by Martha Hooker, B.A. (Hist).

22. Personal interview with Lt Guy de Merlis.

23. Personal interview with Lt Charles Forbes.

24. Personal interview with anon., Hansweert, Zeeland.

25. Anon.

26. Personal interview with Brig W. J. Megill.

27. Pte Roger Mathen, *Memoires d'un Combattant, 1944* (account written in 1944 by a member of the Belgian Resistance attached to the Régt de Maisonneuve); personal interview with Roger Mathen.

28. Personal interview with Lt Robert Saey.

29. Personal interview with Lt Guy de Merlis.

30. Personal interview with Lt Charles Forbes.

31. Pte R. Mathen, *Memoires d'un Combattant.*

32. Personal interview with Lt Charles Forbes.

33. "Copie du Carnet de Campagne, 1944." Pte Jacques Cantinieaux, *Ensubsistance dans la Cie D du Regiment de Maisonneuve, septembre du décembre, 1944.*

34. Pte R. Mathen, *Memoires d'un Combattant.*

35. Jacques Cantinieaux, "Copie du Carnet de Campagne, 1944."

36. War Diary, 1st Glasgow Highlanders, W0171/1296, PRO.

37. Personal interview with Brig W. J. Megill.

38. Personal interview with Maj George Hees.

39. George Blake, *Mountain and Flood: The History of the 52nd (Lowland) Division 1939–1946* (Glasgow: Jackson, Son & Co., Publishers to the University, 1950), 92.

40. Personal interview with Lt Charles Forbes.

41. Jacques Cantinieaux, "Copie du Carnet de Campagne, 1944."

42. *History of the 1st Glasgow Highlanders,* W0171/1296 PRO.

43. Personal interview with Lt Guy de Merlis.

44. Jacques Cantinieaux, "Copie du Carnet de Campagne."

45. Personal interview with Gunner John Colligan.

46. Personal interview with Lt Charles Forbes.

47. Personal correspondence with Maj-Gen Sir Edmund Hakewill Smith, GOC 52nd (Lowland) Div.

48. Personal interview with Pieter Kloosterman, January, 1983; Account by Pieter Kloosterman, 15 August 1946 for Netherlands Interior Forces, Department of His Royal Highness Prince Bernhard. H.A. van Lith, *Liberation of Walcheren.*

49. Blake, *Mountain and Flood,* 94.

50. Personal correspondence with Lt-Col Ian Buchanan-Dunlop, CO, 6 Bn, the Cameronians, 157 Bde, 52 (Lowland) Div.

Comments

We are grateful for the generous assistance extended us by several members of the 52nd (Lowland) Division, and particularly to Major General Sir E. Hakewill Smith, GOC of the 52nd Division, as well as to Brigadier Ian Buchanan-Dunlop, Brigadier D.B. Riddell-Webster and Brigadier Eric Southward of the 157th Brigade for their helpful and interesting information. We would offer thanks, too, to Colonel C.F. "Tiny" Nason of the 7th Cameronians, 156 Brigade, for so freely offering the hospitality of his home in Guernsey.

For his work with the Resistance, Lieutenant Pieter Kloosterman received letters of commendation from Field Marshal Bernard L. Montgomery and General Dwight D. Eisenhower. Kloosterman's account of his actions during the liberation battle was recorded and verified immediately after the war. He was honoured by his own country with several medals, the most prestigious being the Bronzen Kruis (equivalent to the Military Cross). His citation, filed with the Department of National Defence of the Netherlands, specifically lists his contributions in crossing the enemy line to make contact with the Allied forces (52nd Lowland) on South Beveland, as well as with the Canadians at 's-Heer Abtskerke, and, finally, for indicating a "practically unknown fordable lane through the Sloe Channel in order to launch a surprise assault on the island of Walcheren." Kloosterman, now ninety-one, only last year addressed the Prince of the Netherlands in an excellent speech, despite the fact that he was sporting false teeth that had been "installed" only a few days earlier.

16 — Red Hot — Best of Luck

1. Col C.P. Stacey, *The Victory Campaign,* 412.
2. Ibid., 413; Major General J.L. Moulton, *Battle for Antwerp* (London: Sam Allan Ltd.), 139.
3. Dr. A.V. Van Woerden, *Bericht van de Tweede Wereldoorlog* (Water as an Ally), NR 76 Band 5.
4. Ellis, *Sharp End of War,* 77.
5. Reinhardt interrogation, 1st Cdn Army Review re: Clearing of the Scheldt, 39; August Muir, *The First of Foot: The History of the Royal Scots* (The Royal Regiment): (Edinburgh: The Royal Scots History Committee), 335.
6. Maj-Gen H. Essame, *Battle for Germany,* 47.
7. R.W. Thompson, *The Eighty-Five Days* (London: Hutchinson, 1957), 145.

8. Report from Commander K.A. Sellar to Captain A.F. Pugsley; Gerald Rawling, *Cinderella Operation* (London: Cassell, 1980), 100.

9. Personal interview with Brig Bruce Matthews.

10. Personal interview with Bdr John Walker, Gunner, Manchester Regiment, RA, 52 (Lowland) Division.

11. Col Eric Harris, *Mike Wardell and the Canadian Rocket Battery.*

12. Excerpt from *Canadian Army Review* re: "Clearing the Scheldt, 30 October: Report 4 Commando re surrender of Col. Reinhardt," WO 218/66 PRO, 39.

13. AEF/21 Army Group/C/F/Docket II, Clearing of the Scheldt, 24; CAB 44/301: PRO; W.D. G.S. Ops, H.Q. First Cdn Army, October 1944.

14. Col C.P. Stacey, *The Victory Campaign*, 413.

15. Personal interview with Lt-Col W.A.B. Anderson.

16. Report from Commander K.A. Sellar to Captain A.F. Pugsley; Rawling, *Cinderella Operation*, 101.

17. Admiral A.F. Pugsley, *Destroyer Man* (London: 1957), 196.

18. Ibid., 202.

19. Report on Scheldt Operation — Employment of Air OP in Naval Bombardment, WO 205/758 PRO 52579.

20. J.B. Hillsman, M.D., *Eleven Men and a Scalpel* (Winnipeg: The Columbia Press Ltd., 1948), 101; War Diary: 8 Cdn Field Surgical Unit, RCAMC.

21. Shulman, *Defeat in the West*, 198.

22. Hillsman, *Eleven Men and a Scalpel*, 106.

23. Ibid., 108; War Diary, 6 Fd Surgical Unit, RCAMC.

24. Ibid., 108.

25. Anon.

26. Personal interview with Pte Roy Connors.

27. Hillsman, *Eleven Men and a Scalpel*, 111.

28. George Blake, *Mountain and Flood*, 112.

29. Col C.P. Stacey, *The Victory Campaign*, 424.

30. James Ladd, *Commandos and Rangers of World War II* (London: Macdonald and Jane's, 1978), 204.

31. Admiral A.F. Pugsley, *Destroyer Man*, 190.

32. Combined Ops HQ Records DEFE 2/307, PRO.

33. Hillsman, *Eleven Men and a Scalpel*, 96.

General information was gleaned from:
— Cdn Military Ops CAB 44/301.
— The Assault on Walcheren (4 Cdo Brigade).
— An Assault on the Island of Walcheren-Operations Infatuate I and II, 21 Army Group Report, "Clearing of the Scheldt Estuary," October-November 1944, Part VI.
— Report from Commander K.A. Sellar to Captain A.F. Pugsley.
— Report, 4th Special Service Commando, 1 November–8 November, 1944.
— *The First of Foot,* the History of the Royal Scots (The Royal Regiment), by August Muir.

Comments

Contemporary Walcheren is again a sunny beach resort. Its only sinister undertones from the black years of German occupation are in the large number of unexploded mines that are continually being found. About three thousand are uncovered each year in the dunes.

Another reminder, even more incredible, of the efficiency of the German troops lies in the fact that despite imminent defeat, they were able to publish a newspaper about the event! On the 3rd of November, two days after the invasion, the German Occupation Forces on Walcheren published — and had printed right on the island — an accurate, up-to-date account of their battle with the British. This is one of the 1,200 original leaflets published and distributed by both Germans and Allies that Peter Eekman and Hans Tuynman have collected and display periodically. They are also publishing a photographic book on the liberation of Walcheren.

Their interest stems from boyhood, when they stood outside their homes in Flushing and watched the Commandos invade and liberate their city. Mr. Eekman recalls sweating out the initial bombardment in an earthen hole his grandfather had dug under the living room. (During the Occupation, the countraband radio and his bicycle — their two most precious possessions — were hidden there.) When the barrage lifted, the boy joined a crowd of neighbours on the street. A commando running past yelled, "Stay back from the corner. There is a German sniper there!"

"But," Eekman recalls, "everyone was pretty casual about watching the battle in progress — until a lady in the group was shot in the leg. Then the crowd dispersed."

Bibliography

Allen, Ralph. *Ordeal by Fire: Vol. 5.* Toronto: Doubleday Canada Ltd., 1961.

Ambrose, Stephen E. *The Supreme Commander.* Garden City, N.J.: Doubleday, 1970.

Baldewyns, Albert, and André Herman-Lemoine. *Les Batteries de Walcheren.* Brussels: Rossel Edition, 1974.

Bennett, Ralph. *Ultra in the West: The Normandy Campaign, 1944–45.* London: Hutchinson & Co., 1979.

Bradley, Omar N., and Clay Blair. *A General's Life; An Autobiography by General of the Army Omar N. Bradley.* New York: Simon & Schuster, 1983.

Brereton, Lewis H. *The Brereton Diaries: The War in the Air in the Pacific, Middle East and Europe, 3 October 1941–8 May 1945.* New York: William Morrow, 1946.

Bryant, Sir A. *Triumph in the West.* London: Collins, 1959.

Burns, Major General E.L.M., DSO, OBE, MC. *Manpower in the Canadian Army, 1939–45.* Toronto: Clarke, Irwin & Co. Ltd., 1956.

Chalmers, W.S., Rear Admiral, CBE, DSC. *Full Cycle: Ramsay, Admiral Sir B. H.* London: Hodder & Stoughton, 1959.

De Jong, Dr. L. *Het Koninkrijk der Nederlandor in de Tweede Werel Doorlag, Vol. 10A.* Holland: 's-Gravenhage/Staat Suitgeverif/80. Riiksin Stituut V007, Oorlag Documentatie, 1980.

Douglas, W.A.B., and B. Greenhous. *Out of the Shadows: Canada in the Second World War.* Toronto: Oxford University Press, 1977.

Dunkleman, Ben. *Dual Allegiance.* Toronto: Macmillan, 1976.

Dupuy, Col., T.N., US Army, Ret. *Numbers, Predictions and War: Using History to Evaluate Combat Factors and Predict the Outcome of Battles.* London: Macdonald and Jane's Publishers Ltd., 1979.

Eisenhower, General Dwight D. *Crusade in Europe.* New York: Doubleday & Co., 1948.

Eisenhower, John. *The Bitter Woods.* Toronto: Longmans Canada Ltd., 1969.

Ellis, Maj L.F., CVO, CBE, DSO, MC. *History of the Second World War. Vol. 2: Victory in the West.* London: Her Majesty's Stationery Office, 1962.

Ellis, John. *Sharp End of War: The Fighting Man in World War II.* Newton Abbot, Devon: David & Charles Ltd., Brunei House, 1980.

Essame, Maj Gen H. *Battle for Germany.* New York: Scribner, 1969.

Farago, Ladislas. *Patton: Ordeal and Triumph.* New York: Astor-Honour, 1964.

Feis, Herbert. *Churchill, Roosevelt, Stalin: The War They Waged and the Peace They Sought.* London: Oxford University Press, 1957.

Garlinski, Joseph. *Hitler's Last Weapons.* Toronto: Times Book Co. Inc./Fitzhenry & Whiteside, 1978.

Gilbert, Dr. Felix G. *Hitler Directs His War.* London: Oxford University Press, 1950.

Granatstein, J.L. *Canada's War: The Politics of the Mackenzie King Government '39–45.* Toronto: Oxford University Press, 1975.

Hamilton, Nigel. *Monty: The Making of a General.* New York: McGraw-Hill, 1981.

Harris, Col Eric. *Mike Wardell and the Canadian Rocket Battery.*

Hart, Liddell B.H. *The Other Side of the Hill.* London: Cassell & Co. Ltd., 1948.

Hart, Liddell. *History of the Second World War.* London: Cassell & Co. Ltd., 1970.

Harvey, John, ed. *The War Diaries of Oliver Harvey, 1941–1945.* London: Collins, 1979.

Horrocks, Sir Brian. *A Full Life.* London: Collins, 1962.

Horrocks, Sir Brian, with Eversley Belfield and Maj-Gen H. Essame. *Corps Commander.* Toronto: Griffin House, 1977.

How, Douglas, ed. *The Canadians at War.* Montreal: The Reader's
    Digest Association, 1969.

Hutchinson, Bruce. *The Incredible Canadian.* Toronto: Longmans,
    Green & Co., 1952.

Irving, David. *Hitler's War.* New York: Viking Press, 1977.

Irving, David, *The War Between the Generals.* New York: Congdon
    & Lattès, Inc., 1981.

Kaufman, David, ed., and Michiel Horn. *A Liberation Album.*
    Toronto: McGraw-Hill Ryerson Ltd., 1980.

Kelly, Arthur. *There's a Goddamn Bullet for Everyone.* Paris, Ontario:
    Arts and Publishing Co. Ltd., 1979.

Kirkconnell, Watson. *Canada, Europe and Hitler.* London: Oxford
    University Press, 1939.

Ladd, James. *Commandos and Rangers of World War II.* London:
    Macdonald and Jane's, 1978.

Leasor, Sir James. *War at the Top.* London: Michael Joseph, 1959.

Lewin, Ronald. *Ultra Goes to War.* London: Hutchinson, 1978.

Malone, Col. Richard, OBE. *Missing from the Record.* Toronto: Wm.
    Collins Sons and Co. Ltd., 1946.

Munroe, Ross. *Gauntlet to Overload — The Story of the Canadian
    Army.* Toronto: Macmillan, 1945.

Montgomery, Field Marshal Bernard. *The Memoirs of Field Marshal
    Montgomery.* London: Collins, 1958.

Masse, Walter B. *The Netherlands at War, 1940–45.* Toronto: Abelard
    Schuman, 1977.

McKee, Alexander. *The Race for the Rhine Bridges.* London:
    Souvenir Press Ltd., 1971.

Moulton, Maj-Gen. J.L., CB, DSO, OBE. *Battle for Antwerp.*
    London: Sam Allan Ltd., 1978.

North, John. *Northwest Europe '44–55.* London: H.M. Stationery
    Office, 1977.

Panter-Downes, Mollie. *London War Notes.* New York: Farrar, Straus
    & Giroux, 1971.

Patton, George. *War as I Knew It.* Boston: Houghton, 1947.

Pearce, Donald. *Journal of a War.* Toronto: Macmillan, 1965.

Pugsley, A.F. *Destroyer Man.* London: Weidenfeld, 1957.

Rawling, Gerald. *Cinderella Operation.* London: Cassell, 1980.

Shulman, Milton. *Defeat in the West*. London: Secker & Warburg Ltd., 1947.

Sixsmith, E.K.G. *British Generalship in the Twentieth Century*. London: Arms & Armour Press, 1970.

Sixsmith, E.K.G. *Eisenhower as a Military Commander*. London: B.T. Batsford Ltd., 1973.

Smythe, Conn, with Scott Young. *If You Can't Beat 'Em in the Alley*. Toronto: McClelland & Stewart, 1981.

Stacey, Col C.P. *The Canadian Army, 1939–1945: An Official Historical Summary*. Published by Authority of the Minister of Defence, Canada, 1948.

Stacey, Col C.P. *The Victory Campaign, Vol. III: 1944–45*. Ottawa: Queen's Printer, 1960.

Stacey, Col C.P. *Arms, Men and Governments: The War Policies of Canada, 1939–1945*. Published by Authority of the Minister of National Defence. Ottawa: Queen's Printer, 1974.

Stacey, C.P. *A Date With History: Memoirs of a Canadian Historian*. Ottawa: Deneau, 1983.

Thompson, R.W. *The Eighty-five Days*. London: Hutchinson & Co., 1957.

Trevor-Roper, H.R. *Hitler's War Directives, 1939–1945*. London: Sidgwick & Jackson Ltd., 1964.

Urquhart. R.E. *Arnhem*. London: Cassell and Co., 1958.

van Lith, H.A. *Liberation of Walcheren*. Middelburg: G.W. den Boer, 1970.

von Mellethin, F.W. *German Generals of W.W.H.* Tulsa: University of Oklahoma Press, 1977.

Warlymont, Walter. *Inside Hitler's Headquarters, 1939–1945*. Bristol: Western Printing Services, 1963.

Weighley, Russell. *Eisenhower's Lieutenants*. London: Sidgwick & Jackson Ltd., 1981.

Wilmot, Chester. *The Struggle for Europe*, London: Collins, 1952.

Winterbotham, F.W., C.B.E. *The Ultra Secret*. New York: Harper & Row Publishers, 1974.

Woensdrecht en Hoogerheide in de Bange Dagen van Haar Bevrijding (Woensdrecht and Hoogerheide — from Anxious Days until Their Liberation). Woensdrecht: Town Council, 1975.

Regimental and Military Histories

Barclay, Brigadier C.N., CBE, DSO. *The History of the Cameronians (Scottish Rifles), Vol. III, 1933–1946.* London: Sifton Praed.

Barnard, Lieutenant Colonel W.T.T., ED, CD. *Queen's Own Rifles of Canada, 1860–1960.* Don Mills, Ontario: The Ontario Publishing Co. Ltd.

Barrett, LT. W. W. *The History of 13 Canadian Field Regiment. Royal Canadian Artillery (1940–45).*

Bartlett, Jack Fortune. *The Highland Light Infantry of Canada (1st Battalion) (1940–1945).* Galt, Ontario: Highland Light Infantry of Canada Association, 1951.

Bird, Will R., *No Retreating Footsteps: The Story of the North Nova Scotia Highlanders.* Kentville, N.S.: Kentville Publishing Co. Ltd., 1954.

Bird, Will R. *North Shore (New Brunswick) Regiment.* Brunswick Press, 1963.

Blake, George. *Mountain and Flood: The History of the 52nd (Lowland) Division, 1939–1946.* Glasgow: Jackson, Son & Co., Publishers to the University, 1950.

Boss, Lt-Col W., CD. *The Stormont, Dundas and Glengarry Highlanders (1783–1951).* The Runge Press Ltd., Ottawa, 1952.

Brown, Kingsley, Sr., and Kingsley Brown, Jr. *The History of the Royal Hamilton Light Infantry (Wentworth Regiment).*

Buchanan, Lt-Col G.B. *The March of the Prairie Men: Regimental History of the South Sask Regiment.*

Cassidy, Major George L., DSO. *Warpath: The Story of the Algonquin Regiment 1939–1945.* Published under the direction of the Algonquin Regiment Veterans' Association, Canada. Ryerson Press, 1948.

Darby, Hugh, and Marcus Cunliffe. *A Short Story of 21 Army Group.* Aldershot, England: Gale & Polden Ltd., 1949.

Elliot, Major. S.R. *Scarlet to Green: A History of Intelligence in the Canadian Army, 1903–1963.* Toronto: Canadian Intelligence and Security Association, 1981.

Farran, Major Roy, DSO, MC. *The History of the Calgary Highlanders, 1921–1954.* Calgary: Bryant Press Ltd., 1954.

Feasby, W.R., B.A., M.D. *Official History of the Canadian Medical Services, 1939–45: Vol. 1 & 2.* 1956.

Fergusson, Bernard. *The Watery Maze: The Story of Combined Operations.* London: Collins, St. James's Place, 1961.

Goodspeed, Major D.J. *Battle Royal.* Published by the Royal Regiment of Canada, 1962.

Gouin, Jacques, ed. "et quelques anciens du Régiment de Maisonneuve," *Bon Coeur et Bon Bras: Regimental History of the Régiment de Maisonneuve 1880–1980.* Montreal: Régiment de Maisonneuve, 1980.

Grant, Major D.W. *Carry On: The History of the Toronto Scottish Regiment (M.G.) 1939–1945.*

Greenhous, Brereton, *Semper Paratus.* Hamilton: The Royal Hamilton Light Infantry Historical Association, 1977.

Hillsman, J. B., M. D. *Eleven Men and a Scalpel.* Winnipeg: The Columbia Press Ltd., 1948.

Hutchinson, Col. Paul C. *Canada's Black Watch — The First 100 Years (1862–1962).* The Black Watch (RHR) of Canada.

Jackson, Lt-Col H.M., MBE, ED, ed., and Officers of the Regiment. *The Argyll and Sutherland Highlanders of Canada (Princess Louise's) 1928–1953.*

Kemp, Lieut-Comdr P.K. *The History of the 4th Battalion King's Shropshire Light Infantry (T.A.), 1745–1945.* Shrewsbury: Wilding & Son Ltd., 1955.

Mann, Maj-Gen CC, CBE, DSO. *The Campaign in North-west Europe. Vol. 3, No. 4.* Published by the Directorate of Military Training under authority of the Chief of the General Staff, July 1949.

Muir, Augustus. *The First of Foot: The History of the Royal Scots (The Royal Regiment).* Blackwood, 1961.

Nicholson, Col G.W.L. *The Gunners of Canada, Vol. II,* Toronto: McClelland & Stewart, 1967.

Nicholson, Col G.W.L., C.D. *Seventy Years of Service (A History of a Royal Canadian Army Medical Corps).* Ottawa: Borealis Press, 1977.

Queen-Hughes, R.W. *Whatever Men Dare: Regimental History of the Queen's Own Cameron Highlanders of Canada, 1935–1960.*

Ramsey, Winston G., ed. *After the Battle: Walcheren, Number '36.* London: Battle of Britain Prints International Ltd., 1982.

Rogers, Major R. L. *History of the Lincoln and Welland Regiment.* 1954.

Ross, Maj Armand, DSO, and Maj Michael Gauvin, DSO. *Le Geste du Régiment de la Chaudière.*

Ross, Lt-Col Richard M., OBE. *The History of the 1st Battalion: The Cameron Highlanders of Ottawa (MG).*

Roy, R.H. *Ready for the Fray: History of the Canadian Scottish Regiment.* Evergreen Press Ltd., 1958.

Saunders, Hilary St George, and Richards, Denis. *Royal Air Force, 1939–1945.* London: Her Majesty's Stationery Office, 1975.

Sawyer, Lt-Col W. R. *Report on Smoke Screens carried out by First Canadian Army.* Printed in the field by 1 Canadian Mobile Printing Section, RCASC, 15 July 1945.

Warren, Arnold. *Wait for the Waggon: The Story of the Royal Canadian Army Service Corps.* Toronto: McClelland & Stewart, 1961.

Centans d'historie d'un Regiment Canadien-Français, 1869–1969.
Les Fusiliers de Mont Royal, 1869–1969.
The History of 6th (Lanarkshire) Battalion: The Cameronians (S.P.) World War II. Glasgow: John Cossar Publishing.
The Regina Rifle Regiment, 1939–1946.
Royal Winnipeg Rifles Pamphlet, 75th Anniversary, 1883–1958.
Taurus Pursuant: A History of the 11 Armoured Division.
1 Bn, The Essex Scottish Regiment (Allied with the Essex Regt), 1939–1945. The Wellington Press, 1946.

War Diaries: September – November, 1944

2 Cdn Corps HQ
2 Cdn Inf Div:
8 Cdn Recce, Toronto Scottish
4th Cdn Inf Bde HQ: RHLI, Essex Scottish, Royal Regt
5th Cdn Inf Bde HQ: Black Watch, Calgary Highlanders, Le Regt de Maisonneuve

6th Cdn Inf Bde HQ: SSR, FMR, Cameron Highlanders of Canada

3rd Cdn Inf Div:
12, 13 and 14 Field Regt, RCA, Cameron Highlanders of Ottawa
7th Cdn Inf Bde HQ: Regina Rifles, Royal Winnipeg Rifles, 1st Cdn
    Scot Regt
8th Cdn Inf Bde HQ: Régiment de la Chaudière, North Shore Regt.,
    Queen's Own Rifles of Canada
9th Cdn Inf Bde HQ: HLI of Canada, Stormont, Dundas &
    Glengarry Highlanders, North Nova Scotia Highlanders

4th Cdn Armoured Division:
10th Cdn Inf Bde HQ: The Algonquin Regt, Lincoln & Welland,
    Argyll & Sutherland Highlanders

52 British (Lowland) Div: 4 KOSB, 5 KOSB, 7/9 Royal Scots,
    4/5 Royal Scots, 6 Cameronians, 7 Cameronians, Glasgow
    Highlanders, 5 HLI, 6 HLI.

List of Interviews

This book could not have been completed were it not for the unstinting cooperation of the following men and women who provided unparalleled insight concerning so many facets of our subject. It would be impossible to delineate the details of their valuable contributions in the available space; however, we want to express our most sincere and unqualified thanks to them all. The greatest pleasure gleaned from this work has been the opportunity to renew contact with so many old friends. As well, many new friendships have been made in Canada, the UK and northwest Europe.

In order to avoid confusion, ranks shown below were those held at the time of the Scheldt battle. Later promotions are shown in brackets.

Karel Aernondts, Dutch Resistance, Oostburg
Lt-Col Mowbray Alway, DSO, 8th Canadian Recconaissance Regiment
H/Capt Jock Anderson, MC, (Lt-Col) Highland Light Infantry of Canada
Lt-Col W.A.B. Anderson, OBE, CD, (Lt-Gen) 1st Canadian Army
Lieut W.A. Atkinson, Régiment de la Chaudière
Capt Osborne Avery, Royal Hamilton Light Infantry (Wentworth Regiment)

Sgt Wm Bailey, MM, North Nova Scotia Highlanders
Maj William Barrett, 13th Fd Regt Royal Canadian Artillery

Brig G.E. Beament, OBE, ED, 1st Cdn Army

Major David S. Beatty, (Col) Royal Regiment of Canada

Capt Roger Beauvin, Les Fusiliers Mont-Royal

Lieut George Beck, 7th South Staffordshire 59 Br Div

Mr. Eversley Belfield, Historian, Sark, Channel Islands

Capt Thomas Bell, MC, 12th Field Regiment RCA

Capt James Bennet, 13th Fd Regt RCA

Mr. Ralph Bennett

Maj Andrew Bieber, Royal Winnipeg Rifles

Capt George Blackburn, 4th Fd Regt RCA

Sgt Peter Bolus, RHLI

Maj Gordon Bourne, The Black Watch (Royal Highland Regiment)
   of Canada

Sgt Jack Brabbs, RHLI

Cpl E.C. Brownhill, Cameron Highlanders of Ottawa

Lt-Col A.I. Buchanan-Dunlop, CBE, DSO (Brig) 6th Cameronians
   52 British (Lowland) Div

Cpl James Bulmer, RHLI

Cpl Wesley Burrows, MM, RHLI

Capt Herbert Burton, (Maj) RHLI

Pte Al Butler, Royal Regt of Canada

Sgt Jack Campbell, Regina Rifle Regiment

Jacques Cantinieaux, Belgian Resistance, Régiment de
   Maisonneuve

Lt-Col George Cassidy, DSO, Algonquin Regiment

Dr. Jean Leon Charles, Professor of History, Ecole Royale Militaire,
   Brussels

Pte Jack Chew, RHLI

Maj F.H. Clarke, (Lt-Col) Calgary Highlanders

F.O. Tom Clayton, RAF

Maj Jake Clement, 15 Fd Regt RCA

Maj Morris Clennett, North Nova Scotia Highlanders

Gnr John Colligan, 79 Fd Regt RA, 52 Br Div

Lt-Col Eugene J. Colson, Grand Officer de l'Ordre de Leopold,
   La Croix de Guerre, MNR, Belgian Resistance, Antwerp

CSM Jim Coughlin, Essex Scottish Regt

Cpl Harry Connor, 4th Cdn Inf Bde
Pte Roy Connors, RCAMC
B. Cools, Bergemeester, Antwerp
Lt-Col John Craig, MBE, 3rd Cdn Inf Div
Lt-Col James Curry, EM CD, North Shore (New Brunswick)

Regt Maj C.O. Dalton, DSO, KspJ, ED, (Col) Queen's Own Rifles of
    Canada
Maj Elliot Dalton, DSO, EM, CD, (Col) Queen's Own Rifles
Maj James Dandy, DSO, (Lt-Col) Lincoln and Welland Regt
Dr. L de Jong, RIOD, Netherlands Institute of War Documentation,
    Amsterdam, Netherlands
Dr Wisse Dekker, President Phillips N.V., Eindhoven, Netherlands
Lieut Guy de Merlis, Régiment de Maisonneuve
Lieut Frans De Moor, Belgian Resistance, Antwerp
Peter de Winde, Bronze Lion, Dutch Resistance, Amsterdam,
    Netherlands
Sara de Winde, Resistance Remembrance Cross, Dutch Resistance,
    Breskens, Netherlands
Capt Reginald Dixon, Stormont, Dundas and Glengarry
    Highlanders
Capt Lyle Doering, (Maj) RHLI
Maj M.R. Douglas, Regina Rifle Regiment
Dr. Von Druten, Director of the Archief van de Binnenlands
    Strydkrachten (Archives of the Underground), Kerkrade,
    Netherlands
Capt Ben Dunkleman, DSO, (Maj) Queen's Own Rifles

Peter Eekman, Flushing, Netherlands
Maj Ross Ellis, DSO, Calgary Highlanders*
Maj William Ewing, The Black Watch

Pte Robert Favlaro, SD&G Regt
Pieter de Fayter, Dutch Resistance, Sluis, Netherlands
Pte Harry Ferguson, Toronto Scottish Regiment (MG)
Lieut Burton Fitch, North Nova Scotia Highlanders
Col Frank Fleury, CBE, ED, CD, (Lt-Gen) CMHQ

Lieut J. Charles Forbes, Military Order of William, Régiment de Masionneuve
Sgt Roy Francis, Highland Light Infantry of Canada
Lt-Col L.R. Fulton, DSO, Royal Winnipeg Rifles

Pte E. Gale, Algonquin Regt
Capt Maurice Gervais, Royal Canadian Army Pay Corps, attached to RHLI
Capt Maurice Gravel, Fusiliers de Mont-Royal
Mr. John Grodzinski, Hamilton, Ontario
Maj-Gen Sir Edmond Hakewill Smith, KCVO, CBE, MC, 52 British (Lowland) Division
Sgt Harold Hall, RHLI
Maj George Hees, RCA, 5th Cdn Inf Bde
Maj Larry Henderson, DSO, First Canadian Scottish Regt
Pte Roy Hergott, RHLI
CSM Robert Hibberd, (RSM) RHLI
Maj Roy Hodgins, HLI of Canada
Maj J.T. Hugill, 1st Cdn Army

Pieter Jacobs, Ossendrecht, Netherlands

Cpl Arthur Kelly, MM, RHLI
Lt-Col Telford Kenny, Royal Canadian Army Service Corps, 2nd Cdn Inf Div
Lieut Pieter Kloosterman, Bronze Cross, Dutch Resistance, Nisse, Netherlands

Lt-Col Frank Lace, DSO, OBE, (Brig) 13th Fd Regt RCA
Capt William Lees, RHLI
Lt-Col Steven Lett, DSO, Queen's Own Rifles
Capt Guy Levesque, FMR
J.M. De Leeuw, Burgemeester, Woensdrecht, Netherlands
Maj William Lye (Brig-Gen)

Maj Donald McCrimmon, MBE, Royal Canadian Army Medical Corps

Sgt Tom MacDonald, MM (Maj) RHLI
Lieut Fred McKenna, Toronto Scottish Regt
Lieut George McRae, 7th Cameronians 52 Br (L) Div
Brig Richard Malone, OBE, ED, 21st Army Group
Pte Jack Martin, Queen's Own Rifles
Roger Mathen, Belgian Resistance, Régiment de Masionneuve
Brig Bruce Matthews, (Maj-Gen) CBE, DSO, ED, CRA 2nd Cdn Corps
Brig W.J. Megill, DSO, (Maj-Gen) 5th Cdn Inf Bde
Maj D.C. Menzies, The Black Watch
Lt-Col Donald Mingay, DSO, MBE, 3rd Cdn Inf Div
Brig R.W. Moncel, DSO, OBE, (Lt-Gen) 4 Cdn Armd Bde
Sgt William Moriarity, Essex Scottish Regt
Capt Norman Mould, MC, 1st Canadian Army
Lt-Col J.L. Moulton, CB, DSO, OBE (Maj-Gen) 48 Commando,
    Royal Marines
Charles Muysken, attached to RHLI, Den Haag, Netherlands

Lt-Col C.F. Nason, 7th Cameronians 52 Br (L) Div
Cpl Edward Newman, RHLI
Lieut J.A.B. Nixon, The Black Watch

Capt Kenneth O'Hara, 8th Recce Regt
Cpl Austin Oliver, RHLI
Sgt Gerry Ollinger, RHLI
Pieter Ooms, Breda, Netherlands
Lieut Blake Oulton, (Lt-Col) North Shore (New Brunswick) Regt

Dr. A.H. Paape, Rijksinstituut voor Oorlogsdocumentatie (RIOD),
    Netherlands Institute for War Documentation, RIOD,
    Amsterdam
Pte Roy Parry, Algonquin Regt
W.J. Pieters, Dutch Resistance, Oostburg, Netherlands
Maj J.M. Pigott, DSO, RHLI
Louis Pijnen, Woensdrecht, Netherlands
Maj Edouard Pilaet, Belgian Resistance, Antwerp
Brig E.C. Plow, CBE, DSO, RCA
Maj Tom Prest, Highland Light Infantry of Canada

Lt-Col Walter Reynolds, 1st Cdn Army*

Maj Cliff Richardson, RCAMC Essex Scottish Regt

Maj D.B. Riddell-Webster, OBE, (Brig) 6th Cameronians 52 Br (L) Div

Lt-Col Bruce Ritchie, The Black Watch

Brig James Roberts, DSO, (Maj-Gen) 8 Cdn Inf Bde

Brig J.M. Rockingham, CBE, DSO, ED, (Maj-Gen) 9th Cdn Inf Bde

Brig N.E. Rodger, CBE, (Major-Gen) 2 Cdn Corps

Lt-Col Roger Rowley, DSO, ED, CD, (Maj-Gen) SD&G Regt

Lieut Robert Saey, (Lt-Col) Régiment de Maisonneuve

Pte Alexander Schmidt, 6 Para Regt, Germany

Maj Victor Schubert, South Saskatchewan Regiment

Dr. Schulten, Chief of the Army, Historical Section; Mrs. Lea Strik, Sectie Militaire Geschiedenis, HQ Royal Netherlands Army, 's-Gravenhage

Col Charles Simonds, Cdn Army, Ottawa

Pieter I. Simpelaar, Dutch Resistance, Oostburg, Netherlands

Maj-Gen E.K.G. Sixsmith, CB, CBE, Langport, Somerset, England

Maj Kenneth A. Smith, Queen's Own Cameron Highlanders of Canada

Mr. John Smith-Wright, formerly Cryptographer, Bletchely Park

Lt-Col Eric N. Southward, DSO, (Brig) 6th Cameronians, 52nd Br (L) Div

Brig H.A. Sparling, CBE, DSO, CD, RCA (Maj-Gen) 1st Cdn Corps

Maj F.A. Sparks, DSO, (Lt-Col), North Nova Scotia Highlanders

Maj-Gen D.C. Spry, CBE, DSO, OBE, 3rd Cdn Inf Div

Col C.P. Stacey, OBE, CD, PhD, Official Cdn War Historian

Capt Marshal Stearns, 2nd Cdn Corps

Maj S. Steele, Essex Scottish Regt

Capt Jack Steen, RCASC, 2nd Cdn Inf Div

Capt W.D. Stevenson, MC, 4 Fd Regt RCA

Capt Tom Stewart, Essex Scottish Regt

Lt-Col Vernon Stott, DSO, SSR

Lt-Col Phillip Strickland, DSO, HLI of Canada

Maj James Swayze, DSO (Col) Lincoln & Welland Regt

Maj Mark Tennant, Calgary Highlanders
Leo Timmermans, Woensdrecht, Netherlands
Brig P.A.S. Todd, DSO, OBE, ED, CRA 3rd Cdn Inf Div
Dr. Thomas Trumpp, Bundesarchiv, Koblenz, W. Germany
RSM Alan Turnbull, DCM, The Black Watch
Capt Alf Turvey, MC, RCASC, 3 Cdn Inf Div
Hans Tuynman, Flushing, Walcheren

Cornelis van Beek, Woensdrecht
Clement van der Poest, Nisse, Netherlands
Marc van de Velde, Boom, Belgium Leon van Lakwijk,
     Woensdrecht
Lieut Robert Vekemans, MC, La Croix de Guerre, Belgian
     Resistance, Antwerp
Maria Verboven, Woensdrecht
Camille Vervarcke, La Croix de Guerre, Belgian Resistance,
     Knokke, Belgium
Pte Doug Vidler, SD&G Regt
Dr. Carlos Vlaemynck, Dr in de Rechten, Brugge, Belgium
Maj-Gen Christopher Vokes, CB, CBE, DSO, 4th Cdn Armd Div
Lt-Col Friedrich A. von der Heydte, (Brig) 6 Para Regt, Germany

Fl Lt Bill Walker, RCAF
Bdr John Walker, Manchester Regt 52 Br (L) Div
Capt Frank Walton, Essex Scottish Regt
Capt R.J.G. Weeks, (Maj-Gen) 3 Cdn Inf Div (Maj-Gen)
Capt William Whiteside, (Maj) Argyll & Sutherland Highlanders
     of Canada
Capt A.R.G. Wight, RHLI
Capt T.R. Wilcox, Royal Regt of Canada
Lieut John Williamson, (Col) RHLI
F.W. Winterbotham, CBE

Maj Ralph Young, Royal Regt of Canada

Archives

National Archives of Canada
Department of National Defence, Ottawa
Imperial War Museum, London
Public Record Office, Kew, Richmond, England
Bundesarchiv Militararchiv, Freiburg, Germany
BBC Written Archives Centre
Ecole Royale Militaire, Brussels
Centre de Recherches et d'Etudes Historiques de la Seconde Guerre
    Mondiale, Brussels
Rijksinstituut voor Oorlogsdocumentatie (RIOD), Amsterdam
Historical Section, Sectie Militaire Geschiedenis, HQ Royal
    Netherlands Army, 's-Gravenhage
Archief van de Binnenlands Strydkrachten (the Archives of the
    Underground), Kerkrade
Bundesarchiv, Koblenz-Oberwerth, Germany
Royal Canadian Military Institute, Toronto

Translators

Heer Patrick Defauru, Bruges, Belgium
Katrien Goethals, Bruges
Martha Hooker, B.A. (Honours) History, Ottawa
Heer Pieter Ooms, Breda, Netherlands
Heer Leo Timmermans, Woensdrecht, Zeeland
Heer C. Van Elzakken, Woensdrecht
Heer Sjoerd Westra, Moraira, Spain

Canadian Infantry Battalions at the Scheldt

The following regiments served with distinction at the Scheldt battle. The Battle Honours awarded them in commemoration of outstanding service in this single battle are listed following each name (those Honours in italics have been approved to be borne on the regiment's Standard, Guidon or Colours).

2 CANADIAN INFANTRY DIVISION

TORONTO SCOTTISH REGIMENT (MG): (Toronto, Ont): *Antwerp-Turnhout Canal, The Scheldt, Woensdrecht,* South Beveland

4TH CANADIAN INFANTRY BRIGADE

1) THE ROYAL HAMILTON LIGHT INFANTRY (Wentworth Regiment) (Hamilton, Ont): The Scheldt, *Woensdrecht,* South Beveland

2) THE ESSEX SCOTTISH REGT (Windsor, Ont): *The Scheldt,* Woensdrecht, *South Beveland*

3) THE ROYAL REGT OF CANADA (Toronto, Ont): *The Scheldt,* Woensdrecht, *South Beveland*

5TH CANADIAN INFANTRY BRIGADE

1) THE BLACK WATCH (RHR) OF CANADA (Montreal, P.Q.): Antwerp-Turnhout Canal, *The Scheldt,* Woensdrecht, South Beveland, *Walcheren Causeway*

2) THE CALGARY HIGHLANDERS (Calgary, Alta): Wyneghem, *Antwerp-Turnhout Canal, The Scheldt*, Woensdrecht, South Beveland, *Walcheren Causeway*

3) LE RÉGIMENT DE MAISONNEUVE (Montreal, P.Q.): *Antwerp-Turnhout Canal*, The Scheldt, Woensdrecht, South Beveland, *Walcheren Causeway*

6TH CANADIAN INFANTRY BRIGADE

1) LES FUSILIERS DE MONT-ROYAL (Montreal, P.Q.): *Antwerp-Turnhout Canal*, The Scheldt, Woensdrecht, *South Beveland*

2) THE QUEEN'S OWN CAMERON HIGHLANDERS OF CANADA (Winnipeg, Man): The Scheldt, *Woensdrecht, South Beveland*

3) THE SOUTH SASKATCHEWAN REGIMENT (Estevan, Sask): *Antwerp-Turnhout Canal, The Scheldt*, Woensdrecht, South Beveland

3 CANADIAN INFANTRY DIVISION

THE CAMERON HIGHLANDERS OF OTTAWA (MG) (Ottawa, Ont): *The Scheldt*, Breskens Pocket

7TH CANADIAN INFANTRY BRIGADE

1) THE REGINA RIFLE REGIMENT (Regina, Sask): *The Scheldt, Leopold Canal*, Breskens Pocket

2) THE ROYAL WINNIPEG RIFLES (Winnipeg, Man): *The Scheldt, Leopold Canal*, Breskens Pocket

3) THE CANADIAN SCOTTISH REGIMENT (Victoria, B.C.): The Scheldt, *Leopold Canal*, Breskens Pocket

8TH CANADIAN INFANTRY BRIGADE

1) LE RÉGIMENT DE LA CHAUDIÈRE (Lévis, P.Q.): *The Scheldt*, Breskens Pocket

2) NORTH SHORE (NEW BRUNSWICK) REGIMENT (Bathurst, N.B.): Moerbrugge, Moerkerke, *The Scheldt*, Breskens Pocket

3) THE QUEEN'S OWN RIFLES OF CANADA (Toronto, Ont): *The Scheldt*, Breskens Pocket

9TH CANADIAN INFANTRY BRIGADE

1) THE HIGHLAND LIGHT INFANTRY OF CANADA (Galt, Ont.): *The Scheldt,* Savojaards Plaat, Breskens Pocket

2) STORMONT, DUNDAS & GLENGARRY HIGHLANDERS (Cornwall, Ont): *The Scheldt,* Savojaards Plaat, *Breskens Pocket*

3) THE NORTH NOVA SCOTIA HIGHLANDERS (New Glasgow, N.S.): The Scheldt, Savojaards Plaat, *Breskens Pocket*

4TH CANADIAN ARMOURED DIVISION

10TH CANADIAN INFANTRY BRIGADE

1) THE ALGONQUIN REGIMENT (North Bay, Ont): *Moerkerke, The Scheldt,* Breskens Pocket

2) THE LINCOLN & WELLAND REGIMENT (St. Catharines, Ont): *Moerbrugge, The Scheldt,* Breskens Pocket

3) THE ARGYLL & SUTHERLAND HIGHLANDERS OF CANADA (Hamilton, Ont): *Moerbrugge, The Scheldt,* Breskens Pocket

Photograph Credits

Photo Insert No. 1

1. Imperial War Museum, London
2. Imperial War Museum, London
3. Centre de Recherches et d'Etudes historiques de la Seconde Guerre Mondiale, Brussels
4. Centre de Recherches et d'Etudes historiques de la Second Guerre Mondiale, Brussels
5. Imperial War Museum, London
6. Ken or Dean, M. M. Bell/DND/Public Archives of Canada PA-136758
7. Bundesarchiv, Koblenz
8. Courtesy of Heer Peter de Winde, Amsterdam
9. Courtesy of Lieutenant Colonel George Cassidy
10. Courtesy of Dr. Carlos Vlaemynck, Bruges, Belgium
11. Courtesy of Captain Marshal Stearns, ADC to General Simonds
12. Ken Bell/DND/Public Archives of Canada/PA-136755
13. Bundesarchiv, Koblenz
14. Courtesy of Heer and Mevrouw Snepvangers-Snoeke, Martinushoeve, Zandvliet, Belgium
15. Courtesy of Burgomeester J.M. de Leeuw, Woensdrecht
16. Courtesy of Heer Bastiaan Burkunk

Photo Insert No. 2

1. F.L. Dubervill / DND / Public Archives of Canada / PA-136762
2. Bundesarchiv, Koblenz
3. Unknown
4. National Archives of Canada / PA-131246
5. Courtesy of P. Kloosterman
6. Unknown
7. Courtesy of Carlos Vlaemynck
8. National Archives of Canada / PA-131240
9. National Archives of Canada / PA-131252
10. Unknown
11. State Institute for War Documentation, Amsterdam
12. Public Relations Branch, Canadian Military Headquarters, London
13. Courtesy of Eberding family
14. M.M. Dean / DND / Public Archives of Canada / PA-13675
15. Sergeant Edward Goodall, 1945. Courtesy of the artist
16. F.C. Dubervill / DND / Public Archives of Canada / PA-136756
17. Ken Bell / DND / Public Archives of Canada / PA-136761

Photo Insert No. 3

1. Imperial War Museum, London
2. Bundesarchiv, Koblenz
3. State Institute for War Documentation, Amsterdam
4. State Institute for War Documentation, Amsterdam
5. State Institute for War Documentation, Amsterdam
6. Imperial War Museum, London
7. Courtesy of Documentation Group Walcheren, 1939–45
8. Courtesy of Documentation Group Walcheren, 1939–45
9. State Institute for War Documentation, Amsterdam
10. Courtesy of Documentation Group Walcheren, 1939–45
11. Bundesarchiv, Koblenz
12. Courtesy of Documentation Group Walcheren, 1939–45
13. State Institute for War Documentation, Amsterdam
14. State Institute for War Documentation, Amsterdam
15. Imperial War Museum, London
16. Imperial War Museum, London

General Index

Index of Formations

BRITISH FORMATIONS

CANADIAN FORMATIONS

GERMAN FORMATIONS